FROM A SHATTERED SUN

FROM A SHATTERED SUN

Hierarchy, Gender, and Alliance
in the Tanimbar Islands

SUSAN MCKINNON

THE UNIVERSITY OF WISCONSIN PRESS

The University of Wisconsin Press
114 North Murray Street
Madison, Wisconsin 53715

3 Henrietta Street
London WC2E 8LU, England

Library of Congress Cataloging-in-Publication Data
McKinnon, Susan, 1949–
    From a shattered sun: hierarchy, gender and
alliance in the Tanimbar Islands / Susan McKinnon.
344 pp.   cm.
    Includes bibliographical references and index.
    ISBN 0-299-13150-5 (cloth)   ISBN 0-299-13154-8 (paper)
    1. Tanimbar (Indonesian people) – Marriage customs and rites.
2. Tanimbar (Indonesian people) – Kinship. 3. Tanimbar (Indonesian
people) – Politics and government. I. Title.
DS632.T36M34   1991
306'.089922 – dc20   91-50325
CIP

For
Kenneth and Mary McKinnon

Contents

Illustrations

Photographs

Tables

Acknowledgments

I am profoundly indebted to a great many people and institutions whose generosity and support over the years have made this project not only a possibility but also a rich and meaningful experience.

The research was carried out under the auspices of the Indonesian Institute of Sciences (LIPI), and sponsored by the Universitas Pattimura in Ambon. I wish to thank Bapak Rektor M. Lestaluhu, S.H., and Drs. Suyatno S. Kusuma of Universitas Pattimura for their willingness to sponsor my research and for their assistance in easing my way through various bureaucratic matters.

Doctoral research (twenty-two months in 1978-80) in the Tanimbar Islands was supported in part by a Grant for Doctoral Dissertation Research for Anthropology from the National Science Foundation. Both doctoral research and another nine months of postdoctoral research (1983-84) in Tanimbar were assisted by grants from the Joint Committee on Southeast Asia of the American Council of Learned Societies and the Social Science Research Council with funds provided by the National Endowment for the Humanities and the Ford Foundation. I would also like to thank the Wenner-Gren Foundation for Anthropological Research, which awarded me a Richard Carley Hunt Memorial Postdoctoral Fellowship, and the University of Virginia, which has been generous with its Faculty Fellowships for Summer Research. The financial assistance given by all of these institutions and their concern for scholarly research have been sincerely appreciated.

I am particularly indebted to Marshall Sahlins, David Schneider, and Valerio Valeri, who have remained constant sources of excellent advice, sharp criticism, and productive commentary. I wish to express my deepest gratitude to them for their encouragement and patient support over the years. To Harold Conklin, I extend my thanks for his kind assistance while I was carrying out research in the Yale Divinity School Library in 1977–78, previous to my fieldwork. From a distance, Shelly Errington, James J. Fox, and S. J. Tambiah have each, in their own way, lent their advice and support to this project, for which I am most grateful.

The encouragement and enthusiasm as well as the critical commentary of my colleagues spurred me on in my first attempts to create a meaningful representation of Tanimbarese society. I would especially like to thank Greg Acciaioli, Mary Ayres, Jim Collins, Liz Coville, Ann Fienup-Riordan, Mark Francillon, Webb Keane, Ward Keeler, Grant McCracken, Richard Parmentier, Rafael Sanchez, Patsy Spyer, and Bonnie Urciuoli.

More recently, in my efforts to rethink and rewrite this book, a number of people have generously given their support, comments, and criticism. I would like to express my gratitude to Fred Damon, Teresa Holmes, Signe Howell, Webb Keane, Peter Metcalf, Charles Piot, David Schneider, Patsy Spyer, Marilyn Strathern, Valerio Valeri, Roy Wagner, and an anonymous reader for the University of Wisconsin Press. Thanks are also due to Rafael Alvarado for drawing the diagrams.

Without the unflagging support of my parents, Kenneth and Mary McKinnon, and indeed my entire family, this project would have never been initiated let alone completed. My gratitude to them knows no boundaries.

My first steps in the Moluccas were made with the help of Bishop Andreas Sol and Pastor Sträter of Ambon, and I would like to thank them here for their thoughtful regard. Pastor Egging also shared freely with me his knowledge of Tanimbarese culture.

The hospitality, kindness, and generosity of the people of Tanimbar made my stay among them an extremely pleasant experience. From among the many people who patiently took it upon themselves to teach me a new way of thinking about the world, I am particularly indebted to Falaksoru and Ma'ileba Ditilebit, whose keen insights helped to reveal the complexities of Tanimbarese culture. Many people in Awear kept me in food and good company, and, at the same time, shared with me their thoughts about the world. I would like to take this opportunity to express my deepest gratitude not only to Falaksoru and Bo'iteri Ditilebit and their family, with whom I lived, but also to La'urvutu Balia Raa together with her four sons Famalik, Jan, Wa'iseran, and Me'ilaa, and their families; Belyaki and Vatavo'u Oratmangun; Labobar and Wisia Sera-Larat; and Nelangvutu, Asela, and Alfonsius Wearmasubun. I would also like to thank Koda, Josep, and Timotis Balia Roal, Yahabanasu Kabressi, Gabriel Kafroli, Vutlima and Resimaran Laian, Bapak Guru Ngelyaratan, and Artoki Wearmasubun. In villages other than Awear, many people graciously shared both their homes and their ideas with me. These include, in particular, Metaniat Bungaa, Ma'idodu Melatutnan, and Kormasela Ongirwalu of

Rumya'an; Yelar Vuarlela of Waleran; Bapak Guru and Lin Rerebain of Sofyanin; Roos Ongirwalu of Rumngevour; Filik and Lelarenan Labatar of Keliobar; Tutubo'i and Titi Kii Lokraa of Watidal; Ratutranan and Lakatelu Ditilebit-Yafur of Ridoal; Sinyasu and Beri Kuwai, Mo'u Angormasa, Sa'intii Kora, and the Kelvulan and Balak families of Sera; the Huninhatu and Kudmasa families of Makatian; Bapak Guru Areyesam of Sangliat Dol; Efraim Lamera of Sifnana; Wakil Aletaman Luturmela, Lilarat Oratmangun, Mantavar Rahan Koli, and, in particular, Abok and Alarenan Kuwai and their family in Olilit Lama. To all of these people, and many, many more, I extend my deepest thanks.

FROM A SHATTERED SUN

1 Approaching Tanimbar: Visions and Revisions

On landing, the contrast to the Australian shores we had so recently sailed from, was very striking. We left a land covered with the monotonous interminable forest of the eucalyptus or gumtree, which, from the peculiar structure of its leaf, affords but little shelter from the tropical sun. Shores fringed with impenetrable mangroves; a soil producing scarcely any indigenous vegetable, either in the shape of root or fruit fit for food. . . .

We landed on a beach, along which a luxuriant grove of cocoa-nut trees extended for more than a mile, under the shade of which were sheds neatly constructed of bamboo and thatched with palm leaves, for the reception of their canoes. To our right a hill rose to the height of about 400 feet, covered with brilliant and varied vegetation so luxuriant as entirely to conceal the village built on its summit. (Owen Stanley in Stokes 1969 [1846], 1:455–56)

One hundred and forty years later, and approaching Tanimbar from the rain-snatcher islands of the central Moluccas, I found my perspective to be somewhat different from that of Captain Owen Stanley. The lush encircling hills of Ambon and the great mountainous spine of Seram provide a dramatic contrast to the lower-lying islands of the southeastern Moluccas (map 1). As I sailed slowly to the southeast on the government cargo ship—first to the volcanic islands of Banda, and then further to the Kei and Aru archipelagos—the islands seemed to sink lower and lower into the sea. Kei had a profile still, but Aru looked as if it could surely be inundated in a high tide.

Yet, in following the arc of the islands and the route of the government ships back in a westerly direction to the towns of Larat and Saumlaki in the Tanimbar archipelago,[1] I was encouraged to find the islands rising

1. In the early literature, the islands of Yamdena and Selaru were known as Timor-Laut or Timor-Lao, whereas Molu, Maru, Fordata, Larat, and Sera were referred to as the Tanimbar, Tanembar, Tenimbar, or Tenimber Islands (see, e.g., Kolff 1840; Stokes 1969 [1846];

significantly again above the level of the sea. It is nevertheless true that (aside from the high relief of Fordata and the extinct volcanic cone of the tiny island of Labobar) the archipelago presents a relatively low profile along the horizon: the sixty-six limestone and coral islands,[2] which stretch some 135 miles north to south, are rarely elevated more than 150–250 meters above sea level (map 2). Behind the shore-front façade of sparkling white beaches and coconut groves, the islands are covered with primary and secondary growth forests as well as some scattered grasslands that are the result of overworked swidden cultivations. Because of an extended dry season, which arrives with the east winds about May and lasts until November, the forests are far less luxuriant than those of the higher, more mountainous islands of the central Moluccas.

I was hardly the first Westerner to step on Tanimbarese shores or to make these islands home for some time. Indeed Tanimbarese had been in contact with Westerners for more than three centuries before the time of my arrival. In the early seventeenth century, the exploration of the Tanimbar Islands by the Dutch East India Company was undertaken as part of a larger effort to explore the "Southland," which included the unmapped coasts of the Southeastern Islands (Kei, Aru, and Tanimbar), New Guinea, and Australia.[3] Although several voyages were conducted to the "Southland" in the first three decades of the seventeenth century, it was not until July 1636 that Pieter Pieterszoon passed briefly through the Tanimbar Islands on his return voyage to Banda from the northwest coast of Australia (Robert 1973:30–31; *Daghregister, anno 1636,* 1899:228–29).

The first official contact between the Tanimbarese and the Dutch took place in 1646, when Judge-Advocate Adriaen Dortsman, a representative of the Dutch East Indies Company, established an "exclusive contract" with the village heads and elders of the islands concerning trade in slaves, tortoiseshell, shark fins, ambergris, wax, and sapanwood (Riedel 1886:276; the text of this contract is published in Tiele and Heeres 1886–95, 3:303–7). A fort was set up in Rumya'an, on Fordata, and was manned by a garrison under the supervision of Dortsman. In the same year a Protestant missionary by the name of N. Vertregt was sent out to foster "the advance-

---

A. Forbes 1888; H. O. Forbes 1884, 1885; Riedel 1883, 1885, 1886; van Hoëvell 1890). The entire archipelago is now referred to as the Tanimbar Islands.

2. The *Beknopte encyclopaedie van Nederlandsch-Indië* fixes on a total of sixty-six islands (Bezemer 1921:545), and others seem to follow this as an established fact. Nevertheless, it is evident that an accurate map of the archipelago has yet to be made.

3. Documents concerning the Dutch relations with the Tanimbar Islands in the seventeenth and eighteenth centuries can be found in the *Daghregister, anno 1624–1682*; van der Chijs 1885–97; Tiele and Heeres 1886–95; Colenbrander and Coolhaas 1919–53; and Coolhaas 1960–79.

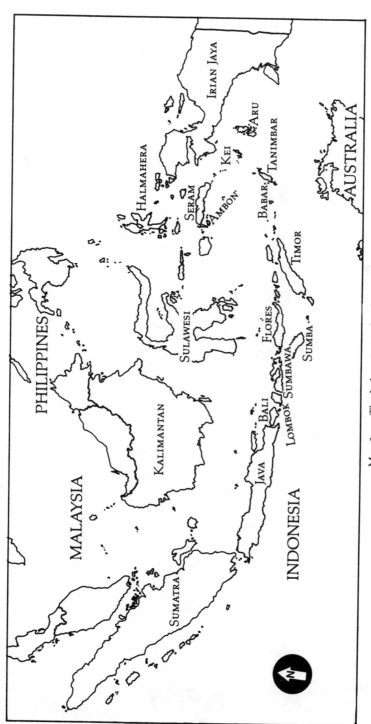

Map 1   The Indonesian archipelago

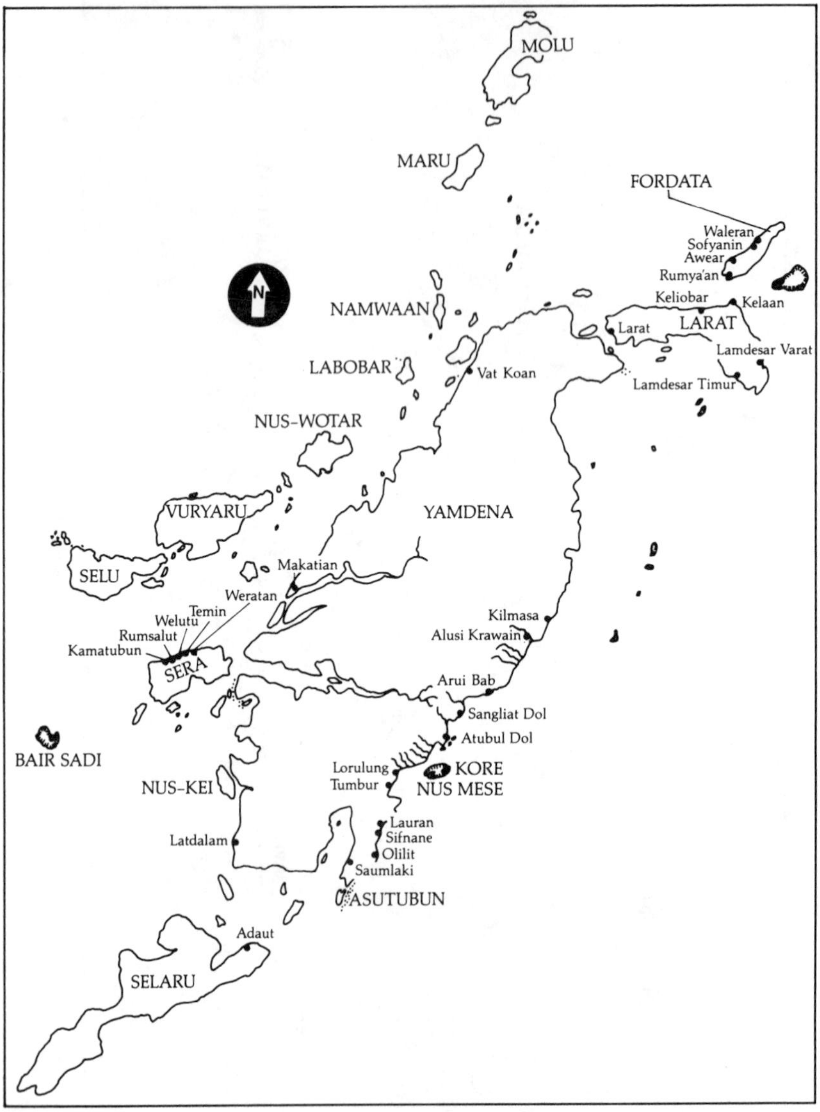

Map 2   The Tanimbar archipelago

ment of religion" among the islanders (Riedel 1886:276–77). According to the Dutch rendition of this history, the intrigues of the Bandanese traders and the unprofitable nature of the trade caused commercial relations in the area to lag and, by the middle of the eighteenth century, to be suspended altogether. The services of a schoolteacher, who had been sent to Fordata in 1683, were likewise withdrawn with the dwindling of the trade (Riedel 1886:277).

The islands were not visited again by the Dutch until Lieutenant D. H. Kolff made a voyage with the Brig-of-War *Dourga* in 1825 and 1826 through the islands of the southwestern and southeastern Moluccas. In his lively account of the voyage (Kolff 1840), he describes his visits to the islands of Fordata, Larat, Yamdena, and Sera, where he attempted to impress upon the inhabitants the idea that – despite appearances to the contrary – the islands stood under the Dutch flag. He was, on the whole, well received, although his party was attacked in Makatian, on the west coast of Yamdena, and one man was killed. Otherwise, he occupied himself with settling disputes and investing village heads with flags and silver-topped staffs as official tokens of office. Between Kolff's visit and 1880, several similar voyages were made for the purposes of renewing friendly relations and settling disputes.[4]

In 1882 the Resident of Amboina, J. G. F. Riedel, sent two postholders south to Tanimbar: one was stationed in Weratan on the island of Sera; the other in Ritabel on the island of Larat (Riedel 1886:277). According to the naturalist Henry Forbes, who arrived in Ritabel with his wife in the same year, these officials wielded precious little authority. This was made evident in the context of Forbes' own work, which was hindered by the state of protracted warfare that existed between the three western and the three eastern villages on the island of Larat. Greatly frustrated in his efforts to make a collection of the local flora and fauna, Forbes sought to intervene in the dispute. Both he and the postholder, however, were entirely ineffectual in their attempts to bring the conflict to a peaceful resolution (H. O. Forbes 1885:298–304; 327–29).

Whether or not warfare in Tanimbar was exacerbated by the increased contacts with the wealth and weaponry of the colonial powers is difficult to determine. Yet, from early accounts (Kolff 1840; A. Forbes 1888; H. O. Forbes 1885; Klerks 1912; Nieuwenhuis 1912; Drabbe 1917; Drabbe 1940: 222–27) and from the accounts of contemporary Tanimbarese, one perceives that intervillage warfare was a persistent fact of life in the islands. Wars or, perhaps more properly, headhunting raids could be instigated by disputes concerning rights over land and reefs, or by disputes relating

4. For accounts of other official and unofficial visits made by the Dutch and other Europeans to the Tanimbar Islands in the nineteenth century, see Stokes 1969 (1846), 1:438–60 and 2:351–53; Stanley 1842; Bleeker 1856; van der Crab 1862; van Doren 1863; Bickmore 1869; Kan and Veth 1878; H. O. Forbes 1884, 1885; A. Forbes 1888; Jacobsen 1896; de Vries 1900; Drabbe 1940:11.

to intervillage thefts, adultery, murder, or insults. Most often they seem to have consisted of intermittent raids, conducted over a long period of time, in a cycle of revenge and counter-revenge.

Although the Dutch undertook numerous punitive missions to "pacify" the intractable Tanimbarese (Drabbe 1940:11, 222–27), it was not until 1912 that they firmly established control over the archipelago. In that year, Lieutenant van den Bossche and forty infantrymen were sent to Tanimbar, where they carried out a punitive expedition of such proportions that even the high martial spirit of the islanders was bent (if not entirely broken) to the will of their colonial intruders (Klerks 1912; Nieuwenhuis 1912; Drabbe:1940:11, 227). "Tens of arrests and convictions were made. No boat departed from here that did not bring whole rows of prisoners to Amboina. All weapons were confiscated" (Drabbe 1940:227).[5] Van den Bossche's new, more draconian form of warfare virtually terminated not only the indigenous form of warfare and headhunting, but also Tanimbarese resistance to the Dutch.

Although the prevalence of wars in the last seventy-five years indeed appears to have diminished greatly, there is nevertheless scarcely a village in Tanimbar that is not engaged in an ongoing border dispute with its neighbor. More recently, intervillage hostilities often find expression in the context of soccer tournaments, which have become a regular part of national holiday celebrations. Indeed, there is hardly ever a soccer tournament that does not harbor the potential for outright violence. Such events can and occasionally do lead to armed conflicts, which, although they no longer involve headhunting, can result in serious injury and death.[6]

With the decline in warfare, the number of missionaries stationed in the Tanimbar Islands increased. The first Dutch Catholic missionaries arrived in 1910 (Cappers 1935) and established themselves on the east coast of Yamdena, which remains their stronghold today. I have no reliable information as to when the Protestant missionaries began their work in Tanimbar. The overwhelming majority of Protestants in Tanimbar belong to what is called the Moluccan Protestant Church (Gereja Protestan Maluku), which was the first and, for a long time, the only Protestant sect to proselytize in the area. More recently, some people have converted to the Seventh-Day Adventist Church, which has established itself in several villages. All Tanimbarese have ultimately converted to one or another Christian denomination.

---

5. All translations of the works of Drabbe and other Dutch sources, here and throughout the book, are mine.

6. Headhunting may no longer be an integral part of armed conflict, but it remains an integral part of people's consciousness. That is, although Tanimbarese no longer practice headhunting, they are convinced that other people, generally from outside the Tanimbar archipelago, do so. During the customary headhunting "season"—the dry period from mid-April or May until the rains begin again in November—headhunting scares are a constant feature of life.

The new European religions stand in a complex relation to the indigenous forms of warfare and religion. On the one hand, headhunting and warfare were central features of indigenous religious practices and these have been almost entirely replaced by Christian religious practices. On the other hand, having banned headhunting and warfare, the Christian missionaries introduced a new kind of ritual enmity—that between opposing Christian sects. Indeed, Tanimbarese appropriated the virulent enmity between Catholic and Protestant missionaries and, fighting their own wars under new religious banners and from different altars, they continued to negotiate and express the identity and opposition of their villages to one another. It is the legacy of this enmity (which has, more recently, abated considerably) that accounts for the fact that villages have allied themselves with one or another faith, but rarely more than one.

The Catholic missionaries not only lived, worked, and proselytized in the islands, they also wrote extensively about the inhabitants. It was from the works of a Dutch Catholic missionary, Petrus Drabbe, that I learned nearly everything I knew about Tanimbar before my arrival. Drabbe, who spent twenty years of his life in the archipelago, wrote not only a substantial ethnography (1940; cf. 1923, 1925, 1927) but also grammars and dictionaries for three of the four Austronesian languages—Yamdenan, Fordatan, Selaruan, and Seluwasan—that are spoken in the archipelago (1926a, 1926b, 1932a, 1932b, 1932c, 1935).

Drabbe's account of the linguistic diversity of the islands contrasts with his representation of their cultural unity, which is, in fact, impressive. This is not to say that local variations do not exist from island to island or from village to village. Yet, on the whole, one perceives an overall continuity in the forms of social organization throughout Tanimbar that differs from the explicitly contrastive forms typical of ethnic differentiation in other areas of Indonesia.

Despite the excellence of Drabbe's ethnographic account, however, it hardly prepared me for what I was initially to encounter. For Drabbe had written about Tanimbarese culture as it was before missionization and, at the same time, he had omitted reference to the effects that his presence (and that of his fellow missionaries) had engendered in the culture he described. There being no other, more recent, sources concerning Tanimbar, I therefore arrived with an image in my mind that dated from well before 1940. I spent my first several months in Tanimbar adjusting the images with which I arrived to those I encountered.

During this initial period, I traveled up the entire length of the east coast of Yamdena, as well as to Makatian on the west coast of Yamdena and to the islands of Sera, Larat, and Fordata. As was evidenced in these travels, the most heavily populated region in Tanimbar continues to be the east coast of Yamdena, which is followed by the island of Selaru to the southwest; Larat, Lutur, and Fordata to the northeast; Sera to the west; and Molu and Maru to the north. According to the 1979 census, the population of the entire archipelago totals 62,704 persons resident in eighty-three villages on twelve islands (see table 1.1).[7] Although villages range in size from under 150 to over 2,500 inhabitants, both the very small and very large villages are few and far between. The population size of most villages falls within the range of 300 to 1,000 persons. Throughout the islands, the majority of the population speaks the dialects of the Yamdenan language, followed by those of the Fordatan, Selaruan, and Seluwasan languages (see table 1.2; and Wurm and Hattori 1981–83).

Before I arrived, I had expected to see the effects of Catholic and Protestant missionization, but I had anticipated neither the extent nor the fervor of the conversion. Although I had perhaps not been at all sure what I would do if I were to meet a headhunter, I was not at all prepared to respond to men and women who were keen to convert me to the Dutch Reformed Protestant Church. The presence of Christianity seemed to dominate the landscape in the form of Catholic hospitals and schools in the towns and of imposing Catholic and Protestant churches in every village.

Similarly, the presence of the "Buginese" and "Makassarese" traders, whose boats were harbored in Saumlaki and Larat waiting for the winds to change, was not unexpected. For these traders were the contemporary emissaries of an enduring system of interisland and international trade that linked the eastern and western parts of the Indonesian archipelago to each other and to the outside. But I was surprised to see the extent to which Chinese merchants had taken over this trade and how firmly they controlled the economy of the towns and villages. Tanimbar had long been one of the furthest eastern outposts of the Indonesian trade routes, yielding copra, tripang, tortoise shell, and shark fins to the international trade. In the nineteenth century these goods were exchanged for cloth, gold, elephant tusks, and other valuables. Currently, however, they exchange for the more prosaic contents of the Indonesian equivalent of a "general store."

Although I had presumed that the Indonesian government would be in evidence, I had not imagined the extent to which its presence would have penetrated into the furthest corners of the archipelago. Indonesian nationalist ideology and language have become forces in every villager's life, primarily through the agency of the school system and through a plethora of national holidays that require the participation of the populace in various ceremonial events. The presence of the national government

7. Riedel (1886:275) reports a total population of 12,732 persons in sixty-eight villages on eight islands. Van Hoëvell (1890:164–68) states that a rough estimate of the population in 1890 was 19,342 persons resident in fifty-eight villages on eight islands. Drabbe notes that the 1930 census established the total population at 27,000 persons distributed over sixty villages on seven islands (1940:2), although the map published at the end of the same volume shows sixty-six villages.

Table 1.1. The population of islands in Tanimbar

Island	Population	Number of Villages
Molu	1,352	4
Maru	323	1
Fordata	3,675	6
Larat	7,163	8
Lutur	1,133	1
Yamdena	35,448	47
Sera	4,072	5
Selaru	8,412	7
Mitak/Teneman	427	1
Labobar	335	1
Nus Wotar	232	1
Maktus	132	1
Total	62,704	83

Source: Population statistics are taken from *Kantor Sensus dan Statistik Propinsi Maluku* 1980:7–10.

Table 1.2. The distribution of Tanimbarese languages

Yamdenan	
Northern dialect	12,019
Southern dialect	16,535
Total	28,554
Fordatan	
Larat-Fordata dialect I	5,534
Larat-Fordata dialect II	6,306
Sera dialect	4,072
Molu-Maru dialect	3,025
Total	18,937
Selaruan	8,268
Seluwasan	2,070
Other/Undetermined	4,875
Total	62,704

and its control over the time and activities of the Tanimbarese increased dramatically in the three years between my initial visit and my return trip in 1983. But even in 1979, it was obvious that much had changed since the time of Drabbe. Not only did things look different (a "Western" style of housing and clothing had been adopted) but the changes in religion, warfare, economics, and government made things more than superficially different.

Yet, the new cultural inventions that were both imposed upon and elaborated by the Tanimbarese have taken shape against the background of what might be called a "conventional" core (Wagner 1975) of social forms. This core comprises the relations of kinship, marriage, and exchange, whose robust continuity was (and is) just as much an explicit act of cultural definition as the more obvious discontinuities I had so quickly perceived.

As I traveled throughout the archipelago, I spoke with many people about the current forms of social organization. Wherever I went, I asked about Drabbe's report that an extended cycle of affinal alliance existed between houses on the islands of Sera, Larat, Fordata, and Yamdena. On Yamdena, most people knew nothing of such a cycle, although some suggested it had once existed, but was presently no longer operating. It was not until I went to Sera that I was told about a double cycle of affinal alliance—called the Lolat Ila'a or "Great Row"—that not only links four houses on the island of Sera with four houses on the island of Fordata, but also gathers together and stands at the apex of a massive network of exchange pathways from the entire archipelago.

Because I had an interest in such networks and cycles of exchange, this new information suggested that it would be best to settle on either Sera or Fordata. Since the five villages of Sera are strung together in a chain and form a large complex of more than four thousand people, I decided that I could better, and more peaceably, work in one of the villages on Fordata. In the end, I settled in the village of Awear (photographs 1.1 and 1.2), which, despite its small size (population 267), is the location of

Photograph 1.1   Bo'iteri Ditilebit and two youngsters paused as they walked along the beach south of Awear, which can be seen on the cape in the background.

Photograph 1.2   The village of Awear viewed from the northwest. Stairs lead from the harbor up to the front gate, which is guarded by the house Oratmangun.

two of the four houses on the Fordatan portion of the double cycle. The size of Awear posed certain drawbacks for the research. It meant, for instance, that simply in terms of the sheer number of events to be observed, there would be some limitations. Yet, because two of the eight houses of the double cycle were present in the village, numerous exchanges that implicated the higher levels of the exchange system took place there. Had I lived in other villages, I would not have had the opportunity to witness these events.

In Awear, I was taken in as a daughter of the house Ditilebit—one of the four houses on the Fordatan cycle. The two elder brothers of this house—Falaksoru and Ma'ileba Ditilebit—were avid participants in the system of exchange and articulate commentators upon their own culture and world events, which they followed through the Voice of America and Radio Australia. Insightful, ironic, and humorous, they gave shape to much of what I came to understand about their culture.

Situated as I was in the Ditilebit house, and in Awear, I soon became well acquainted with the members of houses along the various exchange pathways that led into the Fordatan cycle. Several times a week an exchange would be negotiated, and I spent much of my time sitting with the men who gathered for these exchanges. It was here—amid the palm-wine and the betel nut—that I began to map out the networks of exchange, the complexities of the affinal system, and the movements of people and valuables. Upon the conclusion of each exchange, I sat with the various participants as they told and retold the story of the negotiation and, at the same time, interpreted its significance for themselves and for me. My life was soon focused upon understanding the intricacies of an extraordinarily complex system of exchange and the politics of the men involved in it.

Yet my time was not wholly consumed by attending exchange negotiations. I also maintained several gardens and spent many happy hours with the women planting, tending, and harvesting the wide variety of swidden field crops — corn, rice, mung beans, yams, taro, and other roots and vegetables — that come to fruition over the course of the year. I gradually came to understand something of the movements of the tides (and of fish) and enjoyed accompanying both men and women on their expeditions to the reef (the deep sea fishing, like the pig hunting, remained solely the province of men). But mostly, I took great pleasure from simply sitting with women while they wove cloth, plaited baskets, cooked, chewed betel, and discussed the events of the day and of their lives. Although it was primarily the men who participated in exchanges, nevertheless, the women were often shrewd commentators on the activities they watched from their kitchens. Ultimately, my understanding of village life emerged from listening to the "close, oral, daily history" (Berger 1979:9) that both the men and women told about their lives — constructing, in the process, their own "living portrait" of themselves "out of words, spoken and remembered: out of opinions, stories, eye-witness reports, legends, comments and hearsay" (Berger 1979:9).

To this informal, "living portrait" — which knows neither beginning nor end (Berger 1979:9) — I added more formal and discrete images. As part of my effort to make sense of the exchange system, I conducted a detailed census of Awear, which included information on the marriages, residence, and affiliation of each person in the village, as well as a specification of the exchanges made on behalf of, and the exchange pathways recognized by, each person and each house in the village. Such information was also collected for a number of houses that did not belong to the village but that were situated along the main pathways of exchange I was exploring (these included the houses Bungaa, Melatunan, and Ongirwalu in the village of Rumya'an; Somar and Ba'ir-Sadi in Rumngevour; Vuarlela in Waleran; Labatar in Keliobar; Lokraa in Watidal; Kuwai and Angormasa in Temin and Weratan).

Nearly everyone in the village was an eager language teacher. It was, however, the intelligent and patient work of my younger sister, Maria Ditilebit, that finally converted my initial and awkward efforts into a far more acceptable fluency. After a year or so all my conversations were conducted in the Fordatan language. My ability to speak Fordatan opened the entire archipelago to me, for not only is it spoken on Fordata, Larat, and Sera, but it is the language used in rituals throughout the archipelago. I was therefore able to use Fordatan, instead of Indonesian, with the elder men and women I conversed with when I returned to Yamdena.

Since I was living on Fordata my study naturally assumed a Fordatan perspective. Nevertheless, because the exchange lines (and many other cultural forms) link Fordata intimately not only with Sera and Larat but also with Yamdena, it is impossible for me to say that this study concerns something called "Fordatan culture" alone. On the other hand, it is equally impossible for me to say that it concerns something called "Tanimbarese culture" as a whole, for, despite the similarities across the archipelago, there remain many differences. It should be understood, therefore, that while I found my home in Awear and on Fordata, my study of exchange continually took me beyond the boundaries of a single village, a single island, or even a single archipelago. Conversely, although I occasionally refer to "Tanimbarese" or "Tanimbarese culture," it should be understood that I view the archipelago from the hills of Fordata.

During my first stay in Tanimbar — after my initial tour of Yamdena, Sera, Larat, and Fordata — I did, in fact, confine my efforts primarily to the island of Fordata. In August 1980, however, I returned to Sera in order to accompany the people of Temin and Weratan when they traveled to the village of Latdalam (on the west coast of Yamdena) to renew an intervillage brotherhood alliance. This trip provided an opportunity not only to participate in the marvelous week-long ritual that renewed the alliance between these villages, but also to talk again with the people in Sera about their portion of the "Great Row" and the exchange pathways that feed into it. Not long after I returned from Sera to Fordata I was required by visa limitations to leave the islands in late October 1980.

I was able to return to Tanimbar for another nine months beginning in August 1983. I settled again in the village of Awear, but made many trips from my home there to villages on Fordata, Larat, and the east coast of Yamdena. During this second visit, I focused upon warfare, headhunting, the system of intervillage brotherhood alliances, and their rituals of renewal. I was also able to discuss with many people the results of my previous research on marriage and exchange. I can only hope that their patience and insightful reflections are evident in the present work: for it is to an understanding of the uniqueness and complexity of their lives that the present work is dedicated.

2   Contrastive Forms and Life Processes

A composition from one point of view is a decomposition from another: relationships reduced to a single strand. (Strathern 1988:292)

Social organization itself embodies a playlike component of "alternicity." (Boon 1982:102)

The initial activating force in the world is represented in the form of a spear. It was this spear that differentiated the prior unities of heaven and earth, sun and moon, mainland and island, male and female into their complementary parts. It thereby gave shape to the world, inaugurated temporal cycles, and engendered the attraction of opposites. Set against this process of decomposition, which left the human population in a state of radical mobility and instability, people instituted a process of recomposition, which established new synthetic entities of transcendent unity that came to stand at the core of a newly constituted social life.

There are three such recomposed unities: the stone boat at the center of villages, the altar complex at the center of named houses, and the double cycle of alliance at the center and apex of the archipelago-wide system of exchange pathways. Each is a fixed center that unifies opposed qualities, including those, primarily, of male and female. It is by reference to these new synthetic unities that the forms of what we might otherwise call the elements of social organization — villages, houses, people — are delineated. Neither preexisting nor natural forms, these latter must be continually created and recreated through the processes of differentiation and recomposition that were prefigured in the initial, activating scenario by the spear and that continue to be effected contemporaneously through exchange. Fixed and immobile at the center, each of these transcendent unities anchors this double movement, which is necessary for growth and the continuity of life.

It is an ideology of organic growth, which links source and issue, that engenders Tanimbarese structures of hierarchy and equality. Neither are inherent qualities in the world: rather, both are generated through the

16

relative tension between separation and recomposition, the sociological configurations of which are the various, differentially valued forms of marriage and affiliation. It is in their relative articulation, through the agency of exchange, that the hierarchical order of people, houses, and villages is negotiated.

The structure and movement of this book follow from Tanimbarese representations of form and generative processes. Yet to take indigenous modes of representation seriously is, necessarily, to challenge our own modes of representation and, in particular, the theoretical assumptions that underlie them. The book also seeks, therefore, to allow Tanimbarese understandings regarding such processes as differentiation and the recomposition of unities to challenge the limitations of our understandings of the nature of social units and relations of hierarchy, alliance, exchange, and gender. The aim, in the end, is to make possible a culturally motivated analysis that is informed by indigenous ideas, images, and processes rather than by received analytic categories and typologies.

Nevertheless, any ethnography is inevitably contextualized by the history of the particular anthropological discourses and debates that happen to touch upon the subjects it engages. The various subjects of this book are tied together by the single thread of hierarchy. Indeed, because this book focuses broadly upon the dynamics involved in the creation of hierarchy, it poses several questions concerning its nature. Four issues, in particular, are raised by the complexity of the Tanimbarese material as it bears upon theoretical questions concerning hierarchy and the relation between (1) closed and open asymmetric pathways in systems of generalized exchange; (2) multiple forms of marriage; (3) multiple forms of affiliation; and (4) gender and exchange.

First, since the Tanimbarese system of marriage is, in its own unique way, strictly asymmetric (in the matrilateral direction), the question of the relation between hierarchy and equality is broached straightaway when one considers the relation between closed asymmetric cycles (which imply equality) and open asymmetric pathways (which imply hierarchy). This question arises because of the existence of a double cycle of asymmetric alliance and exchange (called the Great Row) from which emanates numerous open, extended asymmetric exchange pathways of both a more and less permanent nature. Second, since the existence of both closed asymmetric cycles and open asymmetric pathways means that not everyone is marrying their mother's brother's daughter, it is necessary to cast aside the misleading issue of prescriptive and perferential marriages and, rather, consider the relation between different forms of marriage and how their articulation contributes to the creation of a hierarchical order. Third, and as a corollary to the consideration of the significance of multiple forms of marriage, it is also necessary to relinquish the concept of unilineal descent groups and, rather, consider the significance of multiple forms of affiliation and the manner in which their articulation likewise contributes to the creation of a hierarchical order. Finally, since Tanimbarese see the asymmetry of their system as one in which a hierarchical relation between source and issue is created through relations of gender and processes of exchange, it is necessary to explore the relations among hierarchy, gender, and exchange. In the sections that follow, the background of these four issues will each be addressed in turn.

Cycles and Open Asymmetries

It was Lévi-Strauss and Leach who, through a series of writings on the Kachin and related groups, focused attention upon the nature and dynamics of systems of matrilateral cross-cousin marriage and their implications for relations of hierarchy, equality, and social change (Lévi-Strauss 1969; Leach 1965, 1969, 1971). The exchange has spawned considerable commentary on generalized exchange, not only with regard to the Burmese material (see, for instance, Leach 1963; Lehman 1970; Friedman 1975; and Nugent 1982), but also with regard to analogous systems, such as those found on Sumatra in western Indonesia (Singarimbun 1975; Kipp 1983; Lando 1983; Moyer 1983; and Sherman 1987), in eastern Indonesia (Barnes 1974; Valeri 1975–76, 1980; Barraud 1979; Fox 1980c; and Forth 1981), and in India (see, for example, Parry 1979). Nevertheless, despite the extensive writings on the subject, it is to the core of the original debate between Lévi-Strauss and Leach that I wish to return. For in having started from radically different premises and having had, therefore, to explain radically different problems, the two highlight the issues generated by contrasting perspectives upon the nature of hierarchy and equality in asymmetric systems of alliance.

Lévi-Strauss begins *The Elementary Structures of Kinship* (1969) with the institution of the prohibition of incest and the concomitant rule of reciprocity, which requires that a sister be relinquished in exchange for a wife.[1] Throughout the book, the idea of reciprocity in marriage explicitly entails a woman given for a woman received — never a woman given for goods received. The primacy of this understanding of the rule of reciprocity works nicely through the sections on restricted exchange and even those on patrilateral cross-cousin marriage. When Lévi-Strauss reaches

---

1. See Rubin 1975 for a commentary upon the implications of Lévi-Strauss' formulation for an understanding of the structures of female subordination through systems of marriage exchange.

matrilateral cross-cousin marriage, however, he is at pains to show that the rule of reciprocity (of women for women) holds in this case as well (1969:233–34). The dilemma derives from the fact that—because women can only move in one direction (asymmetrically) between exchanging groups and cannot be directly returned (symmetrically) in the same or alternate generations—it is not self-evident where the group that initiated an asymmetric pathway (and gave the first woman) will receive its own wives, or, conversely, where the last group on the pathway will find its husbands. Having presupposed the incest prohibition and the rule of reciprocity, Lévi-Strauss must characterize systems of matrilateral cross-cousin marriage—in their most fundamental formulation—as cyclical (1969:266). That is, the last group on any asymmetric pathway must become the wife-giver to the first, thus turning an open extended pathway into a closed cycle (figure 2.1). The closing of the cycle immediately implies that relations between the groups will be egalitarian in nature. Such asymmetric exchange

> . . . presupposes equality, since the theoretical condition for the application of the elementary formula is that the operation *c marries A,* which closes the cycle, is equivalent to the operation, *A marries b,* which opened it in the first place. For the system to function harmoniously, an *a* woman must be equivalent to a *b* woman, a *b* woman to a *c* woman, and a *c* woman to an *a* woman; i.e., that the lineages *A, B, C* shall be of equal status and prestige. (Lévi-Strauss 1969:266)

Ultimately, having assumed that generalized exchange "presupposes equality," Lévi-Strauss' problem then becomes how to explain the manner in which this egalitarian form developed into the hierarchical forms so often associated with systems of matrilateral cross-cousin marriage.

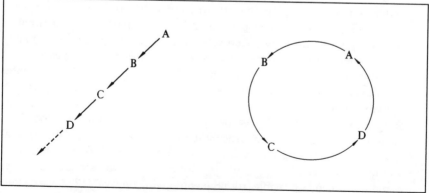

Figure 2.1   An open-ended pathway and a cycle of alliance

Leach begins from a set of assumptions diametrically opposed to those of Lévi-Strauss. What he presupposes is not reciprocity, but rather hierarchy. Characterizing the difference between his own position and that of Lévi-Strauss, he claims that the latter

> . . . perceives that in fact differences of price and differences of status will result, but regards this as the breakdown of the system, and hence as a mechanism in the general process of social evolution. My own argument is almost the reverse of this. As far as the marriage system is concerned, the status of relations between group A and group B must be taken as given factors in the situation; a marriage is only one of many possible ways of 'expressing' those relations. (Leach 1971:101; see also 102)

Rejecting the primacy of equality, Leach must therefore discard the cycle as the fundamental form of matrilateral cross-cousin marriage systems, which he instead characterizes in terms of open asymmetric pathways. As a result, however, he is also obliged to characterize the system of marriage in terms of the exchange of women for bridewealth goods instead of the exchange of women for women (1971:60). The problem for Leach then becomes what forms of reciprocity resolve the instability of a system in which goods tend to accumulate at the top of the system. In the process, Lévi-Strauss' question concerning the forms of reciprocity that allow men at the top and women at the bottom of the system to obtain spouses becomes a muted one.

In short, Lévi-Strauss begins with the incest prohibition and reciprocity (women for women), constitutes matrilateral cross-cousin marriage as essentially cyclical and egalitarian, and must therefore explain the genesis of hierarchy. Leach begins with a rejection of the egalitarian cycle, constitutes matrilateral cross-cousin marriage as essentially hierarchical, and must therefore explain the structure of reciprocity (women for goods.)

Lévi-Strauss resolves the passage from egalitarian cycle to hierarchical system by reference to what he sees as the internal dynamics of matrilateral cross-cousin marriage systems, which he describes in a passage that sounds suspiciously like a characterization of the mentality that animates the movement of securities on Wall Street. Seeing the system as based, fundamentally, on "credit" and "speculation," he argues that it is inherently unstable (1969:265). As the cycles grow longer, the "risk" becomes greater. Yet ". . . one can guard oneself doubly against the risk: qualitatively, by multiplying the cycles of exchange in which one participates, and quantitatively, by accumulating securities, i.e., by seeking to corner as many women as possible from the wife-giving lineage" (1969:265). Hierarchy is thus generated by the breakdown in equality caused by the combination of speculative and accumulative tendencies.

Leach resolves his dilemma, initially, in his 1951 article "The Structural Implications of Matrilateral Cross-Cousin Marriage" (reprinted in 1971:54–104). Here he deals with the problem of the instability of the open asymmetric pathway that results from the fact that bridewealth cattle (not women, as Lévi-Strauss would have it) tend to accumulate at the top of the system. The requirements of hierarchy, however, are met by the structure of reciprocity: in Leach's terms, bridewealth cattle, being "consumer" goods, are converted into prestige and redistributed back down the pathway in the form of feasts (1971:89). The instability of the open asymmetric pathway is thus overcome in a way that strengthens rather than threatens hierarchy.

While Lévi-Strauss' presuppositions force him to seek the genesis of hierarchy in the instability of egalitarian cycles, it is precisely hierarchy that Leach takes as the most fundamental form of asymmetric systems. Conversely, whereas Leach's own presuppositions force him to seek the genesis of reciprocity (in asymmetric systems) in the instability of their hierarchical forms, it is precisely reciprocity that Lévi-Strauss takes as fundamental to all systems of marriage.[2] Indeed, because he sees reciprocity as primary, and in terms of a woman given for a woman, hierarchy must necessarily be a derived form, dependent upon the breakdown of equality. And, because Leach has conceptualized the asymmetry of the system in terms of the exchange of women for goods, rather than of women for women, he does not directly confront the issue of egalitarian cycles (i.e., the forms of reciprocity necessary to allow men at the top and women at the bottom to obtain spouses). As a consequence, in the 1951 article (1971) he never systematically explores the interlocking dynamics of hierarchy and equality that are played out in the relation between the open asymmetric pathways that extend *between* chiefly, aristocratic and commoner classes and the closed asymmetric cycles that exist *within* these classes (figure 2.2). This is so despite the fact that his description of the system, as well as the diagram he provides, clearly presuppose the simultaneous existence of closed asymmetric cycles and open asymmetric path-

2. It is perhaps strange, then, that although Lévi-Strauss understood that hierarchy depends on the opening up of a cycle and the multiplication of exchange pathways, it was nevertheless Leach who understood that the cultural logic and hierarchical force of exchange derives from giving, not from accumulating. Leach called attention to the fact that Lévi-Strauss' formulation depended upon the assumption that hierarchy would be the precipitate of hypergamy rather than hypogamy, and accumulation rather than distribution of women—neither of which is the case for the Kachin (1965, 1971).

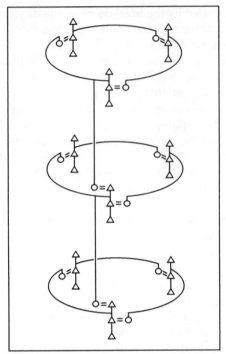

Figure 2.2   Cycles of alliance in combination
with open pathways (after Leach 1971:86)

ways (Leach 1971:82–86). Whereas Lévi-Strauss clearly saw the opening
up of the cycle as a prerequisite for the development of hierarchy, Leach
failed to elaborate the converse—that the closing down of cycles (along
open asymmetric pathways) is every bit as much a precondition for the
existence of hierarchy.

Yet it is precisely the question of the relation between closed cycles and
open asymmetric pathways—between equality and hierarchy—that becomes the central issue in Leach's discussion of the relations among Shan,
gumsa, and *gumlao* forms in *The Political Systems of Highland Burma*
(1965). Here, the accumulation of wealth at the top of a *gumsa* system
tends to push it toward the model of a Shan princedom. However, the contradictions between the two forms of hierarchy—the Shan system of ranks
being based on hypergamy, tribute, and the negation kinship values, and the
gumsa system of ranks being based upon hypogamy, reciprocity, and
the valorization of kinship values—ultimately prove to be too great. These
contradictions, in turn, tend to lead to a *gumlao* rebellion, in which closed

egalitarian cycles replace open hierarchical pathways (1965:203). Here equality is generated out of the structure of the conjunction of two contradictory ideas of the nature of hierarchy and the resultant threat to a kin-based system of reciprocity. But the *gumlao* system, too, is unstable to the extent that the superiority of wife-giver (*mayu*) over wife-taker (*dama*), and the valuation of the matrilateral cross-cousin over the partilateral cross-cousin, contradicts the assertion of an egalitarian ideology. The *gumlao* system only works with any consistency where both cousins are equally valued — that is, where it is no longer a strictly matrilateral system (1965:203, 210–11) and reciprocities are no longer strictly asymmetric. The choice of the matrilateral over the patrilateral cross-cousin, and the resulting asymmetry of exchange, immediately signifies a difference in value and implicates a hierarchical order. Leach's account, in *Political Systems*, thus deals with the manner in which the internal contradictions in the relations of reciprocity among the three systems — the ranked hierarchy of the Shan, the extended asymmetric pathways of the *gumsa*, and the closed asymmetric cycles of the *gumlao* — drives the oscillation between them. What Leach was able to see, here, is that the instabilities of both the closed cycle and the open asymmetric pathway mutually imply one another in a logic that is processual in nature.

In the end, however, both authors deal with the instability of either closed or open asymmetric pathways by placing them and their concomitant egalitarian and hierarchical forms in separate time frames connected by a developmental, evolutionary, or oscillating social dynamic. The historical ascendancy of one occurs thanks to logical contradictions in the forms of reciprocity that require the simultaneous demise of the other. There is little thought given to the structural and historical significance of the simultaneous presence of both hierarchy and equality (open and closed pathways) in the same society.

Against the formulations of Lévi-Strauss and Leach, Tanimbarese material poses the mutual elicitation of closed and open asymmetric pathways — of egalitarian and hierarchical forms. For, on the one hand, it is true (as Lévi-Strauss pointed out) that the cycle is unstable and that hierarchy requires opening new pathways of alliance. Yet, on the other hand, it could also be said (following Leach) that the open, extended asymmetric pathway is equally unstable and (although Leach never explicitly elaborated the point) that hierarchy requires the closing down of cycles at various levels of the system. Tanimbarese ultimately see matrilateral cross-cousin marriage as fundamentally hierarchical, and this hierarchy is manifest in the nature of relations along the open extended pathways of exchange and alliance. But the continuity of this hierarchical form is possible, not because of the breakdown and demise of all egalitarian cycles, but rather because the egalitarian cycle is preserved as a rare and contrasting form.

Yet to see hierarchical and egalitarian forms of alliance as integral to a single system rather than as historical developments of one another is not to deny history. It is, rather, to attend fully to the complexity and internal dynamics of indigenous representations of alliance, which are shaped by an ideology of growth that links source and issue through processes of differentiation and recomposition. For Tanimbarese, these *are* the forces and forms of history.

Contrastive Forms of Marriage

To apprehend the complexity of indigenous relations of alliance is, in the first place, to recognize the full range of contrastive marriage forms that exist within a society. It has been too easy, apparently, to assume that analytic categories — such as "matrilateral cross-cousin marriage" — are, in themselves, sufficient to describe those alliance systems that have come to bear their names. This problem becomes evident once one attempts to understand the creation of relations of hierarchy and equality in such systems.

It is true that if every man in a society marries his matrilateral cross-cousin, the alliance pathways will be cyclical and relations between allied groups will be egalitarian. Yet the inverse is also true: to the extent that relations between groups are hierarchical, not every man can be marrying his matrilateral cross-cousin. The fact that most "matrilateral cross-cousin systems" *are* hierarchical leads one immediately to the conclusion that such hierarchy must be generated not from strict conformity to a rule of matrilateral cross-cousin marriage, but rather from the differential value accorded to contrastive forms of marriage. In some societies, like Tanimbar, an explicit injunction that two brothers (of the same "house") may not marry two sisters (of the same "house") ensures that matrilateral cross-cousin marriage cannot be the only type of marriage accorded value. Lévi-Strauss' problem — that is, how a system of matrilateral cross-cousin marriage generates hierarchy — is misconstrued. More properly understood, the problem is to determine what role matrilateral cross-cousin marriage has, *relative to other forms of marriage,* in the creation of a system of hierarchy.

An acknowledgment of the hierarchical potential of "matrilateral cross-cousin marriage systems" therefore requires a recognition of the crucial role of contrastive forms of marriage. This is true whether one views the system from the perspective of the closed cycle or the open extended pathway. If one presupposes the existence of a closed asymmetric cycle,

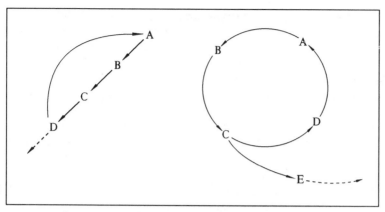

Figure 2.3   Closing and opening pathways of alliance

then to open a new pathway immediately implies marriage with a woman from a previously unallied group — that is, with someone other than a matrilateral cross-cousin (figure 2.3). Such a move further motivates a distinction between new, impermanent affinal relations and old established alliances, and it raises the possibility that the latter might involve marriage with a woman who would be neither a matrilateral cross-cousin nor a complete stranger. If, on the other hand, one presupposes the existence of an open extended pathway, then to close a cycle — to turn the line of extension back around to the point of origin — is to marry the equivalent of one's father's sister's daughter (or "sister") and to reverse the directionality of exchange (figure 2.3).³ The simultaneous existence of both closed and open pathways therefore implies that there must be a range of contrastive forms of marriage.

It is perhaps historical chance that the impetus to explore multiple forms of marriage (and affiliation) presented itself in Indonesia, for one suspects that many other places would have provided equally fertile ground for such an exploration. Because of van Wouden's *Types of Social Structure in Eastern Indonesia* (1968 [1935]), however, the manifest diversity of marriage forms became a focus for research in eastern Indonesia. In his own words, van Wouden ". . . attempted to deal with the erratic distribution and intermingling of patrilineal and matrilineal forms of social organization and of unilateral circulating marriage sytems with mother's brother's daughter marriage, father's sister's daughter's marriage and symmetric

3. Cf. Lévi-Strauss 1966:422, 453 for another interpretation of the covert presence of a patrilateral form in a system of matrilateral cross-cousin marriage.

alliance with brother-sister exchange (1977:184). Van Wouden's analysis
was limited by the historical reconstructions — including circulating connubium, double descent, moiety, and phratry dualism — that he devised
to account for the complexity of the phenomena at hand.[4] He nevertheless clearly understood that the articulation of different possibilities of
marriage and affiliation was integral to the definition of the particular
shape of these societies.

Notwithstanding the excellent beginnings forged by van Wouden, many
subsequent scholars have tended to focus exclusively upon the classification of various societies in terms of a single fixed mode of descent and
a single terminological marriage prescription (Needham 1956, 1957, 1966,
1967, 1968, 1970; Fischer 1957; Barnes 1973, 1977a, 1978; Forth 1981).
Comparative efforts have followed the same lines: for instance, Schulte
Nordholt (1971), Barnes (1980b), and Needham (1980) have catalogued
the relative distribution of, and correlation between, the types of marriage and descent found among societies that belong to related culture
areas in Timor and in Sumba.

Although the insistent focus on the issue of prescriptive marriage has
haunted eastern Indonesian studies, it has long been evident that different
forms of marriage and affiliation are found not only in *adjacent* societies
but also *within* many societies. Encountering a multiplicity of marriage
forms in the societies they study, researchers have dealt with the challenge in several ways. Often it is stated that the marriage rule and the kinship terminology are prescriptive (or that there is a preference for one
type of marriage or another), but that in practice not everyone marries
that way (e.g., Barnes 1974:239–42; Fox 1980b:115–16; Traube 1980a:296;
Traube 1980b:95). Attempts have been made to verify statistically the extent to which practice accords with the rule (Barnes 1974:295–304; Barnes
1978:25).

Such studies have remained mired in a trap that opposes the ideal to
the real, and structure to practice. In this light, contrastive forms of marriage are seen only as deviations from, or manipulations of, the ideal —
they are, in short, practices that do not accord with the structure. Such
an approach makes even less sense when there is an explicit injunction
that two brothers may not marry two sisters. This implies that, by the
rules of the system itself, not everyone should or could marry their matrilateral cross-cousin. Moreover, to deal with these problems by recourse

4. For other early attempts to come to terms with the various forms of kinship and marriage in Indonesia, see, for example, van Ossenbruggen 1930, 1935; and Fischer 1935, 1936.
Remarkably, van Wouden's model continues to be replicated in the historical reconstructions
formulated more recently in Barnes 1979; Blust 1980a, 1980b; van Dijk and de Jonge 1987;
and others.

to accounting methods aimed at determining the statistical frequency of one or another type of marriage — as if numerical preponderance was the only criterion of significance — is to miss the point. For it should be evident that although a type of marriage may not be statistically frequent (it may even be quite rare), it may nevertheless be more highly valued than those that are more statistically preponderant. What is lost, in the rush to statistical verification, is any understanding of the system of ideas that gives differential value and structural significance to the various types of marriage that form a contrastive set in the society under consideration.

Other writers, less concerned with the concept of a prescriptive rule, have more conscientiously recognized the full array of marriage types in the societies they have studied. Marriages that are symmetric and asymmetric in form, marriages that open new alliances and those that renew established, or founding, alliances are seen as part of a system of possibilities (Cunningham 1967b:2–3; Valeri 1975–76; Barraud 1979:149–52; Clamagirand 1980:141–43; Gordon 1980:54–55; Traube 1986). Since one form of marriage often appears to contradict the systematicity of another, there has been some attempt to define the difference between exogamous units and alliance units (Valeri 1975–76; Barnes 1980a, 1980b; Fox 1980b). With a few exceptions (Valeri 1975–76; Boon 1977), however, we are not given a full account of which persons and what units of the society contract which types of marriage, or the manner in which they are differentially valued.

Although it is clear that the various forms of marriage displayed by these societies exist within, and give shape to, a hierarchical order, at best most authors give but fleeting hints of the relationship between the two. Yet commonly it is enough for one brother to renew an established alliance, while other brothers marry women from previously unallied groups (Cunningham 1967b:3; Valeri 1975–76; Barraud 1979:159–61; Gordon 1980:54; see also Leach 1965). It has been noted that the relative wealth of the exchanging group may influence the types of marriage that may be contracted (Geurtjens 1921b:330; Schulte Nordholt 1971:139–40). More to the point, it is evident that in many societies, certain types of marriage, alliance, and affiliation describe the position of rulers, nobles, or elder brothers, and that other, less prestigious forms of marriage and affiliation define the province of their subordinates (de Josselin de Jong 1952:102, 151, 168; de Josselin de Jong 1975:277–78; de Josselin de Jong 1981:10; Valeri 1975–76; Boon 1977; Clamagirand 1980:147–48; Fox 1980b:116).

In face of the complexity of these systems, we are confronted with the rigidity of available analytic categories and with the persistent tendency to define societies in terms of a single type of marriage. As a consequence we are most often left with a sense that there is a radical disjunction between structure and practice, or that strategy operates within a system of differences the values of which are not evident. By contrast, and following Valeri (1975–76) and Boon (1977), I aim to reclaim the complexity and significance of contrastive marriage forms in Tanimbar and, in the process, to explore the manner in which they articulate with one another in the formation of the hierarchical order of society.

Contrastive Forms of Affiliation

Evans-Pritchard may have been the first to formulate the paradox of a patrilineal principle that is so unchallenged that practically everything *except* patrilineality is realized (1951:28); but, in part because of the force of his own rhetoric, he has hardly been the last (cf. Sahlins 1965). Moyer, for instance, has rephrased the Nuer paradox to fit an Indonesian context. Speaking of south Sumatra, he notes that what he calls the "paradox of unilineality" implies that "the more unilineal a system is or becomes the less likely it is to remain unilineal" (1983:256–57). Authors commonly state that in a particular society descent is patrilineal and residence patrilocal, yet in the next breath they note that it is not unusual to find men residing uxorilocally or children affiliating to the patriline of the mother's father. Indeed, the multiplicity of forms of affiliation and residence — in Africa, Indonesia, Oceania, and elsewhere — not only defies the single-mindedness with which we apply our categories, but also challenges the very cogency of the categories themselves.

In many places throughout Indonesia, as in Africa and elsewhere, both the residence of a couple and the affiliation of their children must be established through exchange, since they are linked to a series of reciprocal marriage prestations between wife-giver and wife-taker. Until a specified number of prestations have been completed, the man's residence may remain uxorilocal while his children affiliate matrilaterally. Upon completion of these prestations — often after the second transaction — residence becomes patrilocal for the man and his children affiliate patrilaterally. Depending, then, upon the relative fulfillment of the requirements of exchange, the exchanging units may comprise both patrilaterally and matrilaterally affiliated members (Cunningham 1967b; Schulte Nordholt 1971:116–17; Valeri 1975–76, 1980).

Rather than assuming that the tension between such contrastive forms of affiliation and residence might be central to the dynamics of the society concerned, this tension has been explained away by recourse to the concept of double descent, to some version of "the unilineal paradox," or to related theoretical tropes that differentiate the ideal from the real or structure from practice.[5] It is far more preferable to assume that both patrilateral and matrilateral affiliation have value, and that their value is, in part, derived from their explicit opposition to one another within a common system of relations. From such a perspective, it makes little sense to describe a society in terms of either one or another form of affiliation, since it is the tension between a number of possible forms that is significant. Indeed, in Tanimbar as elsewhere, it is precisely the negotiation of this set of differential values that forms the central focus of social life. Only a marked myopia compels the continued denial of indigenous dynamics in favor of the security of inherited typologies.

Yet the problem lies not only in the rigidity with which analytic categories relating to descent are employed, but also in the assumption that the concept of descent is, in the end, the most relevant one for the description of these basic social units (Schneider 1984; Kuper 1982a, 1982b). The primacy of descent is challenged, in the first instance, by the fact that, in many parts of the world, such units are referred to in the indigenous languages as "houses"—a term that lacks any immediate reference to descent. In fact, the term that has been glossed as "patrilineage" in many of the ethnographies providing the classic models for unilineal descent turns out to be the word "house." Thus, to take just a few examples, the Nuer *thok dwiel* means "the entrance to the hut," the Tikopia *paito* and the Tallensi *yir* mean "house," and the Yapese *tabinau* means either "house" or "landed estate" (Evans-Pritchard 1940:247; Firth 1963a:300; Fortes 1969:10; Labby 1976:15; Schneider 1984:21).[6]

Despite the fact that the term "house" does not, in itself, suggest a descent ideology, nevertheless most authors implicitly or explicitly equate the idea of "house" with that of descent group. Fox, for instance, states that "the category of 'house' defines and often locates a descent group of a varying segmentary order" (1980a:11). Throughout the literature, houses are glossed as patrilineages or matrilineages, notwithstanding the fact that almost everywhere they contain alternately affiliated members who

---

5. Most of the commentators on the Nuer, for instance, have been unable to free themselves from this particular straightjacket. Having defined the ideal/structure in terms of patrilineality, all the other seemingly contradictory social practices engaged in by the Nuer end up being characterized as the failure of the real to accord with the ideal or practice to accord with structure. Such commentators do not appear to recognize that the source of this disjunction is located in their own formulation. Rather, they locate the disjunction in Nuer life—between Nuer ideals and action (see, e.g., Glickman 1971; Karp and Maynard 1983; Southall 1986; and Evens 1989 for different sides of this issue).

6. See also, e.g., Geertz and Geertz 1975 on the Balinese *dadia*; Kuper 1982b on the "house-property" system in South Africa; Lévi-Strauss 1982, 1987, on the Kwakiutl *numayma*; and Parmentier 1984 on the Balauan *blai*.

have been recruited by virtue of the workings of the systems of marriage and exchange. The pervasive ambivalence that abounds with regard to the subject is nicely summed up by Barnes. He first notes that his own preference

> . . . would be to use the phrase "descent group" more broadly, for the reasons put forth by Forde (1963) and Firth (1963[b]): specifically that the aim of establishing discrete corporations may be achieved by allowing descent to operate in combination with other factors. (1980b:116)

Soon thereafter, however, he states:

> Let us in future make our interpretation of collective associations more supple. We are told, after all, very little by being informed that a society has corporate unilineal descent groups. . . . and in Indonesia we are likely to be led well away from the ideas about descent and corporations which have been handed down to us from Maine. (1980b:120)

Rather than tie the concept of the house to a particular substantive definition (given by an ideology of descent), and then be forced to sweep every other aspect of house definition under the rug, it is far more fruitful to foreground the tension between the contrastive social forms that appear to be the most salient features of "houses." As Lévi-Strauss notes:

> On all levels of social life, from the family to the state, the house is therefore an institutional creation that permits compounding forces which, everywhere else, seem only destined to mutual exclusion because of their contradictory bends. Patrilineal descent and matrilineal descent, filiation and residence, hypergamy and hypogamy, close marriage and distant marriage, heredity and election: all these notions, which usually allow anthropologists to distinguish the various known types of society, are reunited in the house, as if, in the last analysis, the spirit (in the eighteenth-century sense) of this institution expressed an effort to transcend, in all spheres of collective life, theoretically incompatible principles. (1982:184; cf. Lévi-Strauss 1987)

Following upon Lévi-Strauss' formulation of the concept of "house societies" various authors have attempted to define, refine, and apply the concept in their own work (see Barraud 1979; Waterson 1986; Errington 1987, 1989; Macdonald 1987). But one senses an unresolved tension between the dead weight of old kinship categories and the effort to transcend them in the face of the integrity of resistant social forms. Fox, for instance, moves between the language of descent and residence and the metaphors of origin and place or location, as if he was uncertain which is more appropriate to the description "houses" (1987:172).

Part of the reason for the uncertainty derives from the nature of Lévi-Strauss' original formulation of the concept. Operating within a more or less explicit evolutionary framework, he situates "house societies" between elementary and complex structures of kinship. He suggests that, although they draw upon the structures of kinship, house societies are nevertheless subjected to the forces of political and economic interests that subvert the elementary language of kinship (1987:151–52). In one sense house societies depend upon the language of kinship; in another, they go beyond and transform this language. Rooted in the elementary structures of kinship, house societies provide the missing link between kin-based societies and those governed, presumably, by the forces of the market.

As if himself trying to transcend the language of kinship, Lévi-Strauss declares that

> Anthropologists have therefore been mistaken in seeking, in this type of institution, a substratum which they have variously thought to find in descent, property and residence. We believe, to the contrary, that it is necessary to move on from the idea of *objective substratum* to that of *objectification of a relation*: the unstable relation of alliance which, as an institution, the role of the house is to solidify, if only in an illusory form. (1987:155)

Extending the rhetoric of the house as a transitional form between elementary and complex structures, the house ultimately becomes a protocapitalist image of the commodity fetishism found in capitalist societies — only here the relations of reproduction substitute for those of production (Lévi-Strauss 1987:155).

To the extent that Lévi-Strauss' concept of house societies is situated in an evolutionary position betwixt and between elementary and complex structures, it will remain in a liminal theoretical position — tied down, at one end, by the old "objective substratum" of ill-fitting kinship categories and suppressed, at the other end, by a vocabulary that turns the "house" into a "fetish" (1987:155). At one end, the house reverts back to a unilineal descent group with an array of awkward appendages; at the other end, the house becomes a protocapitalist transformation of elementary structures on the brink of becoming complex.

Nevertheless, in the opposition between kinship and its transcendence or objectification, I believe Lévi-Strauss has captured something central to our understanding of house societies. Yet this opposition does not define two distinct types of society so much as a tension within a single society that is central to the delineation of hierarchy. Although I am tempted to call the processes involved those of objectification and personification—thereby mobilizing Lévi-Strauss' term—nevertheless, these terms harbor far too many assumptions, particular to Western culture, relating to the nature of persons, subjects, and objects.[7] The contrast I am concerned with here does, in part, implicate something that we could call personification and objectification. Yet it might better be characterized in terms of the particularization of relation and the dispersal of value as opposed to the abstraction and generalization of relation and the concentration of value—where the former is manifested in the form of persons and the latter in the form of houses and valued objects.

It is this opposition, then, that I would like to resituate, removing it from an external, evolutionary framework that makes the "house" a liminal entity caught between two worlds, and instead framing it in terms of internal, indigenous understandings that give to "house societies" their own integral dynamics. In Tanimbar, I find such a framework in indigenous representations of the dynamics of life. For, as will become evident, it is the relative value accorded to the source of life and its issue that differentiates houses—in accordance with their relative ability to generalize relations and concentrate value—and gives shape to the resulting hierarchical order. Framing the issue in this way, it is possible, then, to concentrate upon what Tanimbarese themselves find important: the generation of life and, in the process, the manner in which the markers of value that differentiate a house are established and actively negotiated through exchange. It is also possible to see that what is important in the creation of hierarchical relations both within and between houses is not their transcendence of seemingly "incompatible principles," as Lévi-Strauss would have it, but rather their explicit engagement of the contrast between differently evaluated social forms.

Hierarchy, Exchange, and Gender

In order to understand the hierarchical dynamics of Tanimbarese social relations, it has been necessary to move away from a theoretical framework that conceptualizes social units in terms of a priori, essentialist, and exclusive criteria. In place of these, it has been necessary to substitute a more dynamic conception of social relations that reveals (rather than conceals) the contrastive logic of relatively valued social forms and the processes by which they are brought into being. This move has been possible because a consideration of indigenous ideology has com-

---

7. Recent anthropological works that use the concepts of objectification and personification in various ways include Gregory 1982; Thomas 1985; and Strathern 1988.

pelled a reevaluation of fundamental analytic categories. Quite simply, such categories as unilineal descent and prescriptive marriage extinguish all life from the analysis of a system whose central dynamic — relating unified, fixed, weighted centers to multiple, dispersed, moving, weightless peripheries in an organic figure of growth from source to issue — is capable of precipitating a myriad of contrastive social forms in the process.

In Tanimbar the house is an anchored, fixed, center. But the intergenerational continuity of men within a house cannot, for that reason, be considered to be either a bounded unit or the natural, inevitable result of a principle of unilineal descent. Indeed, the most explicit reason why the concept of descent does not take us very far in Tanimbar does not have to do with the statistical composition of houses (which from an external perspective appear as "patrilineal" as any), but rather with indigenous ideology concerning the constitution of houses. The house as a fixed, enduring unit must continually be created and recreated through exchanges. These effect the differentiation of the prior unity of brother and sister, the establishment of the intergenerational continuity of the male aspects of the house, and the growth and extension of the female aspects of the house (which, though extracted, nevertheless remain part of the estates of the house). The possibility that these effects may or may not be realized yields the contrastive forms of affiliation and residence that otherwise have no place or meaning within the theoretical framework of unilineal descent systems.

Similarly, the closed asymmetric pathways of the Great Row form the anchored, fixed center of the vast network of exchange pathways that wend their way around the archipelago. Yet the cycle cannot be seen as the natural, given form of a matrilateral cross-cousin marriage system. For the very existence of this cycle — as an entity that unifies opposites and anchors the flow of life by turning asymmetry back on itself — both requires and is, itself, the prerequisite for the simultaneous differentiation of opposites and extension of life through alliances that open new asymmetric pathways of exchange. The logic of the contrastive dynamics of variant marriage possibilities that inform such a conceptualization would be suppressed under the more rigid theoretical framework (prescriptive or otherwise) generally applied to matrilateral cross-cousin marriage systems.

All social units in Tanimbar — including not only houses and the Great Row, but also villages and people — are created through a process which involves both the differentiation of a prior transcendent unity into its component parts as well as the subsequent recomposition of new synthetic unities. To apprehend the logic of such a conceptualization of the nature of the world, we need to relinquish static, bounded analytic categories for a more fluid conception of the forms of social organization. We need, in short, not only a concept of hierarchy — the relation between the whole and its parts — but also a way to account for the processes by which both the whole and its parts are decomposed and recomposed.

Such an understanding of hierarchy can be developed by elaborating Dumont's ideas on the subject in the context of Wagner's concept of analogic kinship and Strathern's ideas concerning analogic gender. Dumont uses two images to explain his theory of the hierarchical opposition: one, the creation of Eve from the extracted rib of Adam; the other, the differentially valued polarity of our right and left hands (1980:239–45; see also Dumont 1979, 1982; Barnes et al. 1985). It is the former image that is more helpful here, for the opposed units are not already existent as they are in the latter case. What the Adam and Eve example stresses is that the opposed units must be created out of something that is a prior, undifferentiated unity. That unity must be decomposed — Eve must be created from the extracted rib of Adam — and it is only as a result of this process that their differentiated and opposed natures are brought into existence. Three ideas are important here: first, the idea of a prior, undifferentiated unity; second, the idea (assumed in this example, but not otherwise developed by Dumont) that a *process* of differentiation is a necessary requirement for the existence of a relation between the two opposed entities; and third, the idea that, to the extent that one entity is extracted from another, there will be an asymmetry in the relation between the two such that the one that has been extracted is hierarchically encompassed by the one from which it has been extracted.[8] As useful as it is, Dumont's analysis, which he opposes to a more dynamic Hegelian dialectic, remains a static depiction of the relation between opposed units and "pre-existing totalities" (1980:243). He does not dwell on the processes involved in the differentiation of prior unities, nor does he imagine processes whereby units might be recomposed to form new unities.

Wagner's conception of analogic kinship (1967, 1977) dovetails nicely with the processual implications of the Adam and Eve example and helps us escape the straightjacket of Dumont's structuralism. Like Dumont's hierarchical opposition, Wagner's analogic kinship requires a prior, undifferentiated unity. Yet, for Wagner, the process of extraction or differentiation is explicitly effected through the agency of exchange. Rather than assume that there are natural differences that are reflected in separate, a priori kin categories, which it then becomes the task of exchange to mediate and relate, Wagner assumes that there is an analogic similarity that

8. One can imagine another possibility: that the two units are merely differentiated from one another in which case neither would stand for the whole more than the other and the relation between the two would be one of equality rather than hierarchy.

underlies all kinship relations, which it then becomes the task of exchange to differentiate (1967, 1977). Kinship units are thus defined by a process of differentiation or extraction from a prior, undifferentiated unity.

Strathern (1988) has taken Wagner's model of analogic kinship a step further and, in applying it to the relations of gender, has analyzed the language of the processes of differentiation that are productive of things and people in what she calls "gift societies" as opposed to "commodity societies" (cf. Gregory 1982). Like kinship for Wagner, gender here, does not consist of preexisting, bounded, or natural male and female forms (1988:184).[9] Rather, for Strathern, all entities have the potential for manifesting both a unified, androgynous, cross-sex (male and female) identity as well as a differentiated same-sex (male or female) identity. "Social life consists in a constant movement from one state to another, from one type of sociality to another, from a unity . . . to that unity split or paired with respect to another. . . . Gender is a principal form through which the alternation is conceptualized" (1988:14). Itself a product of a relationship, an androgynous, undifferentiated entity is a completed whole — a unity that contains both male and female parts within itself. "The (androgynous) entity so produced, the object of the relationship, literally evinces their [sic] cross-sex relationship within itself" (Strathern 1988:184). In this condition, however, such an entity is unproductive. In order to be productive, to be able to establish a relation with another, "a composite, androgynous entity has . . . to be reconceptualized as singular, and in being differentiated from another[,] as incomplete" (1988:185). Incomplete same-sex (male or female) entities must therefore be extracted from completed androgynous entities. In this process of extraction, differentiated male and female identities are created. As differentiated, and therefore incomplete, they elicit their cross-sex counterpart. It is through their relation that new, completed, androgynous wholes — which are both the outcome and the containment of the relation between male and female — are created.

Yet it is important not to lose the hierarchy in the processual transformations. For, although the separation, differentiation, or extraction of a part from an undifferentiated whole simultaneously elicits the existence of its opposite, the nature of the relation between the two opposed terms is not yet evident. This relation is potentially either symmetrical and egalitarian or asymmetrical and hierarchical. There are thus two conditions for the establishment of a hierarchical relation between the two opposing parts. First, a part must be extracted from a prior unity such

9. Such a position is, of course, not unique to Strathern; its development has a long history. See, for example, Rosaldo and Lamphere 1974; Rubin 1975; MacCormack and Strathern 1980; and Collier and Yanagisako 1987.

that the remaining part is constituted as the source from which its opposite issues forth. If one cannot be conceptualized as the source of the other, there can be no hierarchy, only differentiation and equality. Second, a tension must be established between the processes of extraction and containment, separation and encompassment. Indeed, it is this tension that holds hierarchy in place. If there were either total separation, on the one hand, or total encompassment—or, more properly, complete reincorporation—on the other hand, there would be no relation whatsoever, and consequently no hierarchy (cf. Valeri 1975–76). Since exchange is what creates this tension, exchange is the motivating force behind the constitution of both the identity of units and the hierarchical relation between units.

In order to apprehend the indigenous logic of processes of differentiation and recomposition that are at the heart of the creation of people, houses, villages, and the Great Row, I have appropriated the form of Dumont's hierarchical opposition, added the idea of a process of differentiation through exchange, which derives from Wagner's analogic kinship, and complemented this with an understanding of the gendered movements of unity and differentiation that are productive of the transforming identities of people and things. It has, moreover, been helpful to complement this formulation with indigenous understandings of hierarchy as constituted by the relations between source and issue that are defined through the processes that decompose and recompose prior unities.

Indeed, Tanimbarese material has required the placement of undifferentiated, androgynous unities at the center of analysis. For these unities—the stone boat, the ancestor altars, the Great Row—stand at the center of society. Yet, as such, they are nonproductive. Their component parts must be differentiated so that they may enter into a productive relation with one another. This differentiation—activated initially by a spear and later by exchange—is effected by the separation or extraction of a part or parts from an otherwise undifferentiated whole. What I am calling recomposition is, of course, the opposite process: that is, the reconstitution of an undifferentiated transcendent unity from an aesthetic synthesis of its parts. Tanimbarese forms of social organization are, in the end, but moments in the unfolding of this double movement.

The book begins, then, with Tanimbarese representations of the original differentiation of the prior transcendent unity of the world, which was effected by the agency of a spear, and which resulted in a condition of extreme mobility and instability for men and women (chapter 3). A new cultural order was established through the recomposition of synthetic, transcendent unities: the stone boats that form the ritual centers of villages (chapter 4), the ancestor statues that form the ritual centers of houses (chapter 5), and the double cycle of alliance at the center of the system of exchange pathways (chapters 6 and 10). The physical and conceptual nature of houses in general, as well as the differential values that distinguish named houses (of nobles) from unnamed houses (of commoners) are discussed in chapter 5. This is followed by an exploration of the pathways that emerge from the flow of blood through female lines, against which the continuity of males in houses must be established (chapter 6). These pathways delineate a network of asymmetric marriage and exchange lines that culminate in the third image of transcendent unity—the double asymmetric cycle of exchange at the center of the entire system of exchange pathways. Having set out the main parameters of the system, the next four chapters analyze the various forms of marriage, exchange, and affiliation that together give shape to the hierarchical relations between houses. The initiation of impermanent affinal relations is discussed first, along with the exchanges that negotiate the extraction of women and children from their natal houses (chapter 7). This is followed by an examination of the relative value of "engendered" valuables and the way their exchange implicates the reciprocal processes of separation and encompassment, which together define the tension that makes hierarchy possible (chapter 8). The manner in which the continuity and asymmetry of affinal relations are effected through both matrilateral cross-cousin marriage and the requirements of exchange is examined in chapter 9; the dynamics of alliance relations along permanent pathways of exchange between named houses and is discussed in chapter 10. Here the hierarchically encompassing nature of alliance and exchange along the top double cycle brings this sequence on marriage and exchange to its final culmination. The book ends with a discussion of rank as the ultimate articulation of the total system of differential values (chapter 11) and a conclusion that develops the implications of the ideas discussed throughout the work (chapter 12).

3 The Differentiation of the World

Logically, and for the Dinka historically, their relations with Divinity
begin with a story of the supposed conjunction, and then division, of the
earth and the sky — the emergence of their world as it is. All the Western
Dinka know much the same version of the myth of this original situation,
which is their representation and ultimate explanation of some of the conditions of human life as they now find it. (Lienhardt 1961:33)

No one ever tells how the world came to be shaped the way
it was before the spear radically transformed it. The world was simply
there — self-contained and static. The moon and the stars were undifferentiated from the great round disc of the sun, which was pinned below the
edge of the eastern horizon by the weight of a sky that pressed so low
upon the earth as to be inseparable from it. Occasionally the sun attempted
to rise over the rim of the horizon, and the rays of a would-be dawn
lightened the world enough for people to move about. But soon the sun
was forced to retreat below the horizon, and the world was enveloped
once again in its primordial darkness. Trapped between the sky and the
earth as it was, the sun held all time and seasonal change within its con-
fines. It also, therefore, reserved the rains, which were yet to be released
according to their seasonal progression. The land, too, was closed in upon
itself, and doubly so: the offshore islands were contained within the mainland, and so were the springs of fresh water, which had yet to flow forth
from the earth. This thoroughgoing containment of the world within itself
was also mirrored in its inhabitants, for male and female, brother and
sister, were contained within one another, rendering social life distinctly
problematic.

Contemporary social forms exist as a result of the forces that acted
to differentiate this initial unity into its integral and complementary parts.
This differentiation is, however, more than the condition for contemporary
existence. It is also the prototype for a process that is necessary for the
generation of life and growth. As such, it is crucial to the dynamics that
shape contemporary social relations.

Yet, for now, it is the manner in which the intial self-contained unity of the world was differentiated that is our focus. We will also be concerned to understand the consequence of this differentiation — the extreme state of mobility and instability that resulted — and its implication for the creation of a new cultural order. It will become evident that the process of differentiation is only one part of a double-edged dynamic that also requires that life and growth be anchored by a process of recomposition that creates new unities, which are as fixed and weighty as the tendrils of new growth are mobile and light.

Origins of the Sacred Spear

It was a spear (*vunut*) — otherwise known the "sacred/taboo spear" (*vunut malmoli*), or the "spear of otherworldly powers" (*vunut sakti*) — that held the power to differentiate the world.[1] The spear is most renowned in connection with the exploits of the culture hero, Atuf, who some say already possessed the spear when he arrived in Tanimbar from overseas. More often, however, it is said that Atuf acquired the spear only later, after he arrived in the archipelago, and that others had held it before him.

The spear is often associated with the people of Olsuin, an autochthonous settlement that is said to have once existed on the southwestern peninsula of Yamdena. Some claim that the Olsuin people obtained the spear from the former village of Ahu Brovu on the island of Maru in the northern part of the archipelago.

The following was contributed by a certain Seranmela of Kamatubun on Sera. Two people from Olsuin, namely Silimela and Lavlovi, took the famous lance away from Ahu Brovu. They tested it on the way and struck the present-day island of Sera off from Yamdena. (Drabbe 1940:320)

---

1. Drabbe notes that the name of the spear is, in Yamdenan, *Ngane-Batin*, for which he gives the Latin gloss, *granum vaginae* (1940:322). It is difficult to determine the exact meaning that he intended to convey by this gloss. In his own Yamdenan dictionary *nganan* means "female genitals" (1932b:74), and *batin* means "heart, pit, kernel, seed, eye (of something)" (1932b:10). It would seem that the most probable translation would be "clitoris," which would give the spear a distinctly female connotation. Drabbe admits that this is an odd name, but then goes on at length to account for the name as a corruption of the name for a famous spear — *Nga'Bal* or "Balinese Lance" — in the Kei Islands, just to the north of Tanimbar (1940:322). His rather lame attempt to explain away the more risque name of the spear is hardly satisfactory. I must concede, however, that I never heard the spear referred to by any name, let alone one with the above connotation. Lacking both a confirmation and an indigenous interpretation of the name reported by Drabbe, I am hesitant to put forward my own interpretation.

Or, more ambitiously:

> At Awear, on Fordata, people say that the lance originated from
> Ahu Brovu on the island Maru. It was taken away by someone who
> was then pursued. He bound the lance in front of the boat and, at a
> rip-roaring speed, they rowed southward up against the northern
> coast of Yamdena. In this way, they struck off various capes that are
> now islands—such as Nus' Lima, Frinun, Itain-Namwaan, Nus'
> Karatat, etc., etc. (Drabbe 1940:320)

The extraordinary powers of the spear are immediately evident, and have
everywhere the same transformative force, opening up the earth and creating the present-day geographical configurations of the archipelago (cf.
Tambiah 1985:303).

People more closely related to the autochthonous population of Olsuin recount yet another, higher, origin of the miraculous spear. From the
village of Lauran, people of the house Das Kormbau (descended from
the old settlement of Olsuin) told Drabbe:

> . . . The elders of Olsuin were: Silimel, Loblobi, Atot, Atumar and
> Batungrof [sic] Mbaretyaman.
>   They tapped palmwine from the sugar [*aren*] palm, but they
> noticed one day that their palmwine had been stolen from the tree.
> They went by turns to lie in wait, but did not trap the thief, until the
> youngest, the blind Ratungrof, got hold of him.[2] It was none other
> than the supreme being himself. He could not deny it and declared
> himself ready to pay a fine. He gave two pieces of gold, Tune (kept
> in Lauran) and Telyawar (kept in Omtufu). Then Ratungrof asked
> for the staff of the supreme being and obtained this also. "And this,"
> he said, "is the power of it: if people make trouble for you, then
> stamp the ground with this staff and their village will sink." When
> Ratungrof went to his older brothers and told of this staff, they did
> not believe him. But soon the truth of it was made clear: they lay the
> staff on the ground in the bush and suddenly a spring issued forth—
> so strongly that the water formed a river that ran out into the sea.
> (1940:320–21; see also 423).

Here it is apparent that the spear has its origins with the supreme being,
Ubila'a, who despite possessing an abundance of gold and other valu-

2. In translating these stories, Drabbe clearly assumes that the supreme being is male,
even though in his discussion of the nature of Tanimbarese perceptions of the supreme deity,
Ubila'a, it is obvious that the deity combines both male and female qualities. It should also
be noted that in Tanimbarese languages, no gender distinctions are marked in pronouns.
Unless otherwise known, the gender attribute of a subject, therefore, is always ambiguous.

ables, is nevertheless caught red-handed as a thief of palmwine. Efraim Lamera, of Sifnane, told me another version of the same history, which (like the above version) also relates the opening up of the main island of Yamdena and the release of a major river from its containment by the land.

At the time of Silimela Batuyaman and his younger brother Loblobi Andityaman . . . we all lived together on the land Olsuin, the village Olsuin. There were no other people there yet. We are a working people, so we made one of our large yam gardens. We made fences, fences, fences of various kinds surrounding the whole garden, so that nothing at all could eat our crops. . . . By chance, each and every night—who knows what in the world it was but—something was pulling up our crops one by one and eating them. . . . We did not really pay attention when people said that something was stealing, something was stealing [our garden produce]. . . . If some people had been there [to watch] we could say that people were stealing. So, they just waited until the crops were completely gone from the garden. Only "itchy taro" was left. . . . Ah, Silimela and Loblobi ordered their three children [to guard the garden]. They ordered Lamera, but [there was] no [result]. They ordered Itran Belakan, but [there was] no [result]. So they ordered the youngest, Iatluri Tibalaman. This Iatluri Tibalaman guarded this garden well. Close to when the cocks crow the third time, [he saw] it was not a pig. There was a person. His beard grew down over his stomach. . . . He held his spear! . . . Then the child wound his hand fast around the beard.

Having caught the thief in the act, Iatluri Tibalaman called upon all his relatives to come take the thief and kill him. But the thief pleaded again and again for his life and promised to give his captors something special if they did not kill him.

"So do you really agree to give us something so that we will not kill you?" . . . "My staff here. I will give it to you." "Ooh, just this staff, and what will *it* do? We already have an abundance of gold earrings and breast pendants, elephant tusks and all kinds of valuables. . . . And your staff, what will it do?" "Ah, it's like this. Ah, you all do not have a dugout canoe, you do not have a sailing boat, you do not yet have even a little outrigger."

So with his spear, the old man made a boat—one of the type that was usually associated with those who possessed the sacred spear. It was a special boat, called Wa'ur Kulit, with a hull made of bark, a sail made of flowered cotton, a ceramic plate for a bailer, and an elephant tusk for a mast (or in other versions for a rudder). But the Olsuin people cried out,

> "Oh, but the earth is still whole, there is no river yet. The sea has not yet been let in. So how could we use a punting pole, or a paddle? How could we use a sail? . . . If we go sailing, we will run aground." . . . Then he said, "Pierce the ground, do it like this." . . . Ah, he did it. He did it. He made the river flow, made the river flow, made the river flow. He pierced [the earth] completely. . . . The earth was split, so that it became a river, like a river. "Go until you reach the sea, the inside of the reef and wait there so I can instruct you."

Having reached the reef edge of the sea, they waited for the old man, and when he arrived,

> he instructed them in everything, the source of absolutely everything. [Then] this person, he was no longer there. . . . The old man was no longer there. Who knows if he was a master [*dua*], or Ubila'a [the supreme being]. At that time, they did not know everything . . . so who knows if Ubila'a showed himself to them. Good or bad, we do not know up to that point. Then he instructed [them] in everything, the sources of absolutely everything.
>
> He instructed them. . . . If you go to sink a village, if the village, the people, do not like you . . . [then] pierce the ground with the spear. . . . So do not mistake this for an ordinary spear, just an ordinary thing. . . . Nevertheless, they did not agree, they did not follow the old man's advice. Later . . . when they met Atuf, they already wanted to exchange. Ah, earlier Sus asked where the sacred spear came from. So, its history is like that. . . . It came from Ubila'a.

These histories, then, recount the transference of the sacred spear from the supreme being, Ubila'a, into the hands of men. In that transference, the power to decompose the primal, self-contained unity of the world and shape its current contours is relinquished by Ubila'a and becomes the power of men.

Ubila'a: Unity and Adrogyny

Although the power of differentiation is relinquished, Ubila'a nevertheless remains the image and force of a completed whole—of the ultimate unity of the world. Now a distant, transcendent deity, Ubila'a is both male and female, the sun and the moon, the heavens and the earth.

As a force, Ubila'a is both the potential for life as well as the keeper of death.[3] The Catholic and Protestant representations of God have now been superimposed upon the figure of this indigenous deity.

Ubila'a is the Fordatan term that derives from the coupling of the root word for all "males and females of the second ascending and the second descending generations" (*ubu*),[4] and the word for "great" or "supreme" (*ila'a*). Ubila'a therefore means "Supreme Grandparent"—the one from whom all originate, and, implicitly, all those (the grandchildren) who have originated from the one. On Fordata, the deity is also known as Duad-ila'a, which would be translated as "Our Great Master." The word *duad* is the first person plural (inclusive) possessive form of the root *dua*,[5] which means "master" or "owner" of persons or objects and, in most contexts, refers to one's life- and wife-givers. On Yamdena, the deity is generally referred to as Ratu, a word that is used commonly throughout Indonesia to signify a deity, a king, or a raja.

On Yamdena, again, Ubila'a is sometimes called the Noble One (*Mele*), and throughout the islands s/he is referred to by the couplings used in ritual language for a noble woman and man, *lemditi-fenreu*, and for the sun and the moon, *lera-vulan*.[6] Using Yamdenan (rather than Fordatan) terms, Drabbe notes that

> . . . some contend that *Limnditi-Fenreu* is the same as *Lere-Bulan*, sun and moon, which is simply unknown by others. Nevertheless, it is quite certain that the terms *Limnditi-Fenreu* mean sun and moon, or better moon and sun, because the moon is thought of as a woman,

---

3. In commenting upon Ambonese cosmology, Jansen remarks: "Finally I would like to draw the bold conclusion that these people have in fact constructed a complete philosophy of life. They view everything in terms of themselves, of a human being, male or female, continually procreating and bringing forth young. High above is a mysterious unit of being, the *uli téru* in which everything originates. . . . Their whole philosophy is founded and logically built on this principle" (1977:114–15).

4. See Barnes 1979 for a discussion of the proto-Austronesian term **e(m)pu* and its contemporary derivatives.

5. Possessive forms appear as suffixes to roots of nouns that denote, among other things, the inalienable body parts or kin relations of a person. Because the root *dua* appears so often in these pages, I will—in this instance—use the root form without any possessive suffix in order to avoid the confusion of variant suffixes. Similarly, plural forms will not be marked on Tanimbarese words, since together with their possessive suffixes, plural forms appear in many and varied guises. That a plural form is intended should be evident by the verbs used in the sentence in which it appears.

6. Throughout the text, there will appear a number of terms that are conventionally used in pairs, and whose linkage I have indicated by the use of a hyphen. Where such a paired term occurs, it constitutes a superordinate category marker, which includes both of the opposed terms (and sometimes others).

> the sun as a man. The two also married with each other, but what
> the consequence of that is, is not said. Just so, one also speaks of
> *langit* and *ombak*, heaven and earth, which are also thought of as
> man and woman, whereby heaven is the man, earth the woman, and
> rain the sperm that fertilizes the earth so that plants sprout. But one
> delves into the matter no further, and fantasizes no tales about it.
> (1940:426)

The gender connection that identifies rain as male and earth as female is
evident in a saying that refers simultaneously to ideas about plant growth,
human conception, and rank: "rain before the earth has content" (*da'ut
bi lanuun ihin*).[7]

Ubila'a is thought to combine not only such contraries as male and
female, heaven and earth, and sun and moon, but also some that implicate the deity more intimately in human social relations. In a story Drabbe
collected in the village of Kelaan,

> . . . we see a man ascend from the earth to heaven, visit God, and
> take one of his ten daughters in marriage. We notice here in God
> nothing other than human and even purely Tanimbarese behavior.
> The only thing that points to something higher is that he is supposed
> to reside in the heavens and that his daughters use golden vessels,
> even to bathe.
>   Another legend is that of Taborat. He noticed that his own and
> his brothers' palmwine was being stolen. They kept watch and dis-
> covered that the supreme being was the thief. His beard hung to the
> ground. Wrapping this beard around his arm with one turn, one of
> the brothers held the supreme being fast. As compensation, the
> supreme being gave them one of his sons, who later married among
> them. (1940:423)

Dwelling in the heavens where all is resplendent with gold, Ubila'a is both
wife-giver and wife-taker to the people of the earth, just as s/he is also
both the greatest of nobles and the most lowly of thieves.

Divided in the human world, such oppositions are united in the figure
of Ubila'a. This unity of opposites is nicely portrayed in the paired terms
(such as woman-man, moon-sun) used to refer to Ubila'a. Here, as generally
in Tanimbarese usage, such paired terms refer to a larger unity—a more
abstract, superordinate category that both combines equally at the same

---

7. See Drabbe 1940:426 for metaphors that refer to the land as female and the rain as
male.

time as it transcends the particularity of the paired elements.[8] Such appellations, therefore, mark Ubila'a as a transcendent figure that contains the world and all potential differentiations within her/himself.

An androgynous image of totality, Ubila'a is unproductive as such (Strathern 1988). Yet s/he contains the power through which the world may be differentiated and thus rendered fertile and productive of life. It is in response to his/her theft—a sign of Ubila'a's inherent lack of productivity—that the spear is appropriated and becomes the tool of male agency. Remaining an image of a prior and transcendent unity, Ubila'a thus becomes the source and possibility for its differentiation.

Of Wives and Offshore Islands

To trace the history of the sacred spear is to trace the history of the differentiation of the original self-contained unity of the world. The power of the spear not only opens the earth so that fresh water might flow forth, it also separates the offshore islands that are held within the mainland and, as a consequence, provides the means whereby sisters are differentiated from brothers and women are separated from their natal houses and given in marriage to the houses of their husbands.

During this time, the Herculean task of striking off capes and opening up channels between the mainland and offshore islands was given to prospective bridegrooms in lieu of bridewealth as the price for the hand of a woman in marriage. Yet the strenuousness of the task, in effect, made marriage virtually impossible. In one of his adventures, after he acquires the spear, Atuf rescues a man who is struggling with such a task.

> Once he [Atuf] traveled with his boat by the little island Dog Cape (Asutubun), which then was still united with [the southeastern tip of] Yamdena to the great inconvenience of the people, since in the east monsoon it stood in such breakers that they could not pass through it with their boats. Atuf saw a man there busy cutting through a stone. He came there in order to marry a woman and the

---

8. The fact that Ubila'a seems to be depicted as a male in some of the above stories does not necessarily contradict this reading. This depiction could be due to any of a number of factors, including (1) the mistranslation of Tanimbarese language pronouns; (2) the influence of Drabbe's and the Christian missionaries' representations of God as male; or, (3) the appearance of Ubila'a as male in particular contexts. It may be noted that Drabbe completely failed to perceive the androgynous nature of Atuf's sister Inkelu, who is otherwise depicted as female (see below). He may well have failed to perceive the androgynous nature of Ubila'a who may have been otherwise depicted as male.

people had demanded that he cut open a channel. Atuf took over the task for him and made the opening with one thrust of his spear. (Drabbe 1940:319)

A similar connection is made between bridewealth and the shattered unity of the mainland in a history of the village of Atubul.

> A part of the *stam*[9] Olsuin also lived at Omtufu. Now there was a woman from this *stam* married at Atubul, but her husband also had a wife from Atubul itself, and since he kept more [wives] than these, he put Tambarsoli, the one from Olsuin, in a pigsty and daily gave her only yam peels to eat. Now it happened by chance that one day the children were playing with some *kaplili* (a tree nut similar to our chestnut), and one of the *kaplili* came directly into the pigsty. The woman seized hold of the *kaplili* and when the youth came to ask for it, it became apparent from their conversation that he was her own brother and she ordered him to report her sad fate to her parents and brothers. He started off at once for home. When he ran short of water on the way, he struck his lance into the ground and there issued forth a spring named Temroli.
>
> Arriving back in Atubul, the youth showed them the pigsty. They released the woman and went to the village. It was in the middle of the night. They stamped the lance on the ground and at the same instant a part of the village flew into the sea with one of the dance plazas: all the people who lived in that part of the village found their death in the waves, but the village was now changed into two islands, Nus' Mese and Kore, between which was the dance plaza that divided the two villages from each other. The part that remained in its own place is the present Atubul. Thus Nus' Mese and Kore became the brideprice of Tambarsoli, and belong to the *stam* Olsuin at Omtufu [which has now split into the two villages of Lorulung and Tumbur]. (Drabbe 1940:319–20)

At this point in time, it is the active agency of the spear, now in the hands of men, that transforms the self-containment of the land and of houses. Penetrating the mainland with their spear, the men open up channels that make possible a separation between the mainland and its offshore islands — the "mother" (*itai*) and her "children" (*yanat*). As a bridewealth payment, such an act of separation makes possible the extraction of the woman from her containment within her natal house, where brother

9. Drabbe uses the Dutch word *stam* in many contexts and it can thus be variously translated as "house," "patriline," "house-complex," "hamlet," or "village." Where it is unclear which of these meanings is intended, I have left the Dutch word *stam* in the English translation.

and sister had previously existed as an otherwise undifferentiated unity. It thus prefigures the role of bridewealth prestations in contemporary social life to separate both women and children from their natal and maternal houses (see chapters 7 and 8).

Atuf and His Sister Inkelu

The transformation of the relation between male and female, brother and sister, is exemplified in the stories of Atuf and his "sister" Inkelu.[10] The events of their lives outline the struggle that takes place, during this time, to demarcate a separate destiny for brothers and sisters and a complementarity of male and female actions in the world.

Not himself a native of Tanimbar, Atuf originated from foreign lands (*nuhu mavu*): some say that he was Buginese, others that he came from Seram or from Luang. But most often it is said that he, together with his three sisters and his slaves, arrived in Tanimbar from the Babar Islands to the west.

> On Babar there lived a family—Atuf and three sisters, Inkelu, Yaum Aratwenan, and Mangmwatabun—with various slaves. They were of high nobility, so high even that (in opposition to Tanimbarese customs) they . . . made no gardens, gathered no wood and fetched no water. The community had to do all that for them, until this began to vex them and they expelled [Atuf and his sisters]. They sailed their boats to Selaru. One of the sisters—Mangmwatabun— remained there, and the company went further on to Yamdena. They left Inkelu behind to the south of the present-day village of Olilit [Lama], on the island Dog Cape (Asutubun). (Drabbe 1940:315)

In the meantime, Atuf himself took up residence in the nearby village of Sifnane. The third sister ultimately made her home further north in the village of Omtufu (now divided into Lorulung and Tumbur). Little is heard about the other two sisters: it is Atuf and, to a lesser extent, Inkelu who become the primary culture heroes of Tanimbarese history.

In these stories there is a double androgyny at play. On the one hand, Inkelu herself turns out to be clearly androgynous. On the other hand, Inkelu and Atuf, together, form a kind of androgynous unity of action and identity. Inkelu's initial identification with her brother and the events that led to their separation are told in the story of Atuf's drinking house.

---

10. Since most of the stories about Atuf and Inkelu collected by Drabbe and me derive from Yamdenan sources, I have retained the Yamdenan version of their names, rather than use their Fordatan names—Tufa and Iankelu.

When Atuf lived in Sifnane, he had a drinking house or *lingat* on Bat'Dedelak, and each day tapped palmwine there. His sister [Inkelu] came there to eat and drink together with him and some [of the men] of the Waran-Masel-Embun *stam* (Olilit), namely Nifangelyaw Amasaman and Tameru Andityaman. One fine day, they had to wait for Inkelu. Atuf was impatient, began to curse her, and steadily poured out the palmwine. Then she appeared, but she spoke not a word. They asked how it was that she came so late, but received no answer. They set her cup of palmwine in front of her, but she did not touch it. After repeatedly invited to drink, finally she flew out at them and cried: "Am I a man, then, that I should drink palmwine? I am but an ugly woman, I am, and come not on time; you pour only in order to drink; I, but a woman, I drink, or otherwise, so there!" <kenum koli merwane yak? feti bat' rot' mbembu yatak yak ye, to weni kmwa, kimline tuak motak ma myenum; bate yak, kenum, tate far ane lo. >[11] With these words, she repeated the curse words with which Atuf had complained about her tardiness and Atuf understood. He offered her all kinds of valuables in order to make up, but all in vain. What then did she really want? "I want," she said, "nothing other than your grindstone <*mandu-ain*>," and what she meant by this was the gold breast pendant in the possession of Atuf, the name of which was Grindstone (Mbumbune). She received this piece of gold and all was forgiven; and after they had eaten and drunk together, she went back to Fanumbi, where that gold is still kept by Awonde Andityaman of the house of Batfutu, *stam* Batmwere. (Drabbe 1940:316)

Not only does Inkelu join her brother daily to drink palmwine in the men's house as if she were, indeed, a man (and then protest that she is but a woman); she also dies a warrior hero's death, beheaded it is true, but not before she single-handedly massacres the entire assembled armies of the villages of Alusi and Kilmasa, which had launched a joint attack upon her (Drabbe 1940:324). Yet, in the episode of the drinking house, Inkelu's identity with her brother is shattered when the latter curses her. Their separation is effected through the agency of Atuf and his gift of a golden breastplate — a "male" valuable which, like an inverted bridewealth prestation, stands in place of him in their relationship and allows them to begin to know how to complement, rather than replicate, one another.

11. The pointed brackets indicate portions of Drabbe's original manuscript that were deleted from the published volume of 1940. They provide the original Yamdenan text. The copy of the original manuscript can be found in the archives of the Missiehuis of Our Lady of the Sacred Heart in Tilburg, the Netherlands.

Although Atuf's curse and gift might have been enough to separate brother and sister, it was not enough to disambiguate Inkelu's sexual androgyny, which was only hinted at in the above passage. The secret of Inkelu's sexuality was related to me by Efraim Lamera of Sifnane. When he was telling me of her bravery in the fight against the Alusi and Kilmasa armies—describing her actions again as if she were a man—I asked explicitly whether she was not, in fact, a woman. He then spoke of Inkelu, and her sisters, in a new way: "Half woman, half man. They [Atuf's sisters] did not marry. The old ones said that we could not know for certain whether they were men or women, because they did not wear loincloths . . . and there were no pants then. . . . So they wore sarongs." Efraim said that their "heads"—that is, their hair—and their chests were like men, but from their "taboo things" (*af malmolinra*), it was impossible to tell whether they were men or women. Atuf was a man, he said, for "we could see that he wore a loincloth," but the three women wore sarongs and therefore it was impossible to know for certain. Efraim then paused, his voice dropped to a whisper, and he began narrating another, more explicit, version of the drinking house story. In this version, her drinking companions (who did not include her brother) devised a plan so as to be able to discover the truth about her sexuality.

> Ah, Lurwembun together with Na'it and the grandchildren, they spoke like this: "Hey, let's not tap, let's not tap palmwine yet. Wait for Inkelu so that when she comes we can send her and she can tap [palmwine] so that we can look up and see whether she is a man or a woman." . . . Alas! These tricky people lured [her] so they would know . . . Inkelu's good and bad. So they said . . . Bwormbaresi's eyes hurt, that they did not know what had hit his eyes, but both his right and left eyes were in pain, and he could not see at all.

On this pretense, they asked her to climb the tree to tap the palmwine, and sent a young boy to stand under the tree to receive the palmwine she would hand down.

> She was up above. . . . This child looked up to see: "Oh! Her taboo things, half woman, half man!" Ah, Inkelu looked down and she was shamed. "Ah, I am completely shamed, I say, he has seen my bad and my good." She was shamed, so they took a named gold piece . . . which is proof, a sign of proof, a sign . . . because they had seen her bad and her good. So they gave the gold piece Mbumbune [Grindstone]. They gave the gold piece—Sifnane's most ancient gold heirloom. . . . So she was ashamed and therefore did not come back again. So when Alusi and Kilmasa came south to burn down

the Village of Canals, all this was inside her. "I will die completely, so I will not see the people who looked at all of my good and my bad." The cause of her death was this. . . . Ah!

Drabbe relates another account of her death. After Inkelu had massacred the Alusi and Kilmasa troops, one soldier remained alive, unnoticed by Inkelu. He feigned death and lay still in the reef. When she leapt over him, however, he looked up (presumably at her "taboo things" under her sarong) and, realizing that it was Inkelu, jumped up and beheaded her (1940:324). Again, it was her sexual ambiguity that betrayed her and ultimately led to her death.

Like the sun that contained both the moon and the stars, and the mainland that contained both the offshore islands and the springs of fresh water, Inkelu contained both male and female attributes within herself. Unlike her brother, who was unambiguously male, Inkelu had a propensity for male activities—drinking in the men's house and excelling in warfare as a true warrior might only dream of doing. Yet, she also maintained the dress and attributes of a woman, including the knowledge of the prescriptions that would release women from their childbirth confinement.[12]

Remaining a self-contained unity, she was, like Ubila'a, sterile and nonproductive in this world: being both man and woman to herself, she could neither marry nor have children. Ultimately, in her shame, she was killed and turned to stone along with the warriors of Alusi and Kilmasa whom she had slaughtered. Their corpses now form the massive shoal of stone outcroppings just offshore from the present-day village of Olilit.

Atuf Spears the Sun to Pieces

In contrast to his sister Inkelu's self-containment, Atuf (together with the sacred spear) was the epitome of the active male agency that effected the separation and differentiation of the world. Indeed, in the hands of Atuf, the spear was yet to accomplish the ultimate act of decomposition.

According to most accounts, however, Atuf was not the original owner of the spear and came to acquire it only through exchange. Some say that the members of the house in which Atuf resided in Sifnane journeyed to Latdalam and bought the spear there for Atuf (Drabbe 1940:317). Others relate that it was Atuf himself who encountered Silimela, the Olsuin man who held the spear, and obtained it from him directly.

12. Drabbe reports that when Inkelu first lived on the island Dog Cape (Asutubun), she met a man of the Fanumbi hamlet to whom she gave her prescription for ending the taboos placed on a woman during her confinement for the birth of a child (1940:315–16).

Then Atuf lived on Selaru, and when he heard of this wonderful lance, he decided to take possession of it. He departed with a great ship; fifty men rowing on one side and fifty men rowing on the other side. They rowed with paddles, which were decorated with small round bells that jingled when they rowed. They shot a polecat and roasted it on the spit on the beach in front of the village of Olsuin. Soon Silimela and Lavlovi came to the beach and asked who they were. "Well," said Atuf, "do you not know me? I am Atuf and come from Tenan, in the middle of the island Selaru." They made a friend-ship pact, which, in the first place, required that they should give each other gifts. Atuf asked for and obtained the wonderful lance, and Silimela obtained two of the paddles decorated with bells. (Drabbe 1940:320)

Originally obtained by autochthones from the supreme being, Ubila'a, the spear now passed into the hands of an outsider. Paying no heed to the warnings of Ubila'a that the spear was no ordinary piece of equip-ment, the Olsuin brothers allowed themselves to be dazzled by the be-jangled paddles. With this trick, Atuf usurped power from the autoch-thones and obtained the spear for a few jingly trifles.

Although there may be some divergence concerning the ultimate origins of the spear and the manner in which Atuf came to possess it, when it comes to the act of heroism for which Atuf is famous throughout the archi-pelago, there is very little divergence indeed. Remarking upon the dark and dismal condition of the world, Atuf fixed upon a plan through which he might release the sun from its captivity beneath the sky at the eastern rim of the horizon. Drabbe recounts his adventures en route:

. . . armed with the lance, Atuf embarked with his slaves in a boat called Silolone. They traveled to the east and, far in the sea on a sandbank, they found an old woman who gave them the advice not to go ashore by the cape of Lamdesar . . . because, she said, that was taboo (*pemali*). They thus went further, and the closer they came to the sun, the hotter it became. But Atuf had taken precau-tions. He had brought with him large shells of coconut milk, and when he got too warm, he scooped out milk from the shell to his left and poured it over his body; and when he stabbed the sun, he rolled himself entirely in the one on his right.

In order to be able to come close to the sun, he had taken a broad plank along, behind which he hid. In the middle of one of the long sides, he had cut out a square in which he lay his lance. When he came close enough to the sun, he pierced it and the sun flew into two pieces. The one was and remained the sun; the other fell into the sea and became the moon; innumerable small pieces flew through the air and became the stars. But the lance remained stuck in the sun and was dragged along with it, until the sun released it on Kei. Atuf followed after the sun and found the lance on a stretch of beach. The blood of the sun dropped there on the beach, and to this day it is therefore called Laran-Lere-Daran, the Sun-Blood-Beach (in the Kei language, Nguur-Ler-Laran). Atuf left behind a female slave — by the name of Ditsamar Aresyenan — and entrusted the lance to her. "Take good care of the lance," he said, "in five days I will come to fetch you." On this place now lies the village Ler-Ohoi-Lim (ler = sun; ohoi = village; lim = five) on the island Yut, Kei Besar.

But when Atuf returned, he stopped off on the cape of Lamdesar. "Wait for me here," he said to his slaves, "I am just going to relieve myself here." He went on land, crouched down, relieved himself, but could no longer move away; he sat fast on the stones.[13] Then he called to his slave Laksusu and ordered him to bring his betelnut basket. The slave came and passed him his basket, but when Atuf held the one end fast, the slave could no longer release the other end. Then Atuf called to the rest of his slaves on the boat: "Turn back, because we sit here stuck fast; but go directly on and stop nowhere until you come to lie at anchor in Nam'Ratu" (a channel in front of Sifnane). The slaves did this and, arriving at Sifnane, they cut off the large sail, which is now the Big Anchor Place (Temyatan Silai); they also cut off the small sail, and that is now the Small Anchor Place (Temyatan Marumat).

The slaves sprang ashore and some became tree bears <*mande*>, some polecats <*lau*>, and some iguanas <*mbuwe*>.[14] The boat itself is the present-day Nus Kese. . . . On that island there is still to be seen the two large shells in which they had taken the coconut milk, but these also turned to stone. The anchor, or anchor stone, is now the smaller Taboo Island (Nus Momolin). (Drabbe 1940:317)

Other accounts differ only in details: in the telling of the incident with the woman who advises them not to stop at the cape near Lamdesar; in a commonly added incident concerning an upside-down mango tree; in the reasons why Atuf went ashore at Lamdesar despite the woman's warnings; and why, moreover, he was turned to stone once ashore there.

13. In Tanimbar, dreams that feature excrement always portend death (dreams of death, however, portend success in hunting or fishing).

14. It is unclear which animals Drabbe is referring to here, since there are neither bears nor polecats in Tanimbar.

The history of the sun-piercing is told somewhat differently in Olilit, and that by Tanati Aboyaman, whose forefathers, whom we have mentioned, daily drank palmwine with Atuf and Inkelu, and who thus should know. . . . They had already sailed a long way, when they came to a small island, where they found an old woman; but she could not speak with them because she had no mouth and also her behind was closed. They went on and close by the sun it was so hot that Atuf and the slaves sometimes crawled completely into the jars of coconut milk that they had brought with them as a precautionary measure. And the sky became ever lower so that again and again they had to cut off a piece of the mast; but they did not lose courage.

Yet they had nothing more to eat and then luckily they found a mango tree. However, this stood upside down and when they hit their bamboo sticks in the branches, the fruit did not fall toward them, but in the direction of the trunk, and therefore they made from their bamboo poles a pitchfork or plucking hook and so mastered the fruit. . . .

And when they arrived at the sun, Atuf pierced it into pieces — just as it has been related above, except where the lance remained was not told.

Then they turned back again and stopped on the little island where the woman lived. But before calling on her, Atuf quickly found somewhere some little crabs, placed them in his palm-leaf case and put it back in his pouch. When he came to the old woman, he took the case out again and offered it to her. The old woman opened it, but the crabs bit so viciously that she screamed from fright and pain. At the same moment, her mouth tore open, and also the other defect she had ceased to exist. "Atuf," she said, "you have made it so that I can speak and I can relieve myself. I will show you my gratitude and give you some good advice. When you return, do not stop over on yonder cape," and she pointed to the cape of Lamdesar, which is taboo.

Atuf departed, but he thought to himself that there should be something behind it, and hoped to find on the cape in question gold or ivory or some other valuable. They went there and he said to his slaves that he must go on land to relieve himself — with the same unlucky results as in the former tale. (Drabbe 1940:318).

People in Keliobar suggested to me that it was not simply because Atuf dared to go ashore at the tabooed Lamdesar cape that he turned to stone, but, more important, because he was no longer carrying the spear. Had he still been in possession of the spear, he might have survived the deadly

effects of the tabooed cape. Without the spear, however, Atuf had lost
the power that had made possible his heroic deeds. He then became incorporated within the very stone of the earth that — in his spear-bearing days —
had opened up before him.[15]

Atuf, like his sister, was a figure of infertility for he neither married
nor left descendants.[16] The connection that might have been made — through
a line descendant from Atuf — between the present and both the primal
unity of the past and the forces of its differentiation was severed when
Atuf turned to stone.[17] The creator of a world of complementary forms,
he himself was destined to find his end in the most self-contained and impenetrable of all forms — imprisoned by the fixity of stone.

Yet, having been turned to stone, the efficacy and power of both Atuf
and his sister Inkelu were not lost to humans, but rather captured and
anchored for all time — or, at least, until the Dutch took control of the
islands. Up to the turn of the century, shrines were made to Atuf and Inkelu in the villages of Olilit, Sifnane, and Lamdesar. There, offerings were
made to them and rituals were carried out in connection with the agricultural cycle and with the control of rain (Drabbe 1940:323–26). Even
after their death, they became an anchoring point for the powers that control rain and the fertility of both crops and women.[18] Thus, although they
were themselves infertile and nonproductive, they nevertheless contained
the conditions for fertility and productivity, just as they had created them
for others in the world.

The Autochthones Unanchored

If this had been a time when the primordial unity of the
heavens and the earth was shattered, broken into its complementary parts,
and set into motion, it was also a time when the unity of autochthonous
settlements of people was shattered and broken into a myriad of migrating

---

15. In Fordatan, the idea of turning to stone is expressed by two phrases: a reflexive
form, which would translate as "she/he/it is transformed/changed into stone" (*nfulak ia na'a
vatu*); and "stone clings to/envelops her/him/it" (*vatu ntafal ia*).

16. Contrary to what everyone else told me, Efraim Lamera of Sifnane claimed that Atuf
did marry in Selaru and had three daughters, including one named Inkelu. Efraim thus con-
tended that the three ambiguous women were not Atuf's sisters, but rather his daughters.
Everyone agrees, however, that none of these figures (whatever their relation might have
been) had any descendants. And, in fact, no one in Tanimbar claims descent from Atuf or
his sisters/daughters.

17. It could be said, then, that the career and the line of the prototypical stranger-king
(Sahlins 1981; Valeri 1982, 1985) was thereby cut short.

18. For the anchoring of supernatural powers in stones, which thereafter become fixed
points of access to these powers, see Hocart 1952:33–38; and Tambiah 1985:303.

groups, which began moving across the Tanimbarese landscape. These groups were joined by still others, which immigrated into the islands from the surrounding archipelagos. Whether the dispersal of these autochthonous settlements occured before, during, or after the herioc period of Atuf, or whether they were indeed a result of his actions, is unclear. What is clear is that Tanimbarese conceive of their own history as marked, initially, by a period in which humans became detached from their places of origin and underwent a long series of migrations before they finally came to rest in their present homes. Thus the history of every house or house cluster is a history of movements across the archipelago, movements which are traced by a trail of intermittent settlements, points where the group stopped for some time — perhaps joining with or separating from other groups — before it moved on yet again.

The names of the autochthonous settlements, from which people were scattered to the four corners of the archipelago, are well known throughout Tanimbar. They include Enos, in the middle of the southern island of Selaru; Makatian, in the center of the main island of Yamdena, and Olsuin, in the middle of the southwestern peninsula of Yamdena; Ba'ir Sadi, once an island and now a submerged reef just to the southwest of the archipelago; and Rumdudun, another former island, now a submerged reef to the northwest of the archipelago (near Nila and Srua).

The moving force behind the original dispersal of the autochthonous settlements and the continued migrations of people is couched, most often, in terms of some catastrophe — a flood (sometimes a flood of palmwine), a plague of mice, or an epidemic illness. Yet underneath these apparent causes, there is usually a more compelling force at work: the action of otherworldly powers, including those of witches.

Although it is said, for instance, that Ba'ir Sadi sunk under a flood of palmwine, this event was not a chance catastrophe, but rather the result of the explicit workings of a disgruntled witch:

> Formerly, Ba'ir Sadi was an inhabited island: three brothers lived there with their families. Their names were: Boki, Limlara, and Masmori. Their house was called Refvutu. One day, Boki was occupied tapping palmwine, when an old woman, an *iwangi*, or witch, asked him for palmwine. However, he refused her. Therefore she made the wine begin to flow in superabundance. He held a long bamboo container under [the tree], but this was soon full and ran over; he set a large ceramic jar under it, but this was also soon full. And even when he set a large boat under it, this could still not contain the palm liquid. At wits' end, he cut the flower cluster off, and when he saw that that still did not help, he even cut the tree down, but the

palmwine continued to flow, so that it soon drenched the ground and flooded it, and the houses began to float. Then the inhabitants fled their submerged land. (Drabbe 1940:69)

The inhabitants of the house Refvutu could, by swimming, fortunately reach the village of Awear, on the island of Selaru, to the south of Adaut, where they settled. (Drabbe 1940:352)

However, the new settlement on Selaru did not last long, and it, too, soon succumbed to a catastrophe that scattered its inhabitants in all directions:

When they had settled at Awear on Selaru, that village also sank and the inhabitants fled — swimming to Adaut, Olilit, Sifnane, Lauran, and Latdalam. The house Refvutu, however, fled to the island of Fordata.

The cause of the inundation of Awear on Selaru is not known here [i.e., in Awear, Fordata]. According to the people of Lauran, however, whose ancestors are also known to have been rescued from the flooding of Awear, it must have happened because of the vengenace of the people of Olsuin on this village. They used the famous wonder lance, which they later sold to Atuf, for this. (Drabbe 1940:352)

For humanity, then, the consequences of the differentiation of the world were unending migrations and perpetual displacements. Just as a group would manage to find a suitable place, some uncontrollable, uncontainable, otherworldly force would disrupt and disperse it. It became clear that, as much as the separation of the world into its complementary parts was necessary for life, nevertheless, some form of anchorage was equally necessary if humans were to escape this condition of continued displacement and dispersal.

Valuables and Otherworldly Powers

However, if this was a time that witnessed the human community unanchored, it was also the time during which men secured the tokens of otherworldly powers that would help to anchor them once again and ensure their enduring place in the world. These tokens of power usually consisted of gold breastplates (*masa*) and gold earrings (*loran*) — both "male" valuables — that were obtained through exploits involving contact with beings from the heavens, the underworld, or from lands far outside the horizon of the Tanimbarese archipelago. Ultimately these valuables would become the heirlooms whose possession is one of the signs of important, named houses and their continued connection to the otherworldly sources of power.

Drabbe tells a history of a named golden breast pendant that was obtained by the ancestors of the house Ditilebit during the time before the
village of Awear had yet been formed.

Behind the Ditilebit house in Awear on Fordata, there stand two
wooden images, of which the one represents a man, Lelamwaan, and
the other a woman, Minanlela. They are two children of deities who
were sent by God down from the heavens to seek a wife in the
Ditilebit house on the rocks of Kelsangur. Lelamwaan took Titiluvu
as a wife, but when he wanted to take her back to the heavens, she
did not want [to follow]; he gave her a golden breast pendant . . .
and then returned to the heavens with Minanlela. Titiluvu and her
son Siavu . . . waited many years for him, but he never returned
again. Since Siavu then no longer had a father who could look for a
wife for him, he took himself to Sera where he took Titi Na'i, from
the house Kuwai in Kamatubun (Drabbe 1940:151).[19]

Whereas the Ditilebit heirloom is reputed to have been a prestation
from heavenly wife-takers, that of the house Temar is thought to have been
stolen from the underworld. Vutlima Laian told me the history of the
Temar heirloom, a small pair of named gold male earrings (*loran*).

In front of the Laian house is a doorstep in the form of a stone called
"the door of the crevice" (*lalahi ni falfolat*), which leads down into the
underworld. One day a man, Itran Rumaenga, descended into
the underworld by way of this door, and there he saw a group of
young children playing a game with golden earrings. He decided
to try to take a pair of these earrings back up with him. He attempted to swallow one pair, but they were too large and did not
go down. Finally, he was able to swallow a very fine pair of small
golden earrings. When the children finished with their game, they
discovered that this pair was missing. They searched everywhere
and began to cry when they could not find them. Finally, it occurred to them to search Itran Rumaenga. They searched him up and
down, and even stripped him of his loincloth [other adventurers
into the underworld have been known to hide coveted grains of
rice tucked in under their testicles], but they were forced to give
up when they still could not find the missing earrings. Itran Ru-

19. The origin place of the Ditilebit house is not on the rocks of Kelsangur (which is
well known as the origin place of the house-complex Weriditi), but rather the rocky bluff
to the south called Ruat ni Dii. The woman Siavu took as his wife from the house Kuwai
in Sera would have been called Titi Ne'i (Kilmasarenan), not Titi Na'i. The wooden images
of Lelamwaan and Minanlela currently reside in the Netherlands.

maenga then returned back up to the earth. The next day he excreted the pair of earrings, which became the heirloom valuables of the house Temar.

Another underworld source of valuables concerns the renowned Golden Snake (Nif Masa) of Makatian, a village now located on the west coast of Yamdena, although at the time of the golden snake it was located in the interior of the island. The ancestors of the house Vuarlela — now located in the village of Waleran (formerly a part of the village of Sofyanin) on Fordata — originally lived in Makatian, where they were the "master" (*dua*) of this famous Golden Snake. The snake, whose scales were made of pure gold, lived in a hole near the village of Makatian.[20] Yelar Vuarlela told me that if his ancestors made an offering consisting of white palm-wine, white rice on a white platter, and their eldest daughter, the snake would emerge to feed on these offerings, at which point it would be possible to scrape off the golden scales of the snake. The scales could then be melted down and made into valuables of various types. This was the source of the Vuarlela hierlooms, and, indeed, many valuables in Tanimbar are thought to originate from the gold of the Makatian Golden Snake.

The otherworldly powers of the gold of the Golden Snake of Makatian were manifest when the members of the Vuarlela house fled from Makatian to Moa. There they deceived the autochthonous people into believing that they were the true autochthones with prior rights on the land. This they did through a trial in which each side called lightning to strike. If lightning struck in the form of a snake then the land belonged to Vuarlela. The deception was effected with the help of the golden tail of the snake, which they had brought with them from Makatian. In this way, they established their claim to autochthonous status in the new land.[21]

It was through deception, or its equivalent in sacrifice, that the gold of the Golden Snake was obtained in the first place and, in the second place, that the gold demonstrated its otherworldly and authoritative powers. Indeed, during this time, deception and trickery were the primary means whereby gold valuables were secured and retained.

The force of deception and trickery is no more evident than in the history of the adventures of So'u Melatunan and his sister Titi Ma'i, who turn out to be trickster figures, much like their predecessors Atuf and Inkelu.

20. I was told by people in Makatian that the snake's hole was five meters deep, and at the bottom of the hole it branched out into four channels, which led out in the four directions from the center point.

21. Drabbe (1940:113–14) also provides an extended history of the Vuarlela house from its origins in Makatian to its final settlement in Sofyanin (which has now separated into two villages, Sofyanin and Waleran). The Vuarlela house is currently located in Waleran.

They acquired the Melatunan hierloom valuables not from heavenly or underworldly beings, but rather from their equivalent on a horizontal plane — foreigners from distant lands, in this case the Dutch. In Tanimbarese renderings of the early contact period of the mid-seventeenth century, the Dutch are referred to as the "Portugis."[22]

The history, as told to me by Metaniat Bungaa and Ma'idodu Melatunan, begins long ago when at least part of the people of what would become the village of Rumya'an had gathered themselves together at a place called Eli, in southern Fordata. The members of the Melatunan house held a feast and the people of the house Bungaa went to Nus Wotar, an island off the southwestern coast of Yamdena, to hunt pigs for the feast. When they set their dogs loose, however, the dogs did not run into the forest, but rather remained on the beach and bayed at a spot in the sand. There they came upon a large piece of ambergris, which they brought home with them and named Fish Excrement (Ian Tean).

Around this time the "Portugis" (that is, the Dutch) came to Tanimbar and began to build a fort on the coast of southern Fordata where the village of Rumya'an now stands. Falaksoru Melatunan, known by the diminutive So'u,[23] soon determined that he would "go off on a sailing adventure" (*nobal*) on one of the Portugis ships. Bungaa gave So'u the large piece of ambergris called Fish Excrement to take with him on his voyage. He went along with the Portugis — some say to Banda (Wadan), or Ambon (Yabun), others say to Dili in east Timor, or even to Batavia, on Java. Among the other things told of So'u's voyages in these foreign lands, it is said that he secured some 160 elephant tusks as the "exchange value of Fish Excrement" (Ian Tean *fiawan*), which he must have considered a neat trick to play on the Portugis. He gave sixty of these tusks to Bungaa as a return on Fish Excrement, and kept one hundred of the tusks for the Melatunan house. Metaniat Bungaa said that he remembered when he was young that four of Bungaa's sixty tusks were still on display in their house. Most of the Melatunan tusks, however, were hidden in a cave in the forest, where they were guarded by a slave. Yet, for some reason, this slave was killed, and the

22. Roos Ongirwalu of Rumngevour, Fordata, in a written history of this period, suggests that when the "Portugis" were defeated by the Dutch in Ambon in 1605, various groups of "Portugis" fled in their ships to different parts of the archipelago — including Irian Jaya, Banda, Kisar, east Timor, and the southeastern Moluccas. One of these groups sailed to Tanimbar and, ultimately, after a number of stops along the way, settled in Rumya'an, where they proceeded to build a fort. In this way, "Portugis" history is adapted to the model of Tanimbarese historical form — i.e., one in which there is an initial settlement that is disrupted, a time of wandering, and finally a second settlement.

23. Falaksoru Melatunan is referred to in the Dutch records as Falcksoor and as Cornelis Speelman, the Dutch Governor-General whose name So'u took as his own when he was baptized.

secret of the location of the cave was lost. The tusks are thus no longer to be found.

The history of the Melatunan heirloom valuables involves a different kind of deception. As Ma'idodu Melatunan tells it, So'u went to Banda, and resided in a place where the Portugis were manufacturing gold valuables. He then tricked the Portugis and absconded with a number of gold pieces, by making them stick to the bottom of his feet (or shoes). These gold valuables later became part of heirloom box (*dolan*) of the Melatunan house.[24]

Sa'intii Kora, of Sera, told me the history of a pair of named golden armbands and a named golden breast pendant, the origin of which he also attributed to So'u's deception of the Portugis. The narrative involves the same deception as practiced above, but the episode is located in east Timor (or alternatively, Roti) rather than in Banda. An added feature of the story is that So'u's sister Titi Ma'i decided — after he had been absent for a long time — to dress herself in the clothes of a man and go search for her brother, whom she found in the process of appropriating the aforementioned valuables.

This was not the only time that So'u would deceive the Portugis, or that his sister Titi Ma'i would cross-dress to take a part in one of So'u's adventures. Indeed, the presence of the Portugis on Fordata is remembered primarily through the stories of So'u's encounters with them. They came, built a fort in Rumya'an (the foundation of which now stands below the Protestant church), and attempted to set up an exclusive trade relationship with the Tanimbarese of the area. In the Tanimbarese version of the history, however, they are remembered only by the ease with which they were deceived into abandoning Fordata and leaving the Tanimbarese to themselves. According to one version I heard, So'u told the Portugis that if they stayed they would have to tough it out and eat only *ngengu* and *karu* — two kinds of shellfish. This they evidently considered to be too much of a hardship, and they departed. In other versions, So'u deceived the Portugis into thinking that the only vegetable available was a particularly bitter kind, and that was enough to convince them that Fordata was not a place they could abide.[25] Although the threat of eating shellfish

24. Cf. van Doren 1863:98–99 for a similar history of So'u Melatunan.

25. From the Dutch side, the history of relations with Fordata, and with So'u in particular, reads quite differently. The Dutch records report, in 1685, that So'u went to Babar, aided in the massacre of the people of the village of Alouta, and sold the survivors into slavery, presumably to the Dutch (Coolhaas 1960–79, 4:793). One wonders, in fact, if the valuables he reputedly obtained abroad were secured in this raid, or as a result of his profits from the slave trade. Later, in the early 1690s and back on Fordata, So'u apparently killed a Fordata man named Masa (literally, "gold"), and the Dutch vowed to capture him and put

or bitter vegetables may appear too insubstantial to account for the departure of the Portugis, that is precisely the point of the story. With such a flimsy threat, So'u demonstrates his own ingenuity and, at the same time, the lack of strength and resolve on the part of the Portugis.

Together with his sister Titi Ma'i, So'u undertook yet another adventure to secure another named gold breast pendant. Here it is not the Portugis they deceived, but rather the people of Lamdesar, a village on the island of Larat. In this case, So'u ordered Tit Ma'i to marry a man in Lamdesar. This she did, but when her bridewealth had been paid with this particular gold breast pendant, she transformed herself into a man — that is, began to wear men's clothing. As a result, her husband refused to keep her as his wife, and "let her down" (*nfasuk ia*) from the house. Titi Ma'i returned home to her brother in Rumya'an, but So'u refused to return the pendant to Lamdesar. It thereby became one of the heirloom valuables of the Melatunan house. Sa'intii Kora of Sera said that ultimately Titi Ma'i married into the house Vavumasa in Sera and, as part of her dowry, she brought the golden armbands and breast pendant, which he said So'u had obtained in Timor.[26]

As for So'u, himself, his fate is ultimately far more mysterious than his predecessor, Atuf. Although So'u is known for other acts of extraordinary cultural import (see chapter 10), in the end he simply disappears. Unlike Atuf, who turns to stone, So'u vanishes into thin air, leaving no trace except for the gold valuables that remained as tokens of the powers appropriated from outside forces.

From Unity to Dispersion

Ubila'a remains the representation of the completed and transcendent unity of sky and earth, sun and moon, male and female. Although the power and agency to transform the world — embodied in the sacred spear — was originally contained within the supreme deity, Ubila'a, this power was surrendered by the deity and given into the hands of men. Thus the differentiation of the prior unity epitomized by Ubila'a became the task of men, and it was through the agency of men, and their actions

---

him into prison for his deed (Coolhaas 1960–79, 5:494, 518). It is clear from the Dutch accounts, however, that the Dutch were not secure enough in the strength of their forces to feel they could withstand the strength of So'u's own allies in Rumya'an. It is not yet evident to me what, in the end, became of So'u, or of his confrontation with the Dutch.

26. This marriage would have been contracted along the Great Row (Lolat Ila'a) exchange pathway (see chapters 6 and 10), in which the Melatunan house on Fordata is the established wife-giver of the Vavumasa house on Sera.

upon fixed, self-contained, and androgynous forms, that the shape of the world and of humanity was radically altered and the conditions for life were created.

Thus it was that the earth was separated from the sky, which then hung high above the land. The moon and the stars were differentiated from the sun and, in the process, time was released from its captivity within the primordial and bounded unity of the sun-moon, so that now day alternates with night, sun with moon. With the movement of the stars across the sky came seasonal change and the rains, which arrive in sequence with the movement of the constellations as they rise on the eastern horizon or set on the western horizon.[27] In releasing the male rain, and in extracting water from the mainland in fresh, flowing springs, Atuf made possible the fertility of its complement, the female land. The generative capacity of the female land was prefigured in the release of her children, the off-shore islands, from their embrace by the mainland. With regard to humans, the bodies of self-enclosed figures were opened up so that they might speak, defecate, and, presumably, procreate. Sister was separated and differentiated from brother, and bridewealth came to be the force through which women were extracted from their natal houses and moved to other houses in marriage. The forces of separation set in motion by Atuf and the sacred spear were mirrored in the dispersal of the autochthonous settlements, which resulted in a period of constant upheaval and forced migrations.

As much as the differentiation of the world into its complementary parts was necessary to foster life, this process ultimately required, and indeed elicited or called forth, its opposite — that is, the recomposition of unities that, as fixed points, would anchor the motion that extended life out from its source. Thus, the epoch of migrations was characterized by the movement of men (and women dressed as men) in search of the signs of otherworldly power that would enable them to secure for themselves a fixed place in the world once again. Named hierloom valuables, acquired by the ancestors through actions that transcended the social order, became signs of the powers that lie before, beyond, outside, and even against society, but also signs of the powers that underlie society and constitute the very basis of its possibility. It was by forays into the heavens, the underworld, and lands beyond the horizon that these men appropriated objects of otherworldly power that would enable them to recompose their own world, the land within the horizon.

---

27. During the season of the east winds, there is a sequence of rains that are called the "fluid" or "liquid" (*vahan*) of a sequence of stars that set during this time of the year. The "stars that set together with their rains" (*narar ravava ovun rir da'ut*) include the Pleiades (*Vun Yanat*), the face of Taurus (*Vun Itai*), the belt of Orion (*Liri Uat*), and a bird (*Manut*), whose outer wing tips are formed by Sirius and Canopus.

4   The Recomposition of the World: Villages

Their piercing through rocks and creating sea passages is a vivid description of the magical potency contained within witches. A recurring Trobriand theme is how these unattached witches (or, elsewhere, dynamic *kula* heroes) representing fantastic speed and motion are finally stabilized as rocks. Rocks are a representation of immobility as well as of permanent *anchoring* (a positive Trobriand valuation). This stabilization of the witches, then, allows for their becoming agents for granting (restricted) benefits, and their locations appropriately become shrines for propitiation by *kula* sailors. (Tambiah 1985:303)

After the initial self-contained unity of the world had been separated into a flurry of fragmented parts, it was some time before it was possible to discover a new order of organization that would bring these parts into a productive relation. Only when humans managed to recompose new cultural images of encompassing unities were they able to create forms that could firmly anchor human activity and productivity.

In the founding of villages, two such images of transcendent unity were created. One, which formed the focal point of the village as a whole, was the central stone boat and ritual center that included an altar to the supreme deity, Ubila'a. The other, which formed the focal point of particular houses in each village, was the ancestor statue and altar complex that was dedicated to the ancestors. Both the stone boat at the center of the village and the altar complex at the center of houses contain the fragments of the old world order in a new synthetic form that becomes a permanent place of access to otherworldly powers.

As such, these points of unity anchor new, culturally constituted processes of differentiation that are necessary for the production of life. Yet the processes that are focused on the stone boat and on the house altar complex are mirror images of one another. The differentiation of the unity of the stone boat generates a mode of productivity in which the mobility of males on the outside is anchored by the fixity of females on the inside. By contrast, the differentiation of the unity of the altar complex of houses generates an inverse mode of productivity — one in which the mobility of females on the outside is anchored by the fixity of males on the inside. Depending upon the context, then, both males and females contain the potential for being either the agent or the anchor of productive action in the world. At the same time, neither agency nor anchorage can be realized without the other.

It is, then, to the first of these two processes that I wish to turn here. The stone boat that forms the ritual center of the village is a brilliant image of a unity that contains both anchorage and potential mobility. To comprehend such an image, it is necessary to explore the manner in which the village and its ritual center were founded, the nature of the stone boat and its crew of ritual officials, and the mode of productivity that is generated by reference to it.

The "Gathering Together" of a Village

As Tanimbarese represent their histories,[1] the period of migrations left the population widely scattered across the landscape in isolated groups that occupied temporary forest settlements. People describe this time as one of great insecurity, when each group was vulnerable to the attacks of others and warfare was always a potential threat. Yet out of this state of fragmentation and instability a new process of consolidation and stabilization began to take place.

This process is generally thought to have been initiated when the members of a particular house found an especially hospitable spot in which to settle. Such a place was usually located atop a cliff on a cape surrounded by the sea on three sides, with a good harbor and a plentiful supply of fresh water. They may have settled there alone or with other named and unnamed houses with whom they were associated as the "elder-younger brothers" (*ya'an-iwarin*) of a single house-complex (*rahan ralan*). In the surrounding forests, there would be other isolated groups settled alone or in association with their "elder-younger brothers."

1. Not only are the details of each village history different, but, within any particular village, historical representations form a tangled mass of contradictory accounts. Any one version will always be countered and contradicted by any number of others. The differences implicate distinctions concerning the status and precedence of a house and its rights to ritual offices and they constitute grounds for serious disputes and even violence. Despite the inevitable contention surrounding these histories, however, the overall pattern of the historical process through which village communities are thought to have been founded is roughly identical throughout the archipelago. Therefore, since it would be impossible to give a complete history (i.e., all possible versions) of any one village, and because I do not wish to "freeze" in print any one or even several conflicting versions, I will present here only this general pattern, rather than any one specific "example."

Finally, the first settlers would decide that they should gather all these dispersed peoples together, in order to form one united village. When I asked why these isolated groups came together to form common settlements, people said that they were desirous of protection in what was otherwise a perilous world of danger and enmity. Another reason why a group might entice others to join them in a common settlement was the latter's possession of important named valuables — evidence of their status, their connection to otherworldly powers, and their "weight."

The first settlers went around, then, and called all the dispersed groups together. If they were hesitant to join, the first settlers "bought them with a portion" (*rfaha ira ovun vaan isaa*). This "portion" consisted of the promise of a ritual office and a "stone" seat (*vatu*) in the ritual center of the newly created village. When they had assembled, the various ritual offices of the village were bestowed upon specific named houses and, with this division of ritual offices, the village was founded. Later, other groups that might happen to sail by — still in search of a place to settle — would likewise be enticed to join the new village with a promise of a "portion" consisting of a tract of land or a ritual office or both.

Thus all villages originally came to be located high on the cliff-tops of capes, which afforded both defensive protection on three sides and a suitable harboring place for boats. As further protection, each village was surrounded by a stone wall that was itself often enveloped by a thick wall of cactus — a combination that made the village virtually impenetrable. Entry to the village was gained through one of its several named gates (*fidu*), which could be closed at night and, during the day, reinforced by a thicket of bamboo spikes set in the ground. Describing his first day in the village of Ritabel, on Larat, in July 1882, Forbes noted:

> All round the village we found a high strong palisade, with a portion removable, however, on the shore side in the daytime. In attempting to pass out by the landward gateway we were at once restrained by several of the villagers following us, who pointed to the ground in an excited manner, demonstrating to us its surface everywhere set with sharpened bamboo spikes, except along a narrow footpath. Their gestures instantly opened our eyes, with an unpleasant shock, to the truth that we were environed by enemies, and the village was standing on its defense. (1885:303)

Most villages have long since moved from their cliff-top sites to beach-side locations.[2] Yet, the old village sites may still be found — often with

2. The only villages I know of in Tanimbar that remain on cliff-top sites are Awear, on the island of Fordata, and Sangliat Dol, Alusi Krawain, Arma, Watmuri, and Batu-Putih

their stone and cactus ramparts still in evidence — on cliff-tops overseeing their proxies below them. After they moved down to the beach sites, and as a result of the peace imposed by the Dutch colonial government, Tanimbarese no longer felt the need to build fortifications around their villages. The new villages nevertheless retained their traditional named gateways, and any island-wide pathway that enters a village will do so through one of these points of access.

Within the walls of the old village, Drabbe noted, the houses were built quite close to one another in more or less regular rows (of which he says there were generally four, although I expect that this varied quite widely). The village was focused upon a central street, where the ritual center was located, and all houses faced this central street (with their gables on a sea-land axis). The two middle rows of houses thus faced each other across the central street, and the outer rows faced the backs of those houses located on the central rows.[3]

Socially and spatially, each village is divided into a number of wards (*arun*). Although the number of wards in a village varies, it is not uncommon to find that there are three in number. These wards are, in turn, made up of a number of house-complexes (*rahan ralan*, the "inside of a house"). It should be stressed, as Tanimbarese themselves do, that the named and unnamed houses that stand as "elder-younger brothers" in a house-complex are not conceptualized as a single descent group or clan (see chapter 5). Rather, elder-younger brothers are generally thought simply to have been traditionally associated with one another through a common history of migrations and settlement. The fact that the ancestors of houses related as elder-younger brothers once resided together on a tract of forest land translates into the spatial organization of the village such that the named and unnamed houses associated in this way continue to constitute a house-complex and are located close to one another as a part of the ward to which they belong in the village. The named and unnamed houses that belong to a single house-complex — like those house-complexes that belong to a single ward — should thus be grouped together and form both the social and spatial units of the village, although there are no obvious boundaries between them.[4]

---

on the island of Yamdena. I cannot speak for the islands of Selaru, Molu, or Maru, which I have not yet visited.

3. In Awear, there appear to have been (and still are) three double rows of houses. Currently, their doorways face each other across the street, rather than all facing toward the center street of the village. Whether or not they all once did face toward the center, I cannot determine.

4. In Awear, however, the relations between wards of the village, and even between house-complexes, has been somewhat obfuscated because the village has twice split into

Aside from the placement of houses within ward and house-complex divisions, the only other specification as to the placement of houses within the village concerns the sites of the houses of ritual officials and of those houses that guard the gates of the village. The houses of the main ritual officials should stand adjacent to the ritual center of the village. Similarly, just as each ward of the village has its gateway, so each gateway has its guardian — a house that stands next to it and acts as the ritual guardian of that particular entryway into the village (photograph 1.2).

The founding of a village out of the whirlwind of migrations and warfare is represented as the consolidation of dispersed groups into a community with a single ritual center.[5] For most places in Tanimbar, this ritual center is neither a place of origin nor one of prior unity, but rather the point where diverse, unrelated groups came together and created a new unity.[6] This idea is expressed in the word *natnemu*, which refers to something that "is whole or complete." People refer to the epoch before the founding of a village as the time when "the village was not yet whole" (*ahu wol natnemu obi*). Once "they had gathered themselves together" (*rasdovu ira*), however, the village was considered "whole" or "complete" (*ahu natnemu roak*).

This model of the origin of villages as a consolidation of diverse groups contrasts sharply with what might be called a segmentary model of village origins. Among the Mambai of East Timor, for instance, the ritual center marks the navel, the point of origin and original unity, and is guarded by elder brothers while younger brothers segment off from the central origin place and disperse into a multitude of lesser ritual centers (Traube 1986).

In Tanimbar, on the contrary, the emphasis is upon the recomposition of a completed whole from a multitude of dispersed parts — the fragments of prior unities. It is by the promise of creating a new ritual and cultural order that a multitude of scattered people and valuables are pulled in from their endless wanderings and concentrated in one place — a place of stillness that is closed against the merciless mobility of the outside.

---

separate villages. With some exceptions, the houses remaining on the old village site may now be built anywhere, regardless of their traditional house-complex or ward association.

5. A few villages — ones which have formed as the consolidation of parts of two former villages — have two ritual centers and two sets of ritual officials. This is the case, for instance, in the village of Olilit, and also Latdalam, both on the island of Yamdena.

6. Pauwels (1990) reports, however, that for the villagers of Hursu (or Fursuy) on Selaru it is precisely the contrast between autochthonous groups and those who arrived later that is crucial in their histories of origin.

Sailing Boats and Stone Boats

This recomposed ritual unity had, as its center and place of worship, a stone platform located in the middle of the village. The stone platform anchored the new cultural order in two ways: by providing an immobilized and weighty center that countered the effects of ungrounded mobility outside the village enclosures, and by providing an altar that made possible direct access to Ubila'a and the transcendent powers represented by the deity.

In most villages this stone ritual center (called *didalan* in the Fordatan language and *natar* in the Yamdenan language) consisted of a circle of stones about fifteen feet in diameter and filled with earth to form a platform raised one or two feet above the ground (Drabbe 1940:50) (photograph 4.1). Although these stone platforms were everywhere conceived as boats, several villages—including Sangliat Dol and Arui—actually constructed their ritual center in the shape of a boat (*natar sori*) and endowed it with finely wrought prow and stern boards (*kora ulu* and *kora muri*) of carved stone (McKinnon 1988) (photographs 4.2 and 4.3). Other villages evoked the image of a boat in innovative ways: Olilit, for instance, invested their circular stone platform with an anchor and chains, which were retrieved from a Dutch steamer that was shipwrecked on the coast of Yamdena (Drabbe 1940:50–51).

Because most of the villages in Tanimbar have moved down off their

Photograph 4.1   Women dancing on the stone boat that was once located in the center of the old village of Arui. (Drabbe 1940: fig. 89)

Photograph 4.2   The stone boat of the village of Sangliat Dol. (Drabbe 1940: fig. 19)

Photograph 4.3   The carved prow board of the Arui stone boat after it was cleared from the forest in January 1979.

Photograph 4.4   The Catholic church and the priest's house in Awear. The old ritual center having been dismantled, the space in front of the church, marked by the flagpole, has become the new ritual center where *adat* ceremonies are performed.

former, cliff-top sites onto beach-side locations, the old stone boat ritual centers have been abandoned. Nowadays the ritual centers of villages consist of an open plaza — usually in front of the church — with a flag pole (photograph 4.4). Conceptually, however, this contemporary ritual center is still conceived of as if it were a stone boat and many of the same activities that were once carried out on the stone boat continue to be carried out on the new ritual center. The latter is, moreover, referred to by the name of the stone boat that once occupied the center of the old village site and it is still thought to represent the village as a whole.[7]

Before the advent of Christianity in Tanimbar, the central stone boat was the only place where the villagers gathered to discuss matters of community concern, and where they danced, worshiped, and made sacrifices to Ubila'a.[8] Toward the bow of the stone boat, which faced seaward, there stood the wooden post and the sacrificial stone that formed the main altar

7. For other works concerning the boat as a symbol for the entire community, see Vroklage 1936, 1940; Steinmann 1946; Adams 1974, Lewcock and Brans 1975:112–13; Barraud 1979, 1985; and Kana 1980:220–24).

8. Now there are, of course, two ritual centers. One is the church, which deals primarily with the rituals and festivals of the Christian order. The other is the contemporary

of Ubila'a.[9] Landward, toward the stern of the boat, were the stone seats of the main ritual officials of the community. Another crucial part of this ritual complex was composed of the "community gold" (*mas kubania*) — the valuables that constituted the common wealth of the village. These were not kept within the stone boat, however, but within the house of one of the ritual officials.[10]

Presently, as in the past, it is only in situations in which the village faced outward that its identity as a unit becomes manifest. These situations include primarily those of warfare and intervillage brotherhood alliance renewals, but also epidemics[11] and, in some villages, agricultural rituals.[12] It is on the stone boat that the ceremonies proper to these events are carried out by the ritual officials of the village. By contrast, all matters internal to the village — involving marriage, sickness (except epidemics), death, adultery, theft, and the like — are handled along the lines of authority demarcated by houses, marriage alliance and exchange pathways, or, occasionally, by church and governmental structures. Thus, what traditional village-wide ritual authority there is — which consists entirely in the ritual officials who have a seat on the stone boat — comes into play only when the village as a whole is actively in a situation of confrontation with forces outside of the village.

That the unity of the village in these situations is represented as a boat is evident in the ritual names used for the village at these times. In the ritual songs sung during intervillage alliance renewal ceremonies, for instance, the village is not referred to by its ordinary name, but rather by a series of special ritual names, including one referring to the village itself, one each for its harbor and its water source, and two boat names. One of these boat names is the ritual name for the stone boat itself. The other

stone boat ritual center — generally adjacent to the church — which deals primarily with the rituals and festivals of the indigenous Tanimbarese order. That Ubila'a is the main deity appealed to in both of these contexts does not appear to be problematic.

9. The Tanimbarese stone boat and wooden altar post can be seen as a variant of the ritual centers found in other Indonesian and Southeast Asian villages that are made of stones and trees. Traube, for instance, writes about the Mambai ritual centers, which are called "rock and tree" (1986), and Leach reports that round stone altars and trees form the ritual centers at the entrance to villages in highland Burma (1965:117).

10. When I visited the stone boat located on the site of the old village of Arui, people indicated that the gold valuables of the village had formerly been kept under the stone that formed a part of the altar to Ubila'a on the bow of the boat.

11. Riedel reports that epidemics were seen as the effluences of the east and west monsoons (1886:278).

12. See Pauwels 1990 for an analysis of the conceptualization of Hursu (Fursuy) village identity in terms of an annual cycle that alternates between agricultural activities and those of marriage and warfare.

is the name for the sailing boat upon which the villagers embark when they engage in intervillage alliance renewal ceremonies. The latter refers not so much to any particular existing boat, but rather to the unity of villagers as they move outward into the world from their own stone boat center and to the unity of the villagers in the boat-shaped dance formation which they assume during an intervillage alliance renewal ceremony (see below). In some villages, this communal boat is named after the boat in which one of the houses of the village is thought to have originally sailed to their present location.[13]

A village was created, then, as a series of successive containments. Not only was it formerly encircled by the stone walls that surrounded it and — often fortified with impenetrable thickets of cactus — bounded it off from the hostile attacks of an outside world, it was also encircled by the guardian houses of the gateways and by the houses of the ritual officials that immediately surrounded the ritual center. Finally, and most important, the village was contained, from its very center, by the stone boat itself. For when the identity of the village as a unity was called into play by outside forces, the internal form of the stone boat became the external form of the village.[14]

The founding of the village — with its communal focus upon the stone boat — created a fixed center, a still anchorage in the midst of what was otherwise a maelstrom of enmity and motion. This was accomplished by recomposing at the very center of the village a paradoxical entity: a sailing boat grounded and immobilized in stone. The weight of the immobilized sailing boat was generated not only through the accumulation of stones, but also, and primarily, through the concentration of people and of the gold valuables they brought with them. In the end, the image is one of a boat so replete with, and completed by, people and valuables that it can no longer move. In its completion it has contained all motion and fixed it in stone.

But the anchorage of the village and a new ritual order was made possible not only by its accumulated weight but also by the fact that the stone boat provided a point of access to, and itself was an expression of, a larger transcendent unity. On the one hand, as an altar to Ubila'a, the stone boat created a permanent place where humans could establish a direct relation-

---

13. In Olilit, for instance, I was told that the name of the boat of the house Luturmela — Lebitlokat — became the name of the village boat because Lebitlokat was a particularly fine boat. Moreover, because Luturmela's boat became the village boat, this house was given the ritual office of "bow of the boat" (*sori luri*), since its members know the boat well and know how to guide it properly through both still and stormy seas. I was told a similar story concerning the village boat of Sangliat Dol.

14. It was Roy Wagner (personal communication) who suggested to me that the stone boat could be seen as a form that contains the village from the inside.

ship with the otherworldly powers of this deity. On the other hand, as the condensation of a contradiction — a moving sailboat immobilized and fixed upon the land — the stone boat itself was an aesthetic and synthetic entity that, like Ubila'a, comprehended the transcendent unity of opposites.

The Community Nobles

As a synthetic entity, the stone boat united not only the contrary forces of mobility and immobility, but also those contrary qualities of gender, space, and time that are central to conceptions of life processes. These qualities are articulated in the organization of the ritual officials who form the crew of the boat.

Tanimbarese currently recognize two sets of village leaders. Those who belong to the indigenous politico-ritual order are called the "landside nobles" (*mela raa*). They are distinguished from those called the "seaside nobles" (*mela roal*), who were appointed by a succession of external authorities — the Dutch East India Company, the Dutch colonial government, and the Indonesian government. The seaside nobles now include the village head (*orang kaya*[15] or *pemerintah negeri*), the government herald (*marinyo*), and the local militia leader (*danton*). It should not be forgotten, moreover, that each village has yet another set of ritual officials whose responsibilities revolve around the workings of the church.

The landside nobles are also called the "community nobles" (*mel kubania*).[16] Although, paradoxically, the term *kubania* derives from the Dutch word *compagnie*, which was used in the Moluccas to refer to the Dutch East India Company,[17] it is clear that the Tanimbarese ritual offices known as the community nobles do not owe their origin to the Dutch East India Company. In Tanimbar, the Dutch origin of the word *kubania* is not known. The word is used to indicate a level of organization that concerns the village as a whole.[18]

Although villages differ a bit in the ritual offices they recognize, nevertheless, throughout the archipelago three main ritual officials appear to be the most important of those called the community nobles. These include the "master of the village" (*ahu dua*), the "sacrificer" (*mela snoba*),

15. See Ellen 1986 for a discussion of the history of the use of this title in the Moluccas.
16. The term "noble" (*mela*) refers to a distinct ranked class. Yet, although it is assumed that those occupying these ritual offices should be of noble rank, the class of nobles is not solely composed of those holding such offices.
17. Valerio Valeri (personal communication) brought this derivation to my attention.
18. Another use of the term, for instance, is found in the context of those hunting parties that include all the men of the village and are undertaken on some village-wide occasion. These are described as hunts in which the men "run [together] as a community" (*rban kubania*).

and the "herald" (*mela fwaak*). The master of the village is the senior representative of the named house that first occupied the land upon which the village stands and that first called the other dispersed groups together from their separate forest settlements when the village was founded. When a new house is built, he should be the first one to dig the earth for the foundation posts; and should the village move to a new site, his house should be the first to be built. The sacrificer is the official who is responsible for making sacrifices, offerings, and prayers to Ubila'a at the central altar in the stone boat. The herald is responsible for making known to the general populace the decisions that have been made by the community officials: these he cries out, with a distinctive cadence, when he makes his rounds through the village. These are the ritual officials whose houses should be located around the stone boat.

Whereas the master of the village could be said to represent the entire village when it comes to temporal precedence on the land, it is the sacrificer and the herald who, together, provide an image of a gendered totality. Drabbe notes that the sacrificer is considered the "mother" (*renan*) of the village, and the herald is thought of as the "father" (*yaman*). Although, as such, they are central to all ritual activities of the village, their authority is nevertheless anything but absolute. "As in questions of war, so it went in other community affairs: 'father' and 'mother' were theoretically the boss, but they did not decide anything without the consent of the community, and often the community went against their decision" (1940:182). Indeed there are other officials who have special roles in any discussion of community matters. On Yamdena, there is an official called the "bow of the boat" (*sori luri*). He is the one who, among his many other tasks, must speak first to open any community meeting. In some villages there is another official—called the "speaker" (*mangatanuk* on Yamdena; *mela ngrihi* on Fordata, Larat, and Sera)—who took up the discussion and spoke after the "bow of the boat" had opened the session. On Fordata, Larat, and Sera there is a special official, called "he answers the voice of the [community] nobles" (*nvalat mel vain*). This man speaks for the general populace, which does not otherwise have a voice in the ritual gatherings, and he has the power to veto the decisions and plans of the main ritual officials. Another official central to various ritual proceedings is the "master of the divisions" (*wahat dua*), who is responsible for the division of meat and rice on the occasion of a communal sacrificial meal.[19]

Just as the ritual officials each have a stone seat (*vatu*) in the stone boat ritual center, so too their ranks are conceptualized in terms of the spatial

---

19. There are many other minor ritual officials whose duties are described by Drabbe (1927; 1940:181–85). See also Pauwels 1990 concerning the ritual officials in Hursu (Fursuy) on Selaru.

organization of a boat. On Yamdena, the "bow of the boat" (*sori luri*) mentioned above has his counterpart in the ritual official called the "stern of the boat" (*sori mudi*). On Fordata, this conceptualization is best realized in the boat-shaped dance formation, where the "bow" (*ulu*) of the boat is complemented by the "rudder" (*wilin*) or sometimes, if there are two, the "right and left rudders" (*wilin mela-balit*). The other main ritual officials — the "owner of the village," the sacrificer, the herald — occupy positions in the middle of the boat.

These three positions — "front/bow" (*ulu*), "middle" (*fruan*), and "back/stern" (*muri*) — not only organize the ritual officials spatially but also temporally. For it is the bow of the boat who must be first in all undertakings: he speaks first in any village or intervillage meeting; he is the first to enter or leave the boat when the village embarks upon a common venture such as an intervillage alliance renewal; he leads when the men of the village go on a communal hunting expedition; and he is the first to plant his gardens. Similarly, where the bow of the boat is first, the stern or the rudder is the last; where the former opens a proceeding, the latter closes it. The boat image thus temporally shapes and contains all significant activities of the village by marking the beginning and end of all events.

The spatial and temporal unity of the village is perhaps nowhere more apparent than in the dance formation the villagers assume when they renew an intervillage alliance. Although only certain named houses have ritual offices and a seat in the stone boat of the village, every house may find a place in the boat-shaped formation of the "great stomp" dance (*tnabar ila'a*) that is always performed on the occasions when intervillage alliances are renewed. The dancers stand in an open circle (figure 4.1; photograph 4.5): the front of the line is the "prow board" (*kora ulu*), and the end of the line is the "stern board" (*kora muri*). The line of dancers is theoretically arranged according to the precedence of arrival of each house at the village site, as conceived in the origin stories. In fact, however, it seems that only the first and last positions are precisely determined. The person who stands second in line, and who calls out the name of the boat (*nfarai*) during the dance, is called the bow of the boat (photograph 4.6). In Yamdenan villages, the ritual official called by that name assumes this position; in other villages that lack such an official, a representative of the house that first settled on the village site should occupy it. Similarly, the person who stands last in line is the "rudder," or, if there are two, the "right and left rudders" (photograph 4.7). The rights to occupy these positions were given to specific houses at the founding of the village, and they remain the hereditary privileges of these houses. Often other positions in this dance boat were given out at that time as well. For example, the privilege to act as lead singer (*kual*), to "beat the large, standing drum" (*nfeffik babal*), to "bail

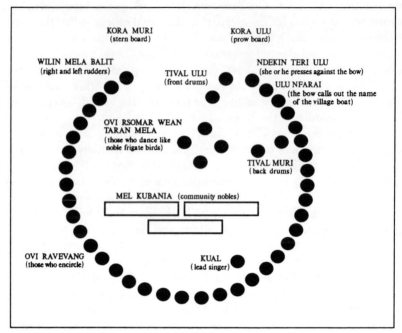

Figure 4.1   The *tnabar ila'a* dance formation

the bilge water" (*nit vaha*), or to "dance on the forefront of the boat" (*nsomar na'a abau ulu*)—when the actual boat is under sail en route to an alliance renewal—are sometimes mentioned as the specific inherited prerogatives of certain named houses.

The boat image of the dance formation is carried even further in the conceptualization of other positions in the dance. The four drummers who stand toward the bow are thought to compose the "sail" (*laar*) of the boat and, just as the sail must fill with wind before the boat can set out, so too the drums must sound before the dance can begin. The dance formation of some villages includes four women who "dance like noble frigate birds" (*rsomar wean taran mela*) in the middle of the boat, toward the front end. They dance with their arms outstretched like the great wings of frigate birds, hovering in place as if they were riding the same winds as the boat itself (photograph 4.8). Finally, the community nobles alone are allowed to sit in the center of the dance formation and, as captains, direct the village boat on its steady course.

The villagers thus represent themselves—not only when they are stationary within their own ritual center but also when they move into the

Photograph 4.5   Standing in a circle, the villagers from Temin and Weratan, Sera, practiced the *tnabar ila'a* dance before renewing their alliance with the village of Latdalam in August 1980.

Photograph 4.6   The dancers from Temin and Weratan paused as the "bow" called out the names of their village boats during the ceremony that renewed their alliance with the village of Latdalam in August 1980.

Photograph 4.7   Holding mirrors in their hands, the "right and left rudder" marked the stern of the Temin-Weratan dancing boat. The "community nobles" sat on benches in the middle of the circle of dancers.

Photograph 4.8   At the bow of the Temin-Weratan dancing boat, the four "frigate birds" danced with arms outstretched as the drummers and gong players on either side of them beat out the rhythm of the *tnabar ila'a*.

outside world — as a boat, a contained spatial and temporal unity. Just as the stone boat stopped all past motion and contains the potential for all future motion, so its crew contains both male and female qualities — epitomized as the father and mother of the village — as well as the beginning and end of time and space. In this way, they draw together all that had been separated, fragmented, and dispersed in the time of Atuf; and they provide a recomposed unity that is powerful enough to anchor a new cultural order.

Female Anchorage and Male Mobility

Yet the new cultural order created by the stone boat ritual center contains a paradox. For while the village was founded as a stabilizing anchorage closed in on itself against a hostile and turbulent world outside, its very identity and existence as a community is predicated on, and realized in, its mobilization and movement back into an outside world of instability and enmity.[20] The immobilized stone boat on the inside and at the center of the village contains its contrary — a mobilized sailing boat that moves out from the village center (see McKinnon 1988).

This paradox is motivated by a double contingency: mobility on the outside is productive only to the extent that the village remains anchored at its center; yet anchorage at the center is productive only to the extent that the village is capable of mobility on the outside.[21] This is to say, on the one hand, that the efficacy of the movement of the village into the outside world depends upon its continued anchorage in, and fixed ritual relation to, the transcendent powers of Ubila'a — and these are achieved through the rituals carried out in and around the immobilized stone boat. On the other hand, the continuity and vitality of this ritual center and its relation to Ubila'a and the ancestors can only be maintained if it is renewed and replenished by outside sources of life and wealth — and this is achieved through the voyages of the mobilized sailing boats of the village.

The occasions upon which villagers sail into a hostile, unstable world outside to obtain vital sources of life include intervillage brotherhood alliance renewals and, formerly, warfare and long-distance trading expeditions from which they returned with precious valuables and (in the case of warfare and trading expeditions) human heads and slaves. It is in the

20. I am grateful for Tambiah's insights concerning a similar dynamic in the relationship between "anchored" and "unanchored" states of existence in the Trobriand Islands (1985:292). See also Pauwels 1990.

21. The same can also be said of the relation between the heirloom valuables that remain immobilized in houses and the valuables that continually move along exchange pathways. Cf. Weiner 1985.

rituals which surrounded the warfare and trading expeditions that it becomes possible to understand the relationship between the stable anchorage of the stone boat at the center of the village and the unstable, but vital mobility of voyagers on the outside.

Indeed, once the identity of the village was called into play by its confrontation with outside forces, the effective unity of the village was realized in the separation of male and female modes of action. Thus whereas it was the men who detached themselves from their fixed ritual center and became its mobile agents in the world outside the village, it was the women who remained still at the center and stabilized the mobility of their men by maintaining a fixed, unmoving relation to Ubila'a.[22]

Success in warfare, or any endeavor, depended upon the establishment of a just cause in the eyes of Ubila'a.[23] Oracles were consulted in order to determine the most auspicious cause for warfare, and this determination had to be affirmed by Ubila'a. When this was done, offerings were made to Ubila'a and the ancestors to ensure the success of the venture (Drabbe 1940). Once the expedition got under way, the fixed ritual relation to Ubila'a — which was crucial to the success of the endeavor and the very life of the voyagers — was maintained by women.

While the men were away at war, two ritual officials — the sacrificer and the herald (the "mother" and the "father") — remained in the village with the older men, women, and children. But it was a woman from the house of the sacrificer (usually an older woman or a very young girl) who had the most important role to play. During the entire time the men were away, she had to remain inside the house of the sacrificer and, in some villages, inside a small walled-off cubicle behind the main altar in the house. Here she maintained constant contact with Ubila'a through prayer and offerings of food and betel nut (Drabbe 1940:230). She also made certain that the fire in the small hearth set up in her cubicle did not go out, since this would signal the demise of the warriors, whose lives depended upon her actions and upon the relationship she maintained with Ubila'a. Moreover, the woman could not speak to persons outside the house, could not leave the house (except to relieve herself), and could not engage in sex-

22. In light of this it is not surprising that the village is thought of as a hen's nest (Drabbe 1940:51–52; Geurtjens 1941:22), or that those villagers who move outside the village for intervillage alliance renewal rituals are referred to as flashing, strutting cocks. The beautiful carved prow boards of sailing boats were also often decorated with an image of a cock (McKinnon 1988). For a similar relation between female fixity and male mobility, see Rosaldo 1980:125–26.

23. In Timor, as elsewhere, the establishment of a just cause was crucial to the success of a war expedition. See, for instance, Schulte Nordholt 1971:332.

ual intercourse,[24] or any other activity, such as weaving, which would threaten the security of the warriors (Drabbe 1940:230). Immobilized and still, she remained completely centered on the task of maintaining the vital link with Ubila'a that would secure victory for the warriors.

A similar arrangement ensured the success of men who embarked on long-distance trading voyages, which were called *inobal*, after the boats that were employed for these purposes. Formerly, Tanimbarese made voyages to the surrounding island groups—Babar, Luang, Ke'i, Aru, Banda—in search of gold, elephant tusks, swords, guns, slaves, bead necklaces, and textiles, for which they traded gold earrings, Tanimbarese textiles, and surplus garden produce (Drabbe 1940:140).

For these trading expeditions, two boats were essential: the one, with a crew of men, which actually undertook the voyage across the seas; the other, with a crew of women, which was formed within a house on land.[25] These trading expeditions could be community undertakings, organized by the ritual officials of the village, or private undertakings organized by a house or a group of houses. The appropriate rituals took place in the house of the man who was the captain of the boat and the organizer of the expedition—whether this was a ritual official or private individual.

Each male voyager had a female representative—usually a wife or a sister—on the land boat, and she carried out activities that paralleled those of the man she represented.

> One is the captain, and she has nothing else to do except to hold her hand on a *vakul*, a betelnut pouch which represents God. It is said of her *nsoba inobal ralan*, "she sacrifices and invokes God for the crew of the boat." Whether she sits or sleeps, she must be careful to hold her hand on the *vakul*. Another woman is the *juru mudi* [steersperson] and sits by the hearth in order to hold the rudder. The hearth is the back side of the house. Another is the *juru batu* [anchor person] and sits on the front side of the house—that is, on the sea side. Yet another is the *juru bahasa* [spokesperson] and she sits in the middle of the house. All these women must remain in the house until the voyagers have returned. The food, water, and wood is fetched for them by other women (Drabbe 1940:141).

The female captain ensured that the fire in the hearth was never extinguished as long as the men were away, lest some misfortune should befall

---

24. What seems important here (as in the preference for a young girl or older woman) is sexual inactivity. This, however, does not mean that the woman is any less female or more male. As far as I know, for Tanimbarese, age and sexual activity are not determinants of gender.

25. See Geurtjens 1910 for a description of a similar ritual configuration in the Kei Islands.

them. One man told me that, for the duration of the expedition, the female captain must keep her right hand cupped in an upright position. Should her hand turn downward at any time, it would indicate that the boat at sea had capsized. All the other women of the crew were further tasked with the obligation to dance and sound drums and gongs without stop (except for meals) during the entire time that their counterparts were at sea (Drabbe 1940:140).

Men were wrested from the village center to face a hostile world outside, but their mobility outside was conditional upon the stillness of the women at the center. The center remained the source of life and, as such, continued to encompass that which was extracted from it and eventually returned to it. Indeed, the life, success, and productivity of the men on the outside depended not only upon this separation but also upon the fixity of the ritual relation that the women maintained with Ubila'a.

Yet, the reverse was also true. The fixity and permanence of the ritual center and of the relation to Ubila'a depended upon the success of the expeditions into the outside world — upon the valuables and heads brought in from the outside to replenish the center. For the enduring identity of the village as a ritual center was as much marked by the gold valuables the village held at its center, as it was by the stones of the ritual center itself. As other villages extracted these valuables through warfare or intervillage alliance exchanges, they had to be replenished from other outside sources. Similarly, although it is difficult to understand the headhunting rituals at present, one suspects that the ultimate offering to Ubila'a was a human head captured in warfare. Heads and other such offerings not only acknowledged the source of the powers whose efficacy allowed for success on the outside, they also secured the continued flow of such powers and thus revitalized the relation between Ubila'a and the villagers. At the same time, these offerings were also a manifestation of the requirement that the center be reconstituted and renewed by forces captured from the outside.

Now the fixity of a village's relation to Ubila'a is also partly secured through the church, but the vitality of the church, like that of the stone boat, is also renewed through outside sources of the wealth. It is significant that a village can activate one of its intervillage alliances for the purpose of securing either valuables which are used to revitalize the stone boat or money which is used to revitalize the church. In either case, the process is the same.

Separation and Encompassment

The stone boat and altar to Ubila'a together constitute an image of a transcendent unity precisely because they contain contraries —

both mobility and immobility, male and female, inside and outside, and the beginning and end of space and time. At the same time, the stone boat provides a permanent place of access to the transcendent powers of Ubila'a, the deity who is both the source of life and contains the potentiality of its productive issue.

Yet as an image of transcendent unity, the stone boat is unproductive (Strathern 1988). When the identity of the village is evoked in confrontation with other villages, productive action requires that what is unified in the stone boat be separated and differentiated. Thus males are extracted from the prior unity of the stone boat to become the epitome of mobile agency on the outside, while their female counterparts remain as an immobile, fixed anchorage on the inside. Nevertheless, although male agency is possible to the extent that it is separated from female fixity, it ultimately must remain encompassed by it, because it is the female form that anchors it to the source of life and power in Ubila'a.

This play of gender identities, of anchorage and agency, of source and issue—all against a transcendent image of unity—is central to the way in which Tanimbarese think about and create the form of the world and the dynamics of productive processes within that world. Yet, in these processes, the qualities of male and female are not fixed: each contains the potential for becoming both anchor and agent, both source and issue. Indeed, Tanimbarese ideas about productivity require two centers of activity and anchorage—the stone boat and the house altars—by reference to which males and females alternately take on qualities once assumed by the other.[26]

26. Such reversals in gender attributes are common throughout Indonesia and elsewhere. See, for instance, Schulte Nordholt 1971, 1980; and Friedberg 1980. Drawing upon Dumont (1979, 1980, 1982), the authors in Barnes et al. 1985 suggest that a reversal is an indicator of a change in context or levels.

5   The Recomposition of
the World: Houses

Kachins in certain circumstances distinguish verbally between the dwelling-houses of ordinary people and the dwelling-house of a chief. The fundamental difference between the two is not in any feature of design but in the fact that the house of the chief contains a special compartment known as the *madai-dap* which is a shrine dedicated to the Madai *nat*, the chief of the Sky Spirits (*mu nat*), who is looked upon as an affinal relative of one of the chief's remote ancestors. (Leach 1965:108)

If the village was created by reference to the transcendent unity of the stone boat that linked it to Ubila'a and the ultimate source of life, the house groups of the village were created by reference to the transcendent unity of the altar complexes that linked them to their ancestors and the sources of life they represented. Both the stone boat and the house are structures of containment, within which disparate, mobile groups are recomposed in a single ritual community, whose unity is defined by reference to the image of totality that is situated at its center.

Between these two ritual centers, however, there is an inversion in the relations between male and female. In the modes of productivity originating in the village and its central stone boat, it is males who move outside and between villages while females remain still at the center. In the modes of productivity originating in houses and their central altar complex, however, it is females who move outside and between houses while males remain still at the center. Indeed, the ability of males to maintain an immobile center and a fixed relation to their ancestors and their patrimony serves to anchor the growth and extension of the productive resources that constitute the externalized "female" aspects, or "estates" (land, trees, outmarried women and their descendents along female lines) of the house.

Yet not all houses are equally able to achieve this double goal of male anchorage and female extension. The status of houses, it will be seen, depends not only upon the relative permanence of the male patrimony that anchors the house, but also upon the relative permanence and extension of its female estates. The difference, in the end, is one that encodes the distinction that separates nobles from commoners and slaves.

Until some decades ago, the qualities of a "house" (*rahan*) were inscribed in its construction and layout, so that the various aspects of a house as a conceptual, social, and physical unit were inseparable. By order of the Dutch, most of the old, raised houses (photograph 5.1) came down in the decades between 1920 and 1940, and those few that still remained during World War II were dismantled for firewood by the Japanese. People now live in bamboo and thatch houses placed directly on the ground or, increasingly, in ovenlike creations of cement with tin roofs—structures that bear little resemblance to their more stately predecessors. The latter are modeled on what they believe Western houses must look like and are an attempt to manifest the physical trappings of "modernity" (inspired by missionary and nationalist influences).

Nevertheless, while the physical structure of the house has changed over the past decades, the conceptual and social attributes of the house have changed little. There is thus a disjunction now between what continues to be the attributes of a house as a conceptual and social unit and those of a house as a physical entity. To understand the significance of

Photograph 5.1   A large Tanimbarese house with ridgepole decorations in the village of Sangliat Dol, probably in the 1920s or 1930s. (Photographic Archives of the Royal Tropical Institute, Amsterdam)

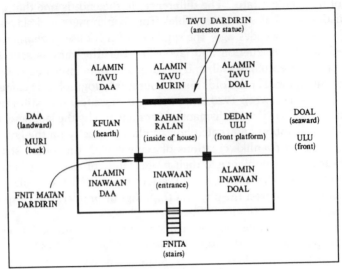

Figure 5.1   Plan of a Tanimbarese house c. 1900

the idea of the house for Tanimbarese, then, we must look to the houses that were last built some fifty or sixty years ago — the likes of which have not been seen since World War II.

Interior Spaces

The placement of a house and its internal arrangement were determined by its orientation relative to the sea and to the ritual center of the village. Formerly, the houses of Tanimbarese villages were ranged in rows that ran landward from the sea. As already noted, the entryway of all houses faced the center of the village — the place of the stone boat (*didalan*) — so that the houses of the two central rows faced one another, and the houses on the outer rows faced onto the backs of those in front of them. The spatial organization of the house followed from this initial placement (figure 5.1): the side of the entrance (*inawaan*), which faced the center of the village, stood opposite the side of the altar panel (*tavu* or *tav dardirin*); the head or front (*ulu*) of the house stood on the seaside (*doal/roal*); and the back (*muri*) of the house stood on the landside (*daa/raa*).[1]

Entrance into such houses, which were raised a meter or so above the

1. There is a considerable amount written on the symbolic organization of the physical structure of houses in Indonesia and Southeast Asia. See Izikowitz and Sörensen 1982, Oli-

ground on ironwood pilings, was gained by way of stairs (*fnita*) that led up through a trapdoor in a bamboo slat floor. Having entered a house, one would have found oneself in the "inside of the house" (*rahan ralan*), a space surrounded on all four sides by raised platforms (*alamin*) used for various purposes. The two platforms on either side of the entrance (*alamin inawaan daa* and *doal*) and on either side of the altar panel (*alamin tavu daa* and *doal*) were the sleeping platforms for the adult married couples resident in the house. On the central platform on the landside of the house stood the hearth (*kfuan*), where women prepared and cooked food. Opposite the hearth, the central platform on the seaside of the house (*dedan ulu*) was the place where guests sat when visiting or on more formal ritual occasions. Behind the altar panel was a platform (*alamin tavu murin*) that was reserved as the sleeping place of the marriageable girls of the house. Young children slept in the space in the center of the house, and unmarried boys generally slept outside on platforms underneath the house—although, if the seaside platform by the door was not occupied, they could also sleep there (Drabbe 1940:18).[2]

The grandest of named houses would have been marked by the presence of two extraordinary structures. Upon entering through the trap door, one would have had to pass through an elegantly carved portal (*fnit matan dardirin*), the two sides of which ran from the floor up to the roof beam on the entrance side of the house (*kalulun inawaan*). A pair of elephant tusks might have been tied on either side of the portal as an indication of the wealth and stature of the house (Geurtjens 1917:67; Geurtjens 1941:18–19; Drabbe 1928:148–49; Drabbe 1940:35).

Upon standing up inside such a house, one would have also been immediately confronted with the striking image of the *tavu*, the exquisitely carved altar panel that stood directly opposite the entrance (photographs 5.2 and 5.3). The "standing portion of the altar" (*tav dardirin*) took the shape of a human figure—abstractly represented in a playful arabesque of spirals—with arms arching gracefully upward. The upraised arms of the figure appeared to support the main roof beam (*kalulun tavu*) on this side of the house, just as the carved structures at the entrance ap-

---

ver 1975, Vroklage 1936, and Waterson 1990 for overviews; and, for studies of particular areas see, among others, Barnes 1974, Barraud 1979, Clamagirand 1975, Cunningham 1973, van Dijk and de Jonge 1987, Drabbe 1928, Errington 1979, Feldman 1979, Forth 1981, Kana 1980, and Vroklage 1940.

2. The interior arrangement of contemporary houses is modeled after an image of European (nuclear family) houses—with a front room for receiving guests and separate, walled-off bedrooms for the adults and children resident in the house. The kitchen is now placed either to the rear of the house or, more commonly, in a separate structure behind the house.

Photograph 5.2   The *tavu* of the Ditilebit house in the village of Awear, probably in the 1920s. This *tavu* is currently in the collection of the Royal Tropical Institute, Amsterdam. (Geurtjens 1941)

peared to support the main roof beam (*kalulun inawaan*) on the other side. On the beam above the altar panel were placed the skulls of ancestors, a plate for offerings to the ancestors, and perhaps small, wooden ancestor statues (*walut*) — often tied together in male-female pairs (Geurtjens 1917:67, Geurtjens 1941:19–20; Drabbe 1928:148–49; Drabbe 1940:36; de Hoog 1959:59).[3] Most likely, the heirloom valuables would have also been kept in a small chest (*dolan*) stored on the roof beam above the altar panel. In front of the altar panel there was a bench (*tav dakdokun*) reserved solely for the head of the house, who sat there on ritual occasions when marriage exchanges and other matters were negotiated.

From this privileged position at the base of the altar panel, the head of the house would have looked out toward the entrance of his house, and toward two other small altars. Above the center seaside platform, in the

3. The atlas and axis bones (*nit botun*) and small wooden statues of one's ancestors were often carried by men in a small betel nut pouch (*luvu*) to ensure efficacy in the hunt, on fishing expeditions, in warfare, as well as in the practice of various trades such as house building, boat building, and metal work (Drabbe 1940:84–101, 105–14; Forbes 1885:324; Geurtjens 1917:67; Geurtjens 1941:20; de Hoog 1959:59). A man's *luvu* might also be hung near the *tavu*, or placed on the shelf above it. See van der Kroef 1952:234 for the similar use of vertebrae among the Marind-anem on the southern coast of New Guinea.

Photograph 5.3   A *tavu* from the island of Sera in the collection of
the Royal Tropical Institute, Amsterdam, shown here during an exhibi-
tion at the Tropenmuseum in 1988. (Photograph courtesy of Greg Acciaioli)

"front loft" (*fngear ulu*), there was a plate (or several plates) for offerings
to the "spirits of the above" (*nit ratan*) — free spirits more or less differentiated from the "spirits of the dead" (*nit matmatan*), or ancestors (*ubu-
nusi*), whose offering place was above the altar panel. In Fordatan houses,
there was also an offering place to Ubila'a that was located on a structure
called the *ubu*, situated on top of the roof beam just to the seaside of
the entrance of the house (Drabbe 1940:36–37). In Yamdenan houses, the
offering place to Ubila'a was apparently located in the front loft on the sea-

side of the house (Drabbe 1940:36, 429). The house, then, as both a physical
and conceptual entity was first and foremost a ritual center.[4]

While acknowledging that people made offerings to the ancestors above
the altar panel, Drabbe is quite adamant that the altar panel (*tavu*) had
no religious significance in itself and had nothing to do with the worship
of the ancestors or Ubila'a (1928:148–49; 1940:36). To say that Tanimbarese did not worship the altar panel itself, however, is hardly to say that
it had no religious significance. Indeed, to understand the significance of
the altar panel, and the entire *tavu* complex, is to understand much about
what the house was, and continues to be (McKinnon 1987).

The Unities of the *Tavu*

Like the stone boat ritual center of the village, so too the
ancestral altar complex of the house is an entity that synthesized the fragments of the old order into a new cultural form. Not only did it provide
an image of the transcendent unity of opposed parts, it also afforded a
place where humans could establish a permanent relation with the otherworldly powers of their ancestors.

Anyone who is the slightest bit familiar with Austronesian languages
might immediately think the word *tavu* is a cognate with the more familiar Polynesian word *tabu* ("sacred," "prohibited"). This association
might be strengthened by the fact that, in the Yamdenan language, the
word for these altar panels is *lamngatabu*. Yet the Fordatan root *tavu*, and
its Yamdenan cognate *tabu*, has a very different set of meanings (Drabbe
1932a:96; Drabbe 1932b:102).[5] The noun form, *tavun*, refers to the "beginning, starting point, base, or root of something" and is often paired seman-
tically with the words *ni tutul*, the "end or tip of something." In verb
form, one finds *al ntavu*, "to begin," as well as *ntavun*, "she/he begins to
clear [a garden plot]." The root *tavu*, then, especially when considered in
relation to *tutul*, suggests several interpretations. One is of a whole, an
entity that has a beginning and an end. Another is that of movement,
from starting point to ending point. Yet another is that of growth, as in
plants that have a root or trunk (*tavun*) and a tip (*tutul*), which is only

---

4. Cunningham (1973:205, 226–27) and many others have made clear that the primary
significance of the house — in Timor and elsewhere in Indonesia — is as a ritual center.

5. Drabbe waivers in his thoughts on the meaning of the word, suggesting that *tavu*
is "from the general Indonesian word *tabu*, prohibited, although it could also be the word
tavu, which means base" (1928:151). It should be noted that the Fordatan language has both
the root *tabu* (as in *ntabu teri*, "he forbids, hinders, blocks, prohibits") as well as the root
tavu (as in the examples cited above).

a provisional ending point, one that has the potential for extending beyond itself.[6]

If one assumes that the word *tavu* — as it refers to the house altar — is
the same root word, then one may well ask what is the beginning, base,
or root represented here, and what is the end, or tip that has grown out
of it? To begin to answer the first part of this question, one might inquire
into the significance of the images that — in the midst of an otherwise
remarkably abstract design — do appear upon the *tavu*. These images are
generally of two kinds: animals and heirloom valuables.[7]

On a number of *tavu*, there appear carved images of rather dapper
fish, dogs, or cocks. The names of houses in Tanimbar often include the
names of animals, who sometimes appear as ancestral figures in the histories of the origins of the house. It is not improbable that the animals
represented on the *tavu* bear reference to the exploits of the ancestors in
the origin of the house.[8]

Many of the *tavu* have images of valuables carved onto them.[9] Most often the valuables represented are either gold breast pendants (*masa*) or gold-
en "male earrings" (*loran*) — the two types of "male" valuables that are kept
as heirlooms in important named houses. Although the history of the named
heirloom valuables of a house is not always known, when it is, it usually
involves — as we have already seen — the exploits of an ancestor who journeyed to the heavens, the underworld, or foreign lands and obtained the valuable from beings invested with otherworldly powers. Heirloom valuables
are not only connected with the actions of the founding ancestors, and therefore associated with the origins of the house, they are also linked to the
sources of otherworldly power. Although the heirloom valuables are usually
kept hidden in a small chest, their representation on the *tavu* stands as a sign
of their underlying constitutive power (cf. Weiner 1985).

6. See Fox 1971 for an analysis of plant metaphors used in relation to kinship among
the Rotinese; see Traube 1980b, 1986, 1989, for explorations of the meaning of the "trunk"
and "tip" metaphors among the Mambai of East Timor.

7. Photographs of *tavu* may be found in *Art of the Archaic Indonesians* (1982), Barbier
1984, *Budaya-Indonesia* (1987), Drabbe 1940, Geurtjens 1941, Heine-Geldern 1966, McKinnon
1987, and van Nouhuys 1924.

8. Patsy Spyer (personal communication) pointed out that both dogs and cocks (but
obviously, not fish) are also associated with settled domesticity and a state of guarded
watchfulness over domestic settlements.

9. Carvings of valuables apparently also appear on certain house beams in at least some
areas of Sumba. Adams notes that on "the upper part of the sacred pillar, and on the beam
(*woaharu*) extending toward the back on the men's side are carvings of plants and various
gold ornaments" (1974:336). Leach also reports sacrificial altars with drawings of wealth objects on them among the Kachin (1965:118).

The *tavu*, with its representations of animals and heirloom valuables, connects the house, in time, to those ancestral actions in which the house originated and, in space, to those sources of power and life in which the continued productive activity of the house is secured. The *tavu* thus represents a "beginning," "starting point," "base," and "root" (*tavun*) that is the ancestral source of life.

But the *tavu* is more than an image of the source and root of all possibility for growth and productivity: it is simultaneously that and an image of its own fulfillment, the tip that has issued forth (Strathern 1988). As such, the *tavu* is an image that defies the distinction between an individual ancestral source and the group of descendants who have issued forth from this source (Wagner n.d.).

This synthesis of individual and group, source and issue is manifest in the remarkable aesthetic tension between realism and abstraction that is the hallmark of these ancestral figures. Indeed, what is extraordinary about the *tavu* is that while it clearly represents a human form, the image is so elegantly overwhelmed by scrollwork abstractions that it seems intentionally to deny reference to any particular human individual. Most *tavu* are dominated by abstract designs: the S-shaped double spirals (*kilun ila'a*) and single spirals (*kilun etal*) that also appear on house posts and in the ikat designs of Tanimbarese weavings. Although Drabbe considers the small ancestor statues (*walut*) to be "soul images" of immediate ancestors, he asserts that the *tavu* itself was not a "soul image" of any particular ancestor (1940:36, 112). When compared to the relative realism of the small ancestor statues, the abstraction of the *tavu* image confirms this.

Visually, the *tavu* played upon a line not only between realism and abstraction, but also between a freestanding image and an integral structural feature of the house. While the image of the ancestor was abstracted to the point where it was almost submerged into the structure of the house, the structure of the house was such that it seemed to emerge out of the image of the ancestor. Conceptually, the *tavu* was the founding ancestor (as a particular individual human form) become a house (as an enduring social group, and thus an abstraction). Simultaneously, the *tavu* was the house (as a structural group) rooted in, and supported by, a particular individual human form (the actions and powers of both the founding ancestor and the present head of the house).[10]

The *tavu* provided an aesthetic form that united not only ancestor and descendants, individual and group, but also male and female. It is true that several *tavu* do show either distinctly male or female forms: one *tavu*

10. I am grateful to Roy Wagner for pointing to this interpretation of the significance of the *tavu*.

pictured in Geurtjens 1941, for example, is obviously male; and in the collection of the Museum voor Land- en Volkenkunde in Rotterdam there is a *tavu* that is carved in an unusually realistic manner and clearly shows a figure of a woman wearing shell armbands (van Nouhuys 1924: opposite p. 5). More generally, however, the *tavu* evokes both male and female associations. In the same Rotterdam collection, there is another *tavu* that is rendered in a highly abstract form but, interestingly enough, has a sun and a moon (male and female symbols) carved on either side where the hands would normally be (van Nouhuys 1924: opposite p. 5). Various commentators have noted that the position of the arms on the *tavu* closely resembles that of women when they dance (*rsomar*) — arms extended and turned upward, it is said, like the wings of frigate birds. In connection with this, Drabbe quotes a riddle which asks: Who is the girl who dances day and night? The answer is, of course, the *tavu* (1940:289). In addition to such female associations, however, there are others that clearly link the *tavu* with males and, more broadly, with the intergenerational continuity of men within a house. Most often, the heirloom valuables represented on the *tavu* are "male" valuables. Moreover, the association between the *tavu* and the male forebears of the house is indicated by the saying quoted by Drabbe: "If someone's father is dead, he says: my *lamngatabu* is gone" (1940:284–85). Drabbe also mentions that, in a reciprocal fashion, *lamngatabu* or *tavu* is an honorific term used for the eldest son of the house — the son whose seat, one day, will be on the bench at the base of the *tavu* (1940:271).

The *tavu* complex represented not so much gender ambiguity but rather the unity of both male and female aspects of the house. The gender unity of the *tavu* complex was represented more realistically by the carved figurines — often in male-female pairs — that were placed on the shelf above the altar panel. It was also represented, socially, by the conjunction of male and female figures on either side of the *tavu* panel. In front of the *tavu* was the bench on which only the male head of the house was allowed to sit, and in back of the *tavu* was a platform on which only the unmarried girls of the house were allowed to sleep.

At the center of the house, then, the *tavu* complex was an exquisitely elegant expression of a recomposed totality and synthetic unity. The *tavu* complex expressed the potentiality contained in the unity of male and female, the power of its roots in the past and the multiplicity of its future growth, the individuality of its ancestral source and the structural mass of its descendants' issue.

The Power of Life and Death

Yet the *tavu* complex was not simply a representation of all these values. It also provided permanent places — the altar panel, the skulls and neck bones, the small statues, the heirlooms, as well as the offering plates — where humans could maintain contact with the spirits of their ancestors.[11] It was thus a kind of bridge or pathway that made possible the active relation between the past and the present, the ancestors and their descendants, the root and the tip.

The spirits of the ancestors were not embodied in, and did not necessarily permanently live in, either the *tavu* or the various objects placed above the *tavu*. During a ritual or an exchange negotiation, however, when the head of the house sat in his place directly in front of the altar panel, his ancestor was thought to descend along the panel itself and sit beside him.[12] While both the past and the ancestors are at once necessarily distinct and separate from the present and their descendants, the ancestors are nevertheless forever present in the present and in their descendants. The *tavu* formed a pathway of time and identity — a pathway that related the actions of the past and the ancestors with those of the present and their descendants.

If the *tavu* was a pathway, a place of active relation between ancestors and their descendants, that relation was (and still is) about something: about the potentiality for life and death. It is in the power of the ancestors, and ultimately Ubila'a, to foster the fertility, growth, and health of humans and crops, as well as to ensure efficacy and success in hunting and fishing expeditions and in warfare. It is also in their power to cause infertility and disease, failure and disaster. The fine line between the two potentialities is constantly negotiated through prayers and offerings. In the past, as at present, offerings — of a betel quid, tobacco, food, or some drops of palmwine — were made in connection with almost every event, from birth through the life cycle to death; during illness and upon recovery; from the beginning stages of a new garden to harvest; from the initiation of a hunting or fishing expedition to its conclusion; from the first to the last steps in the building of a house or a boat; from the commencement of a war to its final resolution (Drabbe 1940). Formerly, the

11. People told me that the voices of the ancestors were heard through their skulls. When, for instance, someone came by and called up to see if anyone was home, they might be answered by the voice of the skull and be fooled into thinking that someone was there. They would then go up the stairs and be surprised to find that, in fact, no one was at home.

12. In other areas of Indonesia and Polynesia, the pathways along which the ancestors and gods descend take other forms, as house posts and cloth (see, for example, Adams 1974:336; Barnes 1974:74–75; Sahlins 1981:118; and Traube 1986:165, 266).

occupants of a house "lifted up offerings" (*rsaka fanera*) onto the ceramic plate above the *tavu* for the ancestors and onto the *ubu* for Ubila'a;[13] currently, they tuck such offerings into the roof thatch of the house. Both Ubila'a and the spirits of the ancestors are thought to eat the "soul" (*ngraan*) or the "image" (*walun*) of the offerings, just as Ubila'a is said to "eat the person" should s/he allow the person to die (Drabbe 1940:429). Indeed, formerly, when a person died, he was laid out for the wake with his head at the base of the *tavu* and his feet pointing toward the door (Drabbe 1925:34–40; Drabbe 1940:252–53). One might almost say that the person formed his own last offering to his ancestors in the process of becoming one of them himself (cf. Cunningham 1973:232; Metcalf 1982:107–9).

The *tavu*, as the place where prayers and offerings were made and received, was the meeting place of two intentionalities: those of the ancestors and those of their descendants. The course of life, and ultimately of death, revolve around the mediation of these two intentionalities. For it is only by establishing a permanent and positive relation with the powers of the ancestors that humans are able to foster the growth and extension of life.

Male Anchorage and Female Mobility

Within the context of a house, life and growth depends upon the achievement of a double objective: the intergenerational continuity of men (and ancestors) within the house and the movement of women outside the house. Both objectives are achieved through bride-wealth prestations, which make it possible not only for males to "sit" or "stay" (*rdoku*) within the house of their father, but also for females to move out from the house of their father and marry into other houses.

If the house is an entity that comprises the prior unity of its male and female aspects, then their differentiation and separate identity can only be achieved when the female aspect is extracted from the house. Yet these externalized female aspects of the house — the sisters and the members of the female lines that issue from outmarried sisters — continue to be "owned" and encompassed by their source — the males of the house from which they originated. They constitute a part of the "female" estates of the "male" house that now stands as their source (see below).

---

13. Although it seems that not everyone still does this, I was told by Ma'idodu Melatunan that once a month he "feeds the gold pieces" (*nfa'an masara*) — his heirloom valuables and, presumably the ancestors connected with them — with rice. The feeding of the heirlooms and ancestors thus establishes a direct connection between the present occupants of the house and the first ancestors who "set down the house master [i.e., the heirlooms] for their grandchildren and great grandchildren" (*rfadoku rahan duan ven ubur-nusira*).

The separated male and female aspects of the house are not only differentiated as source and issue, they also embody distinct relational and temporal modalities. Thus, from their "base" or "root" in the *tavu* complex and their natal house, females (and the female lines issuing from them) should "multiply their sprouts a thousandfold" (*rmela ruburira rivun*). They should multiply and extend themselves ever outward in an organic and irreversible pattern of growth and time (see chapter 6). Counterpoised to this restless, outward movement of females is the inward fixity of the males within the house. Between male ancestors and their male descendants, the movement from root to tip is a not one of extension but rather one of alternation and substitution. Because the names for eldest sons generally repeat in alternate generations, the head of the house (who formerly sat in front of the *tavu*) and his deceased father (whose skull formerly rested on top of the *tavu* and whose spirit descended to sit along side of him) together represent the totality of a dual male identity. Only the relative positions alternate with the cycling of names and identities through time. In relations between males, time and identity are immobilized and fixed in a recursive alternation of forms.[14]

To the extent that the intergenerational continuity of males within the house is achieved, it is also represented in certain "male" objects — heirloom valuables and, formerly, bones — that were part of the *tavu* complex.[15] The hardness, weight, and enduring qualities of these objects not only express the permanence that men hope to secure and retain for their houses, they also serve to anchor the productivity of women as they move away from their natal house.

It is not surprising that — in contrast to the blood of women, which marks the movement and extension of the females outside of the house — it is the bones of men that mark the immobility and permanence of the males within the house. Thus the skull (as well as the axis and atlas bones) of the father were (once) the privileged signs of male continuity within the house, and they were prominently displayed on the shelf above the *tavu*. Although bones are no longer used in this way, heirloom valuables continue both to express and to embody the permanence of identity that males strive to achieve for their sons and for the house as a whole (cf. Traube 1980b, 1986). In the Fordatan language, heirloom valuables are

14. Concerning two distinct modes of thinking about time and relation, Traube notes that, for the Mambai, "the house conceived of as a line of men is both immutable and sterile; the ties that a house contracts through women are both mutable and fertile. Social life is based on a complementary balance between a static male order and a dynamic female vitality" (1986:96). In connection with this, she states that "descent works like Father Heaven to freeze time, while alliance follows Mother Earth and unleashes it" (1986:232).

15. See Errington (1983, 1989) on the significance of regalia in Luwu, Sulawesi.

called the "masters of the house" (*rahan dua*); in the Yamdenan language they are known as the "riggings of the house" (*das ni mbaretar*) (Drabbe 1940:202). Every important, named house attempts to retain at least one named heirloom valuable—although the full complement of one breast pendant and one pair of male earrings is preferable—as a sign of its history, stature, and weight. With its heirloom valuables, a house is considered to be "heavy" (*aleman*), whereas an "empty" house that has lost its heirloom valuables (usually in the payment of a debt) is considered to be "light" (*maraan*) and inconsequential. If a house has been forced to alienate its heirlooms, it is said that "they pull out/uproot their *tavu*" (*redal rir tavu*). The root *edal* usually refers to the extraction of a stone or a pole from the ground. Alienating one's heirlooms is therefore likened to dislodging the foundational supports of the house.

The heirloom valuables and bones—as hard, enduring objects—consolidate a number of associations that have to do with weight, permanence, and anchorage. Yet these objects, and the *tavu* complex as a whole, are but the signs, and the place, of contact with that which is the true anchor—the otherworldly powers of the ancestors that make possible both permanence and growth, root and tip. Falaksoru Ditilebit once told me that when the head of the house says he "leans against the *tavu*" (even today, when there are no *tavu*), he means more than that he literally sits with his back against the altar panel; he means that he has, as his backing and support, the spiritual power of all his ancestors, and thus the weight and enduring strength of their history, their name, their bones, and their heirloom valuables.

Named and Unnamed Houses

Any house can be defined, then, in terms of the unity of its male and female aspects: the intergenerational relation between males (including their ritual relation to the ancestors) and the fertility and productivity of its female resources, or "estates" (including land, tree plantations, and exchange pathways marked by female bloodlines). Yet not all houses are able to achieve the same degree of permanence and continuity with regard not only to the ritual relation to their ancestors, but also to their estates.

The difference is coded by the distinction that is made between people who occupy a house (*rahan*) and people who do not. This is usually expressed by saying that they either do or do not have a house, or alternatively, that their house either does or does not have a name. To say that a group has a house or constitutes a named house is to say, among other things, that the group has an enduring relation with the founding ancestors, which is a sign of its permanence, its weight, and its value. To say that a group does not have a house or is an unnamed house is to say that it lacks such attributes.

The distinction between named and unnamed houses is also represented in terms of the relation between "elder-younger same-sex siblings" (*ya'an-iwarin*). Named and unnamed houses are associated as "elder-younger brothers" in what is called the "inside" or "contents of a house" (*rahan ralan*), or what I have called a house-complex. The elder brother named house, alone or together with its attached younger brother unnamed houses, may also be called a *rahan matan*, where *matan* connotes "origin" and "source" as well as the new growth that issues forth from it.[16] Most important, the relation between elder and younger brother houses codes a hierarchical relation between nobles and commoners (as will be seen below).

Formerly, the members of a named house formed a residential unit, which might include not only a set of patrilaterally affiliated brothers, but also matrilaterally affiliated children and "younger brothers" of attached unnamed houses. Alternatively these latter might live in separate, nearby residences. Currently, patrilaterally affiliated brothers of a named house live in separate, nuclear family residences, as do matrilaterally affiliated members and the younger brothers of attached unnamed houses.

The difference between elder brother named houses and their younger brother unnamed houses is evident in what constitutes their patrimony, including not only the *tavu* complex and heirloom valuables already mentioned but also rights over house sites, ridgepole insignia, and ritual offices in the stone boat. Not all named houses have all of the above endowments; unnamed houses have none of them. (Although I had planned to include an appendix listing the named and unnamed houses in Awear, their patrimony and estate holdings, I have excluded it because of the implications it contains concerning people's rank.)

It is my understanding that, like the Kachin distinction between chiefly and ordinary houses (Leach 1965:108–10), named and unnamed houses in Tanimbar would have been differentiated by the kind of altar complex they accomodated. Named houses would have been distinguished by the

---

16. The root *mata* means "eye, sprout, point of origin." Used in conjunction with other words, it can mean the sucker of a banana tree (*muu matan*), the small buds on the main corm of a taro plant (*ronan matan*), the sprouts of a sago palm that issue from its base (*era matan*), the eyes of a coconut (*nuur matan*), and the point at which a wind originates and from which it blows (*nait matan*). *Matan* thus connotes both the source of growth — the base or kernel of a plant — as well as the sprouts, the new growth, that issues from it. The term *rahan matan* is most likely cognate with the Ambonese and Malay term *matarumah* (see Cooley 1962:102–4; Jansen 1977:102). For a more general discussion of the term *mata*, see Barnes 1977b.

possession of a *tavu*, in the sense of an elaborately carved altar panel such as those described above.[17] Unnamed houses most likely had, in its place, only the small carved images of their immediate ancestors placed on the roof beam opposite the entrance to the house. It is clear, however, that only named houses possessed heirloom valuables as a part of the patrimony that embodied and expressed the powers of the ancestors.

Thus, it was only named houses that maintained, through their *tavu* and their heirlooms, a center for an enduring ritual relation to the founding ancestors of the house-complex as a whole. The relation of unnamed houses to these ancestors existed only to the extent that they remained attached as younger brothers to named houses. The capacity for named houses to stand for and represent the whole depended upon their position as a ritual center. It was their *tavu* and their heirlooms that provided a pathway, both in space and through time, to the founding ancestors — to the origins, the base, and the root of all that had issued forth and should continue issue forth from them.

It should be stressed that neither the intergenerational continuity of males within a house nor the relation between elder and younger brother houses is conceived in terms of an ideology of descent. The intergenerational continuity of males is achieved rather than given in the nature of things, and it is therefore contingent in several ways. First of all, patrilateral affiliation depends upon the completion of bridewealth prestations, for if these are left incomplete, a man's children will ultimately affiliate matrilaterally (to the house of the mother's brother) or step-patrilaterally (to the house of the mother's second husband) (see chapters 7, 9, and 10). Second, if those responsible for the payment of a man's wife's bridewealth refuse to pay it altogether, he would (formerly) be sold into slavery, or would "sell himself" to someone who would agree to make the payments. In the latter a case, he and his descendants would lose their affiliation to his father's house and constitute a younger brother house attached to those to whom he sold himself. Third, should a named house become empty, or should its occupants fall in rank, then a man (usually an adult, but sometimes an infant) would be "lifted" in as head of the house, and the original tenants would eventually be seen to occupy a younger brother

17. The only specific mention I ever heard of altar panels on Fordata was in reference to the houses Ditilebit in Awear and Vuarlela in Waleran. This hardly means that these were the only houses on the island that had them, but it does indicate that it is highly unlikely that all houses (or even all named houses) possessed them. That they were only likely to be found in named houses is indicated by the statement made to me to the effect that the altar panel was comparable to the heirloom valuable of a named house as an indicator of its high status. Unnamed houses would have neither heirloom valuables nor altar panels.

unnamed house. The practice of "lifting" adult men from one to another named house — or what I shall call adrogation[18] — is exceedingly common such that nearly every named house in Awear had at least one man lifted in or out in the past three generations (see chapter 10 and appendix 1). Because of the high frequency of adrogation in named houses, therefore, genealogical continuity is repeatedly undermined by considerations of rank in the determination of house membership. Finally, the intergenerational continuity of males within a named house is contingent upon the relation between the descendants of elder and younger brothers. It is usually said that the descendants of the eldest brother have rights over the patrimony and estates of the house, but it could as well be said that he who establishes effective control over the patrimony of the house is the eldest brother, and his descendants will constitute the senior line. Although Tanimbarese do not at all think of the relation between senior and junior lines in terms of segmentation, the descendants of younger brothers — or whoever fails to control the patrimony of the named house — will presumably eventually constitute younger brother unnamed houses. In the end, therefore, houses must be seen as potentially complex units whose constituency may be established through the contingencies of bridewealth prestations, adrogation, and control over patrimony and estates.

Like the relation between elder and younger brothers within houses, the relation between elder brother named houses and younger brother unnamed houses is explicitly not coded in terms of genealogy, or an ideology of descent and segmentation. In fact, speculation on the possible existence of a genealogical relation between elder and younger brother houses is met with indifference or, more generally, outright denial. Instead, people stress that named and unnamed houses have been traditionally associated as elder and younger since the time of migrations and settlement. It is only where the attachment is more recent that people will whisper that an elder-younger brother relation originated because the younger "sold himself" to the elder. The conventional, performative nature of the relation between such traditional and attached brothers is captured in the word that is often used to differentiate them from "true brothers" (*ya'an-iwarin lalean*): they are "elder-younger brothers [who] treat each other well" (*ya'an-iwarin simaklivur*). That is, the relation exists in, and only in, a conventional understanding that, being hierarchically related, they are mutually obliged to treat each other well.

18. The term *adrogation* (Crook 1967:111–12; Taylor 1968:34; J. Goody 1969:59; and E. N. Goody 1971:340–42) is appropriate to the Tanimbarese practice by which "they lift" (*rsikat*) an adult man into a named house and give him full rights over its estates. This measure — which is intended to prevent a named house from dying out — is extremely common in Tanimbar (cf. Barraud 1979:187–204).

The model that people have of elder and younger brother houses, therefore, is not one of a segmentary system of branching descent lines, but rather one of a conventional pairing of named and unnamed houses hierarchically related as elder and younger. Thus, instead of an organic unfolding of a segmentary system of descent (cf. Traube 1986), with regard to houses, Tanimbarese stress a radical disjunction between elder and younger. The values of permanence and impermanence, which distinguish elder from younger, are given substance in the relative constitution of the patrimony and the estates of named and unnamed houses.

Forest Estates

The patrimony of a house, as already mentioned, is not limited to those objects and relations that define the male dimension of the house. It also includes those productive resources or "estates" that define the exteriorized female dimension of the house. The radical distinction between named and unnamed houses is most forcefully expressed by the relative permanence of their estates, including both those called "forest estates" (*abat nangan*) and those called "village estates" (*abat ahu*). The forest estates of named houses include both land and plantations of long-lived trees; those of unnamed houses comprise tree plantations alone.[19]

Within the borders of the land that belongs to a village, various "tracts of land" (*abat*) or "forests" (*nangan*) come under the ritual control of specific named houses, which are thereby considered the "masters of the land" (*abat dua*) or the "masters of the forest" (*nangan dua*). Whereas not all named houses necessarily control a tract of land, no unnamed houses are ever said to be the master over a tract of land. Unnamed houses will be associated with certain pieces of land only because they are attached, as younger brothers, to the named houses that control those lands.

There are two ways in which named houses come into possession of a tract of land: one in accordance with the system of marriage prestations and the other in accordance with the pattern of original settlement on the land. Although it is uncommon, land may be acquired in the context of marriage exchanges. Land may occasionally be given with a woman in marriage, along with the other "female" valuables that constitute her "adornments." Such a transfer of land can only take place between two named

19. Both land (*lanuun*) and the products of the land (including trees and garden produce) are considered to be "female things" (*af vata*). These contrast, on the one hand, with the "male" rain (*da'ut*) that fertilizes the land and, on the other hand, with the products of such activities as hunting, fishing, and distilling, which are considered to be "male things" (*af brana*).

houses that are related as traditional wife-givers and wife-takers.[20] More commonly, ritual control over land was established during the period of migrations before the founding of villages, when migrating groups came to settle upon specific pieces of land (see chapter 4). After these groups had "gathered themselves together" (*rasdovu ira*) and founded a village, the named houses that had originally settled upon tracts of land remained the masters of that land, although they no longer lived upon it, as such.

Elder brother named houses retain ritual control over the land, but they remain obligated to call together the younger brother unnamed houses that had originally settled with them on the land to participate in any first fruit harvest observances that are connected with it. Thus elder and younger brothers of a house-complex share a common relation to a tract of land on which their ancestors first settled and on which they must continue to gather in order to "feed the dead" (*rfa'an nitu*), to honor the ancestors whose productive powers have yielded the abundant crops they harvest. The hierarchical nature of the elder-younger brother relation is brought out to the extent that the named house is considered the master of the land and retains the primary ritual prerogatives, as the elder, with regard to the land and the ancestors. The younger brother houses are associated with the land through their continued affiliation with the elder.

Unlike estates of land (over which specific named *houses* maintain a fixed relation endowed with ritual prerogatives), plantations of trees constitute properties that are inherited by *persons* who may belong to either named or unnamed houses. The long-lived trees comprised in the plantations (*fau tnanan*) of a forest estate include coconut (*nuur*), sago palm (*era*), breadfruit of both the seedless variety (*ulur vrea*) and seeded variety (*ulur watan*), mango (*faa*), bamboo (*temar*), and betel nut (*isua*).

Ritual control over land and the use of land for gardens and tree plantations are two quite different matters. Gardens and trees may be planted on land whether or not one's house is traditionally associated with the land. In order to open a new garden or tree plantation on a specific piece of land, one need only give notice of one's intention to the members of the house that ritually controls the land. In relation to the gardens, there is a first fruit offering that must be given to the master of the land, but such offerings are not required in relation to trees.

The members of those houses that are associated with a particular

20. It is worth remarking, as well, that it is not uncommon for the two houses to be from different villages, such that the gift of land involves not only its transfer from one house to another, but also from one village to another. Thus, for instance, I was told that the two islands called Kasbu'i and Wolas (off the west coast of Yamdena) formerly belonged to a house in Makatian. A woman from that house married into the house Laian in Sera, and the two islands were given to Laian at that time.

tract of land will have the major portions of their tree plantations on that land or in the adjacent areas (especially if that land is suitable for the planting of trees). But they may also have plantations on land not traditionally associated with their house. Likewise, members of other houses not traditionally associated with one's own land may have their tree plantations on this land. As a result, the plantations of the members of a house may be dispersed over several tracts of land, on which they may, at the same time, be interspersed with the plantations of the members of other houses.

The difference between elder brother named houses and younger brother unnamed houses with regard to their forest estates is that the former maintains ritual control over the fertility of the land, including the crops and trees planted upon it. Thus the fertility and productivity of trees (the sole estates of unnamed houses) ultimately depend upon, and are encompassed by, the fertility and productivity of the land (solely the estates of named houses).

Moreover, in maintaining a ritual relation to the land, named houses maintain a permanent relation with the founding ancestors who first settled upon the land and who are thought still to reside upon the land with the other ancestral spirits. By contrast, through their tree plantations, the members of unnamed houses maintain a ritual relation to only their most immediate ancestors — their fathers and their fathers' fathers — who planted the trees. As the older plantations of unnamed houses die off and are supplanted by newer plantations, so too their older ancestors are forgotten in time and supplanted by more immediate ancestors. Thus the forest estates of named houses always anchor the house (and the entire house-complex) in time and space to the actions of the founding ancestors (even if their names are long forgotten), whereas the forest estates of unnamed houses imply a continual impermanence in the movement of generations through time and across space.

Village Estates

Just as forest estates (*abat nangan*) include tracts of land and plantations of trees, so village estates (*abat ahu*) include "rows" (*lolat*) of affinally allied houses and, as it were, plantations of people — the immediate descendants of the outmarried women of the house — referred to collectively as "sisters and aunts" (*ura-ava*) (see chapter 6). Rights over forest estates entitle the members of a house to the harvest of their fruits, as they also oblige them to tend the estates and ensure their growth and expansion. So, too, with the village estates. The members of a house have the obligation to care for, protect, and foster the growth and multiplication of the descendants of their outmarried women. They also are entitled to harvest the fruits (in the form of bridewealth valuables) borne along the exchange pathways to which these descendants of outmarried women belong.

The village estates of named and unnamed houses are differentiated by the fact that those of the former include both "rows" (*lolat*) of allied houses and the persons who make up one's "sisters and aunts" (*ura-ava*) whereas those of the latter include one's *ura-ava* only. "Sisters and aunts" include the descendants, traced along female bloodlines, of three generations of outmarried women (one's sisters, father's sisters, and father's father's sisters). These female lines are created by the recent marriages of these women to men of previously unallied groups. The affinal relations that delimit one's sisters and aunts are considered provisional and essentially impermanent. "Rows," on the other hand, link named houses along the female lines of women who married out of the house in the distant past (or, at least, more than three generations ago). These rows trace the pathways of enduring alliances between named houses, and they are considered to have been in existence since time immemorial.

A named house thus maintains a permanent relation to, and place in, a fixed order of rows. Named houses are defined, in large part, as permanent entities precisely because they maintain enduring alliances along these rows. Defined differentially in this way, the place of a house in a row exists and continues to exist regardless of whether it is occupied and regardless of who occupies it. By contrast, unnamed houses have no position in the permanent order of rows, but only in the order of sisters and aunts pathways, the permanence of which is not guaranteed. Indeed, unnamed houses have no inherent permanence: they are defined by their constituency only, and if their members die out, the house disappears.

It is thus, in large part, the exteriorized female aspects of houses, which are embodied in both their forest estates and their village estates, that differentiate houses. Named houses are marked by their permanent relation, traced through land and other houses, to distant ancestral sources of power and established lines of fertility. Unnamed houses are, by contrast, marked by their impermanent and fleeting relation, traced through trees and persons, to immediate ancestors and recent lines of fertility.

Nobles and Commoners

This relative permanence and impermanence of named and unnamed houses ultimately expresses a difference in rank. Three ranks are recognized in Tanimbar: nobles (*mela*), commoners (*iria-iwarin*: literally, "slaves and younger brothers"), and slaves (*iria*). The distinction between elder brother named houses and younger brother unnamed houses ideally corresponds to the distinction between nobles and commoners, although the shifting fortunes of rank mean that the correlation is not always exact (see chapter 11).

The rank difference between named and unnamed houses (and between the nobles and commoners who ought to occupy them) is represented in a number of ways. Important, named houses are often referred to as ships (*kabal*), under which lesser, unnamed houses "take shelter," or "harbor" (*rlau*).[21] Similarly, named houses are also known as "buffalo" (*karbaa*), in contrast to unnamed houses, which are referred to as "pigs" (*vavu*).

More significantly, however, the nobles who occupy named houses are thought of as "village people" (*tomat ahu*). It is their province to know "customary law" (*adat*), to sit in their village, in their houses, and negotiate bridewealth and other exchanges — that is, "they talk suits" (*rfallak ngrihi*) according to customary law. In so doing, they negotiate the order of human relations and the enduring form of culture: they create and recreate them with each negotiation.

The commoners who belong to unnamed houses, on the contrary, are "forest people" (*tomat nangan*). It is not their province to understand customary law in any depth, and they are not allowed to talk it (at least not where it concerns the affairs of named houses). Their special province is in relation to the forest — to hunting and agriculture, not to the village and customary law. This, I was told, was more marked a generation or two ago, when the men of named houses would, literally, sit in their houses in the village and "talk suits" all day, while slaves and the commoner men of unnamed houses did the fishing, hunting, and gardening for the members of the named houses to which they were attached.[22] Immobile at the center of a named house, the elder brothers "order them [to] come and go" (*rsinar ira rtii rmaa*). In connection with talking *adat*, the younger brothers were — and still are — the messengers and the errand runners.

---

21. Formerly, the physical structures of named houses were significantly larger and more stately than those of unnamed houses and they were often crowned by elegant ridgepole decorations, which — like the prow and stern boards of sailing boats and stone boats — were called *kora*. The representation of the house as a boat is discussed, in particular, in Vroklage 1936, 1940, and Lewcock and Brans 1975.

22. Apparently, up until recently the forest estates of named houses comprised very few trees. For as nobles who sat and negotiated exchanges all day in the village, the members of named houses did not occupy themselves with the planting of either gardens or trees, which was the job of their slaves and "younger brothers." One man who occupies an important named house told me that his father's father did not make gardens and had only six coconut trees. It was only his father who planted their present tree plantation. A man who belonged to an attached unnamed house confirmed this general pattern when he told

They would be ordered to run and call people to the house, to deliver messages, to fetch palmwine, or, within the house, to stand and pour palmwine for the assembled guests.

In recent years, and as the result of governmental restrictions on slavery and other manifestations of rank, the strength of the differentiation between such elder and younger brothers has been greatly diminished, especially as regards the production and provision of food. Younger brothers are no longer sent for food by their elder brothers, and the latter now fish, hunt, and garden along with the rest. But when *adat* is talked and suits are negotiated, it is very clear (once one perceives it) who sits and talks, and who acts as the runner, the messenger, and the pourer of palmwine.

The difference between the named houses of nobles and unnamed houses of commoners is therefore twofold: it can be seen in both the comparative permanence of their estates and the comparative fixity of their relation to the ancestors. The estates of a named house — its land and its *lolat* — are not only inherently enduring, they also form a bridge between the present and the past, between the current occupants of a house and its founding ancestors, by whose actions and alliances the house was originally established. By contrast, the estates of an unnamed house — its trees and its sisters and aunts — are uniquely impermanent and bear no relation to the founding of the fixed order of the world.

Named houses, moreover, maintain an enduring ritual relation to the founding ancestors through which the potential for life may be realized in the fertility of externalized female estates. The relation of unnamed houses to these ancestors exists only to the extent that they remain attached to named houses as younger brothers. Younger brother unnamed houses remain on the periphery, while at the center, and at the origin, remain the elder brother named houses — their permanence and weight embodied in the hard bones of their ancestors, in the enduring metals of their heirloom valuables, and in their continued connection to their ancestors, once evident in the exquisite altar panels that formed the pathways of their descent.

---

me that it was the people who belonged to unnamed houses who had the large tree plantations. He said that those who occupied named houses sat and arranged *adat* matters in the village and had no concern for tree plantations. This differentiation between named and unnamed houses (village people and forest people), although still very much in evidence, no longer holds with regard to tree plantations.

6   The Flow of Blood

As Mambai say of marital alliance: "Its trunk sits there. The bits of its tip go out again and again." A wife-giving trunk house relinquishes its daughters, whose own daughters later marry out again, and so on over the generations, creating branching lines of maternal affiliation. (Traube 1986:86)

When a Tanimbarese child is born, the question asked of those present at the birth is simple: "Stranger or house master?" (*Mangun te rahan dua?*). Yet the question evokes an image of what lies at the heart of complexity in the world: the difference between what Tanimbarese see as the destiny of "females" and "males." Although their destinies are, in the first instance, united in a house, exchange effects their separation and differentiation. Thus a "male" is meant to "sit" or "stay" (*ndoku*) in the house of his father; he is a "master of the house" (*rahan dua*). Even at birth, however, a "female" is a "stranger" (*mangun*) to her natal house; her destiny is to move between houses.

It is the relative movement or fixity that codes gender, rather than the opposite. For whoever moves between houses is considered "female": if a woman moves by marrying into another house, she is regarded as "female"; likewise, if a man moves by being "lifted," or adrogated, into another house, he too is considered "female." This is important because it indicates that this differentiation is not innate, but rather a product of human agency (Wagner 1977; Strathern 1988).

Yet to say that a female is a stranger is not to say that she is alienated or severed from her natal house. On the contrary, the relative fixity and movement of persons codes an asymmetric and hierarchical relation between source and issue that cannot be severed. To say that those who are fixed and male are house masters is to say that they are the source and that they encompass and ritually control the productive resources represented by the estates of houses—the externalized "female" aspects of the house (including land, trees, and women). To say that those who move and are female are strangers is to say that their movement between houses allows for the flow of blood, the transmission of which establishes the basis for the growth and expansion of the village estates that are encompassed by the male source.

While the fixity of the male aspect of both named and unnamed houses forms the foundation for the extension of the female bloodlines of particular women, the established male continuity of named houses grounds the more enduring pathways of exchange that have grown out of these particular female bloodlines and are conceptualized as "rows" (*lolat*) of allied houses. The distinction between those exchange pathways conceptualized in terms of persons and particular bloodlines and those conceptualized in terms of houses and rows differentiates two of the three hierarchical levels outlined by the system of exchange.

Just as the houses anchor the female bloodlines and the rows that issue forth from them, so the Great Row (Lolat Ila'a) anchors, and gathers together, the entire system of exchange pathways. The Great Row — the double cycle of affinal alliance that stands at the apex of the system of exchange pathways — defines the third and final level of the hierarchy. As a recomposed image of transcendent unity and equality — like the stone boat and the altars of named houses — the Great Row makes possible the productive differentiation and the hierarchical order that it encompasses.

The Great Row stands, at least conceptually, as the source and the foundation of the system of exchange pathways that unfolds from it (and is, reciprocally, enfolded into it). An understanding of this system, however, requires that one begins with its lower reaches and most extended portions, and with the manner in which the flow of life and blood through female lines marks the course along which the pathways of exchange are thought to emerge.

Transcending Differentiation

Although the flow of blood may delineate the course of life as it issues forth from a particular source, the ultimate source of life is Ubila'a. Cosmically, Ubila'a is the representation of the unity of all opposites in the world. For humans, Ubila'a transcends the differentiation between male and female and, as such, stands as the basis for their relationship — containing both male and female, both the unity of the source and the conditions for differentiation and growth. Ubila'a thus represents the potential for life itself as well as the certainty of death.

Hence, for humans in this world, the power of Ubila'a is exercised, in the first instance, at the moment of birth: ". . . it is said that God [i.e., Ubila'a] makes the child descend in the mother's womb" (Drabbe 1940:427). S/he is thus the force that initiates the separation of the child from its mother. Moreover, "it is also said that [s/]he has determined the life span from the beginning of the person's life. When the child is descending in the mother's womb, God lets the placenta know its life span, and before the child leaves the mother's womb, the placenta gives the message to the child that it therefore can never live longer than has been determined by God" (Drabbe 1940:427). In fact, the placenta (*bebun*) is held to have an intimate connection with the person's life. I was told that the placenta, itself, is the creation of Ubila'a, and that it gives breath and sustenance to the fetus while in its mother's womb. After birth the placenta is ceremoniously buried in the house, under the bed or in a place where it is certain not to come into contact with any hot substances that might endanger it. If hot water, for instance, were to be poured on the spot where a person's placenta was buried, he or she would surely sicken and die. The placenta is the place marker of both the temporal and spatial dimensions of a person's life: the origin and ultimate end of a person are contained simultaneously in this single entity.

In fixing a person's life span, Ubila'a not only determines the moment of birth, but also the moment of death: "if after treatment with medicines, after treatment by a spirit medium, the sick person nevertheless dies, one says: you have treated him, but God has decided that he should die now. In a word, it is said: God decides if we die, God decides if we live" (Drabbe 1940:427). I was given a similar interpretation of the role of Ubila'a, but in another context. Certain hunters are capable of seeing the souls (*ngraan*) of extremely sick persons that wander about in the forest when they are close to death. These hunters are under oath — on account of the "hot wood and roots" (*aa-wa'ar ngnea*), or magical substances, they have placed in their spear shafts — to shoot such a soul when they see it. If the shot is true, the person will die; if the shot misses its mark, the person will continue to live. It seemed to me a terrible burden to be placed upon the marksmanship of a hunter. When I asked hunters about it, however, they said that the shot will only be true if Ubila'a has decided that the person's moment of death has arrived. Ubila'a is the keeper of time; the hunter is the marksman of the moment.

Whereas Ubila'a stands at some remove from this world, the ancestors are far more closely associated with the particular fate of their descendants. The term most commonly used to refer to the ancestors means all "males and females of the second and third ascending and descending generations" (*ubu-nusi*) (cf. Barnes 1979). Thus, like Ubila'a, the ancestors form a category of beings for whom both gender and temporal differentiation is neutralized: they include both male and female members and contain their descendants as much as the latter contain them.

Like Ubila'a, the ancestors are also considered both the source of life and death. "To the dead [ancestors] as well as to God one says: multiply us — that is to say, make it that we bring forth children, etc. Thus one asks life itself from the dead as well as God" (Drabbe 1940:427). Although

Drabbe contends that, in contrast to Ubila'a, the ancestors do not fix the moment of death (1940:427), it is nevertheless clear that the ancestors do hold the power to curse their descendants. In fact, many deaths are attributed to the displeasure of the ancestors over the actions of their descendants.

The potency of Ubila'a and the ancestors is, fundamentally, ambivalent. They represent the source and the potential for life as much as death (Strathern 1988). Unifying both male and female, they prefigure a completed and closed entity that is nonproductive, an image of death. Yet as the source of the differentiation of male and female, they prefigure the productivity of relation and hence life itself.

The Flow of Blood

Although one's breath and the very possibility and duration of life originate in Ubila'a, one's vital life substance derives from one's ancestors — and, in particular, one's maternal ancestors. This vital life substance is blood, which Tanimbarese see as central to the conceptualization of the sources of life (and death) as well as the trajectories of growth.

Tanimbarese are not particularly prudish, yet they are extremely shy, embarrassed, and reluctant to talk about anything relating to sexual parts, fluids, or ideas about procreation. The only bodily substance that is freely — in fact, obsessively — talked about in this context is blood (*lara*).

Even though blood does appear to be traced through male as well as female links, people continually stress that the ultimate origin of all blood is the side of the mother. When I asked people where their blood came from, they would almost always say that it originated from their mother. When I pointed to those statements that seemed to contradict this dictum, they would say that they also received blood from their father, but that it was not particularly important. When I asked where their father got his blood, they would say their father's blood derived from his (the father's) mother.

In the midst of what is otherwise a striking vagueness on the subject of bodily substances, one thing stands out with marked clarity: blood is a vital substance that is intimately associated with life, and its flow defines both the universe of kin and the commonality that underlies the idea of relation (Wagner 1977).

Sources and Sprouts

If blood underlies the very identity and commonality of kin, then the directionality of its flow — the fact that there are those who are sources of blood and women, and others who are the receivers of blood and women—delineates an initial hierarchical differentiation between kin. The prior unity of brother and sister stands at the heart of all kinship relations. It is because of bridewealth exchanges that a brother comes to stay in the house of his father, and his sister comes to move, carrying the blood they share, into the house where she marries. Following from this, the house of the brother is considered "male" (brana), and the house into which the sister marries is considered "female" (vata).[1] The house of the brother is the "source" (matan) of a woman, blood, and the potential for life that have flowed to the house of the sister's husband. The sister's children will be the "sprouts" (matan/rubun) that have issued forth from their source in the lifeblood shared by their mother and her brother.

It is significant that the root mata[2] means both the "source" of new sprouts and the new "sprouts" that issue from a source. The reflexivity of the idea of source and sprout is evident throughout Tanimbarese ideas about growth, productivity, life, and death. But this is not to say that the source and the sprout are the same, or that they share the same identity. Rather, growth depends upon the acknowledgment of the hierarchical superiority of the source and its asymmetric and encompassing relation to that which issues forth from it. From an anchored source in the male aspect of a house, the extracted and externalized female aspect (women and female valuables) of the house continues to issue forth, to "multiply its sprouts a thousandfold" (rmela ruburira rivun). As both the result and condition of this multiplication, male valuables flow back to the source, the male who "sits and stays" and thereby anchors the house of origin. To recognize the hierarchical superiority of the source is to realize the potentiality for growth out from the source; at the same time, to realize the potentiality for growth is to recognize the hierarchical superiority of the source through the movement of valuables back to it.

This double, and asymmetric, movement out from and back to a source is evident in yet another metaphor for increase. A pregnant woman is often compared to a boat that makes a long-distance journey overseas and returns to land laden with valuables. In contrast to the gender relations that are centered on the stone boat at the center of the village, here it is the women who are the boats that must sail out from a safe anchorage and journey across the seas in order that they might return bearing their cargo of valuables. Thus women must leave the still anchorage of the

1. In other systems, where the focus is on the husband-wife pair rather than the brother-sister pair, the wife-givers are considered female and the wife-takers are considered male.
2. See Barnes (1977b) for an extended study of the word mata in Austronesian languages.

house of their brothers and journey to the house of their husbands before they may bear children, and before the full complement of male bride-wealth valuables can journey back to the source of life. The two movements mutually imply one another, for the success of the journey depends upon the stability of the source, as much as the stability of the source depends upon the success of the journey.

The movement of people and goods between wife-giver and wife-taker, source and issue, is not only conceived as one that moves out and back, but also one that moves down and up. Thus, a "woman goes down" (*vata nban nsuta*) from wife-giver to wife-taker, and "palmwine goes up" (*tuat nban nrata*) from wife-taker to wife-giver. Palmwine, here, stands for all the valuables that move between wife-takers and wife-givers. It is this movement up and down that gives a vertical dimension to the system of exchange pathways. It is for this reason that the Great Row can be conceptualized as standing at the top of the entire system of exchange pathways.

Continued Asymmetries

Once this asymmetric movement between source and issue has been established, it should be preserved over the generations. This is ensured not so much by an injunction to marry one's mother's brother's daughter (since a man may also marry "other women"), but rather by the injunction not to marry the father's sister's daughter (or any woman who is a "cross-sex sibling" or *uran*). More broadly, it is stated that a man should not marry any woman whose bridewealth he stands in a position to receive, or, as it is said, to "eat" (*na'an*).

The continuity of the asymmetric nature of the relationship is effected, on the one hand, by the continued asymmetric movement of women and lifeblood, and, on the other hand, by the reciprocal, or symmetric, exchange of valuables that are differentially marked as "male" and "female." Thus, once an affinal relationship has been established, a relation of exchange is instituted between wife-giver and wife-taker. Female valuables (including a kind of female earring, bead necklaces, shell armbands, textiles, and garden produce) follow the woman, moving from wife-giver to wife-taker. Male valuables (including a kind of male earring, gold breast pendants, elephant tusks, swords, pork, fish, and palmwine) move in the opposite direction, from wife-taker to wife-giver (see chapter 8).

As a continuation of this system of exchange, the mother's brother is obligated to provide a wife for his sister's son. He may do this either by giving one of his own (classificatory) "daughters" (*yanan vata*) in marriage to his sister's son, or by providing the bridewealth required by the sister's son's marriage to an "other woman" of a previously unallied house. In either case, the sister's son remains, in turn, obligated to pass the bridewealth valuables received for his sister on to his mother's brother.

Furthermore, the representatives of the male line of the brother retain rights to act as the life- and wife-giver not only to the sister's children, but to the members of the female line that has sprouted from the sister and thus constitutes a portion of the externalized female aspect of their house. This means that they are obligated to provide a wife for, or pay the bridewealth of, the men who stand along this female line. At the same time, they maintain the right to receive the bridewealth for the women who stand along this same female line (figure 6.1).

The valuables given between mother's brother and sister's son, therefore, have a further destiny along extended pathways of exchange. These pathways of exchange follow the female bloodlines that mark the affinal relations established between successive pairs of wife-giving and wife-taking houses. The male valuables — including the bridewealth of the sisters — are destined to travel from sister's son to mother's brother, and on to each successive wife-giving house that stands along the female line concerned. Traveling this pathway, the bridewealth of the sister traces the flow of lifeblood through women back to her "place" (*waan*) of origin. Similarly, the female valuables given from mother's brother to sister's son are destined to be passed on to each successive wife-taking house that stands along the female line concerned. Traveling in this way, these valuables make evident the fulfillment of the potential for life that is represented by the multiplication of the "sprouts" of the female line of the sister.

If matrilateral cross-cousin marriage were consistently practiced over the generations, the asymmetry of the system would be preserved by the movement of women and blood alone, and a man would belong to the same female line as his father, his father's father, and so on; they would share the same source of women and lifeblood. Yet, as in most asymmetric systems, marriage with the mother's brother's daughter is, in fact, not con-

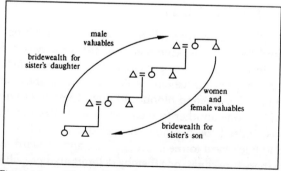

Figure 6.1   The structure of reciprocity along a female line

sistently practiced. Thus, where a man, his son, and his son's son have not practiced matrilateral cross-cousin marriage, then the female lines along which they trace the sources of their lifeblood will all be different. In Tanimbar, the relative rarity of matrilateral cross-cousin marriage is enforced by the injunction that two brothers may not marry two sisters. This institutes, as a matter of course, the differentiation of the female lines along which their children will trace the sources of their lifeblood.

Where matrilateral cross-cousin marriage is not practiced over successive generations, the asymmetry in the relation between the house of the brother and that into which the sister has married would be canceled, but for the reciprocity established in the exchange of valuables. Thus, in lieu of the continued asymmetric movement of women and lifeblood, the asymmetry of the affinal relation is perpetuated by the continuity of the symmetrical exchange of valuables. This symmetrical exchange of valuables will continue over the course of three generations, during which time the representatives of the house of the brother remain implicated in the bridewealth exchanges of descendants of the sister in the house into which she has married (see chapter 7). After three generations, the rights and obligations of wife-giver and wife-taker that have been engendered by the marriage of the sister are exhausted.

Beyond this point, the perpetuation of the asymmetric relation between wife-giver and wife-taker depends upon the fulfillment of one of two conditions: the renewal of the affinal relation through matrilateral cross-cousin marriage or the multiplication of the female line that emanates from the sister. In the latter case, the wife-giving and wife-taking relationship will continue to be acknowledged on account of the exchanges that center upon the new members of the female line of the sister. If neither of these conditions is fulfilled, however, the descendants of the sister in the male line will "fall" (*rleka*) to one side, and the hierarchical relation between the two lines will be canceled and could, potentially, be reversed.

The Affinal Triad

Because matrilateral cross-cousin marriage is not consistently practiced, and because the asymmetry of the system is preserved over three generations through the exchange of male and female valuables, every person recognizes three female lines that trace the sources and the sprouts of his or her life and blood (although these lines will, of course, be collapsed into one another to the extent that matrilateral cross-cousin marriage has, indeed, been practiced over the generations). Tracing the flow of blood backward to the sources of life and forward to the sprouts of life along these three lines, one thereby delimits all those who are thought to share blood and, thereby, share a common identity as kinsmen.

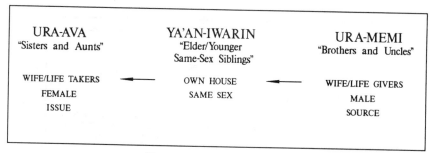

Figure 6.2   The affinal triad

However, the world of "our kinsmen" (*did tiniman*) — as opposed to "other people" (*tomat liak*) — is cut across by a triadic division that distinguishes the members of one's own group from those who have given women and are the sources of one's life and blood as well as from those who have taken women and are the sprouts of one's life and blood (figure 6.2). One's male wife-givers are collectively conceptualized as one's "brothers and uncles" (*ura-memi*) — or one's "masters" (*dua*) — and one's female wife-takers are collectively conceptualized as one's "sisters and aunts" (*ura-ava*).[3] The root *ura* actually means "cross-sex sibling." The translation of the term *ura-memi* as "brothers and uncles" therefore assumes a female or wife-taking perspective, whereas the translation of the term *ura-ava* as "sisters and aunts" assumes a male or wife-giving perspective.[4] Situated in between male wife-givers and female wife-takers are the members of one's own group, who are conceptualized as specifically neither male nor female: they are one's "elder-younger same-sex silbings" (*ya'an-iwarin*).

The various sets of brothers and uncles — or masters (*dua*) — that a person will recognize are reckoned by specifying the members of houses who are related to members of one's own house as wife-givers, the wife-givers of wife-givers, and so on — with regard to the women who belong to *specific* female lines (figure 6.3). The ego's ascending female line traces the pathway that links ego's *dua* on the "side of the woman [or mother]" (*lihir*

3. The term *memi* actually refers to the mother's brother as well as the father's sister's husband, just as the term *ava* refers to both the mother's brother's wife and the father's sister. Nevertheless, in this context, it is clear that *memi* is meant to refer to the maternal uncle only and *ava* to the paternal aunt only. What is being signified here is more a gender differentiation than any particular genealogical category. Note that the Mambai also refer to their wife-takers by the same term, "my sister/my paternal aunt" (*au tbo/au kaia*) (Traube 1986:85).

4. This assumption of a male or female perspective is evident when people sing ritual songs during bridewealth exchange negotiations. Male names are used in the songs to refer to the wife-givers; female names are used to refer to the wife-takers. Moreover, the wife-givers sing "male songs" (*tanlain brana*), and the wife-takers sing "female songs" (*tanlain vata*).

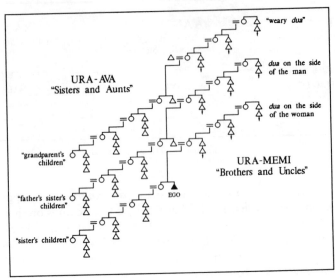

Figure 6.3   Ego's three female bloodlines

vata), just as his father's ascending female line marks the pathway that connects ego's *dua* on the "side of the man [or father]" (*lihir brana*).[5] Finally, his father's father's ascending female line traces the pathway that links his residual *dua*, or what I will call his "weary" *dua*.[6] These three ascending pathways are referred to as *ura-memi*.

The various sets of sisters and aunts that a person will recognize are determined in the inverse order: that is, by specifying members of houses who are related to members of one's own house as the wife-takers, the wife-takers of wife-takers, and so on—by reference to the women who belong to *specific* female lines (figure 6.3). Thus, ego's descending female line traces the pathway that links his "sister's children" (*uran yanan*), and his father's descending female line marks the pathway that connects ego's "father's sister's children" (*avan yanan*). Lastly, his father's father's descending female line traces the pathway that links ego's "grandparent's children" (*ubun yanan*)—i.e., his father's father's sister's children. These three descending pathways are referred to as *ura-ava*.

Facing both one's brothers and uncles, who are the source of women and lifeblood, and one's sisters and aunts, to whom women and lifeblood

5. The *dua* on the side of the woman and on the side of the man are also contrasted as "earth" (*lanuun*) and "rain" (*da'ut*).

6. I use this term—because of the lack of any specific Tanimbarese term for this category—since it is these *dua* who will be paying and receiving the bridewealth prestation called "weariness" (see chapter 7).

have been given, are one's "true elder-younger same-sex siblings" (*ya'an-iwarin lalean*). A person's true elder-younger same-sex siblings are differentiated by reference to the three female bloodlines they recognize, and thus by their relation to specific sets of wife-givers and wife-takers.[7] As a set, they are therefore delimited by the three-generation limit in the tracing of female bloodlines.[8] The first two generations are, again, marked as the side of the woman (or mother) and the side of the man (or father). Hence true elder-younger same-sex siblings on the side of the mother are distinguished by the fact that they have a common wife-giver in their mother's brother, their mother's mother's brother, or their mother's mother's mother's brother. Together, they belong to the same female line (or branches of it) and share a source of lifeblood. They constitute what I shall call uterine brothers and uterine sisters. Uterine brothers, moreover, hold common rights over the sister's children pathways that form the continuation of the female bloodline to which they belong.

True elder-younger same-sex siblings on the side of the father are differentiated from those on the side of the mother by the fact that the wife-givers they share are their father's mother's brother or their father's father's mother's brother. They comprise what I shall refer to as agnatic brothers and agnatic sisters. A person traces *through* male links *to* the female bloodlines — the sources of life — which he shares with his agnates.[9] Furthermore, agnatic brothers share rights over the father's sister's children and the father's father's sister's children that form the continuation of the female bloodlines to which their father and their father's father belong.

The continuity of the relation between uterine sisters is, in theory, indefinitely extensible. For, as blood flows through women, it will always be possible to trace along the female line to their common source of life-

---

7. This is the broad interpretation of the category. True elder-younger same-sex siblings can also be interpreted more narrowly to include only those who have been born of the same mother and father. This is expressed by saying that "they sail with the wind [using] one rope" (*raskolal ua isa'a*) or, more coarsely, that "they come from the inside of one sarong" (*rtali bakan ralan isa'a*). All other, more distant siblings would be then qualified as "attached elder-younger same-sex siblings" (*ya'an-iwarin fareling*). The same holds true for cross-sex siblings (*uran*).

8. In general, a person will remember his father's father and his mother's mother by name (although even here memory sometimes begins to fade). A person may well even remember his father's father's father and his mother's mother's mother, but beyond this point genealogical memory will generally fail in terms of any recognized sequence. Beyond this, there will be ancestors who may be remembered by name, and by the feats they performed, but these ancestors float in the remote past of mythic events and rarely is it remembered whom they married or who their ascendants or descendants may have been.

9. Cf. Barnes's comment concerning the Kédang: "Agnatic ties are based on shared blood originally acquired from another group. Part of the implication of alliance is this transfer of blood, associated with the gift of life and that of physical and spiritual well-being" (1980a:79; see also 1974:248).

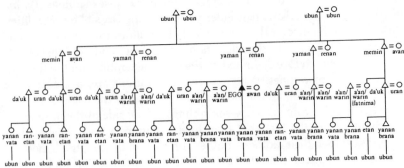

Figure 6.4   Kinship terminology (reference), male perspective

blood. With agnatic brothers, on the contrary, the matter is quite different. Their identity is based on shared sources of lifeblood — the female blood-lines they recognize in common. Because of the nature of the system of marriage exchanges, however, these female lines are acknowledged over the course of three generations only. After three generations, the continuity of the male line can be broken by the female lines that cut across it and distinguish sets of "brothers" who are defined by their differential relation to various female lines.

The asymmetry of the marriage system is revealed by a more general understanding of those persons and groups that belong to these three categories of relatives. The most general rule is that those men of the same generation who belong to groups that are both wife-takers of one and the same wife-giving group are considered elder-younger same-sex siblings, as are those men who belong to groups that are both wife-givers to one and the same wife-taking group. On the other hand, both the wife-givers of one's wife-givers and the wife-takers of one's wife-takers fall into the same category, respectively, as one's own wife-givers and wife-takers.

It is significant for an understanding of the logic of same- and opposite-sex relations that among those in the "same-sex" category — that is, those called "elder-younger same-sex siblings" — are not only one's same-sex siblings, but their spouses as well. Moreover, the classificatory mother's brother's daughter and father's sister's son are both referred to by the special term *fatnima* as well as by the more general term "elder-younger same-sex sibling" (figures 6.4 and 6.5).

Where women are defined as strangers to their natal house, and where the opposition between male wife-givers and female wife-takers defines those same generation members of one's own group as same-sex, it is logical that women of the same generation who may marry or who actually have married into a man's own group should be classified with it as same-

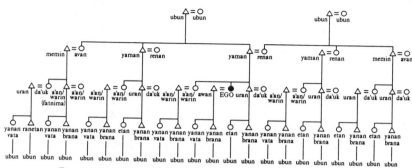

Figure 6.5   Kinship terminology (reference), female perspective

sex siblings. Whereas a man's matrilateral cross-cousin belongs categorically to his own same-sex sibling group because she should marry into it, his cross-sex siblings (*uran*) belong categorically to another group: either that of his female wife-takers or that of his male wife-givers. Similarly, from a woman's perspective, the men of the same generation who belong to groups into which she and her sisters may marry or actually have married are classified as her same-sex siblings. She belongs categorically to this group of same-sex siblings who are the wife-takers of her natal group. By the same token, her cross-sex siblings are men of the same generation who belong to groups which are the wife-takers and the wife-givers of the one into which she has married.

Pathways of Sisters and Rows of Houses

When an affinal relation continues on beyond three generations, a crucial shift in hierarchical levels is marked by characterizing the relations before and after this point in radically different ways. During the three-generational period, affinal relations with one's sisters and aunts are considered to be provisional and impermanent. They are, moreover, traced by female bloodlines that delineate the marriage pathways of specific persons. If relations continue beyond three generations, however, they are thought of as fixed and permanent, and are traced by female bloodlines that connect not specific people, but rather specific houses that now stand along what are thought of as rows that delineate the lines of enduring alliances (figure 6.6).

If one begins by reckoning from the marriage of a man's sister with someone from a previously unrelated house, it is clear that over his lifetime, the sister's children (*uran yanan*) pathway that emanates from his sister will extend down through two or, at most, three generations and will link only two or three houses along a pathway of affinal exchange.

Should his sister, his sister's daughter, or his sister's daughter's daughter have no daughters, then this pathway will soon terminate altogether: it will dissolve unless the affinal relationships provisionally established between the houses along this pathway are renewed through matrilateral cross-cousin marriage.

In fact, sister's children pathways are considered impermanent and highly ephemeral. Although a man will care for his sister's children, in the hopes that the female line that issues from his sister will "multiply its sprouts a thousandfold" (*rmela ruburira rivun*), still there is no guarantee that these pathways will not, on the contrary, dissolve, and the wife-taking groups "fall" (*rleka*) to one side. If, however, a man's sister's children pathways do not dissolve after two or three generations, they will still be in existence during the lifetime of his son and his son's son. They

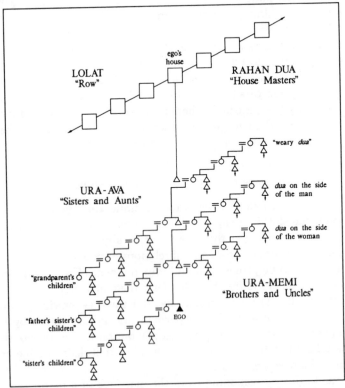

Figure 6.6   The relation between sisters and aunts pathways and rows

will become the father's sister's children (*avan yanan*) pathways of his son, and the grandparent's children (*ubun yanan*) pathways of his son's son.

Blood, particular persons, and bodies are the motivating terms here. These pathways are formed by the descending bloodlines of specific women: one's *uran yanan* are, literally, the children of one's sisters; one's *avan yanan* are the children of one's father's sisters; and one's *ubun yanan* are the children of one's grandparents (or, that is, one's father's father's sisters). As the source of women and blood, a man will, therefore, be considered the "master of the body" (*tenan dua*) of those who belong to the descending bloodlines of the outmarried women of his house.

A man will share at least one female bloodline with those persons who stand among his sisters and aunts. However, unless matrilateral cross-cousin marriage has been practiced over the generations, after three generations the descendants in the male line of the brother will no longer share a female bloodline with the descendants of the sister in either the male or the female line. The descendants of the brother will nevertheless remain the wife-giver and master of the descendants of the sister — even though they no longer share a female bloodline — because they continue to stand as the source of life for the members of the female line that issued from their own house.

Yet those pathways that follow the female line descending from a woman of the house given out in marriage three or more generations previously will no longer be conceived in terms of the bloodlines of specific women. It will be presumed that these pathways are based on female bloodlines and upon the marriages of the women who stood along these bloodlines, but the specific women will have been long forgotten. Unlike sisters and aunts pathways, where it is possible to trace (and indeed people do trace) the relationships involved in terms of the female bloodlines of specific women, such a pathway is thought of as a row of houses that stand in a relation of enduring alliance one with another.[10] Toward such established wife-takers, a man will no longer be considered a "master of the body" (*tenan dua*), but rather a "master of the house" (*rahan dua*).

10. There is a difference of opinion as to when a pathway begins to be considered a row. On the whole, those people who belong to unnamed houses tend to say that a sisters and aunts pathway becomes a row after the passage of three generations. Such a claim fits with the logic of the system and is also, of course, to the advantage of those occupying unnamed houses, since having a row is part of the definition of a named house. People of named houses, on the other hand, claim that many more generations must pass for a sisters and aunts pathway to become a row. Although this claim contradicts the logic of the system, it nevertheless is put forth in an effort to protect the exclusivity of the domain of named houses and their rows. In the end, the point is that it takes some time for a pathway to come to be recognized as a row by all concerned.

Beyond its reference to such a row of allied houses, the term *lolat* refers only to the rows in which corn is planted. In a large plot devoted solely to corn, these rows will stand one next to another. When planted in yam gardens, however, the rows of corn meander through the plot and, especially, run along the border of the plot. The term signifies a row of discrete objects ranged one after another: together they form a line that is differentiated from that which surrounds it and, like the border of a yam plot, they differentiate one space from another.

With reference to alliance, *lolat* refers to a row of wife-taking houses that stand, ranged one after another, along the female line that descends from a woman of the house given out in marriage three or more generations previously. The sprouts of the sister's children pathway have, indeed, greatly multiplied and yielded a row of mature plants.

Lolat are generally conceptualized from the point of view of the superior, wife-giving house. *Lolat* are, like sisters and aunts, the portions of female lines that descend from women of the house; they do not refer to the portions of the female lines that ascend from the house. These latter are called one's masters or, more specifically, the masters of the house.

The entire row may be referred to as the *lolat* of a specific house — the house to which all male valuables traveling the pathway must ultimately flow. Generally, such rows consist of anywhere from six to twelve houses, but one row may feed into another, thereby forming longer pathways that link up to twenty houses. The whole forms a segmentary hierarchy of alliance pathways, in which the initial wife-giving house that stands at each branching node encompasses the houses ranged along the pathways that extend below it.

Unlike sisters and aunts pathways, rows are named. Those that have only recently been sisters and aunts pathways may still bear the name of the woman whose descendants they are: for example, Voru's Grandchildren's Children (Voru Ubun Yanan) or Bo'i's Grandchildren's Children (Bo'i Ubun Yanan). Rows that have been in existence longer may bear distinctive names that no longer evoke the memory of the specific women from whom they originated. Some names have reference to the house-complex, hamlet, village, or island in which the majority of the linked houses are located: Lolat Awear is a row centered in the village of Awear; Lolat Weriditi is a row controlled by the house Urena-Kelianan of the house-complex Weriditi; West Lamdesar (Varat Lamdesar) is a row that runs between the villages of Awear and Lamdesar; and the Contents of the Earth of Sera (Lanuun Sera Ralan) is a row that has its origin on the island of Sera. Others may bear names that refer to the length, inclusiveness, or productivity of a given row: Long Beach (Nguur Blawat); the

Street (Straat); the Value of the Palm Frond Fish Corral (Eat e Fiawan),[11] the Contents of the Common Treasure Stock (Metan Kubania Ralan). Still others may refer to some action performed by an ancestor on behalf of his *lolat*: La'i's Death Motive (La'i ni Matmatan Enan).

Rows are further distinguished according to their size and the length of time they have been in existence. "Small rows" (*lolat ko'u*) — but one step removed from grandparent's children pathways — are still fairly short and comparatively recent in origin. Longer rows that have been in existence seemingly from time immemorial are called "big rows" (*lolat dawan*).

Whereas sisters and aunts pathways are always conceived of in terms of the female bloodlines emanating from specific women, rows are identified strictly in terms of the named houses through which they pass. Thus, every named house possesses, and is a part of, at least one big row of wife-taking houses. At the same time, every named house has at least one "big master" (*dua dawan*) or "house master" (*rahan dua*), along whose row it occupies the first place.

One's *rahan dua* is a house from which a founding (or distant) ancestor of one's own house is thought to have received his wife (even if, as is often the case, one cannot remember the name of this ancestor, or that of his wife). The relation between the two houses is thus one of a founding alliance. Just as rows are differentiated from sisters and aunts pathways by a distinction between houses and blood, so too "house masters" are differentiated from "masters of the body".[12] Although the master of a man's body will share at least one source of lifeblood (one female line) with his sisters and aunts, the members of a named house and those belonging to houses along its rows will not necessarily share any source of lifeblood. The latter relationship is one of a permanent alliance between named houses, and it is maintained regardless of the particular relation between those who happen to occupy them. The continuity of the alliance is respected, even where it has not been renewed by marriage, because the allied houses will continue to be implicated in the exchange of valuables that move along the rows as a result of other marriages: that is, because their houses continue to be regarded as the source of the life of others.

---

11. One's *lolat* (and one's wife-takers in general) are equated with fish, since fish are among those male valuables that move from wife-takers to wife-givers.

12. Concerning the different kinds of *dua*, Drabbe does not mention the "house master" (*rahan dua*), but only the "big master" (*dua dawan*). On the other hand, he also notes that the "master of the body" may be referred to as the "little master" (*dua ko'u*) or as the "master of a sleeping platform" (*dua alamin etal*) — that is, the master of a specific couple, or a specific portion of the house, as opposed to the entire house (1940:154).

Whereas sisters and aunts form pathways whose fecundity and permanence has yet to be demonstrated, the fertility of rows is evident in the multiplication and growth of the female lines, whose very continuity speaks of the enduring nature of the alliances from which they have sprung. The provisional, impermanent character of a sisters and aunts pathway lies in the fact that one can never be certain whether the female line will be extended through daughters and thereby continue on, or whether it will be cut short in sons and "fall" away. On the contrary, the enduring character of a row has been established by the continuity of the female line such that—as I was often told—the world would have to be destroyed before one's rows disappeared.

The distinction between impermanence and permanence, discontinuity and continuity, corresponds to that also drawn between those relations newly established by marriages, which are conceived in terms of the flow of blood, and those relations long established as alliances between named houses, which are realized primarily in the continued flow of valuables. Sisters and aunts are short pathways that are traced through recent marriages and along known blood links. By contrast, rows are extended— often quite lengthy—pathways that follow a progression of alliances traced between named houses. These alliances were formed by the marriages of women long forgotten and by a flow of blood that is remembered only because it continues and, in continuing on, leaves behind a kind of exposed geological record of the strata through which it has cut—the houses through which it has passed. Rows thus become fixed series of houses ranged in order as they stand to one another as the givers and takers of women and life.

The Great Row

In contrast to both the sisters and aunts pathways and the open, extended rows of allied houses, people on Sera, Larat, and Fordata mark a third hierarchical level by distinguishing what is called the Lolat Ila'a, or Great Row—a double, interlocking cycle of affinal alliance that stands at the very pinnacle of the entire system. The Lolat Ila'a consists of the "four source houses of Fordata" (*rahan matan ifa'at Fordata*) and the "four source houses of Sera" (*rahan matan ifa'at Sera*), some eighty miles to the southwest of Fordata (figure 6.7).

Moving from wife-taking to wife-giving house,[13] the cycle proceeds in this way: on the island of Fordata, Melatunan "goes to" (*ntii*) Ditilebit, Ditilebit goes to Koli, Koli to Refvutu, Refvutu to Melatunan, Melatunan

---

13. People always say that the house of the wife-taker "goes to" (*ntii*) the house of the wife-giver. In both text and diagrams, I will follow Tanimbarese usage.

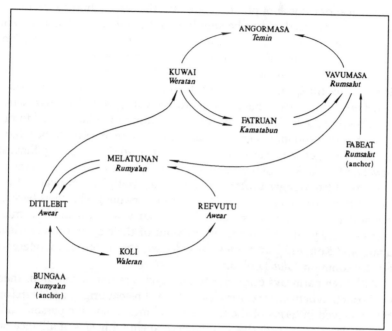

Figure 6.7   The Lolat Ila'a Sera-Fordata

back to Ditilebit. Ditilebit then goes to Kuwai on the island of Sera, where Kuwai goes to Fatruan, Fatruan to Vavumasa, Vavumasa to Angormasa, Angormasa back to Kuwai, Kuwai back to Fatruan, Fatruan back to Vavumasa; Vavumasa then returns to Melatunan on the island of Fordata.[14] In addition, the two houses that are wife-takers to houses on the other cycle — Ditilebit and Vavumasa — each have a house that is its "anchor" (*a'ur*). Each anchor is a wife-taking house that stands at the head of an exceptionally large network of rows that are mobilized when an inter-island alliance along the Lolat Ila'a is negotiated.

Such a closed cycle of alliance as the Great Row is called a *lolat sive-lik* — a row that alternates, or turns back on itself. In this context, the idea conveyed by the word *sivelik* is one of the equality and interchangeability of elements. It is like the wind that blows during the transition period between the east and west wind seasons. At this time, the "winds blow inter-changeably or alternately" (*nait nforuk sivelik*) from all directions with

14. Renes (1977:225–30) notes a similar cycle of asymmetric alliance that links noble clans of the three islands, Letti, Moa, and Kisar, in the southwestern Moluccas. Clamagirand (1980:147) also speaks of interlocking cycles of asymmetric alliance that operate between the chiefly core houses of the Ema in Timor.

equal force: one does not predominate over the others. In the Great Row, each house is considered to be simultaneously *dua* and *lolat*, male and female, to every other house. "One is not more than the other," or, "one does not excel the other" (*isaa wol nrahi isaa*): all are considered to be of equal rank. The stress on the equality of all members of the cycle thus differentiates the Lolat Ila'a from all the other rows and pathways, which are defined by the relative hierarchical order of wife-givers and wife-takers.[15]

Following the logic of the system, in addition to being related to one another as *dua* and *lolat*, certain houses conceive themselves to be related as "elder-younger same-sex siblings" (*ya'an-iwarin*). I was told by Sinyasu Kuwai and Mo'u Angormasa in Sera that the houses Ditilebit and Angormasa are elder-younger brothers because they both have Kuwai as their *dua* and that Angormasa and Melatunan are elder-younger brothers because they both have Vavumasa as their *lolat*. Similarly, Refvutu and Vavumasa must be elder-younger brothers on account of their common *dua* Melatunan, and Koli and Kuwai must be elder-younger brothers by reference to their common *lolat* Ditilebit.

Although pathways of exchange that cycle are not uncommon, there is a distinction between those cycles that are of recent origin, and therefore still conceived in terms of the female bloodlines of specific persons, and those cycles that are conceived as the permanent pathways of alliance between named houses. Aside from the Lolat Ila'a, only a few other cycles are formally recognized as rows. These are the ones that are called *inetal*, "that which cuts through or by-passes." Each of the eight houses that participates in the Lolat Ila'a has its *inetal*. This pathway consists of a number of named houses (five to seven or so) that are linked in a closed cycle of exchange. The express purpose of an *inetal* cycle is to make valuables more readily available to the eight Lolat Ila'a houses, which, because of

15. Drabbe makes no mention of the Lolat Ila'a, but does give one example of what he calls a *lolat sivelik*, which he was told ran from Fordata to Sera and then up along the east coast of Yamdena, to Larat, and then back to Fordata (1940:151). Although this cycle was not recognized by most people I spoke with on Yamdena, people on Sera and Fordata thought that such a cycle had once existed and referred to it as the Great Eastern Row (Lolat Ila'a Timur). This they contrasted to the Great Western Row (Lolat Ila'a Varat), which is otherwise known as the Lolat Ila'a Sera-Fordata and is the one I have here called, simply, the Great Row. Unlike the latter, which unites only two islands in a cycle of alliance, the eastern row supposedly united all four central islands of the Tanimbar archipelago (excluding the islands of Selaru to the far south and Molu and Maru to the far north) in an extended cycle of alliance. Whether this eastern cycle possessed the formal properties of the Lolat Ila'a Sera-Fordata (i.e., two opposing cycles of four houses, each with a fifth house as its "anchor"), it is impossible to determine at this point. The breakdown of the Great Eastern Row, if it ever indeed existed, suggests that the system of alliance and exchange in Tanimbar is always in flux, despite the representation of fixity and permanence that is assumed in the ideology of the rows.

their position at the top of the system, are constantly implicated in the exchanges of their subordinates. If, for instance, the house Ditilebit has been called upon to pay the bridewealth of one of its *lolat* and does not, at that moment, possess an appropriate valuable, one of its representatives may request a valuable from one of the houses along its *inetal* pathway (or, via the Lolat Ila'a, from one of the houses along another *inetal* pathway), and thereby obtain the requisite means for paying the bridewealth requested. Although these *inetal* are recognized as fixed cycles, they are nevertheless subordinate to, and in the service of, the Lolat Ila'a.

The Lolat Ila'a, as a pathway of alliance between equals, stands at the zenith of a vast hierarchy of rows that feed into the eight houses of this closed cycle. In addition to their *inetal*, each of the eight houses possesses at least one main row, along which there are named houses that act as the "ones who meet" (*situan*) other rows that branch off from it. It should be evident that the overall structure of exchange pathways is such that— moving from top to bottom—from the Great Row (the Lolat Ila'a) there extend *inetal* pathways and a number of named, big rows (*lolat dawan*), which branch off into the less permanent small rows (*lolat ko'u*), which in turn branch off into the highly provisional sisters and aunts (*ura-ava*) pathways (see figure 6.8 for a mapping of the rows that feed into the Lolat Ila'a Fordata).

Hierarchy Times Three

Although the system is founded upon the relative superiority of wife-giver over wife-taker, source over issue, nevertheless the relativity of the hierarchical relation between wife-giver and wife-taker is superceded by the delineation of three fixed hierarchical levels. It is the double cycle of the Lolat Ila'a that marks the apex and top level of the system: here the differentiation between male and female, wife-giver and wife-taker, superior and inferior, source and issue are recomposed into a transcendent image of unity. Standing at the top of the system, the Lolat Ila'a encompasses the extended rows of allied houses that stretch out below it. The middle level of the hierarchy is composed of these rows. Here the relation between male and female, wife-giver and wife-taker, superior and inferior is fixed and irreversible, thus marking a permanency and productivity of the asymmetric flow of life from source to issue. The rows of allied houses, in turn, encompass the sisters and aunts pathways that branch out from them and form the lowest level of the system. Along these pathways the relation between male and female, wife-giver and wife-taker, superior and inferior is but a tenuous projection into the future, the permanency and productivity of which are yet to be determined.

That all exchange pathways trace back to the Lolat Ila'a is another way

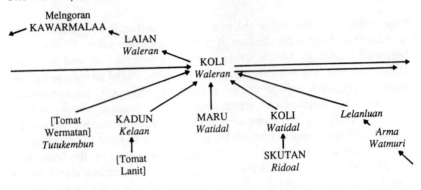

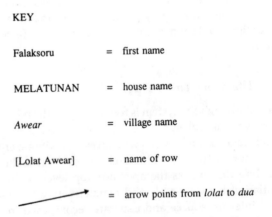

KEY

Falaksoru   =   first name

MELATUNAN   =   house name

Awear   =   village name

[Lolat Awear]   =   name of row

                        =   arrow points from *lolat* to *dua*

Figure 6.8   Rows converging upon the Fordatan portion of the Great Row

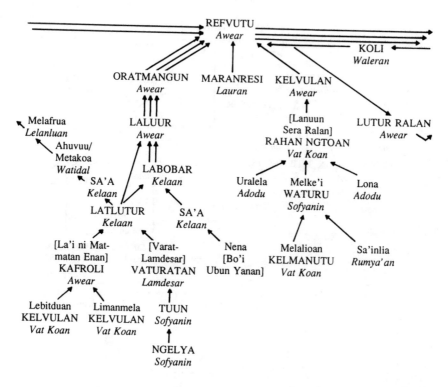

continued on following page

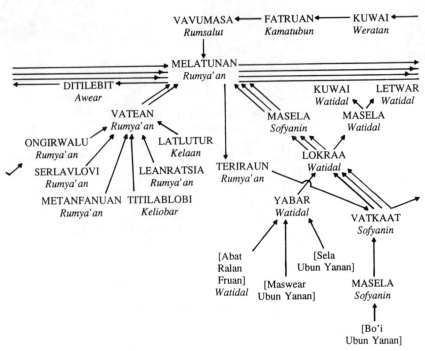

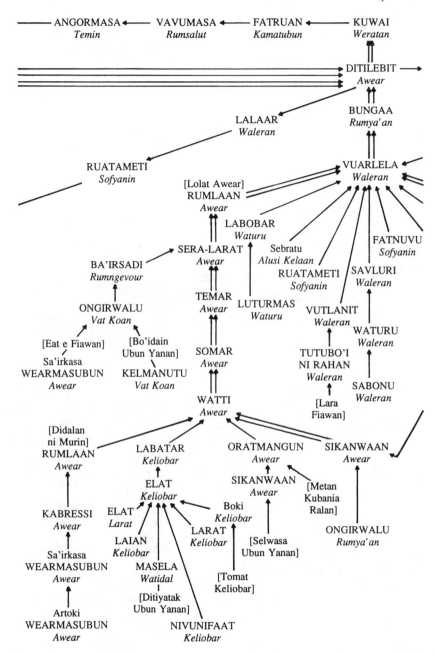

continued on following page

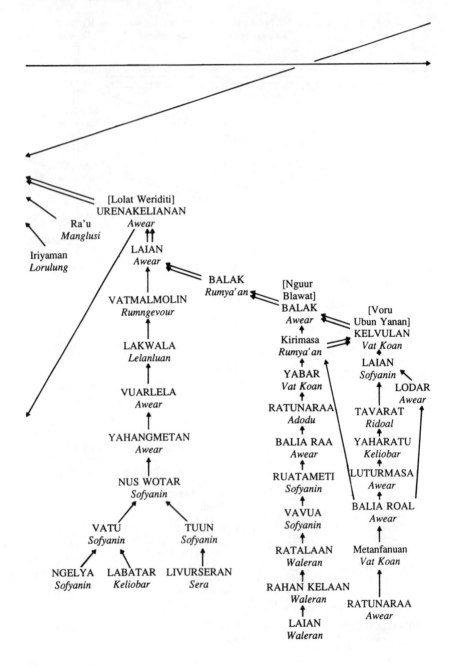

of saying that the Lolat Ila'a is conceptually the ultimate source of all women, blood, and life. I was told by Tutune'i Lokraa—a man who occupies a house belonging to Ditilebit's *inetal* pathway—that another name for the Lolat Ila'a is Soru Matan Iwalu, which might be translated as the Eight Sources (or Points of Origin) That Encompass All. He suggested that the use of *soru* in this context meant that the eight houses encompassed all other houses and comprehended all customary law (*adat*) in Tanimbar.

The Lolat Ila'a thus most closely approximates what, in superhuman terms, is only represented by Ubila'a—the unity of male and female and, indeed, of all opposites. As an image of transcendent unity, the Lolat Ila'a serves as the point of reference and anchor for the entire hierarchical system of rows and sisters and aunts pathways that emanates from it.

Moreover, just as the androgyny of Ubila'a contains the conditions for productive differentiation in the world, so the Lolat Ila'a contains the conditions for productive differentiation of male and female—the growth and expansion of the female bloodlines, the female estates, that belong to male houses. In this way, because the term *matan* means "source" and "point of origin" as well as "sprout" and "issue," the title the Eight Sources That Encompass All could read, in anticipation of their issue, the Eight Sprouts That Are Encompassed. To trace back to origins—ultimately to the Lolat Ila'a—is simultaneously to anticipate that which issues forth (Strathern 1988). The Lolat Ila'a contains the full potentiality of the entire system (see chapter 10).

The mutual implication of source and sprout expresses the explicit asymmetry of growth. The fixity of the double cycle as source makes possible what everywhere else is realized by a restless flow: blood flows forever outward in a pattern of organic growth that is always expanding—"multiplying its sprouts a thousandfold"—and relating still more people and houses in the unfolding of life.

The hierarchical order is created out of the tension between this asymmetric extension—the differentiation of the unity of the Lolat Ila'a—and what might be called an asymmetric recoiling or enclosing—the recomposition of the unity of the Lolat Ila'a. Thus, the Lolat Ila'a is the fixed point in the system, the point from which asymmetric pathways unfold and, in the process, define the lines of hierarchy. In order to constitute itself as a fixed point, however, the Lolat Ila'a must fold asymmetry back on itself to form a cycle that, in the process, demarcates the lines of equality (see chapter 10). The hierarchical order can only be understood in terms of this double process of unfolding asymmetric pathways relative to a fixed source and enclosing a fixed source relative to the asymmetric extension of open pathways. Being unable to capture the dynamics of both processes at the same time, we turn first to those that motivate the unfolding of asymmetric pathways.

7 The Initiation of Affinal Relations

Ngerorod [marriage by capture] represents 'complex' marriages by
individual preference which are not defined by marriage class or
classificatory genealogical position. This complex field sets Bali's
other marriage types into figured relief. Individual unions are
implicitly advocated in rituals of capture; they are not merely the
neutral absence of a more distinct type of marriage. (Boon 1977:122)

Neither the movement of women between houses nor the
continuity of men within houses is given in the nature of things. Both must
be achieved—endlessly negotiated and repeatedly established through the
exchange of valuables. Exchange has force because it effects the movement
of women between houses and the continuity of men within houses in a
system that is defined by multiple forms of marriage, affiliation, and
residence that are differentially valued.

The existence of different forms of marriage is precipitated by the refusal to allow two brothers to marry two sisters. As a consequence of this,
there is a range of women a man might marry. These include: the "women
of one's master" (*vat dua*), who belong to established wife-giving houses;
"elder-younger same-sex siblings" (*ya'an-iwarin*), who include both a man's
matrilateral cross-cousins (*fatnima*) and his brothers' wives and wife's sisters
(if they have been widowed); and "other women" (*vat liak*). In a similar
fashion, there is a range of ways in which a person might be affiliated
to a house: one can be affiliated patrilaterally, matrilaterally, or step-
patrilaterally, and one can also be adopted or adrogated into a house.

It is with the understanding that permanence and fixity of relation are
indices of high rank, that value is given to the different types of marriage
and the different forms of affiliation and residence that will be the subject
of this and the following chapters. In order to achieve this fixity of relation, two conditions must be fulfilled. One must secure the intergenerational continuity of the male aspect of a house so that it may remain the
source of life for others; and one must secure the separation of the female
aspect of the house so that the village estates of the house may grow and
expand. To the extent that these two conditions are fulfilled, the per-

manency of both the house and its affinal relations with other houses will be assured.

We begin, here, with the most impermanent of affinal relations — those newly formed unions that are initiated through a marriage with an "other woman" and that effect the unfolding of an asymmetric pathway from a source. In exploring the form of bridewealth prestations that accompany such marriages, it will be seen how these work to negotiate — through differential forms of residence and affiliation — both the separation of the female aspect of a house and the continuity of the male aspect of a house.

These two conditions are realized within a structure of exchange that is thoroughly asymmetric in form. It is no particular puzzle that in such a system most men marry not their mother's brother's daughter, but rather other women. The puzzle lies, rather, in the fact that all marriages, even those that initiate new affinal relations, presuppose and support an asymmetric system of affinal relations that endures over a greater or lesser period of time. By attending to the dynamics of bridewealth exchange, we will begin to understand the manner in which the most impermanent and tenuous of all affinal relations are established and supported by the permanent asymmetric and hierarchical relations that are so peculiar to the social organization of these islands.

Lovers and Provisional Spouses

There is a constant tension between the desire of elders to arrange politically advantageous alliances through the marriages of their children and the desire of their children to shun such arrangements, follow their own heart — or, rather, "liver" (Indonesian: *hati*) or "insides" (*ralan*) — and marry a person to whom they are genuinely attracted. Indeed, as much as older men and women sit about calculating the politics of marriage, younger men and women go about pursuing those they have come to fancy. I once sat with four or five older women who told — with great delight and still sparkling eyes — of the men their parents had arranged for them to marry, and of the men they had been infatuated with, had run off with and, in the end, had actually married. Some had endured severe beatings and had run off time and time again, but they had eventually won out over the will of their parents. Years later, and despite the fact that some of the women's children may have fallen in rank as a consequence, they did not seem to regret their choices.

It is not at all uncommon for young men and women to engage in several provisional unions before they actually settle down and marry. Nor is it uncommon for them to engage in such affairs even after they have married. Such liaisons, which are initiated in a fashion called "they steal and race away" (*rbori rafraa*), may become known in several ways. In the middle of the night, either the man or the woman may "climb up into the house" (*nva'al rahan*) of his or her lover, in which case, by sharing a sleeping place together, they will signal their intention to establish at least a provisional union. Or, it may happen — especially if the young couple expects some resistance from their parents — that "they flee to the forest" (*raflaa nangan*) in order to make their intentions known. Sometimes, however, an affair is kept a secret until the woman shows the obvious signs of pregnancy and is then forced to name the man who is responsible for her condition.

Once discovered, the man and woman are considered one another's "lover" or "provisional spouse" (*ni dodu*). At this point, everyone will agree either that they should marry (*rsifaa*), in which case the preliminary marriage exchanges will be negotiated, or that they should separate and that the man should "throw the woman off" (*nvatuk vata*), in which case the *dua* of the man must redeem him by paying a separation fine. This fine must also be paid in cases where a man rapes or otherwise molests (*nsitaha*) a woman.

The decision as to whether the couple will marry or separate will usually be made immediately. But the question can remain unsettled for a much longer time, especially if the woman insists upon a match that her parents adamantly oppose. Under such circumstances, for as many times as the woman may run off with her lover, her brothers may bring her back and attempt to beat her into submission. Eventually, one side or the other will tire of the routine.

If it has been decided that the man will throw the woman off, the fine must be paid in full immediately, or, at the latest, within a week or two. The fine, called "the voice of the official" (*tuan vain*),[1] consists of the full equivalent of the four portions of the bridewealth. Each of the four parts is paid and is received, or "eaten," by the same *dua* who would do so in the ordinary bridewealth payments (as discussed below).

From Anger to the Voice of Accord

Marriage with an "other woman" (*vat liak*) may be initiated in two ways. In the first — "they steal and race away" (*rbori rafraa*) — the young couple takes matters into their own hands and makes their desires known in one or another rather explicit fashion. In the second — "they ask

---

1. Because *tuan* is a term usually reserved for Dutch colonial officials (and other foreigners), the name of this fine points to the possibility that it was, indeed, the "voice of a [Dutch] official" that insisted such payments be made. However, I have no evidence for this.

the elders" (*rorat dawan*)[2] – the match is formally arranged beforehand by the parents of the young couple.[3] In either case, the intention that this should be a marriage rather than simply a provisional affair is marked by a series of preliminary exchanges.

There is a certain violence – at least conceptually if not also in actuality – associated with the initiation of a new affinal relationship. It is only with great effort that a woman and the life-giving force she bears are extracted from her natal house and diverted from her marriage destiny along established affinal pathways. The violence of such efforts as well as the resistance to them are evident not only in the preliminary exchanges but also in the main bridewealth prestations that are the hallmark of newly established affinal relations.

Should a man "climb up into the house" of a woman, as is most often the case, her parents and brothers may "sit and block him" (*rdok teri ia*) from leaving until his parents, their elder-younger same-sex siblings, and his *dua* arrive upon the scene to "redeem him" (*rtevut ia*). Whether they actually hold the young man physically hostage matters little: his essential bondage to the woman's family and their *dua* is established the moment his attachment to the woman is confirmed. Indebted for the woman and the potential for life she bears, he is their subordinate until the bridewealth payments are completed. A man's wife-givers are his masters (*dua*), and he is perilously close to being nothing more than a slave (*iria*). In fact, formerly, if neither the separation fine nor the proper bridewealth prestations were made, the wife-givers and their *dua* were entitled to seize him (or one of his brothers or sisters) and sell him into slavery. It is from this fate, and that of continued incorporation within the house of the woman, that a man's own parents and *dua* will, over the course of his lifetime, make great efforts to "redeem him" – along with his wife and children.

In the preliminary exchanges that occur when a man climbs up into the house of a woman, his parents and their elder-younger same-sex siblings will be posed against the woman's parents and their elder-younger same-sex siblings. Each side will be further supported by its *dua*. They will begin by negotiating a series of prestations that will establish the status of the union as a recognized marriage.

Expressing their outrage over the violation of their daughter, the woman's "fathers" (her own father and his elder-younger same-sex siblings)

2. *Dawan* means, literally, "big" or "great." It can be used to refer to adults, elders, and nobles. Here it refers to the parents and *dua* of the girl.

3. Neither form is linked exclusively to marriage with an other woman. Marriage between matrilateral cross-cousins (*fatnima*) may also be initiated in either of these two ways. Marriage with a "woman of one's master" (*vat dua*), however, would only be initiated by a formal request.

will first demand a prestation called "anger" (*ngrova*). This will consist of a pair of male earrings (*loran*) and a sum of money—anywhere up to 20,000 rupiahs (in 1979, US $1 was equal to Rp. 625, so, here, $32), depending upon how truly "angry" they are. *Ngrova* will be paid by the man's fathers and will be received by the woman's fathers. The acceptance of this payment indicates that their displeasure with the match, or at least with the manner in which it was initiated, has been somewhat assuaged and that negotiations may continue.

Another prestation, called "their heads and necks they join together" (*ulur relar ratnemu*) or the "voice of accord" (*vai lolin*), must be made before any of the main portions of the bridewealth can be negotiated. For it is through this prestation that the man and woman are formally united and their union recognized and accepted by both sides as a marriage — even though at this point it is still considered to be a highly tenuous and fragile one. The prestation consists of a pair of male earrings and a small sum of money (Rp. 1,000–2,000), which are given by the man's fathers to those of the woman.

"Their heads and necks they join together" is more symbolically than materially a significant prestation. It cannot fail to bring to mind a headhunting image, for headhunters are called those "who sever necks" (*sierak rela*). When a man steals and races away with a woman, it is an affront to the dignity of the woman and her family. He has attempted to sever the woman from her natal house. "Their heads and necks they join together," then, signifies a reparation for a severance inflicted by the theft of the woman, and, at the same time, it constitutes the act by which the man and woman are officially joined together and a new union is formed. With this payment, the voices of anger are transformed into the voice of accord.

A prestation called the "place" (*waan*) of the woman may also be requested at this time, and it should be paid with a male valuable of good quality. This prestation refers not only to the place of the woman in her natal house that will be left "empty" (*vuu*) when she moves to the house of her husband, but also to the place of origin from which she is the most recent issue in the female line. It is the responsibility of the man's fathers and his *dua* to pay the place of the woman, and it will be received by the woman's fathers. The payment must then be passed along, "following blood" (*norang lara*), to the *dua* who stand as the source and origin along the female line to which she belongs.

The preliminary exchanges are slightly different when a woman climbs up into the house of a man or elopes into the forest and later returns with her lover to his house. In such an eventuality, her parents and those who represent her side must ceremoniously "search for the woman" (*rdava vata*), or "search for the keel of their outrigger" (*rdava rir raa tain*), for she has been swept away onto some foreign shore.

This is one of the marriage exchanges in which women have a prominent role to play. For it is the prerogative of the woman's mothers (her own mother and the latter's elder-younger same-sex siblings) to initiate the preliminaries by a ceremony called "they sit in the space in front of the house" (*rdok lean*). In this ceremony, the women gather together and sit in a mass in front of their daughter's lover's house, where they sing sad laments that, by their very tone, express their loss and demand to know the whereabouts of their daughter who has been so abruptly "stolen" from them. At the same time, the woman's fathers and *dua* stand about and angrily demand restitution. Drabbe notes that, formerly, when "they sat in the space in front of the house," the men who accompanied the woman's mothers came fully armed and expressed their anger at the theft of their daughter by brandishing their swords and spears as if ready to do battle (1940:196).

Eventually, the man's parents and *dua* will request that they come inside the house, but the women and those accompanying them will refuse to enter until they have been offered a bottle of palmwine (*tuat*) with its "cork" (*snibi*), which consists of a small amount of money or a pair of male earrings or both. Once inside, they are again offered palmwine, tobacco, and betel quids. The women continue to sing their songs of lament, but to the extent that their anger is assuaged by the flow of palmwine, betel, and valuables, their songs begin to take on a somewhat lighter tone.

In the meantime, the two sides will begin negotiating the same series of prestations discussed above: "anger," "their heads and necks they join together," and the "place" of the woman. In addition to these, however, if the side of the woman has had to travel some distance in their search for the woman, they are entitled to demand a pair of male earrings for each peninsula they passed en route — a series of prestations that can rapidly become quite extensive, depending upon the distance traveled. Harking back to the time of Atuf, when bridewealth payments consisted of cutting peninsulas free from the mainland, these prestations cut a channel of communication between the two parties and help to diminish the distance separating them.

A marriage that is arranged beforehand is considered far more prestigious and honorable than one that has begun by stealing and racing away with a woman. The negotiations that initiate an arranged marriage are called either "they ask the elders" (*rorat dawan*) or "they sit bending the edge of the bamboo platform" (*rdok sakal ilar wahan*) — a phrase that indicates the respectful posture the petitioners assume. In this event, the principals will be the man's parents, their elder-younger same-sex siblings, and his *dua*, who will be posed in opposition to the woman's parents, their elder-younger same-sex siblings, and her *dua*.

When a marriage is initiated by asking the elders, those representing the side of the man and the side of the woman meet in the house of the intended woman's parents. The man's agnatic fathers and *dua* broach the topic obliquely by offering "just palmwine" (*tuat watan*), which consists of a bottle of palmwine and its cork (a pair of male earrings or some money). When these are accepted, they indicate—in veiled and formal language—the purpose of their visit. If the woman's side is agreeable to the match, then the prestations of the voice of accord and the place of the woman will be paid. Because of the respect with which the marriage has been initiated, the prestation called "anger" need not be requested.

No matter how a union is initiated, however, once it has been formally recognized as a marriage, the next subject of concern that must be negotiated is the residence of the newlyweds. Seemingly a practical matter, the determination of residence is, rather, the beginning of a long series of negotiations that seek to establish the separation of the man, his wife, and his potential children—now characterized as "female"—from their containment within the wife-giving house—which is, relative to their "female" wife-takers, now characterized as "male."

To Make Oneself a Son-in-Law

A preliminary period of uxorilocal residence—described as a time when a man "makes [himself] a son-in-law" (*nafranetan*, from the root *ranetan* for "son-in-law")—may be enjoined in any type of marriage. Officially, a man can be required to live uxorilocally up to the time that the first of the four major portions of his wife's bridewealth is paid. In the rare case where it is evident that a man's *dua* are unwilling or unable to pay even a single portion of his wife's bridewealth—and his agnatic or uterine brothers are likewise unwilling or unable to redeem him—then he will have no other choice but to live uxorilocally (or, formerly, be sold off as a slave).

Yet the question of uxorilocal residence hinges not only upon the willingness and capability of a man's *dua* to redeem him of his bridewealth debts, but also upon the willingness of the woman's parents and *dua* to allow the man to be redeemed and their daughter to be separated from them. Their decision in this regard will depend upon the current composition of their household and also upon how much they trust their daughter in the hands of this young man. If there are no other children or, especially, if there are no adult men in the house, then they may request their daughter's husband to live uxorilocally for some time. Or, if the woman's parents are extremely unhappy with her choice of a husband, they may require him to live uxorilocally, so that they can keep an eye on him and subordinate him to their will.

Another reason for an enforced or prolonged uxorilocal residence has to do with the politics of exchange. The woman's fathers and *dua* may refuse to accept the valuables offered to redeem the man. They may do this not only for the reasons previously mentioned, but also, and more likely, because they have their eye on one particular valuable and will accept nothing less. The redemption of the man may then become stalled for some time.

In any case, the period of uxorilocal residence rarely exceeds a few years. A man who lives uxorilocally is too "embarrassed" and "ashamed" (*nma'it*) in face of his wife's parents and brothers, who are his "masters." He is in debt to them and, until his bridewealth has been paid, he is consequently in a position not unlike that of a slave (by definition, a person whose *dua* refuse to redeem him of his bridewealth debts). Indeed, men who live uxorilocally say they feel much like slaves. They comment that, although they must work until they are "half dead" to provide fish and pork for their wife's family, nevertheless, they themselves can go hungry because they are too ashamed to ask for food. What is true with regard to food is even more true with regard to property and the rights held by the members of the woman's house: a man living uxorilocally has no rights in the house of his wife's father and brothers.

Thus a man will persuade his *dua* to pay a portion of his wife's bridewealth as soon as possible in order that he might be redeemed from his subordination within the house of his master.[4] The payment of the first portion of the bridewealth firmly establishes the residential continuity of a man within his own father's house and initiates the separation of his wife and children from their containment within the house of her father and his master.

4. Two points should be made here. One is that, depending upon how well the couple's parents know and trust one another, a portion of bridewealth may not be required before the couple is allowed to live patri-virilocally. On the other hand, a couple may choose, for various reasons, to continue living uxorilocally even after at least one portion of the bridewealth has been paid. In such a case, however, it can no longer be said of the man that he "makes himself a son-in-law" (*nafranetan*), because his reasons for residing in the house of his wife's parents are no longer consequent upon the payment of bridewealth. In these, as in most cases, Tanimbarese are exceedingly flexible in the interpretation of conventional precepts.

Blocking and Following the Woman

If a man and a woman are both of high rank, and if their marriage initiates an alliance between two important named houses, then two further events may happen before the woman can move from her natal house to that of her husband.

First of all, her parents, her father's agnatic brothers, and her *dua* may "adorn her" (*rfalahar ia*) — that is, they may dress her in as many female valuables as they can muster, so as to indicate her "weight," or rank. At the very least, a woman should wear an indigenous woven sarong (*bakan*) and, if possible, one draped across each shoulder and another wrapped around her hips. Complete attire would include a pair of shell armbands (*sislau*), a bead necklace (*marumat*), and female earrings (*kmena*). However, only the highest-ranking women would likely emerge dressed in this way (and generally, also, only if her marriage established a new affinal relation between two important named houses).

For commoner women, a more modest version of this ritual may occur during the preliminary exchanges. The woman's mother may take an indigenous woven sarong (*bakan*) or an Indonesian sarong and a blouse (*kabaya*) — the dress of a mature woman — and put these on the young bride over her dress. As this is accomplished, her mother and her mother's sisters will wail, for their daughter is no longer an "unmarried girl" (*vat mnelat*), but a "daughter-in-law" (*etan*) to the house of her husband. In marriages with "other women" (as opposed to marriages with *fatnima* and *vat dua*), the adornments (*bareat*) of a woman cannot be considered the main reciprocation for the bridewealth prestations made by the side of the man. Rather, they constitute an additional flow of female valuables that further indebt the wife-takers and ensure the continuity of relationship.

The struggle for, and resistance to, the extraction of the woman is made even more explicit in the other ritual that may occur when a woman is formally taken to her husband's house. This is called *larlera*, and it involves the blocking of the woman's path of departure from her house. This is done because her family "has compassion for her" (*nsilobang ia*) and wishes to "hold her back" (*ntaha teri ia*). As she leaves her house, her parents, any of their same-sex siblings, and her *dua* may block her path with a bamboo pole, over which is hung either an indigenous woven sarong (*bakan*) or a piece of store-bought clothing. In order to clear the path of the obstacle, those on the man's side must give the person holding the bamboo either a pair of male earrings (*loran*) or an amount of money — depending upon whether it is a woven sarong or a piece of store-bought clothing — in exchange for which they receive the cloth. As with the adornment of the woman, this ceremony would most likely be performed only if the woman is high-ranking, and the number of people who would participate would depend upon the resources available to them.

Whether or not the woman is adorned or her path is blocked, the woman will be accompanied to her husband's home by her parents, their same-sex siblings, and her *dua*. The women will bring with them tumpline baskets filled with garden produce—yams, bananas, coconuts, and rice cooked in small packets of plaited coconut fronds (photograph 7.1). As the women enter their daughter's husband's house, they sing—swaying from side to side with the rhythm of their song—and refuse, quite vigorously and with great playfulness, to be relieved of their loads until they are given some recompense for their efforts. The man's parents, their same-sex siblings, and sisters and aunts will give each woman a small amount of money (about Rp. 500), and her basket is then let down. Before departing, the side of the woman is presented with a "dried coconut frond torch" (*ulu*) with which to light their way home. This consists of a bottle of palmwine, possibly a pair of male earrings, and Rp. 1,000 or more. The women, melancholy at the prospect of their impending separation from their daughter, wail together with her for some time and then, with their "torch" to light their way, they finally depart, their tumpline baskets now empty.[5]

In a similar fashion, some time after the woman has moved to her husband's house, her parents, their same-sex siblings, and her *dua* will "follow their daughter" (*rorang yanar vata*) in order to provide her with clothing and all the paraphernalia proper to woman's work. Their efforts are reciprocated by the man's parents, their same-sex siblings, and sisters and aunts.

There are two other times in which a woman's mother and her same-sex siblings follow their daughter and support her with food and the instruments and products of female labor. Some days after the preliminary exchanges have been concluded, they will "make the remainder of the eating dish" (*rotu feng teran*), a kettle of rice, for their daughter's husband. They will also "go pay a visit" (*rtii rsilola*) to their daughter when she gives birth and, at that time, bring her baskets of food and firewood to support her during her confinement. In each of these cases, the female goods brought by the woman's mothers will be reciprocated by male goods given by the man's fathers.

The prestation of food and household goods from the mothers allows their daughter to fulfill her role as a mature woman capable of providing

---

5. If the woman has climbed into the house of the man and it is assumed that she will ultimately remain there (without an intervening period of uxorilocal marriage), then the mothers of the woman will bring baskets of food to be exchanged on the day when they "search for their daughter." Before they leave, they will also be presented with a torch to light their way home.

Photograph 7.1   Women brought tumpline baskets laden with food in order to "follow their daughter," Bo'ivuka Sera-Larat, when she maried Be'i Maru in Awear in 1980.

food. But it also makes known to her husband's family that although she may have finally been physically separated from her natal house, she does not come without the continued support of the members of her house and of the female line to which she and her mothers together belong. The gift of food between the women gives substance to what it means to be sisters, to be mothers to their daughters, and to be women who share the same female blood and the same female substances — the garden produce created by the labor of women. It is also an expression of the insistence of the wife-givers upon the continuity of their position as life-givers — as those who have given women and who continue to feed, grow, and care for those women and their issue.

The Shares of Bridewealth

Unlike the preliminary marriage exchanges just described, in which most of the valuables and goods given bear no further exchange destiny beyond those who receive them, the major portions (*wahat*) or shares (*vaan*) of the bridewealth follow extended pathways of exchange. However, what is unique about the exchanges entailed by a marriage with an other woman (*vat liak*) is the particular alignment of the exchanging parties. Here, it is the *dua* of the wife-takers who must pay bridewealth on behalf of the man to the *dua* of the wife-givers. Yet, as will be seen, the efforts of the former are not reciprocated by the latter but rather by the bridewealth paid for that man's sister. That is, the new affinal relation is supported by the reciprocity that continues to operate along the old pathways of exchange that link people related as *ura-memi* and *ura-ava.*

It is only in marriages that involve an other woman that bridewealth, or "the value of the woman" (*vat velin*), as such, is paid. The major portions of bridewealth consist of a large share (*vaan dawan*) and a small share (*vaan ko'u*), each of which follows a separate pathway of exchange. Each share is further divided into two major parts: "bow"[6] (*vuhur*) and "water" (*wear*) together constitute the large share; "spear" (*ramat*) and "sword" (*suruk*) make up the small share (see figure 7.1).

Not only the portions of the bridewealth but also both those who pay and those who receive them are differentiated according to whether they belong to the "side of the woman" (*lihir vata*) or the "side of the man" (*lihir brana*), where the woman and the man referred to are ego's mother and father. The large share is thus also called "the value of the woman belonging to the side of the woman [mother]" (*vat velin lihir vata*), and the small share is referred to as "the value of the woman belonging to the side of the man [father]" (*vat velin lihir brana*). This division of bridewealth payments is correlated with a differentiation between two sets of *dua*: those who stand on the side of the woman or mother (*dua lihir vata*), and those who stand on the side of the man or father (*dua lihir brana*). The ascending female line of ego (and ego's mother) traces the pathway that links ego's *dua* on the side of the woman, just as ego's father's ascending female line traces the pathway that links ego's *dua* on the side of the man.

Thus, "bow" and "water"—the large share, which belongs to the side of the woman—will be paid by a man's *dua* on the side of the woman and will be received by his wife's *dua* on the side of the woman. Likewise, "spear" and "sword"—the small share, which belongs to the side of the man—will be paid by a man's *dua* on the side of the man and will be received by his wife's *dua* on the side of the man.[7]

In addition to the four main portions of the bridewealth, two small, residual payments called "weariness" (*farea*) will be paid by the male

6. Given the prevalence of boat metaphors, it needs to be said that this prestation is not named after the bow of a boat but rather after the weapon.

7. It should be noted that in 1967 the government convened a meeting to which representatives from all over Tanimbar were invited, for the express purpose of determining a uniform bridewealth for the whole of Tanimbar. Previous to this, although there had been four major portions of the bridewealth on the island of Yamdena, there had only been three main portions on the island of Fordata. (I am not certain of the situation on the other islands.) Formerly, on Fordata, the bridewealth on the side of the woman comprised two portions ("bow"

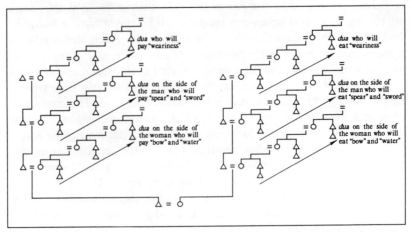

Figure 7.1   The exchange pathways implicated in a man's marriage with an "other woman"

representatives of the houses that are linked along the ascending female line of the man's father's father. They will be received by the male representatives of the houses linked along the ascending female line of his wife's father's father. The two "weariness" payments — also called the "front flag" (*sa'ir ulu*) and the "rear flag" (*sa'ir muri*) — are not, however, considered to be significant portions of the bridewealth. They constitute the final recognition of a set of relationships that determined the *dua* that stood on the side of the woman relative to ego's father's father and stood on the side of the man relative to ego's father. Once "weariness" is paid, this set of *dua* will no longer be implicated in the bridewealth payments that concern the descendants (reckoned through male links) of the father's father's mother.

The four portions of the bridewealth are not equally valued. "Bow" is the most important of the four. "Spear" is second in importance to "bow," and is the primary of the two accorded to the side of the man. The portions called "water" (which "follows bow") and "sword" (which "follows spear") are both subsidiary to those they are destined to "follow." The value of the prestation given for "bow" should therefore exceed that of each of the other three portions, and "spear" should be second in value only to

and "spear"), and the bridewealth on the side of the man comprised only one portion ("sword"). This was changed so that, in addition to "sword," the "spear" portion would now go to the side of the man. To the "bow" portion, which remained on the side of the woman, was added a new payment called "water."

"bow." "Water" and "sword," as subsidiary payments, are roughly equivalent in value. The portion called "weariness" is of negligible value, as it represents but a token gesture of recognition.

Following Blood and Bridewealth

In order to understand who may possibly be involved in the payment of a particular portion of the bridewealth, as well as the manner in which they will be called to action, we would do well to follow the process through from the beginning. With reference to figure 7.2, let us focus upon the "bow" payment that is entailed by the marriage of A1 with a woman from a previously unallied house.

Bridewealth negotiations will be initiated when A1 makes a prestation called the "lifting of the bottom" (*saksikat dii*) to his most immediate *dua* on the side of his mother. This will be the current representative of the house from which his mother originated—his mother's brother (B2) or, let us say, his mother's brother's son (B1). With this prestation, he will request that his *dua* "redeem him" (*ntevut ia*) of his debt for the bow portion of his wife's bridewealth. The "lifting of the bottom" (to make light, because one becomes heavy and lazy if one is allowed to sit too long) consists of a bottle of palmwine and either a pair of male earrings or Rp. 500–1,000 or both.

If B1, himself, is unable to redeem A1, he will pass the prestation and the redemption request to the representative of the house from which A1's mother's mother originated. In this way, it will pass from one house to

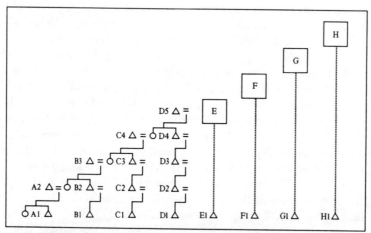

Figure 7.2   The *dua* involved in the "bow" portion of the bridewealth

another as they are linked along the female line appropriate to the bow portion—that is, the female line to which A1 himself belongs. Thus, for instance, it will be passed from B1 to the representatives of the houses C, D, E, F, and onward along this pathway. Depending upon the importance of the marriage concerned and the resources of the men who represent these houses, the prestation may travel through as many houses as necessary until it reaches someone who is capable of redeeming A1.

The "lifting of the bottom" prestation is said to "follow blood" (*norang lara*). In the case of the bow portion, it follows the female bloodline to which ego belongs. The first steps along this pathway will be reckoned genealogically, through remembered blood links. After three generations or so, however, the limits of remembered blood links will be reached, and further steps along the pathway will be reckoned in terms of the alliances that relate houses with reference to the female line in question.

The redemption request initiated by A1 for the bow portion of his wife's bridewealth, for example, will follow blood to B (because this is the house of his mother's brother), on to C (the house of his mother's mother's brother), and on to D (the house of his mother's mother's mother's brother). Beyond this, neither A1 nor D1 may remember the particular people whose marriage related houses D and E. D1 will, most likely, pass the redemption request on to E because, relative to the female line of which A1 is a member, E is the house master (*rahan dua*) of D. At this point, it will continue to follow blood, but no longer in the sense of tracing the remembered genealogical links between specific persons. It will generally have already entered a "row," which, although founded on the female bloodline concerned, is conceived in terms of the relations between houses and not in terms of the blood relations between particular persons. The "lifting of the bottom" prestation and the redemption request will follow this pathway until a representative of one of the houses linked along it agrees to assume the final responsibility for redeeming A1.

When a man makes the prestation of a bottle of palmwine and his *dua* accepts it, the former relinquishes his responsibility for the debt incurred: both the debt and the responsibility for paying it are wholly assumed by the man's *dua* from the moment he accepts the bottle of palmwine. When, in turn, the man's *dua* passes the bottle on to his own *dua*, he does so as if the debt were his own. Often a bottle of palmwine representing a redemption request will pass through a good many houses and, in the process, enter a row and come to rest only when it has reached one of the houses near or at the very top of the hierarchy of exchange pathways— somewhere near or along the double cycle of the Lolat Ila'a. The members of houses higher up will accept the bottle with two thoughts in mind. First, they may accept it not so much out of concern for the person who initiated the request, but because it is presented to them by their immediate *lolat*, who represent the debt as their own. Although the particular relationship between the initiator of the request and the wife-givers to whom he is indebted may — on account of its recent origin and relative impermanence — be of little import in the on-going scheme of things, the permanence of the relation between a Lolat Ila'a house, for instance, and its most immediate *lolat* is valued so highly that a *dua* cannot refuse to accept a request from his *lolat*. To refuse would constitute a complete severance of their relations, and a *dua* would thereby cut himself off from the source of his strength. Second, a *dua* will accept the bottle because all those who have passed it on — including those at the bottom of the line — are reckoned as "his people" (*ni tomata*). He is responsible for the life, growth, and multiplication of these people and he must therefore accept their requests for the redemption of their men. But, by the same token, he is also entitled to receive the bridewealth of their women. As much as they are a drain on his supply of valuables, they are also the source from which valuables flow into his hands.

Negotiating the "Value of a Woman"

Once a *dua* has been found who is willing and able to accept responsibility for redeeming a man, then upon an appointed date all the representatives of the houses along this pathway — that is, all the men whose "bottoms have been lifted" by receiving the bottle of palmwine — will gather together to begin negotiating with the corresponding set of *dua* of the man's wife (photographs 7.2 and 7.3). Bridewealth negotiations may be carried out with both parties meeting face to face in the house of either the man's or the woman's parents or that of any of their *dua*. More rarely, they may proceed with the two sides sitting in separate houses and a messenger mediating between the two. (On Yamdena, this is apparently common practice.)

There is a definite sequence of prestations that occurs both before and after the main portion of bridewealth is accepted. Generally, the man's side will open the proceedings by offering "just palmwine" (*tuat watan*), which will consist of a bottle of palmwine and a small amount of money as its "cork" (*snibi*). After some time, they will make their first offer for the portion of the bridewealth that is at issue. This preliminary offer, which they do not expect to be accepted, is called "the tip of the bamboo container [used to tap palmwine]" (*vovar tutul*). They will eventually make an offering that is accepted, and this prestation is considered the "body" (*tenan*) of this portion of the bridewealth. Once the body has been accepted, small additional prestations may yet be requested. Where the bow portion is

Photograph 7.2   On November 10, 1979, men gathered in the house of Falaksoru and Ma'ileba Ditilebit to negotiate an exchange. The overturned plate on the table indicates that the exchange was unsuccessful.

Photograph 7.3   Men negotiating an exchange in the house of Beliaki Oratmangun late in the afternoon on June 26, 1980.

concerned, the body is not complete without something to elevate it: a man's fathers or *dua* must "give it a foundation" (*rlata ia*) that will lift it off the ground and keep it from tipping to one side. Thus, to balance the bow prestation, they must add what is called the "front foundation" (*latlata ulu*) and the "back foundation" (*latlata muri*). Likewise, to seal the spear prestation, a man's fathers or *dua* must "provide an elephant tusk to plug it" (*rala lela al rsibi ia*); and to round off the sword prestation, they must "give a chain to measure the fit of the fist" (*rwika rsara ngungu*). For each of these, a pair of male earrings (*loran*) will suffice. In addition, the man's fathers and *dua* will also "join together [to strengthen]" (*rbabar*) the bow, spear, and sword prestations, as well as the water prestation, with yet another small offering of money. The father of the woman, who is the first to receive both the body of the prestation and the supporting prestations, is entitled to retain the latter, but must eventually pass the body on to those *dua* who are entitled to receive it. Although these additional prestations are all considered minor, they nevertheless add weight to the body of the prestation, giving it a secure and sturdy foundation.

The payment of a portion of bridewealth is never accomplished at once, but is rather the subject of long negotiations that may take hours or days (and, even then, the negotiations may not end in success). The *dua* of both the man and his wife must be supplied continually with palmwine, tobacco, and betel quids, and negotiations progress under the increasing influence of the strong liquor, which is thought to free a man's tongue and allow for fluidity in speech and in the ritual songs (*tanlain*) that accompany all negotiations.

There is no strict specification of what kind of valuable must be paid for each of the four major portions of the bridewealth, except that it should be a male valuable — among which are included elephant tusks, gold breast pendants, male earrings, and antique swords (although the latter are extremely rare nowadays and are generally kept as heirlooms). Lacking a male valuable of suitable quality, a female valuable, such as a pair of shell armbands, may occasionally be substituted.

What matters far more than the type of valuable offered, and what becomes the subject of intense negotiations, is the relative quality of the valuable, and whether or not it bears a name. In this, all depends upon rank, and upon the skills of the negotiators. Where the woman and her *dua* are of high rank, the latter can rightfully demand high quality, named valuables to be paid for her bridewealth (especially if her mother's bridewealth was also paid with such valuables). These demands may be more or less fulfilled to the extent that the man and his *dua* are also high ranking (and named valuables were also paid for his mother's bridewealth). A commoner woman could never command a bridewealth consisting of named valuables, nor would her *dua* require it.

Whatever the rank of the parties concerned, a good deal of rhetorical skill is needed to bring a negotiation to a satisfactory conclusion. For, amid a fair abount of bravado, bluff, and good humor, any negotiation hinges upon the evocation of feelings of shame and honor, the expressions of which may swing as easily to outright anger and wounded pride, as to compassion and enforced humility.

It should be said, as well, that because a man's redemption request (like a woman's bridewealth) may travel up to the houses situated at the top of the exchange hierarchy, the *dua* involved in a bridewealth negotiation — both those who stand together on the paying or the receiving side and those who stand opposed to one another — may, for political reasons that have nothing to do with the particular exchange at hand, engage in a kind of competitive one-upmanship. This can result in either a total stalemate or a prestation, the value of which has been tremendously inflated.

Reciprocities New and Old

When the prestations that form the body and the support of a particular portion of a woman's bridewealth have been accepted, the negotiations between the man's set of *dua* and that of the woman are brought to a close. It remains, however, the responsibility of the members of the man's house to reciprocate, at least in some small way, the efforts their *dua* have expended on behalf of their housemate. In this, they may call upon their sisters and aunts (*ura-ava*) for assistance.

A man's *dua* may rightfully demand to be feasted with fish or pork, and at the successful conclusion of a negotiation, the members of a man's house and their *ura-ava* should provide a meal — which must include either fish or pork — for both their own *dua* and those of the man's wife. If the prestation has been particularly costly, or if it represents the culmination of a long and especially difficult series of negotiations, the man may slaughter a pig and present the thighs to his *dua*.

In addition to a meal, the members of a man's house should "pour out palmwine so that their *dua* may drink" (*rlii tuat ma duara renu*). By this, it is meant that they should present the *dua* who has just paid a portion of a man's bridewealth with a bottle of palmwine and a male valuable or some money or both. The value of the prestation need in no way be equal to the valuable given for the bridewealth and, indeed, it need not necessarily be made at all. It is simply a sign by which a man acknowledges his indebtedness to his *dua*: it does not reciprocate his *dua* for the valuable paid out on his behalf. Thus, men say that if the "palmwine has liquid" (*tuat vahan*) then the *dua* will drink, but if the "palmwine has no liquid" (*tuat wol vahan*), they will not. That is, the prestation is made in accordance with the resources of the members of the man's house — and those of their sisters and aunts, upon whom they may also draw. Their *dua* may receive, in addition to a bottle of palmwine and money, a male valuable of some worth — perhaps even one that bears a name; or, on the contrary, their *dua* may go home relatively empty-handed. In the latter case, the *dua* may well grumble, but there are many occasions upon which "palmwine may be poured out," and the more a man's *lolat* and *ura-ava* are indebted to him, the more he will be in a position to demand a valuable of worth at some point in the future.

Indeed, the reciprocation for a portion of the bridewealth paid on behalf of a man is not to be found in the palmwine that is poured out on such occasions. Rather, it is to be found in the fact that the *dua* who "redeem" (*rtevut*) a man of a specific portion of his bridewealth are entitled to "eat" the equivalent portion of that man's sister's bridewealth. The various portions of a woman's bridewealth must "travel following blood" (*rbana rorang lara*) along the same pathways that her brother's redemption requests have traveled. Just as her brother's "lifting of the bottom" prestation was passed from the representatives of one house after another linked along the female line appropriate to a specific portion of the bridewealth, so too the same portion of her own bridewealth will be passed from house to house along this same female line. The valuable may be held in one house or another along this pathway for weeks, months, or even years. Ultimately, however, it must be handed on to the next house, and travel along its destined pathway until it reaches the *dua* who was responsible for paying her brother's wife's bridewealth. A *dua* who has paid bow for a man will, therefore, eventually eat the bow portion of the bridewealth paid for that man's sister. It is in what he eats on behalf of the sister that a *dua* is reciprocated for what he has paid on behalf of her brother. In this way old reciprocities established between mother's brother and sister's children support the initiation of new reciprocities between the sister's son and his affines.

It of course happens that some men have no sisters whose bridewealth will form a return on the bridewealth paid out on their own behalf. In such cases, the prestation called "they pour out palmwine so that their *dua* may drink" assumes special importance. A woman who had four sons and no daughters once told me that each time their *dua* redeem one of her sons of a portion of his bridewealth, she insists that "palmwine so that their *dua* may drink" be paid with a male valuable that is roughly equivalent in value. For, in lieu of the bridewealth of a sister, this is a way of making a return on the valuables paid out to redeem a set of brothers.

The importance of what is called *wadu-bebun* also increases when a set of brothers has no sisters and, more especially, when they are unable to pass on substantial valuables as "palmwine so that their *dua* may drink." *Wadu* refers to the "catch" resulting from a fishing or hunting expedition. *Bebun* — or, more fully, *ta'a bebun* — refers to the half shell of a coconut in which the fish or pork portion of a meal was formerly served. *Wadubebun* therefore signifies the fish and pork that sisters and aunts are obliged to give their *dua*. Men without sisters are doubly obliged to provide their *dua* with these goods and with others such as palmwine. Moreover, they cannot refuse their *dua* when requested to perform a service, and *dua* may use such men freely whenever a message or errand must be run, or when hands are needed as, for instance, in the construction of a house. Another woman once commented to me that her sons, who had no sisters, were indeed "like slaves" (*wean iria*) to their *dua*.

Over the years, the negotiations that concern each of the four major portions of the bridewealth will be initiated, carried out, and brought to a conclusion in the same manner. The only difference will consist in the set of *dua* who will be called upon to make and eat the various portions. Both bow and water will be paid by the set of *dua* whose houses are linked with reference to the man's own ascending female line and will be eaten by the set of *dua* whose houses are linked with reference to his wife's own ascending female line. The *dua* who will pay and eat spear and sword, on the other hand, will be determined by the fact that their houses are linked with reference to the ascending female line of the man's father and that of his wife's father, respectively.

Of Spears and Bridewealth

In the epoch of Atuf, marriage was made possible not by the payment of bridewealth valuables, but rather by the completion of a formidable task — the separation of an offshore island from the mainland and the creation, thereby, of a passage between the two. It was through the separation of islands from the mainland, which was ultimately effected by the powers of the sacred spear that Atuf came to possess, that it was possible to separate women from their natal houses and effect their movement to other houses in marriage.

Bridegrooms are no longer required to sever complementary parts of the landscape in order to achieve the separation of their prospective spouses. They are, however, still required to effect the separation of complementary (male and female) parts of a house in order to extract a woman from her containment within her natal house. No longer able to use Atuf's sacred spear, other instruments of separation have had to be substituted. Thus Atuf's spear has been replaced by bridewealth prestations, whose affinity with the original instrument is evident in their names: "bow," "spear," and "sword."

That these bridewealth prestations (and the more recently added "water") actively shape the social world as much as Atuf's spear shaped the physical world can be seen in what they accomplish: the movement and separation of men, women, and children from one house and their attachment to another, and the simultaneous creation of a channel of relation between the two. The shape of the social world and of social relations must continually be created, and this is accomplished by the movement of bridewealth valuables.

Once a man has initiated a relationship with a woman whom he intends to take as his wife, he becomes assimilated to her as "female" in relation to the "male" aspect of her natal house—her father and brothers. It is this female aspect of the house—including the man himself, his wife, and their prospective children—that the man's *dua* must extract through bridewealth payments. This process of separation—and the resulting differentiation of the prior androgynous unity of the brother-sister pair— takes place in stages and generally is stretched out over the course of the couple's lifetime and, occasionally, beyond.

Although there is no specific timetable for the payment of one or another part of the bridewealth, there is one negative provision that enforces a delay in the completion of all four portions. There is a saying: "Wait until she sails off [and comes back] and beaches her boat before [you pay off her bridewealth]" (*Naban ma ia nobal ia ntavu ia veka*). This is to say that a portion of a woman's bridewealth should not be paid off while she is pregnant and, moreover, that all four portions of a woman's bridewealth should not be fully paid off until after she is past childbearing age. To do either would be to condemn her and her children to an early death. The payment of bridewealth is an act that serves to detach a woman from the source of life and blood that flows through her. Hence, to pay bridewealth while a woman is pregnant or to complete bridewealth payments while she is still bearing children is to cut her off from this source and thus cut off her own life and the life that might issue from her. In order for life to flow and sprouts to multiply, a separation must be effected, but it must not constitute a complete alienation.

Aside from these provisions, as long as relations are amicable, neither side will particularly concern itself with the question of exactly when payments should be made. Both will await an auspicious positioning of valuables before making a move. If a man's *dua* come into possession of a valuable that seems appropriate to a particular part of his bridewealth, or if his wife's *dua* take note that his own hold a particular valuable they deem suitable (and, perhaps, covet), then one side or the other may make haste to initiate negotiations before the valuable is forced by other necessities to move out of reach in another direction.

Residence and Affiliation

The payment of bridewealth effects changes in both residence and affiliation for those who are considered the female aspect of an affinal relation. These changes occur within a system that, from the man's perspective, poses patrilocal (or, now more commonly, virilocal) residence against uxorilocal residence, and affiliation to the house of the father in opposition to affiliation to the house of the mother's brother.

The residence of a man, his wife, and children is the first aspect of their life to be affected by the payment of bridewealth. We have already seen that one portion of the bridewealth should be paid to effect the transition from uxorilocal to patrilocal (or virilocal) residence. Change of residence is not tied to the payment of a specific portion of the bridewealth — any portion will suffice. This change in residence removes the man from the immediacy of his slavelike incorporation within the house of his wife's father, and it firmly establishes his residence and rights in the house of his own father. It is also the first step in the extraction of his wife and children from their encompassment within her father's house.

Although payment of only one portion of the bridewealth is necessary to effect a change in residence, all four portions of the bridewealth are considered integral to the determination of the affiliation of the children of a union. Yet because of the nature of the timing of bridewealth payments, the question of affiliation often remains an open one throughout the lifetime of a couple and may not be settled until after their death, when the children — whose affiliation is at stake — are married with children of their own. Upon the death of one or the other parent, however, only one portion — bow — is crucial to the determination of the deceased children's affiliation.

What is at stake in the question of affiliation is the rights over the patrimony and estates of a house. Children who affiliate to the house of their father inherit full rights over the patrimony and estates of their paternal house. These rights are lost entirely when children affiliate to the house of their mother's brother. Matrilaterally affiliated children (*vat yanan*) are said to "have no father" (*wol yaman*) and are considered female and inferior relative to those who have affiliated patrilaterally. The latter are considered male and superior as the rightful heirs of their fathers. Matrilaterally affiliated children can be ordered about at will — "they order them to come and go" (*rsinir ira tii-maa*). Their rights in the maternal house are always secondary and depend, to a large extent, upon the discretion of their mother's brother, and upon the demography of the house. As long as there are heirs in the male line, matrilaterally affiliated members of the house will not gain full rights in the estates of the house — its *lolat* and *ura-ava*, its land, trees, heirlooms, and ritual offices. Rights over the *lolat*, land, heirlooms, and ritual offices will always remain the prerogative of patrilaterally affiliated members. Rights over *ura-ava* and trees may be extended — to one degree or another — to those who have affiliated matrilaterally. If there are very few patrilaterally affiliated occupants of a house, for example, those who have affiliated matrilaterally will, in all probability, receive rights to use the trees of the house, and their rights will most likely be inherited by their sons. If there are many patrilaterally affiliated members, however, matrilaterally affiliated men acquire only limited rights of usufruct in their own generation, and otherwise are left to establish their own plantations, which will then constitute the inheritance of their sons.

The only instance in which an inmarried man may assume rights in his wife's house is when there are no male heirs. In such cases, it is said that "the woman goes out walking and takes a man" (*vat nbana nala brana*). The man will then live uxorilocally on a permanent basis. Being totally incorporated within his wife-giver's house, no bridewealth will be paid, and the man and his children will inherit rights over the estates of the house as well as acquire rights to speak on behalf of the house.

Matrilateral affiliation also entails certain consequences regarding the payment and receipt of bridewealth. A woman's *dua* on the side of the man (or father) will no longer be entitled to eat the spear and sword portions of her bridewealth if she has affiliated matrilaterally, nor will they be further obligated to pay these same portions of her brother's wife's bridewealth. Both of these portions, as well as those that belong to the side of the woman (or mother), will fall to the *dua* on the side of the woman.

The Rope of the Dead and Divorce

Since bridewealth payments are made over the course of a lifetime, two eventualities may arise before all four portions are completed: either the husband or wife may die in the meantime or the couple may wish to divorce.

It is considered imperative that efforts be made to pay all four portions of the bridewealth during the lifetime of a man and his wife. Yet it is only the bow — the main portion on the side of the woman — that is, in the end, the decisive one for the establishment of the patrilateral affiliation of the children. If the bow has already been completed when either a man or his wife die (even if none of the other portions of the bridewealth has been completed), then the patrilateral affiliation of the children will be assured.

Should a man or his wife die before the bow has been paid (even if all the other three parts have been completed), then the man's *dua* on the side of the woman must make an equivalent prestation, called the "rope of the dead" (*tuur nitu*), to the man's wife's *dua* on the side of the woman in order to establish the patrilateral affiliation of the children. If the *tuur nitu* is not made, then the children will affiliate matrilaterally. When a man dies and the *tuur nitu* is paid, his wife will continue to reside in her husband's house with their children. If it is not paid, however, she will "step down from the house" (*nsuta rahan*) of her husband and return, with their children, to the house of her father or brother.

Three generations ago, a man from a house in Waleran was "lifted" into a house in Awear (see figure 7.3). His son, L, had two daughters—A and B—but no son. The house into which he had been lifted therefore again lifted in one of their sister's sons, M, so that the two women would have a brother to look after them. M then married a woman from a house in Awear and they had one son, N. However, M died suddenly and, because only the sword portion of his wife's bridewealth had been paid and the rope of the dead was not accepted, she stepped down from her husband's house and returned with her son to the house of her father. M's death again left his two sisters without a brother. To add to the tragedy, A's husband, her eldest daughter, and her eldest son all died, and she was left completely bereft, with two daughters and a young son to support, but no adult man in her house to help her with the work of a man. Consequently, after M's wife herself died, A resolved to adopt M's son, N. The problem, however, was that M's son was not technically his son. Because his wife's bridewealth payments had not been completed and the rope of the dead prestation had not been made, N had "no father" (*wol yaman*). Some time after I had first arrived in

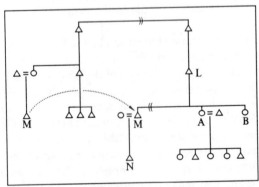

Figure 7.3   Relations involved in a contested affiliation

Awear, in July 1979, negotiations were convened in order to make M's rope of the dead prestation. Yet the negotiations were unsuccessful, and A's tears and sorrow could not avert the fact that M's son remained incorporated within the house of his mother.

Once a woman has stepped down from the house of her deceased husband, she is free to marry once again. If she does remarry, she and her second husband may wish to have her children by her former marriage affiliate to the house of her second husband. The woman's father or brothers may not agree to the plan, in which case the move will be blocked and the children must affiliate matrilaterally. If they do agree, however, the second husband and his *dua* on the side of the woman should make a prestation called "they sprinkle water on their [the children's] heads" (*ral wear na'a ulurira*). Like the rope of the dead, this prestation should be equivalent in value to the bow portion of the bridewealth and should be given to the woman's *dua* on the side of the woman. The second husband's *dua*, who made this prestation, would then be entitled to eat the spear portion of his wife's daughters and, at the same time, be obligated to pay the spear portion for their brothers. To establish a woman's children's affiliation to the house of her second husband, it is sometimes enough for the latter's *dua* to assume responsibility for the spear portions of her sons' bridewealth. As long as they are willing to assume this responsibility, woman's *dua* may not be particularly concerned with whether they receive the "water on their heads" prestations.

There was a woman in Awear whose husband died suddenly, as a consequence, it was said, of having been enticed and deceived by a dangerous female *sebraa* spirit (union with whom causes death by sundown). At the time of his death, no bridewealth prestations (or only the spear portion) had been completed and his *dua* did not make the rope of the dead prestation. For, not only did the couple have four sons and no daughters, but the man's brother also had five sons and only one daughter. His *dua* were therefore faced with the prospect of paying bridewealth for nine brothers and receiving bridewealth for only one sister. Because they decided not to make the rope of the dead prestation, the woman was forced to step down from her husband's house. Eventually she remarried. Her second husband apparently never formally adopted her four sons; rather, he simply began to assume responsibility for the spear portions of their bridewealth prestations. This in effect established him as their father and they affiliated to his house. Because there were no daughters whose bridewealth would reciprocate that paid on her sons' behalf, the woman stressed that each time their *dua* have redeemed one of

her sons of a portion of his bridewealth, she has insisted that a
return prestation (or *wawaul*) be made. Her sons are in a precarious
enough position, she feels, and she does not want this exacerbated
by an overwhelming debt to their *dua*.

The status of children who have affiliated to the house of their mother's
second husband is far better than that of matrilaterally affiliated children.
Unlike the latter, who are said to have no father and who have been rein-
corporated as the female aspect of their mother's father's house, the former
have gained a new father and will be considered a part of the male aspect
of their new house. They will gain full rights over both the forest estates
and the village estates as well as the patrimony of their new house, and
their status will be on a par with those who have patrilaterally affiliated
to the house.

Not all unions with other women last until one or the other spouse
dies. Indeed, because of their tentative and provisional nature, marriages
with other women can be easily dissolved without breaking established
affinal pathways. It is usually repeated instances of adultery, theft, or
slander that will instigate negotiations for reconciliation or separation.

The relation between bridewealth and affiliation differs depending on
whether the couple intends to continue their relationship or intends to
separate. It also differs in accordance with whose fault lies as the basis
for the potential break. There are cases of adultery, theft, and slander in
which the couple nevertheless decide to remain together and not divorce.
If the man is at fault, her parents and *dua* will most likely demand that
he pay another portion of the bridewealth to show his renewed good intentions toward his wife. If the woman has been at fault, however, her
dua must make a prestation called "they lift up his face" (*rsaka wahan*)
to her husband, in order to cover over the shame he feels on account of
his wife's behavior. Once her *dua* have lifted the face of her husband, they
can still require that the full complement of bridewealth be paid. If, however, her *dua* are unable or unwilling to lift his face, then one portion of
the bridewealth is cut from the total amount that her husband owes these
dua.

If the couple decides to divorce, the situation is more complex. When
a woman is not at fault, and her husband wishes to "throw her off"—for
example, because he intends to marry another woman—then the man's
dua must pay the "voice of the official" (*tuan vain*) fine in addition to
whatever bridewealth they have already paid. The man has no rights over
his children, who will follow their mother when she steps down from the
house of her husband and returns to her father's house. In rare instances,
a woman will herself decide to step down from the house of her husband

because he has repeatedly committed adultery or some other offence. More often, her fathers, brothers, or *dua* will force her to leave her husband's house on account of his unseemly or insulting behavior. Her *dua* cannot, then, demand either bridewealth or the separation fine, but the children follow their mother and affiliate matrilaterally to her father's house.

When the woman is at fault and the man decides to divorce her, then the latter need pay no further bridewealth, and her *dua* cannot demand further payment because they will be too "ashamed" and "embarrassed" (*rma'it*) in face of the woman's transgression. They will, nevertheless, be entitled to demand either bridewealth or the voice of the official fine from the woman's lover, depending upon whether the two intend to marry. In such cases, the woman will be obliged to step down from the house of her former husband, and the children will affiliate to the house of their father.

The Value of Extraction

The creation of a differentiated "female" identity through the payment of bridewealth establishes, at the same time, the possibility for the enduring "male" identity of *both* the wife-giving and the wife-taking houses. From the perspective of a wife-giving house, the continuity of its male identity is dependent upon the separation and productivity of its *own* female aspect—here the village estates composed of the female lines that issue forth from outmarried women. From the perspective of a wife-taking house, the permanence of its male identity is dependent in several ways upon the extraction of the female aspect of *other* houses. First, the payment of bridewealth effects the residential removal of a man and his wife from their incorporation within the house of her father. It establishes the man's residence and rights within his own father's house, and it is the final step in a long process that achieves another generation of male continuity for his house. Second, the separation of his wife and her differentiation as a female identity is necessary for their own cross-sex union and thus for the realization of their productive and reproductive potential. And third, the payment of bridewealth establishes the patrilateral affiliation of the couple's children to their father's house and is the first step toward securing yet another generation of male continuity within his own house.

The outward growth and extension of the female side of a house and the simultaneous continuity of a male identity of both the wife-giving and wife-taking houses are the necessary prerequisites for ensuring an enduring affinal relation. For, where affiliation is established by bridewealth, the failure of bridewealth to effect a separation is simultaneously a failure to perpetuate an affinal relation (Valeri 1980). The reincorporation of the sister's children within the house of the mother's brother dissolves not only the continuity of the male line of the sister's husband but also the continuity of the affinal relation itself. Bridewealth is therefore truly the analogue of Atuf's spear, which separated the offshore islands from the mainland and, in the process, created a channel or passage between them.

The fact that, statistically, patrilocal residence and patrilateral affiliation *are* achieved in most cases (see appendix 1), does not at all lessen the fact that they *must* be achieved. They are not given in the shape of social relations. On the contrary, the realization of these conditions is the focus of the overwhelming portion of the creative activity in which people are engaged. To read the statistical outcome as if it were a given would be to deny the integrity of the efforts and achievements that Tanimbarese place at the very center of their social life.

The permanence and continuity of a house as a male source of life depends upon the differentiation and extraction of the female aspect of both one's own house and other houses. Yet the bridewealth exchanges that effect these processes can have variant results, and these are accorded differential value. Thus failure to separate and extract the female aspect of other houses results in the low status alternatives of uxorilocal residence and matrilateral affiliation, whereas success in this regard results in the high status alternatives of patrilocal residence and patrilateral affiliation.

Yet the relative value of the alternate forms of residence and affiliation only make sense within a wider hierarchical order of values that opposes named houses to unnamed houses and permanent alliances along the rows to recent marriages between members of previously unallied houses. Within this hierarchical order, patrilocal residence and patrilateral affiliation establish a fixed relation to the founding ancestor and the founding alliance of the house, as well as to its patrimony and estates. It is the high status of such an enduring and productive anchorage that is at stake in the differential rights linked to alternate forms of residence and affiliation. And it is for this reason as well as to escape the slavelike consequences of the alternatives, that men seek their "redemption."

8 Valuables and the Ideology of Exchange

The best way to acquire notoriety as the owner (ruler) of an object is publicly to give possession of it to someone else. The recipient, it is true, then has the object, but you retain sovereignty over it since you make yourself the owner (*madu*) of a debt. In sum, the possessor of wealth objects gains merit and prestige mainly through the publicity he achieves in getting rid of them. (Leach 1965:142–43)

What from the donor's point of view, then, is a part of himself with which to enter into exchange, from the recipient's is something to be separated and extracted from the donor. (Strathern 1988:198)

The marriage of a woman does not, in the first instance, separate a woman from her house; rather, it incorporates her husband and potential children as part of the female aspect of her brother's house. It is through bridewealth exchanges that this female aspect is extracted from its source, and the relation between wife-takers and wife-givers is constituted as one between separate "female" and "male" entities.

Moreover, the exchanges between the two sides manifest a marked tension between seemingly contradictory impulses. From the wife-taker's point of view, the payment of bridewealth is an act that is meant to sever the more immediate effects of the incorporation and subordination of the husband, his wife, and their children, and to establish their own separate identity. Yet the payment of bridewealth, in itself, both assumes and requires the simultaneous acknowledgment of relation back to, and continued encompassment by, the source of life. From the wife-giver's point of view, their own prestations counter this act of severance with gifts that stress the continuity of relation and the inevitability of the encompassment of the issue by the source. At the same time, these prestations both assume and require the simultaneous acknowledgment of the separate identity and independence of the wife-takers.

This double-sided nature of exchange was well recognized by Mauss in *The Gift* (1967). While commentators have focused on the paradoxical relation between persons and things (Sahlins 1972; Weiner 1985), they have rarely noted the clarity with which Mauss represents the tension between the forces of encompassment and separation.

Tanimbarese material fits nicely with Mauss's characterization of the relation between persons and things. This is most clearly evident in the marriage of a woman, where her brothers, the male aspect of their house, give a part of the androgynous unity that constitutes the whole — here, a part of the female aspect of their house. In giving a woman in marriage, they have truly given a part of their persons in the form of the female lifeblood they share with their sister. In giving female valuables, they also exteriorize a part of what forms their identity as persons. For the female valuables are not only seen as an embodiment of the "weight" and value of the woman herself, but as we shall see, their qualities exemplify the life-giving attributes that constitute the female aspect of the house.

As Mauss indicates, it is impossible to truly alienate the persons or things given, since they are alive and partake of the giver. Indeed, for Tanimbarese, those who are the source of life — in the form of women, blood, and female valuables — remain the master and owner of all that issues forth from the female aspect of their house. At the same time, the necessity of a return derives from the fact that the very life of that which issues forth depends upon a continued acknowledgment of its source. This is achieved through the reciprocal movement of male valuables, which travel back along the lines that trace the course of lifeblood to its "place" (*waan*) of origin. In this sense, Mauss was right: to fail to reciprocate is to invite death (1967:11).

Yet, in a later section of the work, entitled "The Three Obligations: Giving, Receiving, Repaying," Mauss formulated the deathly consequences of a failure to reciprocate in another way — one which stressed the hierarchical implications of the gift and its return. The impulse to give derives from the precept that a man can demonstrate his authority, persona, and rank "only if he can prove that he is favourably regarded by the spirits, that he possesses fortune and that he is possessed by it. The only way to demonstrate his fortune is by expending it to the humiliation of others, by putting them 'in the shadow of his name'" (1967:37–38). It is therefore not accumulation, but rather prestation, that establishes one's identity and status (Leach 1965:142–43). Moreover, the gift establishes the status of the giver at the same time that it effects the subordination and humiliation of the receiver.

In face of this subordination, the receiver is obligated to receive. For in refusing the gift, one "would 'lose the weight' of one's name by admitting defeat in advance" (Mauss 1967:39). But in accepting the gift, "you do so because you mean to take up the challenge and prove that you are not unworthy" (1967:40). Thus, to accept the gift is to take up the challenge to reassert a separate identity, to counter the effects of subordination.

This challenge is answered by the repayment of the gift. It is here that it becomes evident what the consequences of the gift are for the receiver, should he fail to repay. "The sanction for the obligation to repay is enslavement for debt. . . . The person who cannot return a loan or potlatch loses his rank and even his status of a free man" (1967:41). That is, the person is absolutely subordinated and completely incorporated by the giver, whose challenge he has failed to answer.

Putting the two parts of Mauss's analysis together, and reading them through Tanimbarese material, it is possible to formulate their conception of exchange. To give is indeed to give a part of one's self. But one does not thereby alienate that part of the self, as we might see it. Rather, one encompasses the receiver as a subordinate part of oneself. To receive is to acknowledge the threat inherent in the gift—the potential for complete and absolute subordination. And, to repay is to answer the challenge, to effect the redemption of a separate identity. Should the receiver fail to reciprocate, he will remain permanently incorporated as a subordinate part of the giver. By Tanimbarese logic, this meant enslavement.

This dynamic of exchange—the tension between encompassment and separation—is conceptualized in terms of gender. Exchange involves a movement of gendered parts of an androgynous whole. Wife- and life-givers become a male source when they give, or exteriorize, the female part—women and female valuables—of the prior androgynous unity of their house. Similarly, wife- and life-takers become female not only because they receive women and the lifeblood they bear and are thereby encompassed as a female offshoot, but also because they give, or exteriorize, the male part—the male valuables—of their house.

Moreover, the female valuables given by the wife-givers and the male valuables given by the wife-takers are themselves icons of the processes they are meant to engender. For male valuables speak of severance and the permanence of houses, whereas female valuables speak of relation and encompassment. Their exchange negotiates the tension between these two forces that is necessary for the continuity of life.

This chapter seeks to explore the Tanimbarese system of exchange, and, in particular, the manner in which the tension between encompassment and separation is expressed in the qualities of valuables, themselves; in the nature of male and female action in the world; and, in the general character of exchange itself.

The Relative Qualities of Valuables

From early on, observers of Indonesian societies have noted the pervasiveness with which gender has been used to differentiate activities, social groups, and the goods and valuables used in exchanges between social groups.[1] In this regard Tanimbar is no exception: here everything, or nearly everything, has a gender.

There are very few unisex activities in Tanimbar: most activities are either male (*brana*) or female (*vata*). Men hunt and do the deep sea fishing, clear and burn off the gardens, and make palmwine. They build houses and boats, negotiate marriage exchanges, hunt heads (or used to), and, on occasion, still engage in warfare. Women, on the other hand, fish on the reef and do the planting, weeding, and harvesting of gardens. They carry food and water, cook, take care of children, plait baskets, and weave textiles.

Like the social groups involved in exchanges, so too all valuables are given a gender. In everyday life and on festive occasions, "female" wife-takers give the products of male activity — meat, fish, and palmwine — to their "male" wife-givers, while the latter reciprocate with the products of female activity — garden produce and betel nut. Similarly, in the more formal prestations, the gifts of the female wife-takers consist of male valuables, which include a particular kind of earring, gold breast pendants, elephant tusks, and swords. These are reciprocated by the gifts of the male wife-givers, which consist of female valuables and include another type of earring, bead necklaces, shell armbands, and textiles.

An analysis of the contrasting qualities of male and female valuables reveals much about the nature of what Tanimbarese conceive to be male and female qualities, as well as about the processes they see to be integral to the meaning of exchange.[2] I suggest that each type of valuable can be paired, conceptually, with an opposite-gender counterpart. Tanimbarese have not explicitly formulated it for me in this way, nor have they characterized the differences in quite the way I set out. Nevertheless, the values

1. See, for instance, Drabbe 1923; van Ossenbruggen 1930, 1935; van Wouden 1968 (1935); Fischer 1938; and van der Kroef (1954) for early examples of discussions of male and female categorizations.
2. Although the differences in various grades of each type of valuable will be discussed, the more political aspects of the evaluation of valuables will not be analyzed here. Moreover, while this is an analysis of valuables that, in the context of affinal exchanges, are categorized as male and female, it is not an examination of what men and women wear. Not only is there a whole range of other decorations that were formerly worn by men and women (Drabbe 1940:20–33) but some male valuables (breast pendants and, formerly, earrings) are occasionally worn by women, just as some female valuables (primarily textiles) are worn by men.

that are considered in connection with the qualities of valuables discussed here resonate with those found in many other aspects of Tanimbarese social life, and they will be recognized as part of a more general pattern found in other eastern Indonesian societies as well.

Perhaps the most easily contrasted set of male and female valuables is that of earrings: *loran*, which are thought of as male earrings, and *kmena*, which are thought of as female earrings. As with all valuables, there are many different grades of both *loran* and *kmena*: some are very fine, antique pieces with names and histories; others are newer, nameless, and rather coarse in their construction. Gold earrings, of both types, are always valued more highly than silver or mixed species. *Loran* (photographs 8.1–8.3) are all of one basic form: pear-shaped, with an opening slit through the center that is sometimes filled with a swatch of red European cloth, which is said to make the metal "flash like lightning" (*nfitik*). They also have small appendages or "eruptions" (*kamoa*) that protrude from the top, the base, and the sides — in the latter case these are called "wings" (*manin*). Although *loran* may appear to take an essentially female form, nevertheless, when compared with female earrings, their salient characteristics are more their solidity, density, and weight than any particular graphic image they might evoke. This becomes evident when they are placed beside female earrings, *kmena* — especially the most valuable type, "shield" earrings (*kmena ngelya*) — which are a dance of filigreed curvilinear forms composed of thin gold or silver wires (photographs 8.2–8.4). The airy, light, and open qualities of the "shield" *kmena* are only slightly muted in the second type — the "stone" or "pebble" earring (*kmena vatu*), which is formed by an elegant clustering of small dots of gold or silver around an open circle of wire. In addition, some highly prized *kmena* have a string of beads (*kmena ni lean*) that connects the two earrings of the pair and is worn across the woman's back (photograph 8.4). In place of the solid density of the male earrings, female earrings present a composition of light, swirling small bits of metal that dovetail into and around one another. The fluid and connecting qualities of female earrings are further accentuated by the string of beads that joins the two earrings to one another.

Necklaces also come in two basic forms: male breast pendants, which are made of solid, hammered, or cast gold — and, in fact, are simply called "gold" (*masa*); and female bead necklaces (*marumat*). The breast pendants most often represent a human face (or full human figure), alone or in conjunction with horn, boat, or moon motifs (photographs 8.1 and 8.5). But they are also sometimes found in the form of a simple, circular, flat gold disk, a golden kris handle, or in the shape of some animal, such as a turtle (photograph 8.2). The most valuable gold pendants boast a large gold link chain (*wika sitana*) and clasps, which are said to represent "shrimps" (*sngu-*

Photograph 8.1   Drabbe's photograph (taken in the 1920s or 1930s) showing a man wearing a pair of male earrings, a gold breast pendant, a shell necklace (worn by old men), and a textile as a headdress. (Drabbe 1940: fig. 48)

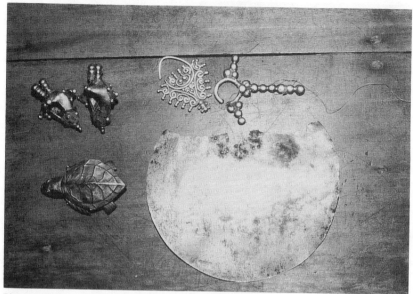

Photograph 8.2   Clockwise from top left: a pair of male earrings; an odd-matched pair of female earrings including a "shield" *kmena* and a "pebble" *kmena*; a disc-shaped gold breast pendant; and a gold piece in the shape of a turtle.

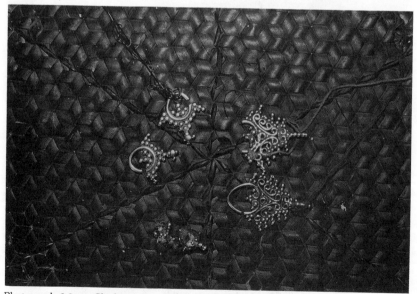

Photograph 8.3   Clockwise from top left: a pair of "pebble" *kmena*; a pair of "shield" *kmena*; a small pair of male earrings.

Photograph 8.4　　A woman from Sera wearing a pair of female earrings ("shield" *kmena*) linked by a strand of beads, a female necklace, a pair of shell armbands, and a sarong of the *bakan inelak* type with flag and half-moon motifs.

ran) (photograph 8.5). *Marumat* are made of imported Venetian glass beads or, most often, of beads made from sard, a variety of reddish-orange chalcedony, known in Indonesia as *muti-salah*. They should be distinguished from the simple, single-strand bead necklace, called a "tie for the neck" (*kakeat rela*), formerly worn by both men and women (photograph 8.6). *Marumat*, which are far more valuable, are composed of double or triple strands of beads, joined together at regular intervals by a larger bead (*knaa ila'a*) or a thin tube of gold. From the center of the necklace there hangs a triangular mass (*laun*) of beads and fragments of gold that have been woven together (photograph 8.4). The most valuable of *marumat* are those known as *ungrela*, which have an additional long strand of beads — called a "tail" (*kikurn*) — that hangs down the back of the woman. Whereas male necklaces are of solid gold, often of a single integral piece or at least all of the same material, female necklaces are made up of tiny pieces of heterogeneous materials — beads and gold — strung together into two or three strands that are alternately united and separated.

The third pair of valuables to be contrasted include elephant tusks (*lela*), which are considered male, and shell armbands (*sislau*), which are considered female. Obviously, an elephant tusk is long and hard — a heavy, penetrating sort of object. Tusks are valued in accordance with their length:

Photograph 8.5   Four gold breast pendants. Three of the pendants boast gold link chains, and two of these have "shrimp" figures at the end of the chains.

Photograph 8.6   Men with swords and spears (photographer and date unknown). They are wearing male earrings and single strands of beads. The two men on the right are also wearing chestcloths. (Photographic Archives of the Royal Tropical Institute)

the longest ones (*lel refa*), which measure a full arm span of a man (or more) are most highly prized. Others, which measure from the fingertips of one arm to the wrist (*lel naran did tanuvur*) or elbow (*lel ti'i nala*) of the other, or which only reach the trunk of the body and thus divide a person in half (*lel daa narut ita*), are less valued.[3] The female shell armbands come in pairs, each consisting of ten shell rings that were, formerly, cut by Tanimbarese women from a variety of *Conus* shell, rounded and polished, and then lashed together along a thin bamboo lath (photographs 8.4 and 8.7). Again, there are various grades of armbands. The most valuable, called *sislau vetit*, fit on the upper arms of a woman and have a dark ring (*diti*) made from coconut shell or thick Venetian glass added at the top. Other, less valuable sets have no black rings or fit only on the lower forearms (*sislau uvur*), or on the arms of young girls. The contrast between elephant tusks and shell armbands is evident. The tusks are single, uncut pieces, whereas the armbands are a composite of numerous rings, each cut from a different shell. The tusks are dense and penetrating; the armbands are open and encircling.

The characteristics implicit in the contrast between tusks and arm-

3. Cf. Maxwell's (1981) comments on the role of elephant tusks in Flores.

Photograph 8.7   Titi Ne'i Balak of Kamatubun, Sera, is shown assembling a pair of shell armbands in March 1979.

bands become even more evident in considering the next pair of valuables: swords (*suruk*) and cloth (*eman-bakan*, "loincloth-sarong"). Even if Tanimbarese may not know what a tusk is to an elephant, they do know what a sword is to a man (photograph 8.6). People say the swords were of "Portugis" origin, although there were never any Portuguese in Tanimbar (see chapter 3). What this means is that they are extremely old and, indeed, the few swords left in Tanimbar are such antique pieces that they are no longer used in exchange, but rather kept as heirloom valuables. A sword is a long, hard, sharp metal weapon. It is used to kill people and to sever heads from bodies: it is, in short, an instrument of death. Whereas swords are the epitome of fierce inflexibility, cloth is the epitome of softness and pliability. Swords are meant to penetrate and sever; cloth is meant to encircle and bind.

All indigenous textiles in Tanimbar are woven by women and are considered to be female valuables — despite the fact that some kinds are worn by men.[4] Of those worn by women there are presently two major types. The first is a sarong (*bakan*) made from two tubes of cloth that are subsequently joined together at the selvages. The resulting cylindrical form is from four to six feet long. There are three main kinds of *bakan*: the most highly valued is the *bakan mnanat*, followed by *bakan maran*, and finally *bakan inelak*.[5] They are differentiated by the relative distribution of the warp ikat and colored bands that run through the indigo-blue or soot-black ground (McKinnon 1989). The second type of textile worn by women is a latter-day invention — a small piece of cloth known as a *shal* (from the Dutch *sjaal*, "shawl" or "scarf"), which is worn over the shoulder. In contrast to the *bakan*, which is predominantly dark in color, the *shal* is woven in "living color" — the brighter and more fluorescent, the better. Sarongs are still worn today, primarily on ritual and festive occasions (photograph 8.8). In full dress, a woman will wear one *bakan* as a skirt (folded over at the waist, and secured with a cloth tie), one or two *bakan* draped diagonally across the shoulders, and sometimes another wrapped

4. Using the Yamdenan language, Drabbe (1940:187) notes that the wife-takers are obliged to "cut palmwine" (*raflait*) and the wife-givers are obliged to "give loincloths-sarongs" (*ral umbin-tais*). In this, it is evident that textiles worn by both men and women were traditionally included within the general category of female goods given by the wife-givers. Today, as Western store-bought clothes increasingly replace indigenous woven textiles in at least some exchanges, the prestation of cloth is occasionally referred to, in the Fordatan language, as "pants-shirts" (*kadar-ravit*). Again, it includes both men's and women's clothing and remains a category of female valuables.

5. A few people I spoke with suggested that, in the past, these three major types of sarong were worn by women who belonged, respectively, to the class of nobles, commoners, and slaves. There was, however, no general agreement on this point. Moreover, although this may have once been the practice, it certainly is not so today.

around the hips. Often the modern-day *shal* replaces the sarong draped across the shoulders. The two forms of textiles traditionally worn by men are a loincloth (*eman*) and a chestcloth (*sinuun*). The *eman* is a narrow, nine-foot-long strip of plain indigo-dyed cloth embellished with ikat designs — and often red cloth appliqué work as well as small shells — at the very ends (photograph 8.9). Loincloths were woven by Tanimbarese women and also imported from the southwestern islands of Babar and Luang (Drabbe 1940:21). They are sometimes worn today on ritual occasions, but rarely in the traditional manner. The chestcloths, which have practically disappeared, are composed of two woven panels joined together along their selvages; they are considerably shorter and broader than the loincloths (Drabbe 1940:22) (photograph 8.6).

Since the textiles traditionally worn by men are no longer woven by Tanimbarese women or imported, the few that still exist are generally kept in houses as heirloom valuables and are rarely circulated in exchanges. However, the women's sarongs of all three types (as well as the shoulder cloth) are still being woven. In fact, textile production is quite active, partially because cloth is an important valuable used in marriage exchanges, but also because it is the only valuable, of any type, for which there is an on-going supply.

Photograph 8.8   A circle of women from the villages of Temin and Weratan, Sera, dancing in the village of Latdalam in August 1980. The picture shows a variety of Tanimbarese sarongs.

Photograph 8.9   Men and women from the houses that make up the Lolat Ila'a Sera gathered in Laiyaman Watutma'an's house in Temin on March 12, 1979, to tell me about the Great Row. For the occasion, the men dressed in loincloths.

The composite, binding, and encompassing qualities of female textiles is evident not simply in the obvious way that one must weave together a great number of yarns to make a textile or that the resulting cloth encircles human bodies. It is also evident in a less obvious way: that is, in the way that Tanimbarese women construct the ikat motifs with which they decorate their sarongs (for an analysis of this, see McKinnon 1989). These motifs are built up from a multitude of tiny dots that are strung together, or spaced out, as if they were beads on a necklace. If one thinks, for instance, of Sumbanese ikat motifs — comprised of large, integral figures of humans, plants, and animals — and contrasts these with Tanimbarese motifs, the particular logic of the latter becomes clearer. Tanimbarese women string together a number of beadlike dots to create fairly simple and abstract forms — flags, half-moons, fish, lizards, and such. Often, these simple forms are then strung together into larger, composite images: a double-headed fish, for instance, with a flag on its head. This stringing together of dots sometimes dominates the piece, so that it is overcome in a mesh (actually called a *fuat*, or "fishnet") of dots, which, though difficult to read from close up, presents a striking image from a distance. The contrast between the hard, deadly, cutting edge of men's swords, and the binding, composite quality of women's textiles could not be more striking. This is doubly so: for not only in the weaving, itself, but also in the creation of the ikat motifs, women string together many discrete bits, form the relationships between one thing and another, and tie them into a significant pattern of relations.

The contrast between what Tanimbarese characterize as male and female valuables can thus be drawn along a number of dimensions. First of all, male valuables are hard metal and ivory objects: they are solid, dense, and heavy. Female valuables—even when they are made of hard substances—deny that hardness, solidity, and density. They are, on the contrary, light, filigreed, and open forms. Second, male valuables are of one piece, the epitome of singleness and permanence as well as of inflexibility and immobility. Female valuables, however, are pieced together from many elements. They speak more of multiplicity, flexibility, mobility, and, perhaps, impermanence. The density and weight of male earrings contrast with the light, delicate, and open filigree patterns of female earrings. The unity of a man's gold breast pendant finds its counterpart in the multiplicity of beads and small bits of gold that are strung together into a woman's necklace, just as the solidity of an elephant tusk or a sword contrasts with the numerous open rings that are lashed together to form shell armbands (not to mention the multiplicity of yarns that must be woven together to form a finished textile). Finally the long, pointed, and cutting qualities of male valuables such as tusks and swords complement the encircling, receptive, and binding qualities of women's necklaces, armbands, and tubes of woven cloth.[6]

In looking at the contrast between swords and cloth—or any pair of male and female valuables—we can understand the ways in which they can be seen to epitomize the most essential characteristics of what it means to be male and female in Tanimbar. The outright sexual symbolism is evident enough. But there are several other values that are expressed through these valuables. One is the relation between life and death, which will be dealt with below.

Another is the relationship between permanent entities, on the one hand, and those that relate them—that make the ties that bind—on the other. Like the valuables that speak of their qualities, males come to occupy single, permanent, and fixed places in the world: they remain in the houses to which they are born. The place of females in their natal house, however, is impermanent—for they are destined to move to the houses

6. Speaking of the Atoni of Timor, Schulte Nordholt (1980:239–40) comments: "Hard, sharp, and pointed objects are symbols of manliness. Like the horned buffalo and the metal gifts that wife-taking houses give, they are classified as male objects. Similarly a woman offers a betel and areca nut to the warriors. In this offering of *puah manus*, the areca nuts (*puah*) are female and the tapering betel leaves (*manus*) are male."

of their husbands upon marriage.[7] In contrast to males, then, the place of females is always shifting and composite: their role — like the lashings of armshells, the threads of a necklace, or the yarns of a textile — is to bind together a multiplicity of discrete houses through the encircling flow of the lifeblood they bear.[8]

Yet, as stressed throughout, neither the fixity of men within houses nor the movement of women between houses is automatically assured. Both must be created through exchange — through the play of the forces of encompassment and separation. Thus the gift of a woman and female valuables encompasses the wife-taker as a subordinate female aspect of the wife-giver's house. The valuables that move from wife-giver to wife-taker express and effect this encompassment in their encircling, binding, relational, and composite qualities. They stress the continuity of the relation between the source and issue of life — a relation that is based in the unseverable quality of blood. For this relation to continue, however, the wife-takers must answer the challenge of absolute subordination and, formerly, potential enslavement. They must redeem their separate identity and effect the continuity and permanence of this separate identity. This they do with bridewealth prestations that, in both their names and their qualities, express and effect a semblance of severance. It is no surprise that bridewealth prestations are named after weapons: "bow," "spear," and "sword." Nor is it a surprise that male valuables refer to the qualities of hardness, permanence, and singleness, which the wife-takers wish to achieve for their house; or that they refer to actions of killing and severance, which are necessary in order to achieve a separate, enduring identity for their house.[9]

In this way, the qualities of valuables speak of more than just the categorical differentiation of male and female. They also speak of the man-

7. It should be remembered that this differentiation between males and females does not necessarily correspond to that between men and women, for men who are "lifted" into other houses are likewise considered female, just as matrilaterally affiliated men are considered part of the female aspect of the house to which they have affiliated.

8. Note Adams' reflection (1980:220) that "the Sumbanese consider textiles, as they do women in a clan household, impermanent. Thus, cloths provide the feminine counterpart to masculine metal goods, which are regarded as permanent." Similarly, Traube discusses the "crucial distinction between the lasting, perduring, 'hard' character of agnatic connections and the more perishable, 'soft' connections established through women" (1980a:98). The former find their representation "in metal objects which mythological traditions trace back to the bones of Father Heaven" (1980a:99).

9. It should be noted that this contrast between the severing qualities of male bridewealth prestations and the encompassing qualities of female counter-prestations — represented in the opposition between weapons and cloth — is very common and not limited to this area. See, for example, Wagner 1967 and Weiner 1985. Battaglia's (1983:301) differentiation between individuation and corporation is also relevant here.

ner in which encompassment and separation are part of a single process of exchange, in which each depends upon the other for its realization, and for the realization of life.

Male and Female Production

The relation between the severance implied by male valuables and the encompassment implied by female valuables is evident more generally in the nature of male and female productivity. Here, however, the contrast is coded in terms of work that is carried out under conditions of heat and results in death as opposed to work that is carried out in coolness and results in life.

The production of male goods and valuables specifically requires the use of "hot wood and roots" (*aa-wa'ar ngnea*) — that is, hot, magical substances — to effect the death of a living being, which is itself then permeated with heat such that it must be cooled before it is converted into an object that has exchange value. The production of female goods and valuables, on the contrary, either does not involve the use of hot magical substances or specifically requires a ritual process that cools (*nfangridin*) the object concerned and creates a cool (*radridin*) condition in which the growth of a living thing is possible. In order to clarify the difference in the two modes of production, it will be useful, first, to compare the processes whereby women make textiles and shell armbands with those whereby men make male earrings and cut elephant tusks, and, then, to compare the processes involved in gardening and hunting.

Neither Drabbe's informants nor mine ever mentioned the use of "hot wood and roots" by women during the course of weaving a textile (photograph 8.10). In the past, a woman might have given the ancestors an offering of rice, a knife, and an armband when she undertook to weave her first sarong, and thereafter might have offered them a betel quid upon the completion of each piece, or during the weaving of one, if the yarns became sticky (Drabbe 1940:126–27). But these offerings were meant to facilitate the ease and smoothness with which the weaving was carried out. They had nothing to do with the creation of a hot condition or, conversely, with the cooling of an object permeated with heat. Lacking a condition of heat, weaving is an activity that is intrinsically cool.

The situation is quite different in the process of smelting gold (and other metals), which was carried out by men to produce male earrings and other objects. The only type of male valuable ever actually produced in Tanimbar was a particular form of male earring known as "our" *loran* (*loran dida*). Although male earrings were, on the whole, obtained in trade from outside Tanimbar, this inferior model was formerly produced

Photograph 8.10   Nelangvutu Wearmasubun weaving outside her son's house in Awear, July 1980.

locally, from foreign coins, by men who possessed the inherited right to practice metal work. In this work, which is now only very rarely performed, small ancestor images (called *kukuwe* in Yamdenan and *walut* in Fordatan) were used to invoke the ancestors — both in order to produce the required heat for smelting and to protect the producer from the heat of the object once it had been made (Drabbe 1940:112). Thus Drabbe states that the smelting of metal "was a trade practiced by only a few, [sic] For it, a man had his *kukuwes*, soul images, without whose help the hottest fire could smelt no gold" (1940:112).

Not only did the production of earrings involve a situation of intense heat, it also involved the "killing" of the gold. "Just as in the working of an elephant tusk, one speaks of killing, *rfen mase* [Yamdenan: "they kill the gold"], and if one kills something, it is said, one must take care that the ancestors help so that the heat of the object killed does one no harm" (Drabbe 1940:112). In contrast to weaving, the production of male earrings is clearly seen to involve a process in which the heat of the fire kills the gold and creates an object whose heat — but for the protection rendered by the ancestors — is dangerous for the person who has caused the death of the gold.

The mention of elephant tusks is of interest, for they were occasionally sawed into armrings and bracelets by men, and the process was conducted in a very different manner from the cutting of the *Conus* shell by women in the production of female shell armbands. Armbands are no longer made in Tanimbar, but even from Drabbe's notes concerning their production (1940:134–35), there is no indication that the process might be conceived to involve the killing of the shell, or that it might create or take place in a condition permeated by heat and danger. In fact, Drabbe's commentary seems to indicate that no ritual mediation whatsoever was involved in the making of shell armbands.

By contrast, a rather complex series of offerings made to Ubila'a and the ancestors accompanied the cutting of an elephant tusk. Although the resulting ivory rings were never used as exchange valuables (but rather were worn by men as adornments), the production of these rings still provides a good example of the way men work in the world. Drabbe states that the tusk itself was known as *fenreu* — the ritual language word for a noble man — and that the process of cutting the tusk into rings was called, literally, "they kill the tusk" (*rfen lela*) (1940:135). Furthermore, when the men cut off the wide end of the tusk — which is too thin to make rings — it was said: "they sever the head [of the tusk/man]" (*rtetak ulun*) (1940:135). Before the commencement of the work, the owners of the tusk went on a pig hunt to provide pork for an offering to Ubila'a and the ancestors. A small and a large rice cake were made: the former was offered to the ancestor images of the man who did the cutting, and the latter was offered to Ubila'a together with an invocation for help in the cutting that was to begin (1940:136). The cutter invoked his ancestors in the following way: "if I go to kill this man, make it so that he bewitches neither me nor the owners of the tusk, cool us off with coconut and candlenut and also the owners of the tusk, so that we may not become sick and that we may finish the work, you my ancestors there" (Drabbe 1940:136). Here, again, it is evident that the killing of the tusk involved a process characterized by intense heat and danger, from which the workers could only be protected by the use of cooling substances and the intercession of the ancestors.

The offerings were repeated at the beginning of each new day of work and again once the work had been completed. During the entire process, the workmen were accompanied by the beat of a drum and a gong, as well as by the singing and dancing of a group of men assembled at the spot. The words of the songs reported by Drabbe do not refer to head-hunting, but simply to the process of cutting the tusk (1940:137). One is nevertheless tempted to draw the comparison between this dance and the one that followed the taking of heads in warfare. Moreover, at the time of the final offering made to Ubila'a and the ancestors, the man who cut the tusk also made an offering to the sawdust, not unlike the way men made an offering to the heads captured in war. Thus, Drabbe notes that when the cutter fed the sawdust, he said:

> "You sawdust of the elephant tusk, I sweep you up now, I have killed you already, and you have died, I have divided you up completely; if I feed you rice cake and pork now and give you [something] to drink, if I sweep you away outside the village wall, outside the fence, then do not desire to bewitch me — neither me nor the members of my house nor the owners of the tusk, you man there."
>
> Then he takes a little handful of the sawdust, goes with it to the village wall, invokes God there, and counting to nine, on the count of nine he throws the sawdust away saying: remain sitting here forever, so that you become tired of it. (1940:138)

Like a head captured in warfare, the sawdust of the beheaded tusk was fed and then thrown outside the village wall, where it was asked to remain contentedly and to refrain from seeking vengeance for its death.

The productive action of men is always carried out with the help of "wood and roots," or an ancestor image, both of which are considered to be "hot" (*ngnea*). Indeed, the very conditions of production are hot and dangerous, for they involve the killing of the object. On account of its death, that object is, itself, considered hot. The heat and anger of the object killed can only be cooled, and rendered harmless, through ritual mediation and through the protective intercession of the ancestors and Ubila'a.

By contrast, because women do not work through the agency of "hot" magical substances, and their productive activity does not require the killing of the object concerned, both their work and the resulting object are considered to be inherently cool. More generally, the heat and danger of men's action in the world derives from its focus upon the processes of killing, separation, and division. The coolness of women's action in the world, on the other hand, derives from its focus upon the processes of uniting, encircling, and binding.

Configurations of Life and Death

Although death is produced in an atmosphere of heat and through the agency of men, it cannot be said that life (and the coolness it requires) is produced solely through the agency of women. Rather, what is productive of life requires the union of male and female. The contrast between processes that result in death and those that result in life can be seen most clearly in connection with hunting and gardening. The elaborate rituals involved in hunting and gardening that are reported by Drabbe are, for the most part, no longer practiced, at least not in Awear. Furthermore, an analysis of these complex rituals would require several chapters in itself. Here, I only want to note what conditions are necessary for success in hunting and gardening.

Hunting is, again, an exclusively male activity that takes place under conditions of heat and danger, requires the use of "hot wood and roots" and appeals to the ancestors, and results in the death of a living being (photograph 8.11). Because men primarily hunt pigs, it is important to understand something of the complicated relation between men and pigs. Besides normal pigs, there exist other kinds of pigs that are manifestations of souls and spirits. It has already been seen that the soul (*ngraan*) of a person who is near death often wanders about in the forest and may assume the form of a pig. If the soul-pig is shot by a hunter, it signifies the death of the person concerned; but if the soul-pig escapes the spear of the hunter, then the person will continue to live. Liana masters (*aa warat duan*) — tree spirits of the forest — also often transform themselves into pigs, which may be shot by hunters. As inhabitants of the forest depths, pigs and hunters participate in a world where the lines between spirit and flesh, life and death are fluid. Where souls, tree spirits, and death are concerned, the situation is conceived of as one imbued with heat and danger.

Men who enter such a world arm themselves with the "hot wood and

Photograph 8.11   A group of men from Awear gathered together just before setting out to hunt wild pigs for a feast that celebrated the opening of their large yam garden in August 1979.

roots" that they have inherited from their agnatic ancestors—who may have obtained them originally through exploits with tree spirits or even the corpses of infants. Certain men's hot magical substances enable them to see the soul-image of a human as it transforms into a pig and obliges them to attempt to shoot it. They also enable a hunter to compete successfully against other hunters in drawing a pig into his range and ensuring that his shot will be true and kill the pig.

After a pig has been killed, a ceremony called "the dog's feast" (*yaha ni fafa'an*), or "the dead's [ancestor's] feast" (*nitu ni fafa'an*), is carried out. This offering feast (like that given when a sea turtle is caught) is one of the few activities in which women are strictly forbidden to take part. For this ceremony, the pig's taboo parts (*vavu ni malmoli*)—the internal organs, fat, and the meat from the central strip that runs from the neck to the belly of the pig, all of which are considered "hot"—are boiled and eaten by all the adult men who happen to be around at the time. An offering is made to the ancestors, who are invoked and beseeched to help in whatever hunting endeavors may be undertaken in the future. The rest of the pig may then be divided and eaten by anyone without harm.

The productiveness of men depends upon their entrance into a world that is hot, upon the effectiveness of their hot wood and roots, and upon their realization of the death of a living thing. The heat of the object so produced must be isolated from women, who may be endangered by it, and who may, also, cool the effectiveness of the men's hot wood and roots, such that they will not be successful in the hunt thereafter. Furthermore, by isolating the hot, taboo parts — by making of them an offering feast to the ancestors — the men ensure their effectiveness in other hunts, at the same time that they render the rest of the pig free from the hot, tabooed parts and convert it into a cooled object that has exchange value.

In contrast with effectiveness in the hunt, success in gardening depends upon a condition of coolness that fosters the growth of plants. In general, it is thought that plants will only grow when the "earth [is] cool" (*lanuun radridin*). This coolness arrives when the "west [winds] begin to blow" (*varat mulai naluan*) in November or December and bring the cooling rains that relieve the heat of the long dry season, which has caused the garden crops to wither and die off.

Drabbe's description of the planting ritual for yam gardens shows nicely the manner in which the coolness of the garden land was brought about.

> When the planting is finished, a man goes to the middle of the garden, where a little place has been left free. There he makes three planting holes in a little circle, in which are planted, respectively, an *ubi* [yam], a *keladi* [taro], and a *kembili* [another kind of tuber]. In the middle of this, he sets the planting stick in the ground with a top of a kind of tree, which is called *fndirin*, [Yamdenan] literally cold-maker, and he lays a candlenut next to it. Then he says: "O God, I have now cooled off my garden already with *fndirin*, make it so that there come into it fruits that I can eat in the dry season." With his wife, he now takes a meal near what is called the *fini* ([Yamdenan] seedlings), with which the whole is indicated, throws a small piece of food for God, a small piece for the dead [ancestors], then takes with his wife a betel quid and also gives a small piece to God and the dead. At the harvest, the fruits that originated from the *fini* are kept apart and eaten only by the man and woman and their children. (1940:75–76).

The objective of gardening — the generation of living things, the growth of plants — is achieved through the medium of cooling substances and requires the union of male and female actors, and of male and female goods. In opposition to hunting rituals, where men alone are the actors, in the garden ritual noted above a man and his wife must both be present and eat together. In fact, gardening rituals are always accompanied by a hunt and, although Drabbe does not mention it in the above passage, it is not unreasonable to suspect that the meal the couple ate at the end of the ritual included both pork and tubers.

Certainly this was the case in the first fruit harvest feasts I witnessed on the occasions when the large communal yam gardens (*arin*) were opened in Awear. When these gardens—in which anywhere from five to fifteen households may have a plot—are first harvested near the beginning of August, a thanksgiving feast called "feed the dead [ancestors]" (*fa'an nitu*) is held. On the day the feast is to take place, all the men who have a garden plot on that particular piece of land go hunting together for wild pig while the women begin to harvest the yams and taro of the new gardens. For each garden plot, five cooked yams and fifteen cooked taro must be contributed to the communal feast. Eventually the men return, and if a pig has been captured, it is slaughtered and boiled. The cooked pork, yams, and taro will be shared out equally among all those present and the men and women will eat together of a meal made up of foods that are categorically male and female—and that are the result of male and female modes of working in the world. A similar feast takes place for the gardens located in the lowlands along the coast (photograph 8.12). But there it is called "they give recompense for the land/earth" (*rarean lanuun*), rather than "feed the dead [ancestors]," and fish is usually substituted for pork. In other respects, the feast is the same.

Such a feast, celebrating the successful growth and fruition of a gar-

Photograph 8.12   A group of men and women from Awear held a feast to "give recompense for the land" at the harvest of their lowland gardens in 1980.

den crop, contrasts sharply with that which celebrates the conclusion of
a successful hunt, in which men alone participate to the exclusion of women,
and in which only male food (pork and, more specifically, the taboo parts
of the pig) are eaten to the exclusion of female food (garden produce).

What I am suggesting here is that death involves the denial or absence
of sexual complementarity, whereas growth and life explicitly requires the
complementarity of male and female. The process that is productive of
death always turns in on itself — it pits heat against heat, man against man
(or pig, as the case may be). The process that is productive of life always
turns toward an other, which is complementary in nature: it requires the
union of male and female as well as the union of objects that have been
generated out of heat and death with objects that have been generated
through coolness and growth.

The Shape of Reciprocity

Like gardening, the object of the exchange of valuables between affines is the production of life, and this is accomplished through
the complementary movement of male and female valuables. Like gardening, the production of life through exchange requires the union of male
objects that have been generated out of heat and death — and that speak
of penetration, severance, and homogeneity — with female objects that
have been generated through coolness and growth — and speak of encompassment, relation, and the binding together of heterogeneous elements.
This union of male and female objects is enacted in the many instances
of exchange that take place between wife-givers and wife-takers.

Once an affinal relationship has been initiated, a system of reciprocity
is established between the wife-givers and wife-takers (and their descendants) that is not limited to exchanges focused upon marriage. The on-
going reciprocity that characterizes the relationship between the two sides
becomes manifest not only in the little exchanges that occur from day to
day, but also in the larger exchanges that accompany almost every event —
such as life-cycle rituals, the thanksgiving feasts given on the occasion of
a person's recovery from a severe illness, the raising and roofing of a house,
and the death of a person. Since all such exchanges follow a similar pattern, I will use the roofing of a house as an example to demonstrate the
manner in which they are carried out.

At the time when a man roofs a new house, he will request the at-
tendance of this *dua* (including both his *ura-memi* and his "house masters"),
his *ura-ava* and his *lolat*. His *dua* will be charged with bringing a specific
number of packets of cooked rice (*tufat*), the number of which depends
upon the scope of the event. If, for instance, he asks each of his immediate

dua to bring five hundred packets, those *dua* may then divide the responsibility between their own *dua*, such that each will bring one hundred
packets, and this responsibility may even be further subdivided. In addition, his *dua* will bring female valuables. His *ura-ava* and *lolat*, on the
other hand, will be required to bring palmwine with a "cork" (*snibi*) of
Rp. 500–1,000, as well as male valuables. They will, depending upon the
scope of the event, call upon their own *ura-ava* and *lolat* to bring palmwine and male valuables.

As the day progresses and the male elder-younger same-sex siblings
of the man and his wife roof the house, his *ura-ava* will begin to arrive,
bringing their palmwine, money, and male valuables, all of which will be
duly noted down. If they are slow to come, a man—called "he who sits
by the hearth ash" (*ia ndok kfuan*)—begins going about calling out the
names of those *ura-ava* and *lolat* who still have to make their appearance.
In the meantime, the *dua* will begin arriving as well, with their female
valuables, and their wives will bring strings of rice packets, or even tumpline baskets heaped full of them. Eventually the accumulated rice packets
begin to form veritable mountains and hang from the rafters in great
masses. All that is brought by the man's *dua* is also carefully noted down.
At one point, one of his *dua* will "raise a flag" (*ntawak sa'ir*) from the
rafters of the house. This flag will consist of at least several indigenous
woven sarongs. Sometime later, one of the *ura-ava* or *lolat* will lower this
flag and receive the sarongs in exchange for an appropriate male valuable,
which is given to the one who raised the flag in the first place.

During this time, the female elder-younger same-sex siblings of the
man and his wife will be in the kitchen cooking and preparing food, which
together they have contributed to make a feast. This usually consists of
a large portion of rice, which is topped with a dash of vegetable and a
small portion of either fish or pork. Each woman will have supplied a specific amount of rice, vegetables, and spices, and their husbands will have
supplied the pork or fish for the meal. (In addition, the man's *ura-ava*
should bring whatever fish or pork may be available to them.) Everyone
who has put in their appearance at the event will be given a heaping plate-
ful of food. The hosts and their elder-younger same-sex siblings must also
see to it that there is an ample supply of betel nut and tobacco on hand
for their guests.

This is the occasion upon which the man's *dua* make the final payment—called the "head [or main portion] of the house" (*rahan ulun*)—to
the master carpenter whose chief responsibility it was to build the house.
This payment must consist of a valuable (any category will do) that is
equal in value to a bow or spear portion of a woman's bridewealth—that
is, a valuable of some worth, although it need not necessarily be a named

valuable. In the negotiations regarding this payment, the *dua* may be requested to add other valuables — usually pairs of male earrings of lesser value.

As the evening wears on, calculations will begin to be made regarding the division of goods and valuables brought by the man's *dua*, *ura-ava*, and *lolat*. These divisions will be made proportionate to the relative amount brought by each person. The rice packets and the female valuables brought by the man's *dua* will exchange against the palmwine (or that portion of which has not been drunk), money, and male valuables brought by his *ura-ava* and *lolat*. In addition, the man's *dua* who have made the payment to the master carpenter should each be presented with a pig's thigh. The elder-younger same-sex siblings who have contributed the bulk of the food consumed at the feast are not reciprocated. The value of this food is not in exchange, but in consumption.

The tripartition of the world into male *dua*, same-sex siblings, and female *ura-ava* and *lolat* — together with the obligation of reciprocal exchange that binds them, ensures that all events of import will be mediated by the complementary movement, and symbolic union, of male and female goods and valuables. Such exchanges make evident the fertility of the relation, at the same time as they make possible the continuity of the flow of life.

The success of such exchanges — their effect in fostering growth and life — results not only from the joining of male and female valuables. This effect is also due to the fact that, in being a reciprocal (but not necessarily balanced or equivalent) exchange, the tension between the forces of separation and those of encompassment is maintained rather than resolved into complete alienation on the one side or complete incorporation on the other. It is this explicit reluctance to resolve the tension between separation and encompassment that is the condition for the continued flow and extension of life.

The Elicitation of Encompassment

The tension between separation and encompassment is realized in yet another fashion. For although the forces of separation and encompassment are opposed to one another, it is important to understand that each side also elicits and contains its opposite. That is, while male valuables and bridewealth payments are meant to sever the more immediate effects of encompassment and subordination, they also assume and require the simultaneous acknowledgment of relation back to, and continued encompassment by, the source of life. Similarly, female valuables and the counter-prestations of the life-givers not only resist complete severance and stress the continuity of relation and the inevitability of encompassment, they also assume and require the simultaneous acknowledgment of the separate identity and independence of their wife-takers. This section, and the one following, explores the manner in which these contradictory impulses are contained in the reciprocal prestations of lifegivers and life-takers.

Although the male valuables that comprise bridewealth prestations both express and effect the severance of a man, his wife, and children from absolute encompassment and incorporation within the house of his wife-givers, they have a further destiny in exchange, as they travel back to the source of life, that serves to delineate the lines of encompassment. It is considered to be of utmost importance that the lifting of the bottom prestations of a brother and the bridewealth prestations for a sister travel along the correct pathways. In this, they are said to "travel following blood" (*rbana rorang lara*), and, to the extent that they do, they are thought to "touch the place" of a person (*rkena waan*). The place (*waan*) of a person is defined both by the pathway that traces his or her female bloodline back to the point of origin and by that point of origin and source of life itself.

The recognition of the source of life is synonymous with the growth and extension of life (Strathern 1988) and, thereby, with the very permanence of the wife-taking group as a separate identity. The power of a man's *dua* is absolute and is compared to that of Ubila'a in both its lifegiving and death-dealing potential: "They say we live, we live; they say we die, we die" (*Rfallak itvaat, itvaat; rfallak itmata, itmata*). Through the functioning of exchange, their power is rendered life-giving; where exchange fails, it becomes the curse of death. This is to say that, as a source of life, a *dua* also has the power to curse those who receive life but do not reciprocate. People say that if a *dua* curses (*near*) a descendant of his sister, it may take some time — weeks, perhaps months, or even a year — but eventually the curse will take its toll. "The fire will burn down to the end [of the stick]" (*yafu bi vek ngarang orang*), and when it reaches the end, sickness and death will follow. The continuity of the wife-taking group will thereby be negated and end in barrenness and death.

A person's life, health, and well-being depend, therefore, upon the flow of valuables — upon their "touching" his or her place. Where valuables "travel straight" (*rbana malolan*) along the correct pathways to the proper *dua*, they remain "cool" (*radridin*) and ensure the continuity of life and health. Where valuables "travel wrongly" (*rbana sala*) and cease to follow the correct pathway to the proper *dua*, they become "hot" (*ngnea*) and "asphyxiate" (*rumak*) the person whose place they were meant to mark. Sickness and death result when valuables do not touch the place of a person, when their passage is blocked or reversed, and when they are diverted onto another pathway.

People speculated that such was the likely cause of the death of one woman from Rumya'an. A pair of earrings that had been used for her mother's bridewealth had traveled following blood (on the side of the woman) from her brother to their *dua* in the next three ascending houses. The earrings then remained for some time in the third house. When the woman's son requested one of the portions of his wife's bridewealth to be paid, he passed his redemption request along this same pathway. For some reason, the representative of the third house took the same pair of earrings that had been received for her mother and redeemed her son with them. Within a week the woman was dead. The valuable that had been a part of her mother's bridewealth had ceased to touch her place. It had ceased to follow her female bloodline and, with its diversion onto another pathway of exchange, the result was that "blood asphyxiated her." Presumably, the *dua* of the third house, who were entitled to receive the bridewealth, had just cause for retribution. Having been denied recognition as the source of life, they became the agents of death.

Indeed, I was told that a *dua* who should have received the bridewealth of a woman, but did not, could justifiably say "some others might eat the bridewealth, but I eat the person" (*boku ki ra'an velin, ya'a uan tomata*). When it is said that a *dua* "eats a person"—just as when it is said that Ubila'a "eats a person"—the meaning is clear. Instead of bridewealth acting as a substitute for the person, the person becomes a substitute for the bridewealth and sacrifices his or her life. When bridewealth and the lifting of the bottom prestations travel wrongly, the consequence is that "people die" (*tomata ramuu*) and "houses die out" (*rahan ramudut*).[10]

Not only is it prohibited to use bridewealth received for the women among one's *ura-ava* or *lolat* to redeem men who stand along the same pathway, there is also a sanction against holding onto bridewealth for inordinately long periods of time and refusing to pass it on to the *dua* who are entitled to eat it. Thus, it is said that if the representative of a house "holds and blocks the bridewealth for a long time" (*ntaha teri vat velin mnanat*) and does not pass it on along the pathway that it is destined to travel, then blood will asphyxiate the woman concerned or one of her immediate family.

---

10. These are special terms used to refer only to death resulting from the improper passage of bridewealth and lifting of the bottom prestations.

The death of a woman from the village of Keliobar who had married a man in Awear was attributed to this. In a maneuver that necessitated a certain amount of shrewdness — but, in the end, backfired — the man's fathers paid two portions of her bridewealth with one large, named gold breast pendant. However, the two portions had an exchange destiny along two separate pathways. This was at a time, in the early 1950s, when only one portion of the bridewealth (sword) followed the pathway on the side of the man, and two (bow and spear) followed the pathway on the side of the woman. This particular valuable was given as both sword and spear. Since the piece obviously could not be divided so as to travel along two separate pathways, it meant that, in order to receive the valuable, the *dua* on the side of either the woman's father or mother would have to give another piece to substitute for the missing portion. Neither side has, up to now, been willing to do so and, as a result, the pendant has remained in the woman's brother's house for the last thirty years. When she died suddenly in 1978, one of the reasons put forth to explain her early death was the fact that the valuable had, for all these years, been held and blocked from traveling along one or the other of its pathways. Blood, it was said, had asphyxiated her.

The importance of knowing and recognizing one's *dua* and, therefore, one's debt for life and one's place, was first suggested to me in a conversation I had with a man from Rumya'an.

This man had been lifted at birth from a named house in Awear into one in Rumya'an, where he had been brought up in ignorance of his true origins. Eventually, he came to know his brothers in Awear, but up until 1931, he still did not know his sisters or his mother's brother. In that year, he became extremely ill and was close to death. It was finally determined that the cause of his illness was the fact that he neither knew, nor recognized, his "true" (*lalean*) mother's brother. When the man finally brought palmwine to his true mother's brother, as a sign of his recognition of him as his *dua*, and of his own place as his sister's child (*uran yanan*), he quite promptly became well again.

The destiny of valuables, then, is to trace and fix the relations between the houses to which a person is indebted for his place — for the very possibility of life.

Yet there is a limit in the distance that a particular woman's bridewealth valuables will travel along a given pathway back to the source of life. A valuable must travel following blood along its appropriate pathway until it is said to "die" or "stop" (*nmata*). The *dua* with whom one's bridewealth dies is called her "death place" or "stopping place" (*matmatan waan*). I was told, on the one hand, that a valuable dies at the point when it reaches the *dua* who paid the equivalent portion of the woman's brother's bridewealth, and, on the other hand, that it dies at the point where it enters a row. These two points are not necessarily congruent, for the man who paid the woman's brother's bridewealth may be situated along the pathway at a point before or after the pathway has entered a row.

One issue here is how far a woman's bridewealth must travel before it can be safely used for other purposes and diverted onto other pathways without requiring a substitute. My understanding is that it must travel until both provisions are satisfied: that is, it must travel at least as far as the *dua* who has paid the woman's brother's bridewealth and it must also travel until it has reached the limits of recognized blood links. If, for example, an immediate *dua* (say, a mother's brother) has paid a man's bridewealth and eaten his sister's bridewealth, the latter cannot yet be diverted without evoking the anger of the *dua* further along the pathway who consider the woman among their sisters and aunts. For, in such cases, a *dua* lower down along the pathway redeems a man in the name of his own *dua* who are situated higher up along the pathway. In such cases, it is only after the woman's bridewealth has entered a row that it can be diverted for other purposes.

> One woman told me of her concern over the misdirected movement of a pair of named male earrings that had been used to pay the bow portion of her bridewealth. Her brother had passed the earrings on to their *dua*, but instead of passing these on in the female line along which they should have traveled, their *dua* used them in order to "ask the elders" or propose a marriage between his son and his mother's brother's son's daughter, whose father then received the earrings. The woman claimed that the fact that her bridewealth had not continued along its proper path, but had been diverted for other purposes, was the cause of the sickness that plagued her family at that time.

Properly speaking, if their *dua* was to divert the pair of earrings from its pathway without incurring the wrath of those who should have rightly received it, he should have found a substitute for the pair and passed the substitute along in its stead. The concern, here, was not so much that the woman's *dua* had diverted her bridewealth to other purposes, but that everyone knew that he did not have a valuable to substitute in its place.

There is, in fact, nothing wrong with diverting a valuable from its intended pathway before it has died, as long as a substitute for the original valuable is found and passed along. The process by which a person replaces one valuable with another is called "he substitutes the place" (*nkati waan*), or "he changes the cloth" (*nkati maloli*). A substitution must also be made when someone outside the appropriate pathway redeems a man or when a man's *dua* borrows a valuable from someone outside the pathway in order to redeem him. By rights, the person who actually redeemed the man or supplied the borrowed valuable should drink the palmwine passed on by the man and eat the bridewealth of the man's sister. In order to prevent this, the man's *dua* must give the person who redeemed him (or the person from whom the valuable was borrowed) a substitute for the valuable originally given, in order that the palmwine of the man and the bridewealth of the sister will continue to travel along the proper pathway to the point where it dies or stops. Once both conditions have been satisfied and the valuable has died, it can either be passed along the same pathway as "fish and palmwine set traveling" or it can be diverted onto another pathway in order to meet the bridewealth requirements of other members of their village estates.

Another issue related to the passage of a man's lifting of the bottom prestations and his sister's bridewealth involves the relative claims of *dua* to be the source of life, and their relative ability to actualize those claims by paying and eating the bridewealth of those who constitute their village estates. In a system where the asymmetry between source and issue codes a hierarchical relation, to be able to pay and eat bridewealth — to actively assert one's status as the source of life and the death place — is also to actively assert one's hierarchical superiority. It is the movement of valuables along pathways of exchange that fixes the hierarchical order of houses related as source and issue.

Most bridewealth prestations are ultimately paid and eaten by members of houses that stand either at the very top of the system of rows or at those meeting (*situan*) places of several different rows. This is true because it is generally only these houses that control enough exchange pathways — and therefore enough valuables — to have the flexibility to assume responsibility for a great number of bridewealth prestations. By redeeming men of their bridewealth debts, such houses establish their claims as the source and origin of life. At the same time, they establish their rights to harvest even more valuables — the bridewealth of these men's sisters — as they travel up the pathways of exchange. In this way, the hierarchical relations of houses along pathways of exchange are established as a system of ever more encompassing sources of life.

In sum, bridewealth prestations effect the severance of the wife-takers from their absolute encompassment and incorporation within the house of the wife-givers and establish the continuity of the former as an independent identity. Yet at the same time, the exchange destiny of bridewealth prestations also stipulates that the continuity and growth of the wife-takers as an independent identity can only be achieved by acknowledging that the source of life forever encompasses its issue and that marking the extension of this encompassment constitutes the very condition for the continuity of life.

The Elicitation of Separation

From the wife-givers' point of view, their acceptance of bridewealth prestations, their counter-prestations to their wife-takers, and their redemption of the bridewealth debts of their sisters' children all serve to substantiate their claim that their wife-takers are indeed "their people." The latter constitute a portion of the village estates of the wife-giver's house and, as such, the wife-givers are their masters or owners (*dua*). Yet while the inward and outward flow of valuables on behalf of these people indicates their continued encompassment by their *dua*, these prestations also effect the separation of the wife-takers and make possible their continued existence as an independent unit.

This is true in the immediate sense that their initial acceptance of bridewealth for an outmarried woman allows her husband to establish both patrilocal residence and the patrilateral affiliation of his children within the house of his own father. At the same time, their payment of the bridewealth debts of the sister's son — should he marry an "other woman" — effect the latter's patrilocal residence and the patrilateral affiliation of the sister's son's children. It is only because these prestations are accepted and made that any continuity in the male line of the wife-takers can be maintained and the permanence of their house as a separate unit be assured.

But a *dua*'s role in assuring the independent existence of his wife-takers is also evident in another, more general, sense. For the continuity of the wife-takers is contingent upon their health, well-being, and fertility — upon their multiplying and not dying out. The power, and responsibility, of *dua* to ensure these conditions for their sisters and aunts (and *lolat*) can be seen in the relation between the forest estates and village estates of a house.

Like plantations of trees, one's sisters and aunts must be cared for in order that they "multiply their sprouts a thousandfold." Just as the established trees of old plantations bear the fruit that contains the seed from which new plantations grow and expand, so the daughters of sisters become the basis for the growth and expansion of new exchange pathways. The wealth of a man and a house depends precisely upon the continued growth and expansion of their plantations of trees and their plantations of people. Where there are no trees, there is no fruit; where there are no women, there are no valuables. Wealth comes from these two sources.[11]

It is with this understanding that people say: "We take from the forest estates in order to look after the village estates" (*Tala abat nangan ala tsi'ik abat ahu*), or, "The trunk belongs to us [the *dua*], the fruit belongs to them [the sister's children]" (*Ita dida ni dii, ira rira vuan*). These statements do not mean, for example, that the sister's son has the right to harvest a coconut crop for his own benefit. They do indicate, that, for their immediate use, a sister's child may always request the fruits of their mother's brother's trees (and gardens). A sister's child may also make a sign on a tree belonging to the mother's brother's forest estates: from then on it belongs to him, and the mother's brother may no longer use it. But this applies to a single tree and can not be extended to the entire estate.

That the harvest of the forest estate exists at least in part to be passed along exchange pathways to the village estate, to care for the well-being of one's sisters and aunts, is most explicit in relation to sago and at what might be called "starving time." Sago trees are harvested at the end of the yearly cycle, when all other food stores have been severely depleted, and when people are truly close to starvation. The explicit assumption is that the sago harvest is meant for one's *ura-ava*, to keep them from starving and dying out. Thus when sago trees are harvested, the working party may include one's elder-younger brothers along with one's *ura-ava*, or it may be composed entirely of the latter. Most of the trees that were harvested when I was in Awear belonged to people who had moved away from Awear when the village split in 1969. Yet the trees were still recognized as belonging to their original owners, and the working parties were formed entirely by the sisters and aunts of those persons.

The relationship between the forest and village estates, then, is not a static one. The harvest of the forest estates assures, especially in times of famine, the continuity and well-being of the village estates — that is, of the *ura-ava* of the house. While the flow of the fruits of tree plantations to the *ura-ava* ensures their life and expansion, it also ensures the continued harvest that is the yield of the village estates — the ongoing flow of bridewealth valuables from the *ura-ava*. Continuity and life depend upon exchange as much as exchange depends upon the continuity of life.

Just as the impermanent forest and village estates of both named and unnamed houses — their trees and their *ura-ava* — stand in a dynamic rela-

---

11. Note Sahlins' comment on Dumezil's observation: "Riches, of course, are the economic counterpart of the powers of growth and agricultural fertility, hence indicative, as Dumezil observes, of the female side" (1981:116). Productive resources in Tanimbar, although controlled by men, are indeed female by nature.

tion to one another, so too do the permanent forest and village estates of named houses – their land and their *lolat*. Not only does land constitute one of the female valuables that may be given from *dua* to *lolat*, but the first fruits of the land must also be ritually bestowed upon the *lolat* (and, secondarily upon the *ura-ava*) that belong to the "master of the land" (*abat dua*). At the time when the thanksgiving feast for the harvest of the large inland gardens is celebrated, each couple that has a plot in the garden must give ten large yams to the master of the land. He will then redistribute his share of the yams first to his *lolat* and, when there is enough, then to his *ura-ava*, if they have brought a bottle of palmwine or some fish or pork or both.[12] The gift of garden produce, then, like all the female valuables given to one's *lolat* and *ura-ava*, is a gift of life – one that marshals the wealth of one's forest estates in order to ensure the continuity of one's village estates as separate, permanent units that will grow and multiply rather than wither and die out.

The asymmetry between the prestations given by wife-givers and wife-takers is evident when people say that, in giving female valuables, *dua* "cool" their *lolat* and *ura-ava*. It is not possible to say that, in giving male valuables, *lolat* and *ura-ava* "cool" their *dua*. For whereas the male prestations of the latter emphasize separation through metaphors of heat and death (at the same time that they require acknowledgment of the source of life), the female prestations of the former emphasize encompassment though metaphors of coolness and life (at the same time that they effect the separate and enduring identity of an independent unit).

Gender and Life-Giving Hierarchies

It is the tension between separation and encompassment that allows the female wife-takers to establish their independent identity at the same time that they continue to acknowledge their dependence upon their male wife-givers, who remain their source of life. In the process, where exchanges are effective, both groups are able to achieve the intergenerational male continuity of their house that ensures its permanence.

---

12. The fact that the rights of the *ura-ava* and the *lolat* over the harvest of their *dua* are part of a larger structure of exchange was made explicit in the case of the harvest and threshing of rice. Formerly, the harvested rice from a field was measured out in containers made of lontar palm fronds (*besi lalaun*). Should one have a harvest that yielded more than one hundred such containers, then at the time of threshing, one's *dua*, *lolat*, and *ura-ava* were called together. The *dua* would raise a "flag" (*sa'ir*) consisting of female valuables, and then the *lolat* and *ura-ava* would "cut down the flag" (*rtavar sa'ir*) with male valuables, which were exchanged for the female valuables. At this time, too, the *lolat* and *ura-ava* – who had been the threshers – were given a portion of the rice harvest to take home with them.

Yet even when the male core of both houses has been reasserted, they continue to be differentiated by gender, as male and female to one another.

The question remains why it is that the wife-givers—who effect encompassment by giving female valuables—are nevertheless, themselves, considered male, and the wife-takers—who sever and separate by giving male valuables—are themselves considered female. In terms of exchange, it is through the movement of opposite-gender aspects of one another that houses transform the unproductive androgynous unity of a house into a productive differentiation of female wife-takers and male wife-givers. By exteriorizing the female aspect of their house (women and female valuables), the wife-giving house constitutes itself as male. Similarly, by exteriorizing the male aspect of their house (male valuables), the wife-taking house constitutes itself as female. When one aspect of a whole is externalized, a house not only establishes its own same-gender identity, but also makes possible a new form of relation with the opposite-gender part that has been externalized. The prior, unproductive cross-gender relation *within* a house is thereby transformed into a productive cross-gender relation *between* houses.

The encompassing quality of wife-givers and the separating quality of wife-takers thus derives not from the aspect that they retain, but from the aspect that they give away. When the focus is upon encompassment, it is those entities that contain the potential for life and relation (women and female valuables) that must be exteriorized. When the focus is upon separation, it is those entities that contain the potential for death and severance that must be exteriorized. It is, therefore, not because males are inherently superior that they encompass females, but rather because, in giving the encompassing, life-giving female aspect of a house away, a male identity is elicited and constituted as the source of life. Likewise, it is not because females are inherently inferior that they are encompassed by males, but rather because, in giving the separating and death-dealing male aspect of a house away, a female identity is elicited and constituted as that which has issued forth from the source.

The simultaneous achievement of both separation and encompassment—the continued tension between the two forces—is the condition for productivity, growth, and the extension of life. Because these depend upon the dynamics of relation and exchange between a source and that which issues forth from it, the conditions of productivity also delineate the form of hierarchy. This is to say that hierarchy *is* the form through which life and its extension are realized.

9   The Continuity of Affinal Relations

. . . a new marriage renews all marriages concluded at other times, and at different points in the social structure, so that each connexion rests upon all the others and gives them, on its establishment, a recrudescence of activity. (Lévi-Strauss 1969:65)

The village estates of a house need tending, not only to foster their growth but also to harvest the fruits borne by their offshoots. Yet neither the growth nor the harvest is assured. In order to nurture their village estates, the men of a house must continue to give women, lifeblood, and female valuables to the descendants of their sister. It is only to the extent that the growth of their village estates is achieved that they will harvest their fruits — the male valuables that are passed back to the source of women and life.

The effort to effect the continuity of affinal relations makes sense within this larger context of the double movement of growth out from the source and return to the source. Growth is possible only to the extent that it is rooted to a source. At the same time, a source exists only to the extent that growth continues to issue forth and differentiate itself. The mutual implication of this asymmetric relation is played out in the forms of marriage and the exchange of valuables.

Matrilateral cross-cousin marriage is neither a rule to be broken or followed nor an ideal to be enacted or not in practice. It is, rather, one particular manner of creating relation that has a number of particular consequences.[1] Whereas marriage with an "other woman" pushes out the tendrils of growth into new terrain, matrilateral cross-cousin marriage extends an established direction of growth at the same time that it strengthens its connection back to the root and the source of life. Both matrilateral cross-cousin marriage and the exchange of valuables replicate and rein-

---

1. Catholic and Protestant missionaries had divergent views on the permissibility of first cousin marriage: the Catholics have prohibited such marriages; the Protestants have permitted them. As a consequence, in recent generations, matrilateral cross-cousin marriage in the first degree is rare in Catholic villages and more common in Protestant villages.

force the pattern of movement in a way that begins to transform a provisional relationship into a more permanent asymmetric pathway between the source of life and the trajectory of growth.

The value of matrilateral cross-cousin marriage and asymmetric exchange can be gauged not only by comparison with other forms of marriage but also by contrast with those forms of relation that turn asymmetry into symmetry and open pathways into closed cycles. A consideration of relations with the father's sister's daughter and of the point at which the directionality of exchange may be reversed motivates a discussion of the distinction between persons and houses. For it is here that the transformation is effected from a system of relativized hierarchical relations (between wife-givers and wife-takers) to one of fixed hierarchical relations (between named and unnamed houses, on the one hand, and between *lolat* and *ura-ava* pathways, on the other).

Continuity and Limitations

Part of the system of reciprocity established between mother's brother and sister's son is the former's obligation to continue as the life- and wife-giver *to* his sister's son. He is, at the same time, entitled to continue to act as the life- and wife-giver on behalf *of* his sister's daughter. This is to say, among other things, that he is obliged to provide a wife for his sister's son and is entitled to receive the bridewealth paid for his sister's daughter.

A man's obligation to provide a wife for his sister's son may be fulfilled in one of two ways: either he may give one of his own "daughters" in marriage or he may provide the primary (bow and water) portions of the bridewealth necessitated by the sister's son's marriage to an other woman. In the former case, the mother's brother continues to act as the primary source of women, lifeblood, and female valuables given to the sister's son. In the latter case, the mother's brother "redeems" (*ntevut*) his sister's son's debt for another source of women, lifeblood, and female valuables. In either case, however, the mother's brother remains entitled to receive the male valuables that constitute the primary (bow and water) portions of the bridewealth paid for his sister's daughter, and it is in this that he is reciprocated for his efforts on behalf of his sister's son.

All this means, on the one hand, that a marriage between members of previously unallied houses is supported and made possible, at least initially, not by a reciprocity established between these houses, but rather by a reciprocity based upon the continuity of old chains of alliances — that is, between houses linked along the pathways described by the female lines of both the bride's and the groom's mother and father. On the other hand, this means that these old alliances are supported as much, or more, by the movement of valuables along these pathways of exchange that link houses as they are by the renewal of alliances through the marriages of members of the houses concerned.

Yet, the exchange obligations that are engendered by the initial movement of a woman between houses are certain to endure over the course of three generations only. While ego's mother's brother retains the right to act as his primary wife-giver, nevertheless, should ego marry an other woman, this right will be ceded to the members of ego's wife's house, who will become the primary wife-giver to ego's children. Toward these latter, the role of ego's mother's brother will begin to diminish: he will pay and eat only the secondary spear and sword portions of the bridewealth of ego's sons and daughters. If, in the following generation, the relationship between the two lines has not been renewed through marriage, the role of ego's mother's brother toward ego's son's children will diminish still further. He (or his descendants in the male line) will pay and eat only the weariness portion of the bridewealth of ego's son's son and daughter.

With reference to figure 9.1, A1 and his descendants A2 and A3, and their *dua* on the side of A1's mother (the representatives of houses X and Y, etc.) will pay and eat the primary bow and water portions of the bride-

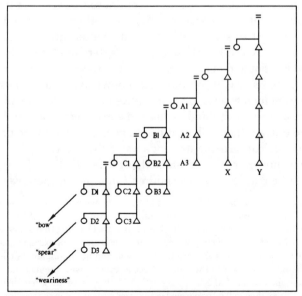

Figure 9.1   The continuity and limitations of bridewealth obligations

wealth of B1, C1, D1, and so on. They will pay and eat the secondary spear and sword portions of the bridewealth of B2, C2, D2, and so on. And they will pay and eat the residual weariness portions of the bride-wealth of B3, C3, D3, and so on. Thereafter, they will cease to be involved in the bridewealth exchanges that center upon the children of B3, C3, and D3.[2]

Thus while the rights and responsibilities of the descendants of the brother extend indefinitely in relation to the descendants of the sister traced through female links, their rights and responsibilities in relation to the descendants of the sister traced through male links may be limited to three generations. After this time, these latter "fall" (*rleka*) to one side, and their bridewealth exchanges will no longer concern the descendants of the brother. It was once explained to me in the following way: "Ubila'a gives a granddaughter, [the pathway] goes on and on; Ubila'a gives a grandson, [the pathway] already falls [to one side]" (*Ubila'a nala ubun vata, nbana trus; Ubila'a nala ubun brana, nlek roak*).

Although the specific obligations of exchange engendered by the marriage of the sister extend over three generations only, the affinal relation between the side of the brother and that of the sister may be perpetuated far beyond three generations. The continuity of the affinal and asymmetric relation between the two depends upon either of two factors: whether the relationship is renewed through matrilateral cross-cousin marriage, and whether the female line of the sister continues to grow and multiply. In lieu of matrilateral cross-cousin marriage, the affinal and asymmetric relation between the two sides will remain intact after three generations only to the extent that the female line of the sister "multiplies its sprouts a thousandfold." For in that case, the representatives of the side of the brother and that of the sister will continue to acknowledge their own asymmetric affinal relation *by reference to* the members of the female line of the sister, toward whom they both stand as *dua* and wife-givers. They, and their relationship to one another, will continue to be implicated in the bridewealth exchanges that concern the descendants of the sister.

There is, however, no guarantee that the female line of the sister will continue to be fruitful. Sister's children (*uran yanan*) pathways are con-

2. In this, I have outlined the structure of the exchange pathways in which a man and his descendants in the male line (together with his *dua* on the side of the woman) will be involved relative to his sister's children. It should go without saying that a man and his male descendants will continue to be implicated in the same structure of exchange pathways that center upon his father's sister's children (*avan yanan*) and his grandparent's children (*ubun yanan*), although in relation to them he will act in concert with the *dua* linked along the pathways described by his father's and his father's father's ascending female lines, respectively. Furthermore, they will be implicated in the same structure of exchanges for the descendants of each woman who belongs to any of these female lines.

sidered impermanent and ephemeral. Should there be no issue along this line, the pathway will terminate altogether after the last weariness exchanges have been completed on behalf of the son's son's son of the last woman. Where the female line of the sister bears no issue, and where the relation between the male lines of the brother and the sister's husband has not been renewed by matrilateral cross-cousin marriage, the two lines will — after three generations — have no further cause for association. The continuity of their affinal relationship — and the asymmetric and hierarchical order engendered by it — will dissolve and be superceded by more current affinal arrangements. If the relationship is ever reinitiated, there is no reason why the asymmetric order of wife-giver and wife-taker may not be reversed.

To the extent that a house is defined by the expansion of its village estates, both the dissolution of affinal relations after three generations and the dissolution of the female line that issues from a woman of the house have a negative effect on the definition and status of that house. Hence the high value placed on the continuity and permanence of these relations. The two strategies for ensuring the relative permanence of affinal relations — matrilateral cross-cousin marriage and the expansion of the female lines of outmarried women — thus become crucial to the continuity of the identity and status of a house.

Matrilateral Cross-Cousin Marriage

Matrilateral cross-cousin marriage is the most obvious way of reaffirming the affinal relation between the descendants of a brother and a sister. The pivotal role of this form of marriage in the establishment of a permanent affinal alliance can be seen in a number of different ways. Structurally speaking, marriages between *fatnima* (classificatory mother's brother's daughter and father's sister's son) are situated midway between those in which a man marries either an "other woman" (*vat liak*) or a "woman of his master" (*vat dua*). Unlike marriage with an other woman, which establishes a new relation between persons, that with a *fatnima* reaffirms a relationship between persons that was initiated in a previous generation. However, unlike in a marriage with a woman of one's master, which is based upon a permanent alliance between named houses regardless of the genealogical relation between the persons involved, it is precisely the genealogical relationship between specific persons (a man and his mother's brothers, or *memi*) that a *fatnima* marriage traces, regardless of the houses to which they belong. Thus in making such a marriage, a woman is said to "follow her aunt" (*norang avan*). Although still reckoned in terms of persons (rather than houses), matrilateral cross-cousin marriage nevertheless replicates the movement of women in a way that begins to establish the relation as a more enduring entity in the world.

In the exchanges that accompany *fatnima* marriages, it is the man's *ura-ava* who stand opposed to his *dua*—or, more specifically, his *ura-memi*. That is, *fatnima* marriage is supported by the reciprocity of exchange between mother's brother and sister's son that was established in a previous generation by the payment of bridewealth. Like the replication of the movement of women, the continued movement of valuables cuts a more deeply furrowed pathway between the two sides, one that is increasingly less likely to be erased by the passage of time.

As in marriage with an other woman, marriage with a *fatnima* can be initiated either by the parents through formal negotiations called "they ask the elders" (*rorat dawan*) or by the couple themselves through rather less formal negotiations, otherwise known as "they steal and race away" (*rbori rafraa*). Where the marriage has not been arranged beforehand, the man and woman can make their wishes known if one "climbs up into the house" (*nva'al rahan*) of the other, or if "they flee to the forest" together (*raflaa nangan*).

Whether a *fatnima* marriage has been inaugurated by asking the elders or by stealing and racing away, the preliminary exchanges will proceed in much the same manner. Because the mother's brother and sister's son are already in a wife-giving and wife-taking relationship, there should be no need to "search for the woman" (*rdav vata*) or to "sit in the space in front of the house" (*rdok lean*) to learn the whereabouts of the stolen woman. If a man's daughter is in the house of his sister's son, she is where she belongs. There should also be no cause to demand the prestation called "anger" (*ngrova*), for, on the contrary, the woman's father should welcome the union of his daughter and his sister's son.[3] The preliminary negotiations, then, will concern the prestations of "just palmwine" (*tuat watan*), the "voice of accord" (*vai lolin*), and the "place" (*waan*) of the woman (see chapter 7). The palmwine, money, and male valuables that constitute these prestations will be drawn from the resources of the man's fathers, brothers, and *ura-ava*, and they will be given to his mother's brothers. The latter may keep just palmwine and the voice of accord, but should pass on the place of the woman to the *dua* who stand along the female line to which she belongs.

---

3. If a man steals and races away with his *fatnima*, it may happen that her parents are insulted that they were not consulted beforehand, in which case it is possible that they would "sit in the space in front of the house" and ask for the payment of *ngrova*. However, this would likely happen only if relations between the two sides were already strained for other reasons.

Palmwine Overflows

In *fatnima* marriages, the bridewealth paid for the mother's brother's daughter is no longer called the "value of the woman" (*vat velin*). The value of the woman has already been established in the previous generation and has laid the foundation for a system of reciprocity centered upon the current generation. In this, the woman, lifeblood, and female valuables that the sister's son receives from his mother's brother find their counter in the male valuables that are given in connection with the marriage of the sister's daughter and that must travel back to the source of life — to the mother's brother and onward to the *dua* of the mother's brother.

Thus it is said that "palmwine simply overflows" (*tuat nvoat watan*). That is, the sister's son stands under a renewed obligation to pass on the valuables received for his sisters (*uran*) and his sister's daughters (*uran yanan vata*), so that they continue to overflow into the cups of the mother's brother. At the same time, by giving his daughter in marriage to his sister's son, the mother's brother retains his primary place as life-giver to his sister's son's children, instead of ceding this place to another house, as he would if his sister's son married an other woman. The mother's brother then remains entitled to eat the primary (bow and water) portions of the bridewealth of the sister's son's daughter (and to pay the equivalent portions for the sister's son's son), rather than being entitled to the secondary (spear and sword) portions only.

Although it is said that a man is not required to pay bridewealth as such, I was told that the palmwine should overflow in such a way that four valuables — equivalent in value to the four parts of an ordinary bridewealth — should be given to the mother's brother by the sister's son over the course of his lifetime. The sister's son will not call a particular prestation bow or spear: it will be called simply "palmwine overflows," but it will be given over with the understanding that it is the equivalent of the bow or spear portion of the bridewealth, and the mother's brother will pass it on to his own *dua* accordingly.

The ambiguity concerning the status of these prestations — whether they are to be considered bridewealth (*vat velin*) or palmwine that simply overflows — derives from the intermittent practice of matrilateral cross-cousin marriage.[4] It is readily apparent that if matrilateral cross-cousin

4. It will be noted that I have not provided statistical data relating to the various types of marriage. A meaningful statistical account could only be compiled by means of a detailed analysis of Drabbe's census material in connection with my own. For in a system where women often marry outside the village, and where some forms of marriage occur only once every other generation, an accurate picture cannot be gained from data that relate only to persons currently living in the village. Such an analysis will have to await another time.

marriage is practiced by one son consistently in every generation in each house in the system, then each of the male lines concerned would find its place in a single fixed pathway of wife-givers and wife-takers, rather than in a series of differentiated exchange pathways. The female bloodline to which each man belonged would link the same houses on a single pathway of exchange along which all portions of the bridewealth would travel.

However, not everyone can marry his matrilateral cross-cousin, and such marriages are, in any case, practiced more sporadically than systematically. Therefore, in cases where matrilateral cross-cousin marriage is practiced for the first time between cousins of either the first or second degree, the *dua* who would redeem the man of his wife's bridewealth would only partially overlap with those who would eat his wife's bridewealth. In an initial matrilateral cross-cousin marriage, for instance, the *dua* who would make a man's bow prestation are the same as those who would eat his wife's spear prestation. Following figure 9.2, M, N, and their *dua* would both pay B's bow and eat D's spear. In such a case, these *dua* will "let [the] spear portion fall' (*rfaleka wahat ramat*). Palmwine will simply continue to overflow along these lines. However, because the woman's mother's *dua* are not in a position to both pay and eat bridewealth, the bow portion of the woman's bridewealth must still be paid. Again following figure 9.2, M, N, and their *dua* will pay the bow portion of B's wife's bridewealth to E and his *dua*.

It is true that if all men consistently married their matrilateral cross-cousins, palmwine would simply overflow and no bridewealth prestation as such would be made. But it is also true — both historically and at the present time — that since such marriages are not consistently practiced, a kind of intermediate resolution to the question of bridewealth is reached. Where *dua* would both pay and receive portions of the bridewealth, then palmwine simply overflows; where *dua* have the right to receive bride-

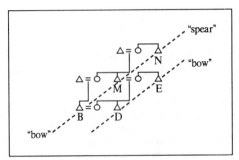

Figure 9.2   Overlapping prestations in an initial
matrilateral cross-cousin marriage

wealth, but are not simultaneously in a position where they are obligated to pay bridewealth for the same marriage, then their demands should be satisfied.

Residence, Affiliation, and Reciprocities

A man who has married his *fatnima* can be asked to "make himself a son-in-law" (*nafranetan*) and live avunculocally for some time in the house of his mother's brother. This is not a prerequisite of the marriage, but will depend upon the needs of the mother's brother's household at the time. Certainly, once a substantial valuable has passed from the sister's son to his mother's brother as palmwine overflowing, the avunculocal residence of the former can no longer be insisted upon.

Whenever a man and his mother's brother's daughter move to his own house or to that of his father, the blocking of the path ceremony (*larlera*) may be performed (see chapter 7). Whether or not the woman's path will be blocked depends upon her rank, the resources of the *ura-memi* and *ura-ava* along this pathway, as well as the resources of the elder-younger same-sex siblings of the couple's parents. The *larlera* ceremony exemplifies, in a single moment, the double movement of all affinal exchanges. On the one hand, there is an effort to extract a woman and the life-bearing potential she bears — to separate the female aspect from the male aspect of the house of the wife-givers. On the other hand, there is resistance to a complete severance of the woman and her life-bearing potential from their encompassment by the house of her brothers. The latter, together with their *dua*, insist upon the recognition of their position as the source of life through the continued prestations of female valuables.

This insistence is even more evident in another event that should happen when the couple changes residence. The woman's *dua* on both the side of her mother and father should "adorn her" (*rfalahar ia*) with the female valuables that she is to bear with her to the house of her father's sister's son (see chapter 7). Again, the extent to which a woman is adorned with female valuables will depend upon her rank and the status of the houses concerned. To the extent that she is a high-ranking woman, her *dua* will endeavor to "make her weighty" (*rfalemang ia*) with a full array of female valuables. These valuables do more than express a woman's rank: in a sense, a woman is made a *lemditi*, a high-ranking woman, by the weight of her adornments. Without these, even a woman who, by birth, is of the highest rank will carry no weight in the world, and neither she nor her *dua* will be able to command the respect of their sisters and aunts.

Just as the palmwine that overflows from the sister's son comprises the male valuables that are, in any case, due to the mother's brother in acknowledgment of the source of life, so too the adornment of the woman comprises the female valuables that are due to the sister's son to foster the continued growth that issues forth from the source. In both the small, daily exchanges of fish, meat, and garden produce and the larger prestations of valuables on more momentous occasions, the reciprocal flow of valuables will continue throughout their lifetime and the lifetime of their children. When a valuable is given as palmwine overflowing, it should be reciprocated by what is called the "small sarong" (*bakan ko'u*) — that is, by an indigenous weaving or any other female valuable. Moreover, just as the male valuables given from the sister's son to the mother's brother bear a further exchange destiny along the pathway described by their ascending female line, so the female valuables given by the mother's brother are destined to travel further along the pathway described by their descending female lines.

Thus, when a man marries his mother's brother's daughter, the movement of valuables is contained within established pathways. As palmwine continues to overflow and as women are adorned and made weighty, the pathways and the houses linked along them are themselves made weighty — which is to say, more enduring and less likely to fall to one side. In this way, the exchange of valuables along a pathway both anchors the flow of life in the continued acknowledgment of its source and ensures its continued expansion and growth.

Although less permanent than the established alliances between houses related as *dua* and *lolat*, a relation between two houses that has been reaffirmed by matrilateral cross-cousin marriage is still regarded as far more stable and enduring than one that has only recently been opened by a marriage between members of previously unrelated houses. The reciprocal exchange of female and male valuables expresses the value both sides place upon the continuity of the affinal relationship, which, as Valeri (1975–76, 1980) has pointed out, implies the perpetuation of the line of the sister's son as distinct from — but in continuous and complementary relation to — the line of the mother's brother, which is its source of life. The anchoring of the flow of life within an established pathway, therefore, requires a second movement in which the continuity of relation is established by the separation of the wife-takers from their potential incorporation within the house of the wife-givers.

Consequently, as the continuity of the affinal relation becomes more assured through matrilateral cross-cousin marriage, so too the differentiation between the two affinally related houses becomes more assured. Although the affiliation of the sister's son's children is still dependent upon the movement of valuables, nevertheless, with such marriages, the question of affiliation is far more muted than in marriages with other women.

In *fatnima* marriages, the patrilateral affiliation of the sister's son's children will not be questioned as long as the mother's brother and sister's son remain on good terms, palmwine overflows, and exchange continues unhampered. Yet—because of the sporadic nature of matrilateral cross-cousin marriage—should either the man or the woman die before the equivalent of the bow portion of the bridewealth has been paid, then the rope of the dead prestation should be made to the woman's *dua* in the female line. Since it is the responsibility of the man's mother's brother and his *dua* to make this prestation, however, there is little likelihood that it would not be paid. For the whole point of matrilateral cross-cousin marriage is to assure the continuity of an affinal relation between the two houses, and this assumes the permanence of the distinction between them — and hence the patrilateral affiliation of the sister's son's children.

In light of the continuity of relation that is established through matrilateral cross-cousin marriage, divorce takes on a highly negative value. A divorce between *fatnima* would entail the complete severing of relations between mother's brother and sister's son and, more precisely, the complete severing of the pathway that links all the *ura-memi* and *ura-ava* connected along the female lines concerned. In rare cases, a provisional union (*ni dodu*) between *fatnima* might be ended by the payment of the voice of the official fine without damaging the relation between the two sides (the more so as the *fatnima* concerned are only very distantly related). But once *fatnima* are married, the sanction against a break in relations between *ura-memi* and *ura-ava* makes divorce as rare as it is difficult. Should there be a divorce, however, and a consequent break in the exchange relations between the two sides, the sister's son will no longer have an avenue for extracting his children from the house of his mother's brother, and they will therefore affiliate to the latter's house.

The breakdown in affinal and exchange relations between the mother's brother and sister's son has a number of serious consequences for both sides. On the one hand, the mother's brother would relinquish a portion of his village estates and would no longer be in a position to harvest the bridewealth paid for his sisters' daughters and their children. On the other hand, the sister's son and his brothers would lack a source of bridewealth to marry other women, and would be forced to "sell themselves" (*rfeddi ira*) to another *dua*—a strategy that essentially puts them in the position of being a slave (*iria*) to their new *dua*.[5] Moreover, in severing his relations with his mother's brother, a man cuts himself, his sister, and their descend-

---

5. When a man sells himself to a new *dua*, the latter is said to "buy his new estate" (*nfaha ni abat ngorva'an*). Because the new *dua* redeems the man of his bridewealth debts, he is then entitled to eat the relevant portions of the bridewealth of the man's daughters. He is not, however, required to pass their bridewealth on, for it stops or "dies with him"

ants off from their source of life. Such a divorce, then, implies a total breakdown in the relations that are productive of life, and opens the way for sickness and death to follow in its wake.

The Fruitfulness of the Female Line

In addition to matrilateral cross-cousin marriage, what makes an alliance — what turns a provisional affinal link into an enduring alliance between houses — is the fruitfulness of the female bloodline that grows out of it. The relation between the two can be stated in the following terms. The growth of the female line depends upon the continued acknowledgment of the source of life. This involves a double movement of valuables — of women and female valuables out from the source and of male valuables back to the source. It is the continuity of this double movement of valuables that ensures the permanence of an alliance.

As the encompassing male aspect of a house and as the point of origin of the life borne by the outmarried women of a house, a man remains (with his descendants in the male line) the life- and wife-giver of the descendants of the sister in the female line. They are "his people" (*ni tomata*) and constitute a portion of the estates of his house. He is, therefore, implicated in a system of reciprocity whereby he is obligated to give women and female valuables (or the requisite male valuables necessary to secure other women) and is entitled to receive male valuables on behalf of the men and women who are "his people."

Because the continued growth of one's village estates depends upon the movement of valuables back to the source of life, the directionality of this movement is guaranteed by the prohibition against using the bridewealth received for a sister to pay the bridewealth of her brother's wife, when the latter is an other woman. I was told that "we may not take their [the sisters'] blood just to redeem them [the brothers] back again" (*wol bis ma tala lararira ma tatevut ira ewal watan*). For when a man marries an other woman, the bridewealth of his wife and that of his sister are destined to travel along different pathways of exchange back to different sources of life. If, on the contrary, a man does marry his mother's brother's daughter, the bridewealth of his sisters and sister's daughters will form

---

(*nmata na'a ia*). Koda Balia and Agus Kabressi said that "if you wanted to sell yourself on Fordata, the big fish would swallow you right down" (*sadane mane fweddi oa na'a Yaru, ian dawan rtelas falolang oa*). That is to say, there are only a few houses to whom anyone would sell themselves on Fordata. These include: in Rumya'an, Melatunan, Bungaa, and Ongirwalu; in Awear, Ditilebit, Refvutu, and Watti; in Sofyanin, Nuswotar, Lalin, and Vatkaat; in Waleran, Vuarlela and Koli.

a portion of the bridewealth of his wife. It will travel along the same pathway of exchange back to the same source of life.

Thus, where a man marries his matrilateral cross-cousin, both his own marriage and the passage of his sister's bridewealth reiterate the value of an established affinal relation and source of life. Where a man marries an other woman, the value of this relation is realized to the extent that a man lifts the bottom of his *dua* and his sister's bridewealth follows the pathway that links those whose bottoms have been lifted. This means that the flow of valuables precipitated by each new marriage at the lower reaches of the pathway not only establishes the conditions for this new affinal relation but also reasserts the significance of every preceding marriage and gives to the relationship between the houses linked by them the quality of an enduring alliance.

It is because of the asymmetric flow of women and blood that houses are hierarchically related. Yet there is no inherent fixity in relations based upon the flow of blood, for these would be lost to the onward movement of the current, unless the memory of their former existence could be traced. It is only because alliances are renewed by marriages and, even more so, by the reciprocal movement of valuables along exchange pathways that the hierarchical relations between houses can become more or less fixed and not simply shift, be drawn under, and submerged as blood flows on.

Whereas marriage with an other woman involves an expansion of the differentiation of the original unity of a brother-sister pair, both matrilateral cross-cousin marriage and the continued movement of valuables along the pathways involve a retraction of that differentiation. The one entails the dispersal of persons and valuables along a new branch pathway, the other the concentration of persons and valuables on an older, established pathway that is strengthened and given weight by their travel upon it. Implicating the reciprocal processes that differentiate and recompose an original unity, the two forms of marriage are opposed at the same time that they are dependent upon one another for their realization.

To Shatter One's Palmwine Cup

Although the foundation of an alliance is reinforced by the continued asymmetry in the movement of women and valuables, it is undercut by the reversal of the established asymmetry between wife-giver and wife-taker. It is also undercut by the denial of the necessity for a distinction between wife-giver and wife-taker. That is, such an alliance is undermined not only by a symmetry in affinal relations but also by what might be called incest.

The interdiction that forms the basis of the asymmetric system of marriage and alliance is this: a man is prohibited from having sexual or marital relations with any woman whose bridewealth he stands in a position to eat. It is said of a man who engages in a relation with such a woman that "he shatters his palmwine cup" (*nfeffar ni kobi*). A good many women can shatter a man's palmwine cup, but he will call them all "sister" (*uran*: cross-sex sibling).[6]

In the context of the tripartite division of relatives — female sisters and aunts, male brothers and uncles, and elder-younger same-sex siblings (see chapter 6) — the relevant distinction here is that between cross-sex siblings and elder-younger same-sex siblings. A man's "true elder-younger same-sex siblings" (*ya'an-iwarin lalean*) include both his agnatic and uterine brothers. They also include his matrilateral cross-cousins (*fatnima*) who, by right, should marry into his own house — or, more broadly, marry one of his agnatic or uterine brothers. His cross-sex siblings, by contrast, are those women who, as "strangers" to their natal houses, should follow their aunts to marry men in the houses that are already established wife-takers. In these latter houses they are not strangers but rather same-sex siblings who have a rightful place there. A man's "true sisters" (*uran lalean*) include all the cross-sex siblings of his agnatic and uterine brothers (i.e., his sisters, father's brother's daughters, and mother's sister's daughters), the female descendants of his mother's mother's sisters, as well the female descendants of the sisters of his father and his father's fathers brothers (i.e., his father's sister's daughter, etc.).

A man is the "master of the body" (*tenan dua*) over his true sisters and the men of houses into which these women should marry. As a member of a male wife-giving house, he is in a position to continue to give women, life, and female valuables to his female wife-takers (i.e., his *da'uk* — his father's sister's sons, etc.). He is also in a position to receive the male valuables given as bridewealth for his own outmarried sisters and those of his wife-taking *da'uk*. With these people he shares at least one female bloodline and therefore at least one line of *dua*. Similarly, although a man's uterine brothers belong to other houses, his identity with them, like his identity with his agnatic brothers, is based upon this double movement of shared substance: lifeblood received from categorically "male" brothers and uncles, and bridewealth valuables received from categorically "female" sisters and aunts. As a consequence, their sisters are also his "true sisters," and he is the "master of their bodies."

The consequences of a man's relations with his true sisters is slightly different, depending upon whether they belong to his own house (and the

6. The discussion will be limited to a consideration of women who belong to ego's own generation. Obviously, what will be said here will also apply, for instance, to all those of the descending generation whom a man calls "daughter" (*yanan vata*).

houses of his uterine brothers) or to an established wife-taking house. What is at issue in a man's relation to his sister, his father's brother's daughter, and mother's sister's daughter is not so much the reversal of established relations between wife-giver and wife-taker but a denial of their relevance altogether. To establish sexual or marital relations with these women would be to say that one need not receive life and blood from others or give life and blood to others: it is enough to "eat" one's own lifeblood. For a man to engage in sexual or marital relations with these women is considered particularly reprehensible. Such behavior, people say, is "like dogs and pigs" (*wean yaha-vavu*). And because it takes place between persons who share valuables, no compensation can be made for such a transgression. The only manner in which such behavior can be punished is to expel the offending party from the house — at least for a period of time. A transgression of this sort can also lead to a permanent split between the agnatic brothers of a house, in which case the offending brother is disinherited from the estates of the house (Drabbe 1940:213).

The situation is different when relations are established between a man and his father's sister's daughter. The directionality of the flow of women and lifeblood has been established in the previous generation, and the structure of the reciprocity engendered by this determines that the asymmetric relation between wife-giver and wife-taker must remain fixed over the course of at least three generations. Were a man to marry his father's sister's daughter, the flow of women, lifeblood, and female valuables would reverse, turning back upon itself. The hierarchical and asymmetric relation between the two sides would be inverted, or altogether neutralized: the two sides would be simultaneously wife-giver and wife-taker, male and female, superior and inferior to one another.

> Falaksoru Ditilebit told me that one of his sons had wanted to marry his father's father's sister's daughter's daughter, who was also from the house Bungaa, Ditilebit's immediate *lolat*. Falaksoru had been furious with his son, and he had blocked the marriage. He said that if his son had married this woman, then their *lolat*, Bungaa, would "repudiate us" (*rafen ita*) and break off the long-established alliance between the two houses. He indicated that such a marriage would have been a serious breach of relations and could not have been carried out. "If we eat the bow portion, we eat blood" (*Ta'an vuhur, ta'an lara*). This could not be tolerated.

In a system where reciprocity is based upon the perpetuation of asymmetric and hierarchical relations, a symmetric marriage not only denies hierarchy but also shatters the very possibility of reciprocity. Hence the significance of the phrase used to describe such unions: "he shatters his palmwine cup." In reversing the relation between wife-giver and wife-taker through father's sister's daughter marriage, a man and his *dua* forfeit their rights to be reciprocated with the bridewealth of this woman, for they themselves would have to pay for it. Palmwine cannot overflow their cups, for their cups have been shattered. It is impossible that where, as wife-giver, one has already given a woman and female valuables one should also be obliged to give male valuables. The hierarchical and asymmetric relations upon which the entire system of reciprocity is founded are totally undermined.

Therefore, when a man engages in sexual relations with his father's sister's daughter, compensation can and must be made in order to reestablish the preexisting form of the relationship. If, for example, a man takes his father's sister's daughter as "his lover" (*ni dodu*) — that is, has a brief affair with her and then "throws her off" — then, in place of the ordinary voice of the official fine, another fine called "they cover and clothe her" (*ruung reluk ia*) or, alternatively, "he joins together his palmwine cup [and makes it whole again]" (*nfatnemung ni kobi*), must be paid. This consists entirely of female valuables (four in number, like a voice of the official fine), and it must be paid by the offending man and his *dua* to the girl's father (their *ura-ava*). The prestation reasserts the position of the man as the *dua* of the latter. If this prestation is not made, the woman's father will cease to recognize the members of the offending man's house as his *dua* and, in the exchanges that implicate the two houses, the woman's father will thereafter skip over the house of the man and go directly to the latter's *dua*.

At one point W had a brief affair with his father's father's sister's daughter's daughter, M (figure 9.3). Because the fines that would "join together his palmwine cup" were not paid, M's mother's brother's son, A, refused to speak to (*nma'ir*) or recognize W as his *dua*. Then, in December 1979, A's sister R had an affair. Under normal circumstances, W would have received the portion on the side of the man of the voice of the official fine paid on account of this affair. Yet, because A refused to recognize W as his *dua*, he skipped over W and passed this portion on to K, who stands as the local representative of W's actual *dua*, from a house on the island of Sera. Half a year later, in June 1980 when a group of men from the Sera house arrived in Awear, it was decided that their aid should be enlisted to cover and clothe W's sisters and aunts. At that time, W and his Sera *dua* gave one indigenous woven sarong and seven pieces of store-bought clothing to A. With that, W's palmwine cup was joined together again, and his relations with his sisters and aunts had been restored.

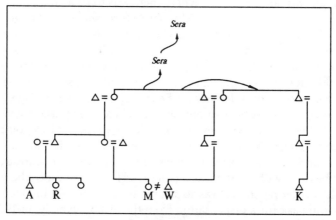

Figure 9.3   An affair that shatters a palmwine cup

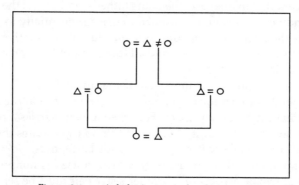

Figure 9.4   A father's sister's daughter marriage

Although it is not unheard of for a man to engage in a brief affair with his father's sister's daughter, it is extremely rare that they would actually marry, or be permitted to marry. I have no records of anyone in Awear having married his sister, his father's brother's daughter, or mother's sister's daughter, and there is only one case where a man married his father's sister's daughter. The marriage was accomplished, however, only after a determined struggle on the part of the woman.

Even after the couple had already had a provisional affair (*ni dodu*), the woman's parents forbade her to marry her lover, since he was her mother's father's son's son (figure 9.4). A marriage was arranged for her with a man from the Ke'i Islands who was living in Larat. The woman was taken to Larat, where there was to be a church wedding on a Wednesday. But on the Monday before, she refused to go ahead with it and ran away. When she was brought back, her brother beat her until her arms and legs were swollen. Still she persisted and again ran away. She was brought back on the condition that they would not beat her again and that they would consult with the Catholic priest for a decision. If he consented to the marriage, it could go ahead. A big conference was held at the priest's house, and he informed them that they could not be married. At this point, the woman replied that if they could not be married within the church, then she would go ahead and marry according to Tanimbarese *adat* and be done with it. She was again severely beaten. Since the priest could see her resistance was so strong, he said they should wait and he would ask for a dispensation from the bishop. Finally, in 1959 when the bishop came on a tour of the Tanimbar Islands, he said that they could be married, and so they were.

It is significant that in this case, the man's father's mother and the woman's mother's mother were different women married sequentially to the same man. Thus their female lines, on both the side of the mother and the father, were completely divergent and all four parts of the woman's bride-wealth were, in the end, paid.

The return of blood, the inversion of the hierarchical relations, and the impossibility of reciprocity entailed by marriage with a true sister are thought to have dire consequences. For when a man marries a true sister he eats his own blood, and it is said that "blood asphyxiates them" (*lara numak ira*): the couple will be plagued with barrenness, sickness, and death. Forming an androgynous unity, which in itself is nonproductive, the male and female aspects of a brother-sister pair must be separated in order to be productive. Because the distinction between male and female has been collapsed, the flow of blood cannot be mediated or cooled by the reciprocity established in the passage of valuables that are differentially connoted as male and female. Only where the asymmetric flow of women and lifeblood and the relative hierarchy of indebtedness are preserved over at least three generations can the flow of blood be mediated by the asymmetric and complementary movement of male and female valuables and the potential for life represented in the woman be fulfilled.[7]

7. Similarly, among the Ema, Clamagirand notes that if a marriage reversed the asymmetry of affinal relations, "it would be impossible . . . to engage in discussions or to make the necessary payments and counterpayments, for, as they say, 'buffalo cannot meet buffalo.' Reversing the direction of alliance would be 'giving against' instead of 'giving to meet.' The regular flow of exchanges evokes an image of the flow of life which circulates by means of

Sisters and Other Women

In considering what constitutes a reversal of asymmetry, it is crucial to understand who are considered sisters and who are not. There are two sets of criteria for making the relevant distinctions. One concerns whether a bloodline is shared; the other concerns the line between blood and houses, or between bridewealth (*vat velin*) and "fish and palmwine set traveling" (*ian e tuat fabana*).

The first distinction is between those cross-sex siblings who share a bloodline (and whose union would therefore confound reciprocity) and those who do not. Indeed, a man has many sisters (*uran*) aside from the women he calls his true sisters (*uran lalean*), with whom he shares at least one female bloodline. Unless matrilateral cross-cousin marriage has been practiced, after three generations the descendants of the brother will no longer share a source of lifeblood with the descendants of the sister. The bridewealth exchanges that center upon these people will no longer implicate the same ascending female bloodlines. Yet as long as the descendants of the brother continue to eat the bridewealth of the female descendants of the sister—especially when this is the primary bow portion—they will consider these women sisters, regardless of their distance. To marry one of these women would be to "shatter one's palmwine cup."

Because the system of reciprocity presupposes the continuity of the asymmetric relation between wife-giver and wife-taker over three generations, there is a significant difference between the consequences entailed by marriages that reverse the relation between wife-giver and wife-taker before the passage of three generations and those which do so after that time. When in the latter case, a source of lifeblood is no longer shared between those who marry, such a reversal may well confound hierarchy, but reciprocity again becomes possible. No longer "like dogs and pigs," the man who marries a more distant sister no longer eats his own blood. Because a man and such a sister share no source of lifeblood, the female lines along which her bridewealth must travel will not be the same as those along which he will pass his redemption request.[8]

The distinction between true sisters and more distant sisters is signifi-

women. If there were no way by which payments and counterpayments could be exchanged, the transmission of life could not normally take place and the child would remain within the mother's womb for he could find no 'way out'" (1980:145).

8. The same can be said of a man and those sisters to whom he is related because their houses stand as elder-younger brothers to one another. There are many grounds upon which two or more houses may be related as brothers. Most significant, in this context, are the houses that are considered to belong to the "inside of a house" (*rahan ralan*), or house-complex, in which certain younger brother houses are said to "harbor in the space beneath"

cant because to the extent that symmetric marriages do occur, they occur with women of the latter rather than the former category. I was told by some that if a man does marry a more distant sister, then no bridewealth would be paid, but rather the prestation called "they cover and clothe her" must be made. Yet in all the cases, for which I have records, where a man married a woman who was categorically his sister, bridewealth was paid: in each case, the female lines along which the man's redemption requests were passed differed entirely from those along which the woman's bridewealth valuables were to travel.

If a man's sisters are defined by the fact that he is in a position to eat their bridewealth (whether or not they still share a female line in common), the question remains as to when a man is no longer entitled to eat the bridewealth of a woman. The second and more important distinction, therefore, has to do with the differentiation between sisters and those women whose relations have become so distant as to be considered other women. Here, again, the distinction between blood and houses, between *ura-ava* and *lolat*, and between bridewealth and "fish and palmwine set traveling" is critical.

Logically, the distinction between *ura-ava* and *lolat* — blood and houses — is drawn after the passage of three generations. In practice, however, this distinction is not so easily drawn. Once when I was trying to discuss this issue with Falaksoru Ditilebit, we got into a heated debate as to where the line could be drawn. In calmer moments he agreed that after three generations the bow portion of a bridewealth prestation would be paid or eaten not because of a shared bloodline, but because of the relations between houses. Still, at other points he vehemently denied that, after three generations, relations traced through blood would be converted into relations traced through houses.

Several considerations were important in his resistance to the abstract logic of my argument. The key, however, is whether a *dua* — despite a three-generation separation along the female line — is still paying and eating the bridewealth (in particular, the bow portion) of the descendants of his sister. For where there is bridewealth, there is blood; and the bow portion of the bridewealth marks the movement of blood in a direct line, one that has not yet fallen to one side through male links.

---

other elder brother houses. The men who occupy such houses are "attached elder-younger brothers" (*ya'an-iwarin fareling*) who "treat each other well" (*rsimaklivur*). The sisters of one are considered the sisters of the other. One should not marry such a sister, but since no female bloodlines are shared in common, such marriages do occasionally occur.

The question then is how far the bridewealth of a woman must travel before it can be diverted or passed on—no longer as the bridewealth of a specific woman, but rather as "fish and palmwine" given from *lolat* to *dua*. For one definition of the boundary between blood and *lolat* is the place where "the value of the woman" (*vat velin*) dies and subsequently is diverted or passed on as "fish and palmwine set traveling" (see chapter 8). This is, in part, a political issue. In calling valuables bridewealth, a man commits himself to passing them on to the next *dua*; in calling them fish and palmwine set traveling he will not be so compelled and may be free to divert them for other purposes. The relative characterization of a valuable as one or the other and the distance traveled before it is no longer considered bridewealth are matters for interpretation and matters of politics; and, as a consequence, so too is the line that separates one's sister from the women of one's *lolat*. In the end, however, the crucial distinction is that where a man eats a woman's bridewealth, that woman is still considered a sister, whatever the distance between them, and the two should not marry. She will no longer be considered a sister, however, if the man is in a position to eat the valuables given for her bridewealth only after they have been transformed into fish and palmwine set traveling along the rows. This is a sign that she has become an other woman and the two may marry without fear of being asphyxiated.

From Blood to House

It nevertheless remains the case that four generations marks the first point at which the identity shared between the descendants of a brother and a sister becomes diffused and differentiated and the relations between the two lines may be rejoined in reverse without subverting the complementarity of exchange, in which the very potential for life resides.

There are, however, two related problems in all of this. First, to the extent that there are sanctions against closing the cycle and reversing the hierarchical order between wife-giver and wife-taker, men who occupy houses toward the top of the hierarchy of exchange pathways (and women who occupy houses toward the bottom) would find themselves in the awkward position of having increasingly fewer houses to which they may turn for spouses. Second, to the extent that cycling does (and must) occur, the entire hierarchical order threatens to be undermined.

For a house located along the double cycle of the Great Row (Lolat Ila'a), for example, all other houses—except those of the Great Row itself—are its wife-takers. Thus, in terms of the relation between houses, for a man of such a house to marry anyone except a woman from another Great

Row house would be to invert the hierarchical order between wife-giving and wife-taking houses, male and female, superior and inferior. Yet because two brothers cannot marry two sisters, not all brothers are able to marry women from their traditional wife-giving houses, and such marriages are, in any case, quite rare (see chapter 10). As a consequence, it is not uncommon for men to marry women from houses that stand along the rows of their wife-taking houses.

The solution to this dilemma became evident to me when I attempted to understand the significance of the marriage of a man from the house Ditilebit in Awear to a woman from the house Labatar in Keliobar. This marriage was especially confusing to me, since at first glance it seemed to involve not only a reversal in the relation between wife-giving and wife-taking houses, but also what might be considered a direct exchange of sisters.

Labatar has as its "house master" a house in Awear named Watti, which in turn belongs to the row called Lolat Awear, which ultimately feeds into the Lolat Ila'a house Ditilebit (figure 9.5). Labatar is thus located along a row of wife-taking houses that ultimately ends — albeit in eight steps — in the house of Ditilebit. I thought, at first, that when the Ditilebit man married a woman from Labatar, he had shattered his palmwine cup and reversed the established relations between wife-giving and wife-taking houses.

To complicate matters, some time after his marriage, a woman — who through agnatic links was his father's father's brother's son's daughter — was given in marriage from the house Watti to that of Labatar (figure 9.6). Because of the agnatic connection between this man and woman, it seemed to me that together the two marriages represented a direct exchange of sisters.

To consider this an instance of sister exchange, however, or even to consider the man's marriage an instance of the reversal of relations between established wife-givers and wife-takers would be to miss several important points.

First of all, it is true that the Ditilebit man and the Watti woman still consider one another cross-sex siblings on account of their agnatic connection, which is, on occasion, still effective as such. Yet the man's father's father's brother was lifted from Ditilebit into the house Watti, and his son occupied that house when his daughter's marriage was arranged. As opposed to whatever relationship can be traced through agnatic links, from the point of view of the relationship between houses, the Ditilebit man and the Watti woman are placed in quite different positions in regard to the Labatar house.

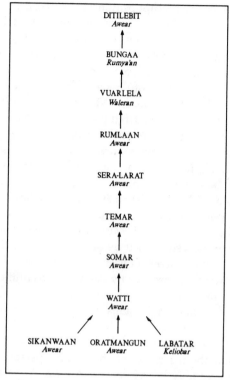

Figure 9.5   The row called Lolat Awear

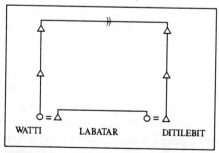

Figure 9.6   Relations of persons and houses

Second, the explicit presuppositions underlying the two marriages were quite different. The Watti woman belonged to the house that is the immediate house master of the Labatar house. She was considered her husband's *vat dua*, and their marriage was explicitly arranged to renew the alliance between the two houses Watti and Labatar. By contrast, the Ditilebit man's marriage to a woman of the Labatar house did not implicate the relations between their two houses. With regard to bloodlines, his wife was too far removed to be considered his sister: she was an other woman (*vat liak*). With regard to the relations between houses, Labatar is considered Watti's *lolat*, not Ditilebit's. Furthermore, even though — or, rather, because — she was from what was ultimately a wife-taking house, she could in no way be considered his *vat dua*, and their marriage was not thought to pertain to the established system of relations between houses. From Ditilebit's point of view, his marriage was motivated with regard to his *person*. The marriage of the Watti woman, however, was politically arranged to renew an established alliance within the fixed hierarchical structure of relations between *houses*.

Alliances between houses are, by definition, asymmetric and irreversible in form. The only marriages that activate the relations between houses are those in which a man marries his *vat dua*, a woman from the house that stands as the traditional wife-giver to his own. The asymmetry and irreversibility of the alliance relations between houses remain fixed, despite the fact that the marriages of the specific persons who happen to occupy these houses may be symmetric in form. Just as the persons (or "bodies") who belong to a given house are distinguished from the "house" itself, so to the marriages that specific persons may make are distinguished from the alliances maintained by particular houses. In the fixed order of things, the former is always subordinate to the latter: the alliances between houses are not contradicted by the marriages of those who occupy them. Valeri has made evident the necessity of the distinction between permanent alliances, which are asymmetric and irreversible, and marriage exchanges, which may involve a reversal in the asymmetric order of affinal relations (1975–76). This distinction — which, at least in Sera, Larat, and Fordata, the people themselves make — is crucial to an understanding of the complexity of such systems as exist in Tanimbar and other eastern Indonesian societies.

Indeed, the entire hierarchical order would be threatened by the potential for cycling if not for the distinction between houses — and the alliances they maintain — and the particular people who occupy these houses — and the marriages they themselves engage in. Although a marriage such as the one between Ditilebit and Labatar would appear to close a cycle along the rows, and reverse the relation between traditional wife-giver and wife-taker (with its consequent implications of equality), in fact it can do nothing of the kind, since this marriage implicated a relation between persons (and their particular bloodlines) rather than an alliance between houses (and their rows).

Nevertheless, cycles do — and must — occur. This is true not only because of the problem of where men at the top and women at the bottom of the system of exchange pathways will find their spouses, but also because the asymmetry of the movement of male and female valuables requires their recycling back through the pathways of exchange. Yet cycles are also differentially valued. The only cycles that implicate houses and relations of permanent alliance between houses are those constituted by the Great Row and its subsidiary *inetal* pathways. All other cycles are seen to implicate only the bloodlines of particular people and the more ephemeral affinal relations of recent marriages. The latter are given a subordinate value and, at least for those who occupy houses at the top of the system, are not thought to involve the fixed order of relations between houses.

One of the pathways implicated by the Ditilebit-Labatar marriage did indeed involve a cycle, but the cycle was not located where I first suspected. It did not close a cycle between the *houses* Ditilebit and Labatar along the row called Lolat Awear. Rather, a cycle had already been closed along the more recent *bloodline* that formed the pathway on which his wife's bridewealth moved (figure 9.7). Moreover, the Labatar woman's brother claimed to be in a position to both pay and eat his sister's bridewealth. For the Ditilebit man's redemption request for the bow portion of his bridewealth would travel (following the female bloodline of his mother) back along the pathway called Ditiyatak Ubun Yanan to the members of the house Masela and then, entering a row, potentially on to the houses Elat and Labatar. At the same time, the bow portion of his wife's bridewealth was destined to travel (following the female bloodline of her mother) from Labatar through a number of houses to the members of the house Nivunifa'at and then, entering a row, potentially back to the house Elat and on to Labatar.

It should be noted that — as Lévi-Strauss might well have predicted (1969:265–67) — where cycles do occur, the longer they are, the more fragile they will be. Thus if they extend beyond four or so houses and enter into a row, the valuables that move along these lines will "die," and they will most likely be diverted to other uses rather than being passed on to complete the circuit. To the extent that marriages do not renew the affinal relations along this cycle, its pathway will therefore rarely be fully realized by the passage of valuables, and it will eventually cease to be recognized as a cycle.

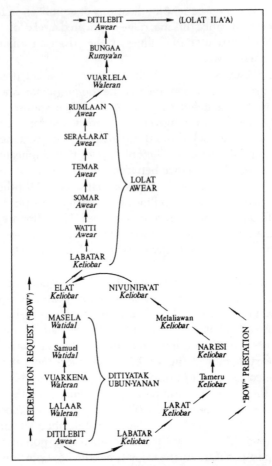

Figure 9.7   Bloodlines relative to rows of houses

What is significant here, however, is that the relations mobilized by the marriage of the Ditilebit man and the Labatar woman are placed at the subsidiary level of the system. Rather than implicating the fixed relations between houses along the rows and closing a cycle at the top of the system, the newly formed affinal pathways are grafted on at the lower reaches of the system. While it is true that Labatar may well be the master of the Ditilebit man's body as reckoned along bloodlines, the fact that Labatar has given him a woman in marriage cannot controvert the fact that the Ditilebit house remains in a superordinate position to the house of Labatar along the rows.

Relative and Fixed Hierarchies

It is this differentiation between person and house that generates the distinction between the two major hierarchical levels of the system: the unnamed, younger brother houses that control only the impermanent pathways made up of sisters and aunts; and the named, elder brother houses that control both sisters and aunts pathways and the rows that mark the permanent alliances between houses.

Indeed, on the island of Yamdena, where there is a tendency not to recognize one's *dua* past three generations, the system of rows is much attenuated. The hierarchical structure that is supported by the differentiation between person and house is therefore far less in evidence. Although this is not to say that the people on Yamdena do not recognize nobles and commoners, it may account for the fact that relative to the people of the islands of Sera, Larat, and Fordata — where this distinction between person and house, and the resulting system of rows, is highly elaborated — the people of Yamdena are considered (and often consider themselves) to be of lesser rank.

This difference between the island of Yamdena and those of Sera, Larat, and Fordata became evident to me in 1983 when I returned to Yamdena. While there, I had extended conversations with a school teacher who had been the first person from Yamdena allowed to teach on the island of Fordata. Previous to his tenure there, the Fordatans had refused to accept Yamdenan teachers, who they felt were far below them in rank. Others on Yamdena also described how difficult it was to marry a woman from Sera, Larat, and Fordata. In order to even propose such a union, the man's side would have to provide a slave in order to "open the door."

It may well be that the ability of people on the islands of Sera, Larat, and Fordata to elaborate an enduring superordinate level of named houses and rows was facilitated by their geographical position in the north and west of the archipelago — at the forefront, as it were, of contact with outside traders and colonial forces through which valuables made their way into the islands. Whether or not historical contingency had a role to play in the efflorescence of hierarchical values, it was the genius of the people of these islands to use those valuables in such a way as to create a crucial contrast between relations that are particularized in terms of specific persons, bodies, and blood and those that come to be increasingly abstracted and generalized in terms of valuables, houses, and rows.

By insisting upon a differential valuation of persons and houses, the people on the islands of Sera, Larat, and Fordata transform the relative hierarchical order of persons (wife-givers and wife-takers) into an absolute hierarchical order of houses — one in which a superordinate structure of named houses and *lolat* encompasses a subordinate structure of un-named houses and *ura-ava* pathways. For all named houses — despite the fact that they may be related to one another as wife-giver and wife-taker along the rows — are considered to be more or less equal. Similarly, and by contrast, all unnamed houses are more or less equal — despite the fact that they may be related to one another as wife-giver and wife-taker.

Named houses and their *lolat* hierarchically encompass unnamed houses and their *ura-ava* pathways in two ways. First, the former continue to maintain their position as sources of life — recognition of which is the condition for new growth among the latter. Second, the former control the full range of types of marriages and modalities of exchange which is denied to the latter. Thus members of unnamed houses may marry other women and their *fatnima*, and also may engage in the types of exchange appropriate to these marriages and their *ura-ava* pathways. But it is only members of named houses who, in addition to these types of marriage and exchange, may also marry a woman of their house master and engage in a modality of exchange that is found only along the rows. They can, in short, travel the rows.

10 The Recomposition of the World: Permanent Alliances and the Double Cycle

In Balinese cosmology the gods marry in the most preeminent fashion: a husband-wife consort = brother-sister of the nearest kind, boy-girl twins. The legendary maharaja can practice brother-sister incest. But well formed ancestor groups actually practice nothing closer than first-cousin unions. . . . Thus, cousin marriage appears to be a compromise between incest and outmarriage. (Boon 1977:139)

In moving from the relations between *ura-ava* and *ura-memi* to those between *dua* and *lolat*, we move from the impermanent pathways of exchange that link persons (of either unnamed or named houses) to the permanent pathways of exchange characteristic of the rows that link named houses only. If the former is expressed in terms of persons, bodies, and blood, the latter is seen in terms of houses, valuables, and rows. It is the increasing concentration of value as well as the generalization and objectification of relations along the open rows and the Great Row that is, in part, the subject of this chapter.

At the same time, the movement from sisters and aunts pathways to the rows of houses and the double cycle is also a movement from relations of hierarchy to those of equality. If, along the sisters and aunts pathways, the tension between encompassment and separation maintains a hierarchical order, this tension is subject to negotiation and temporary resolution along the open rows, and is permanently resolved in the egalitarian form of the double cycle of the Great Row, which, in itself, grounds the entire hierarchical order.

In Tanimbarese terms, the relation between hierarchy and equality is another way of talking about the relation between a source of life and that which issues forth from a source. Thus the hierarchical tension between encompassment and separation is the form that growth out from the source necessarily takes. The resolution of this tension into relations of equality is, by contrast, the form that marks a source and its ability to act as an anchor for the flow of life.

This chapter explores the significance of these movements from the dispersal to the concentration of value, from the particularization to the generalization of relations, and from hierarchy to equality, as they are manifest in relations between named houses along the rows. The concern, in the first place, is with the form of marriage called "to launch a ceremonial boat," which can only be contracted with a woman of one's master, and with the ways in which the permanence of named houses and rows is effected through residence, affiliation, and adrogation. This is followed by an analysis of the particular form and significance of the exchange of valuables as it is practiced along the rows. The chapter ends with an investigation of marriage and exchange along the Great Row and an analysis of the relation between the rows and the double cycle that stands at the apex of the system of exchange pathways.

Women of One's Master

The most prestigious form of marriage, and the one that is the sole prerogative of members of named houses, it that arranged between a man and "a woman of [his] master" (*vat dua*) — a woman who belongs to a house that is the "house master" (*rahan dua*) and traditional wife-giver of the man's own house. The marriage renews the alliance through which the position of the house in a particular row was originally established.

Like matrilateral cross-cousin marriage, a *vat dua* marriage preserves the asymmetric and hierarchical relation between wife-giver and wife-taker. Yet the two forms of marriage differ in significant ways. Matrilateral cross-cousin marriage has reference to a man's own female bloodline and entails a reciprocity established between specific persons — the *ura-ava* and the *ura-memi* who are linked along his own female bloodline. By contrast, a *vat dua* marriage has exclusive reference to the row that connects specific named houses and it entails a series of reciprocal exchanges between the *dua* and *lolat* related along this row. In marrying her father's sister's son, a woman follows the bloodline of a particular person: "she follows her father's sister" (*norang avan*). In marrying a man from a house that is the traditional wife-taker of her own house, a woman "follows the row" (*norang lolat*) of named houses that are wife-takers relative to her own. Here, the relation is no longer particularized in terms of specific persons and the bloodline that connects them; rather, it is generalized in terms of houses and the row that links them.

Had *vat dua* marriages been consistently practiced over the generations since the time of the founding alliance, then in marrying his *vat dua* a man would also be marrying his matrilateral cross-cousin (*fatnima*). The female bloodlines of the man and the woman would then coincide with the row that links their houses. *Vat dua* marriages, however, are not consistently practiced over the generations. This is so, on the one hand, because a proper *vat dua* marriage requires the mobilization of such a vast quantity of valuables that most houses can only afford to renew an alliance once every other generation at most. On the other hand, it is also true that the permanence of an alliance between two houses does not depend strictly upon marriage, for it is continuously renewed through the movement of exchange valuables along their row. As a consequence, two houses will not consider it necessary to renew their alliance every generation by contracting a marriage. Although it is therefore conceivable that in marrying his *vat dua* a man would also be marrying his matrilateral cross-cousin, this, in fact, rarely happens and is more or less irrelevant. A *vat dua* marriage concerns the relations between houses exclusively, regardless of the genealogical relation between the persons involved.

Yet precisely because of this, when a woman's *dua* along her own female line and the *dua* of her house do not coincide, the former must be dislodged so that the valuables intended for the *dua* of her house will not be diverted from the row onto the pathway constituted by her own female bloodline. Her father pushes aside (*nrii*) her mother's brother and his *dua* by presenting them with a valuable that is the equivalent of the bow portion of her bridewealth. In this way, the female bloodline of the woman will no longer be implicated in the exchanges that follow, and these exchanges will henceforth solely concern the houses that stand along the relevant row. This ability to push aside the woman's mother's brother is a graphic representation of the subordination of relations through persons to relations through houses that is the hallmark of such marriages.

Just as a man's *vat dua* need not necessarily be his matrilateral cross-cousin, she also need not belong, at least initially, to the house that is the immediate house master of his own house. There are two reasons why this might be the case. First of all, there may be no available woman in the house of a man's *dua*, or a man may have a preference for a particular woman who happens to belong to a house further up the row — the house of the wife-giver of the wife-giver of one's own wife-giver, for instance. In either case, it is possible for a woman to follow the row through several houses and ultimately marry a man who belongs to a wife-taking house that is several steps removed from her own house. The result is described by saying that the woman "wipes her feet" (*na'i ean*) at the doorstep of each intervening house until she reaches her final destination.[1] In this way, when both Taru and her brother's daughter Titi Kii Ditilebit followed the row which is Ditilebit's *inetal* pathway, they wiped their feet at the doorsteps of the houses Melatunan and Masela before they arrived at the house Lokraa, in which they found their husbands (see fig. 6.8). In a similar fashion Vat Meti, from the house Vatu in Sofyanin, wiped her feet at the doorsteps of the houses Ngelya, Oratmangun, and Seri in Sofyanin before she followed this row south to Sera, where she married a man of the house Refwalu.

Second, it can also happen that a high-ranking noble man takes a fancy to a lower-ranking commoner woman. If he is intent on the match, then it is possible to have her taken into a high-ranking house — preferably that of his house master — in order that she might be "adorned" as a high-ranking woman and be given in marriage from the house as if she were a woman of that house and the *vat dua* of her husband. When a commoner woman marries out of a noble house in this way, it is said that "they mold her into a finely worked rice cake" (*rtotak ia na'a vurat basalan*). Such a rice cake was used as an offering to Ubila'a on ritual occasions, and the implication is that the woman is transformed into a suitable offering for Ubila'a — or, that is, his/her earthly proxy, a man of noble birth. In order to make her worthy of a marriage with a high-ranking man, "they adorn the commoner woman to make her noble" (*rfalahar vata iwarin ala rot mela ia*), "to make her big" (*ala rfadawan ia*), and "to make her weighty" (*ala rfalemang ia*). This means, quite literally, that upon her marriage she would be weighted down with valuables. She would be dressed in cloth and gold befitting a noble woman, and her betelnut basket (*luvu*) would contain important named valuables. Such a procedure can be carried out for a commoner (*iria-iwarin*) woman, but not for a slave (*iria*). Nor can it be carried out for a low-ranking man — be he a commoner or a slave — who might wish to marry a high-ranking woman.

The strategy of transforming a commoner woman into a noble woman emphasizes that it is the relation between houses that is more important than the particular people concerned. A particular woman becomes, in a sense, a vehicle for expressing the worth and weight of the relation between houses as it is objectified and concentrated in the valuables with which she is adorned and which she carries with her into the marriage.

---

1. Cf. Traube (1986:255), who reports a similar practice among the Mambai, where it is called "to walk by the doorway" (*lolai damata*).

To Launch a Ceremonial Boat

In order for a woman to be considered truly a *vat dua* and for a marriage to take the form called "they launch a ceremonial boat" (*rtolar tutuk*), it must be negotiated beforehand and be agreed upon by the immediate *dua* and *lolat* houses along the row concerned. This is especially true where the house of the man and that of the woman are separated by several intervening houses along the row. It is not enough that a man happens to belong to a house located along the row attached to the house of the woman for her to be considered a *vat dua*, or for their marriage to be treated as one in which they launch a ceremonial boat.

When I first thought about the marriage of a woman from the house Ditilebit and a man from the house Sera-Larat, I assumed that it was a *vat dua* marriage. For Sera-Larat is located just four steps below the Ditilebit house along the row called Lolat Awear (see figure 9.5). I was quickly corrected, however, for their marriage had been initiated when the young couple eloped into the forest. Although the woman could technically be considered the man's *vat dua*, nevertheless because their marriage was not negotiated and arranged beforehand between all the *dua* and *lolat* concerned, it was not considered a *vat dua* marriage, and it was as if the man had married another woman.

Thus, if a woman is married — as the representative of her house — to a man of a wife-taking house and wipes her feet at the doorsteps of the intervening houses, then the exchanges that accompany the marriage will take the form called they launch a ceremonial boat. But if a woman simply runs off with her lover who happens to be a man who belongs to a house further down along the row to which her house belongs, then the exchanges entailed by their marriage will proceed as in any ordinary marriage with another woman.

In the negotiations, exchanges, and ceremonies that occur in connection with the renewal of an alliance between two named houses, the side of the man will consist of representatives of his house, of houses that are the elder-younger brothers of his own house, and of all those houses that are related as *lolat* along the row implicated by the marriage. These will be posed against the side of the woman, which will consist of representatives of her house, of houses that are the elder-younger brothers of her own house, and of all those houses that stand as *dua* along the row. The configuration is slightly different when the alliance being renewed is one between houses of the Great Row (Lolat Ila'a). For in such cases, not only will the Great Row cycle itself be implicated but also all the rows that lead up to the two houses concerned (see below).

The degree to which the launching of a ceremonial boat is elaborated depends upon both the relative wealth of the houses involved and their relative proximity. When the alliance is one that exists between two named houses that occupy the same village, the events and exchanges involved will be far less elaborated than when the houses occupy different villages, and this less elaborated still than when the houses are from different islands. It is only when the houses belong to separate villages, or more especially, to separate islands, that it is possible to launch a ceremonial boat in the fullest sense that the phrase implies. Thus it is rare for this form of marriage to be fully realized; more often some form of intermediate realization is achieved.

I should note that my description of the events and exchanges peculiar to such marriages derives from people's accounts of what should happen when they launch a ceremonial boat. Neither I nor a good many of my informants have ever seen the most complete realization of this form of marriage, which takes place when the alliances between the Lolat Ila'a houses of the two islands, Sera and Fordata, are renewed. Other alliance renewals, while perhaps less rare, are also less encompassing of the entire system of exchange.

When a man marries a *vat dua* from another village or another island, the representatives of his house, their elder-younger brothers, and *lolat* will sail together to the woman's village, where they will launch the ceremonial boat or, as is also said, "launch the woman" (*rtolar vata*). This happens at the time when the side of the man intends to bring the woman back to their village — either immediately after the marriage is agreed upon or after an initial period of uxorilocal residence on the part of the man, should this be requested of him.

The exchanges commence immediately as the visitors disembark from their boats. They must pull their boats ashore and put them in order, for their stay in the host village is expected to be a prolonged one. They must first "tie the paddles and punting poles" (*rkeak vahi la'it*). This is done for the paddles and punting poles of each boat when the side of the woman presents a female valuable — most likely an indigenous woven sarong (*bakan*) or a pair of female earrings (*kmena*) — and is reciprocated with a male valuable given by the side of the man — a pair of male earrings (*loran*) or a sum of money. A similar exchange must be made for each log used as a "skid" (*lunur*) to haul the boats ashore.

The visitors may stay with their hosts for days, weeks, or even months, and it will be the responsibility of the woman's side to house and feed their guests for the duration of their stay. An occasion like this presents an opportunity not only to consider the alliance that is being renewed by the marriage in question, but also to consider the condition of all the houses and alliances along the row. If there are problems along the row — unresolved disputes, for instance, or houses that have become empty — then these problems may be settled at this time.

The marriage itself entails a series of reciprocal prestations between *dua* and *lolat* that will continue over the lifetime of the couple and, usually, on into the next generation. Of the male valuables that are due from *lolat* to *dua*, it is said "fish and palmwine simply overflow" (*ian e tuat nvoat watan*) or "fish and palmwine are set traveling" (*ian e tuat fabana*). These find their counter in the female valuables that constitute the "adornment" (*baiyau* or *bareat*) of the woman and that are to be given from *dua* to *lolat*.

With regard to the fish and palmwine that overflows on account of a *vat dua* marriage, four major prestations must be made, and these bear names that distinguish them from all other types of marriage prestations. Following from the image of the woman as a boat, these are her "great sail" (*laar ila'a*) and "small sail" (*laar ko'u*), together with her "right rudder" (*wilin mela*) and the "left rudder" (*wilin balit*). In addition, there are two subsidiary prestations called the "great shading branch" (*imut ila'a*) and the "small shading branch" (*imut ko'u*).[2] Each prestation must consist of a high quality, named, male valuable. A golden breast pendant (*masa*), preferably one with a large gold link chain, should be given for the great sail, and a large elephant tusk (*lela*) should be presented as the right rudder. The other portions may consist of a golden breast pendant, an elephant tusk, or a pair of especially fine male earrings. These prestations need not be made all at once, but certainly at the time when they launch the woman several, at least, will be made.

This, too, is the time when the *dua* of the woman must ceremoniously "adorn her" (*rfalahar ia*, or, *rareat ia*). When she is actually taken from her house, they will dress her in the valuables that constitute her adornment. These valuables should likewise all be high quality, named valuables, but categorically female in nature: woven sarongs, bead necklaces, shell armbands, and female earrings.

By dressing a woman in such valuables, her *dua* "make her weighty" and make evident, for all to see, that she is a *lemditi*, a high-ranking woman of a noble house. These valuables compose the "contents of the betelnut basket" (*luvu ralan*) that the woman will bring to the house of her husband. Given from *dua* to *lolat*, they will, in time, be passed on

2. The word *imut* refers to the new shoots that issue forth from a branch or trunk of a tree that has been trimmed back.

to the *lolat* of her husband's house that belong to the row. The valuables are given, as the woman herself is given, "in order to look after/care for the row" (*ala rsi'ik lolat*), and they "make weighty" the row and the houses that belong to it just as much as they make the woman, herself weighty.[3] A woman's *dua* may, at the same time or later, "give weight to her betelnut basket" (*rta'i ni luvu*) with another prestation, such as the gift of a tract of land or a certain type of magic.

Loaded down and made heavy with valuables in this way, a woman embodies far more than her own person. She epitomizes the weight of the relation and, as she follows the row, her footsteps create an even more deeply furrowed pathway, leaving an imprint that will not soon be forgotten. The weight, names, and number of both the valuables she bears and those that travel in the opposite direction transform a marriage of persons into an alliance of houses: they concentrate and objectify the value of the relation between houses, giving to it a sense of entrenched permanence. This entrenchment is also achieved by the concentration of valuables along a single pathway. For whereas the valuables that move in connection with marriages with other women are dispersed along three separate pathways and those that move in connection with matrilateral cross-cousin marriages generally travel along two separate pathways, those that move in a *vat dua* marriage travel along a single row only. This concentration of valuables recomposes a kind of unity of movement (in face of potential dispersal) that is the essence of an objectified permanence.

At the time that a woman is adorned and taken from her house, the exchanges that constitute what is called *larlera* will take place. Indeed, it is precisely in those marriages where they launch a ceremonial boat that the *larlera* ritual is most appropriate and most likely to occur. In this ceremony, as mentioned previously, the people who represent the side of the woman will block her pathway with bamboo poles over which are hung woven sarongs. The side of the man must reopen the pathway and free it of obstacles by presenting male earrings in exchange for the cloth. The tension in this ceremony between continued encompassment and effective separation is given even more importance here to the extent that the relations involved implicate the continuity of named houses and the rows that link them.

Once the man and his new wife have arrived back in his own village,

3. It is unclear to me whether the number of female valuables given as the woman's adornment at this time is strictly in accordance with the number of male valuables given as the sails and rudders. On the whole, the exchanges between *dua* and *lolat* entail a strictly balanced and immediate reciprocity. However, I was also told that the adornments of the woman are given, in part, to encourage the *lolat* to expedite the sail and rudder prestations that are due on behalf of the woman.

the woman may refuse to disembark until all the *dua, lolat,* and *ura-ava* of her husband's house in the village come to honor her. They do so by making prestations to her — either of woven sarongs or of palmwine and male earrings, depending upon their relation to her husband's house.

People say that when a high-ranking woman of a noble house disembarks in the village of her husband, the pathway from the harbor to her husband's house should be set with a line of porcelain plates. It is on top of these plates that she should walk to her new home. Although this trial appears to occur more often in accounts of the distant past than in the present, it is nevertheless indicative of what Tanimbarese expect of a high-ranking woman. For a woman of high rank, it is assumed, should be able to manage this feat without breaking a single plate. It is curious, however, that a woman who is considered so weighty should be subjected to such a test. The trial is required as evidence that the woman is of high rank and that she is not a witch (*iwangi*). This makes it all the more curious, since witches are paradigmatically the most featherweight of all people. Yet there is a classic story of a witch who murdered a high-ranking woman as she was being taken back to her husband's village. The witch took all the adornments of the woman and successfully impersonated her, but when it came time to walk the line of porcelain plates, she shattered them to pieces and her deception was thereby discovered.

A woman who has followed the row and married a man of another village or another island is not permitted to return to her village in just any way or at just any time. She may not visit her village again until her husband and the *lolat* of his house are prepared to make another major presatation to their *dua.* When she does return, the occasion is called "she sets foot in the village" (*ntaa ahu*). She will sail to her village accompanied by her husband, representatives of his house, their elder-younger brothers, and their *lolat.* As they enter the harbor and approach the shore, they must "throw out an elephant tusk bridge" (*rleta lela*) into the waves that are breaking on the beach. This is their first offering to their house masters, who await them on shore and who will reciprocate with a "small sarong" (*bakan ko'u*) composed of any type of female valuable. Just as before, they must tie the paddles and punting poles by means of an exchange of male and female valuables, which exchange must also accompany each log used as a skid to haul their boats ashore. They will again stay in the woman's village for some days or weeks while they negotiate another sail or rudder prestation.

Once the initial marriage prestations have been made, further exchanges will be stretched out over a lifetime and occur as occasions present themselves for the two sides to come together — for instance, at a house-raising feast, at the death feast of an important person, or even at the death feast of the man or woman concerned. Since the exchanges involve a balanced and immediate reciprocity between the two sides, their progress will depend upon the resources of both houses over the course of the years.

Looking back upon a series of exchanges between two houses, however, what assumes importance is not so much whether all the named prestations have indeed been made, but rather that momentous occasions have been marked by the movement of important named valuables that give weight to the persons and the events involved. In talking about the death feast for their father, Siavu, the Ditilebit brothers recounted the various named valuables that had passed between Ditilebit, their *dua* Kuwai, and other closely related houses:

> Kuwai gave its *lolat* Ditilebit a gold breast pendant called Ulun Itelu, an antique sarong, three pairs of armbands, a pair of male earrings called Vuarmerah, and a pair of female earrings called Ngova. Ditilebit gave their house master Kuwai two gold pieces, including Lim Ila'a and Siku Wahan Sian, the latter of which had moved from Vuarlela to Bungaa to Ditilebit for the occasion. The event also gave Ma'idodu Melatunan the opportunity to give a pair of named female earrings to Kuwai (by way of Vavumasa and Fatruan) and a valuable named Ti'i Sela ni Laar to their house master Ditilebit.

The movement of so many named valuables between Ditilebit and Kuwai on the occasion of Siavu Ditilebit's death feast followed not only from the status of the two houses concerned but also from the fact that Siavu's brother Metlia had married Masvahan Kuwai. Indeed, her father, Seran Kuwai, had lived in Awear for several years with the hopes, people said, that the Ditilebits would pass on the gold breast pendant Lim Ila'a. However, it was not until after Siavu, Metlia, Masvahan, and her father, Seran, had all died and the younger generation of Ditilebits gave Siavu's death feast that the valuable was finally surrendered to Seran's son Sinyasu Kuwai. Whether Lim Ila'a was considered Masvahan's sail or rudder is not remembered, and it is irrelevant. What is significant is that important named valuables continue to move on such occasions, giving weight to the people, the houses, and the rows involved.

Residence, Affiliation, and Divorce

The permanence of named houses and that of the rows which link them mutually imply one another. Efforts to maintain the continuity of one are also, and simultaneously, efforts to maintain the continuity of the other. This is evident in the manner in which people think about residence, affiliation, and divorce relative to *vat dua* marriages.

Because *vat dua* marriages renew the alliances that link houses along the rows, it is understood that such marriges will also contribute to the permanence of the houses concerned. Therefore, as long as the continuity of the relation between a wife-giving and a wife-taking house is assured by the movement of valuables along the row, the implied continuity of the wife-taking house will be preserved both by the patrilocal residence of the man and his family and by the patrilateral affiliation of his children.

It may happen that the couple will reside uxorilocally for a time, especially if, for whatever reasons, the woman has not yet been properly "launched" and at least one portion of her marriage prestations has not yet been negotiated and completed. But the logic of *vat dua* marriages — that they are high status unions and that their very nature implies the continued separate identity of the allied houses — militates against the likelihood that uxorilocal residence would be practiced in connection with them, at least for any extended period of time. Continued uxorilocal residence would contradict the intention of the marriage — the renewal of an alliance, which presupposes the separate identity of the two houses.

A similar logic applies to the question of affiliation. The permanence of the alliance being renewed assumes that the continuity of the wife-taking house will be reaffirmed through the patrilateral affiliation of the children of the marriage. Matrilateral affiliation of the children would imply the breakdown of all exchange along the row between the two houses (and the incorporation of the children of the marriage within the house of the wife's father). It would thus contradict the very point of the renewal of the alliance.

In the normal course of events, then, the affiliation of the children depends upon the continuity of exchange, but not upon the completion of any specific prestation. Whether the woman's great sail, small sail, right rudder, and left rudder have all been completed at the time when she and her husband die is of little consequence. No rope of the dead prestation need be made: the patrilateral affilation of their children will remain unquestioned. Certainly, the great sail and the right rudder should be made and accounted for during the couple's lifetime. But the alliance outlasts the particular people whose marraige happens to renew it at any given time: fish and palmwine will continue to overflow from *lolat* to *dua* whether or not the valuables are called a particular woman's great or small sail; and *dua* will continue to make weighty their *lolat* whether or not the valuables they pass on are called the adornment of a particular woman.

To say that the logic of *vat dua* marriages is such that the permanence of both the rows and the houses standing along them implies one another is not to say that their permanence is invulnerable or automatic. The fragility of rows becomes evident in the event of a divorce. In the extremely rare case that a divorce should take place between a man and his *vat dua*, relations between the two houses along the row would completely rupture and, depending upon the relative completion of exchanges, open up the possibility for the matrilateral affiliation of the children. The only just cause for a separation is adultery on the part of the woman, in which case the members of her house would be obliged to provide another wife for the man, their *lolat*. Any other cause for divorce would result in a total break in relations between *dua* and *lolat* and the consequent dissolution of the row.

Such a break in a major row occurred some three generations ago. The Lolat Ila'a house Refvutu, in Awear, had as one of its major *lolat* the house Maranresi of Lauran in southern Yamdena.

> Three generations ago, Melamnanat Maranresi came to Refvutu to take a *vat dua* in marriage. Because Refvutu had no unmarried woman available at the time, a woman named Lalin from the house Ditilebit "wiped her feet" at the doorstep of the house Melatunan and was given in marriage from the house Refvutu to Melamnanat Maranresi. After the two were married, they stayed for a long time in Awear, but they never had any children. At one point, Melamnanat wanted to return home to Lauran, but Lalin did not want to follow, I was told, out of fear for the witches who are thought to abound in certain villages of southern Yamdena. In the end, Melamnanat returned alone to Lauran.

To this day, people in Lauran and Olilit still remember the insult — and the valuables they paid and lost in the ill-fated match. Lalin's great sail was the gold breast pendant called Lebit Funlia; her small sail was the gold breast pendant, Masa Bibi (and, some said, Lim Ila'a); her right rudder was a large elephant tusk named Savaluri; and her left rudder was a piece called Tavaleka (I am unsure what type of valuable this is). In addition, they gave a female slave, named Ritngongoan, who "opened the door" (*nvadil falfolat*) to the engagement.

On account of this breach in relations, the house Maranresi no longer goes to or recognizes Refvutu as its house master, and all movement along this row has ceased.[4] In order for the row to be activated once again, Refvutu would have to "make good" (*nfalolin*) the relationship with Maranresi by means of a prestation of at least one important named female valuable. This has still not been done.

---

4. Some people said that the row connecting these two houses was part of an eastern cycle of the Lolat Ila'a. If this is true, the divorce might account for the discontinuance of the eastern cycle (see chapter 6).

The force of relations involved in *vat dua* marriages militates against divorce and for the continuity of exchange—and thereby the continuity of the wife-taking house, as realized through patrilocal residence and patrilateral affiliation. Yet the fact that divorce can happen, and that it has such catastrophic effects for the row, is a reminder that even here along the rows where the fixity of relations is assumed, this is possible only to the extent that the continuity of exchange gives it weight and form.

Empty Houses and "Lifted" Men

Like the permanence of a row, that of a house is vulnerable and may be threatened in several ways. First of all, the occupants of a named house may have no heir, leaving the house empty. This may be seen as the result of simple demographic chance. But it is more likely to be viewed as the result of the perceived difficulty high-ranking people are thought to have in bearing children, the curse of a *dua*, or a curse laid on the house itself generations ago on account of excessive or unjustifiable bloodshed perpetrated by its former occupants. In the latter instance, it is said that the "house kills off [its occupants]" (*rahan nfakinan*), in which case, it is extremely difficult to keep it occupied in any continuous fashion.[5] Second, the continuity and status of a house may be threatened because its occupants have fallen in rank such that the *dua* and *lolat* of the house refuse to recognize the legitimacy of the occupant's claims to represent a named house in *adat* matters. Third, those occupying a house may simply be so inept in negotiating the concerns of the house that they are unable to act as the representatives of the house.

There are two solutions to such threats to a named house. One is accomplished through marriage, the other through adrogation. Because of the frequency with which adrogation is used to reestablish the continuity of named houses, it has assumed a tremendous importance in Tanimbarese social relations.

It is not uncommon that a house will lack male heirs yet be blessed with a surfeit of daughters. A daughter on her own, however, cannot act as a representative of her natal house, for she is destined to marry a man of another house and, with her husband, become the representative of his house. The situation is different if a "woman goes walking and takes a man" (*vata nbana nala brana*). In such a case, her husband marries into

5. Usually, in the history of such houses there has been one or more cases of unjustified bloodshed. The "hot blood" (*lara ngnea*), which is the result, continues to avenge itself. Thus it is said: "hot blood demands its price" (*lara ngnea ntuntut ni fiawan*). This causes a house (or a valuable) to be hot and thereby to "kill off" (*nfakinan*) those who represent it.

and becomes the heir of the house of his wife's father. As the logic of bridewealth prestations would have it, when a man is completely incorporated into the house of his wife, no bridewealth need be paid. If the *dua* and *lolat* of the house are agreed, this man will (together with his wife) become the official representative of the house and will speak for it in all negotiations that concern it.

The more common solution to the problems that threaten the continuity of a named house is found in the practice of adrogation, a term taken from Roman law. Adrogation in Tanimbar shares a number of features with the practice observed in ancient Rome. It "concerns the nobility almost exclusively" (E. Goody 1971:340); its purpose is to prevent a house from dying out; the act of adrogation requires public sanction (Crook 1967:112); those adrogated are usually adult and male; the concern of adrogation is to "substitute one legal status for another" with regard to rights over property and a cult of worship (E. Goody 1971:341); and adrogation is used — in a fashion similar to marriage — to establish alliances between the houses related by the adrogation.[6]

When a person is adrogated, it is said "they lift him" (*rsikat ia*) from one house to another. Adrogation is almost exclusively a practice that is the concern of named houses. A man may, in rare instances, be lifted from an unnamed house into a named house, but the idea of lifting a man into an unnamed house is counter-intuitive, since unnamed houses are thought of as inherently impermanent and their continuity is therefore not an issue. Those lifted are generally men, and most often adults, although it does occasionally happen that a young child will be lifted, or that an infant will be born, into another house. In such a case, it is said that "they lift him together with his swaddling clothes" (*rsikat ia ovun ni sikar*).

Because a named house is defined by reference to its *dua* and *lolat*, and because the purpose of adrogating a person into a house is to preserve its permanent position and status in a row, no person may be lifted into a named house without the consent of all the *dua* and *lolat* of the house. This is true even if the house is still occupied. It is often, though not necessarily, the case that the person adrogated will be chosen from a house that belongs to the same row as the house into which he will be lifted — whether or not he is related by recent blood ties to the occupants

---

6. It should be mentioned that adrogation differs from adoption, which is known in Tanimbar as *rlaing* ("they adopt" a child as their own). This practice is extremely rare, such that in all the genealogies I collected in Awear, there is only one instance of a child being adopted in this way. "Orphans" (*watat*) are taken into the house of their father's brother or mother's brother — depending upon the state of bridewealth exchanges at the time of their parents' death — or of other close relatives, who "bring them up" (*rfawatat ira*). But this is not called *rlaing*.

or former occupants of the house. A sister's son, or a person who is in one way or another related as an elder-younger brother is also a good candidate for being lifted into a house. But various other criteria mark a good candidate for adrogation — including rank, knowledge of and ability to talk *adat*, and more general political concerns — and these may be cited as reasons for lifting in someone who may otherwise be unrelated to the occupants or former occupants of the house.

If the person adrogated is unrelated to the ocupants of the house and their *dua*, then the prestations called "water–breast milk" (*wear-sus vahan*) should be made. This is given by the *dua* of the adrogating house to the *dua* of the person who is adrogated. "Water" is the "portion of the man" (*brana ni wahat*) and is given to the man's father's *dua*; "breast milk" is the "portion of the woman" (*vata ni wahat*) and is given to the man's mother's *dua*. Once these payments are made, and the man is lifted into his new house, he will no longer (at least officially) recognize his old *dua*, and his new *dua* will take responsibility for redeeming him of his bride-wealth and other debts.

Upon being lifted into another house, a man loses the rights and prerogatives he enjoyed as a member of his natal house and gains full rights in his new house. These include rights to negotiate all matters that have to do with both the forest estates and the village estates of the house, to hold the heirloom valuables of the house, and to carry out all ritual offices that pertain to the house. In this way, the new head of the house assumes a position as the inheritor of the patrimony — the *lolat*, the land, the heirloom valuables, and ritual offices — of the ancestral founders of the house. Through the ritual observances connected with this patrimony, he maintains the continuity of relation between the ancestors and himself. In the genealogy of the house, he is now their descendant, the inheritor of their patrimony and estates.

Adrogation is extremely common. The greater proportion of named houses have had at least one person lifted in or out of them, and often many more (see appendix 2). One consequence of the prevalence of adrogation is that the genealogies of named houses very often begin where they had broken off: that is, they often commence with a man lifted in, and it is usually no longer remembered who the original or former occupants might have been.

Although adrogation is a means of preserving the continuity of named houses along rows, it is also a means for renewing the links between these houses. In fact, adrogation is explicitly thought of in the same terms as marriage alliance. As mentioned before, whoever moves out of a house is considered female — whether this be a woman who moves in marriage or a man who moves through adrogation. When a man is lifted into another house, therefore, he becomes related to his house of origin as a female. Like all *ura-ava* and *lolat*, he must bring palmwine to his former house on those occasions that require it.

Adrogation is indeed important as a substitute for marriage in renewing the bonds of alliance between named houses along a row. Yelar Vuarlela noted that if, for several generations, the women of a house do not follow the row and marry a man from one of their *lolat*, there may be a tendency for the bonds of these old alliances to weaken in favor of new ones. Adrogation, as much as marriage, renews these old alliances and gives weight and permanence to the rows.

The effectiveness of this strategy can be observed in the double adrogation involving the three houses Vuarlela, Bungaa, and Ditilebit. Vuarlela is the *lolat* of Bungaa, which is the *lolat* of Ditilebit.

> For as long as anyone can remember, no Bungaa woman has actually ever followed the row and married a Vuarlela man, and only one Ditilebit woman, Luvu, has married a Bungaa man within living memory. Yet in the generation of Luvu's father, So'u (three generations ago), a double adrogation was negotiated, which linked all three houses as elder-younger brothers. Nifmasa Vuarlela was lifted into Ditilebit, and his brother Metaniat was lifted into Bungaa, while their eldest brother, Temar, remained behind in Vuarlela. Temar's great grandson Yelar is currently the head of the Vuarlela house, and Metaniat's grandson Metaniat (the son of Luvu Ditilebit and Sabonu Bungaa) is the head of Bungaa. Nifmasa was lifted into Ditilebit as the brother of Falaksoru: the latter's grandsons—Falaksoru and Ma'ileba—head the Ditilebit house alone now, since Nifmasa's line has died out (and the third grandson, Luraleman, has been lifted into Refvutu).[7]

The men of these three houses continue, to this day, to consider themselves closely related on account of this double adrogation. In place of, and in addition to, marriage, these adrogations reaffirmed the alliances between the *dua* and *lolat* houses along this row.

Yet adrogations not only strengthen an alliance, they also add another dimension to it. For houses related as *dua* and *lolat* thereby also become linked through men who are, by blood, related as elder-younger same-sex

---

7. It will be noted that the relations engendered by this particular adrogation are potentially problematic. For not only have men moved "as females" out of a wife-taking house into wife-giving houses but also it was the younger brothers who moved out into the houses of their *dua* while the eldest brother remained in their own house. Ordinarily, people said, the elder brother should be in the house of the *dua*, and the younger brother should be moved into the house of a *lolat*.

siblings. Although a brother who is lifted out of his natal house severs his relations with the house, as such, he can never sever the blood relation between himself and his brothers who have remained in his natal house. Indeed, part of the political force of adrogation stems from the fact that the representatives of houses related as *dua* and *lolat* come, through adrogation, to be also related by the more intimate bond of brotherhood, which is more conducive to the political machinations so common in the negotiation of exchanges. Although the strength of the bond between elder-younger brothers cannot be denied, nevertheless it is also true that by compounding the complementarity of the affinal alliance with the potentially competitive relation between brothers, as many problems may be created as solved.

Despite whatever ambiguities might be created by adrogation, its prevalence speaks of the tremendous concern Tanimbarese have with maintaining the permanence of named houses and the rows that link them. In a world of motion and flux, they are conceived as fixed points of concentrated value that are defined by their village and forest estates, their heirlooms, and ritual offices. Adrogation is the fortification of such houses in the face of the contingencies of individual lives and personal histories.

Dispersed and Concentrated Valuables

The permanence of named houses is a cultural value rather than a functional value. At issue is the ability of named houses to foster their identity as an enduring source of life and therefore their hierarchical superiority over those who have issued forth from them—their *lolat* and their *ura-ava*. Where women have not moved in marriage from *dua* to *lolat*, a *dua*'s life-giving capacities and continued hierarchical superiority must be continually demonstrated through the movement of valuables lest he be disavowed by his *lolat*. Indeed, it is the movement of valuables—far more than the movement of women in marriage or men in adrogation—that renews the relations between named houses along the rows. The burden of the continuity of the relationship rests with the *dua*: it is he who must first give a woman or valuables in order to entice and further indebt his *lolat*. If neither is forthcoming, then the *lolat* will not "be afraid of" (*nbobar*) or respect his *dua* and will not feel at all obliged to pass on valuables to him.

As a consequence, the nature of exchange along the rows is seen as qualitatively different from that along the *ura-ava* pathways. A set of brothers will refer to their *ura-ava* as "the contents of our wallet" (*ita dida dompet ralan*). The relationship between *dua* and their *ura-ava* is based upon recent marriages and remembered blood links between specific persons. *Ura-ava* are therefore obliged to pass on palmwine and male bride-wealth valuables when these are demanded by their *dua*. One's *ura-ava*, so the saying goes, are like the half of a coconut shell that contains the eyes (i.e., the holes): valuables must flow out. They represent an assured source of valuables that will be passed on, upon demand.

One's *lolat*, on the other hand, are described as the half of a coconut shell that contains no eyes: there is no assurance that valuables will flow out at all. In contrast to *ura-ava*, who form the "contents of our wallet," people say of *lolat*: "We buy before we receive" (*Tfaha betii tala*), or "We pound so there may be sago" (*Tfalu bo ma era*). Some additional effort is required. Thus where the movement of valuables does not answer to a recent flow of women and lifeblood, *lolat* are not indebted to their *dua* in an immediate way that obligates them to pass along valuables upon demand. Not fearing their *dua*, they must be impressed in other ways with a sense of indebtedness. In lieu of women, then, it is the continued giving of valuables that "buys" the relation and the reciprocation.

Yet, in the nature of exchange along the rows, there is a tension between the imperative that a *dua* must continually demonstrate his generosity in order to further indebt his *lolat* and the equally important injunction that a *dua* must not be so generous as to empty his house of all valuables and thereby lose the respect of his *lolat*. This tension involves, on the one hand, the dispersal of valuables that fosters the flow of life and, on the other hand, the concentration of valuables in houses and along the rows that anchors that flow.

When a *dua* neglects his *lolat*—by not giving women or female valu-ables, or by not taking responsibility for redeeming "his people"—he runs a far greater risk than simply reciprocal neglect by his *lolat*. For if his *lolat* truly despair of receiving the proper attention from their *dua*, then they will find themselves another *dua* and move the whole row to the new *dua*. The movement of an entire row to a new *dua* is different from an indi-vidual selling himself to a new *dua*. Whereas the latter move makes a virtual slave out of the person who has sold himself, the former move has no such connotation. The movement of a row goes a long way to express the contingency of the status of a *dua* relative to his *lolat*, since the *dua* depends upon the existence and fruitfulness of the *lolat*.

> Falaksoru said that *dua* could not be considered "big" (*dawan*) as a matter of course. They were big if they acted in a big way and gave out many women and valuables. *Dua* are also big, he said, because of their *lolat*. If *lolat* go elsewhere, then *dua* are nothing. He gave, as an example, a named house in Lamdesar. Apparently its *lolat* brought a case against its representative, because they felt that

he had been less than forthcoming in light of what his *lolat* had given. When everything that had been given and taken was tallied up, it turned out that the man owed some Rp. 150,000 to his *lolat*. Falaksoru commented tersely, *"Dawan akaa?"* which might be translated as "What bigness [is that]?" He then went on to quote a ritual song, sung by Lamdesar people about a boat whose sideboards had fallen apart and whose keel had been broken. The song had been created to describe the condition of this house.

Falaksoru also mentioned a named house in Awear whose *lolat* has begun to shift to a new *dua*. Since the old *dua* had not been carrying out his responsibilities satisfactorily, his *lolat* had begun to go to the house Bungaa, which assumed the responsibilities of a *dua*. Falaksoru said that if the *lolat* had only gone to Bungaa once, it might still be possible to reestablish relations with his old *dua*. But he had already gone several times and, at this point, in order for the old *dua* to reclaim his *lolat*, he would have to reimburse Bungaa for all the valuables Bungaa has already paid on behalf of his *lolat*. This becomes difficult as time goes on and Bungaa expends more and more valuables. It therefore becomes increasingly certain that the old *dua* has lost his *lolat* to Bungaa for good.

It should be noted that such a move tends to reinforce the position of those houses at the apex of the system of exchange pathways, because it is highly unlikely that a disgruntled *lolat* would take his row to any other but the very top houses. In this way, too, longer rows tend to get shortened and feed into the system toward the top.

Although a *dua* must reassert his life-giving capacity and hierarchical superiority by further indebting his *lolat*, this is not done, at least initially, by an outright prestation of a big named valuable. Rather, it is done through innumerable prestations made on behalf of people much lower down in the system of exchange pathways. Thus one plays for big stakes with a lot of little chips.

Ditilebit's *lolat* is Bungaa, whose *lolat* is Vuarlela. At the time of my stay, Ditilebit held (among other valuables) the breast pendant Mas Batavi, Metaniat Bungaa held one called Laksilu, and Yelar Vuarlela held one called Lebit Fenu. The Ditilebit brothers were keen to get their hands on Laksilu, which was traveling the row in their direction. But in order to do this they felt they had to indebt both Bungaa and Vuarlela to the point where Vuarlela would finally release Lebit Fenu to Bungaa, thereby bumping Laksilu into Ditilebit. Mas Batavi would be the counter that would move in the opposite direction. Because of Yelar Vuarlela's position along the rows, he was extraordinarily cautious of releasing a valuable, since he knew that once it went up the row further to Bungaa and Ditilebit, it would most likely disappear into the Lolat Ila'a, and he would not see it again. A big man in his own right, one who controls a vast system of exchange pathways, Yelar Vuarlela was not particularly concerned with his *dua*, and he resisted mightily the sense of obligation to pass on Lebit Fenu or any other important named valuable to his *dua*.

The only way to force the hand of someone as powerful in his own right as Yelar Vuarlela is to compel him to recognize his own *dua* on as many occasions as possible. When redemption requests come up the row, it is Yelar Vuarlela who would generally take responsibility for them and redeem his people of their bridewealth debts. But the Ditilebits can also attempt to force Yelar Vuarlela to pass on the redemption request and, in the process, make Yelar recognize them as his *dua*, to whom he is indebted. Such a strategy, however, is only possible given a number of conditions. First of all, the higher *dua* must be in cahoots with those who are destined to eat the bridewealth, so that it can be agreed that the latter will refuse whatever is offered by the lower *dua*. If the lower *dua* is thereby blocked and unable to pay the bridewealth, he is forced to pass on the redemption request to his own *dua*. Second, the exchange must involve people belonging to one's own village. For instance, the Ditilebits could manage such a maneuver in their own village, Awear, but not in Vuarlela's village, Waleran. Third, it is easier to carry off such a scheme if those who will eat the bridewealth have one as their *dua* along another, different pathway that does not include the *lolat* whose hand one is trying to force.

The point of all this is that a lot of little valuables are moved around, not so much with an eye to obtaining an exact reciprocation from the people one redeems. Rather, one redeems a great number of people further down in the system of exchange pathways in order to increase the indebtedness of one's immediate *lolat*. Thus the Ditilebits may pay out a fair number of valuables to redeem their people of their bridewealth debts, but the motivation, at least in part, is eventually to increase Vuarlela's sense of indebtedness to the point that Lebit Fenu, or some other big named valuable, will move from Vuarlela into Bungaa, thereby bumping Laksilu into Ditilebit. These valuables will still not move without ones of equivalent value moving in the opposite direction, nor generally will they move unless there is a clear sense of indebtedness already established.

This is not to say that other, lesser named valuables will not exchange hands, or rather houses, in the meantime.

When So'u Ditilebit roofed his house, the Ditilebit brothers took the opportunity to give the female earrings La'it and a pair of shell armbands to their *lolat* Bungaa and a small elephant tusk named Aran Laan to Melatunan, their *lolat* along the Lolat Ila'a. These more than reciprocated the pairs of male earrings brought by Bungaa and Melatunan on this occasion and were clearly meant as yet another effort "to buy them" (*ala rfaha ira*) and "to make them fearful" (*ala rfabobar ira*).

But such exchanges are, in a sense, mere preliminaries foreshadowing the eventual movement of bigger named valuables that travel the rows far more slowly (see below).

While it is imperative for the continuity of the relationship that *dua* give valuables to their *lolat*, it is equally important that they do not empty their house of all valuables — most especially their heirloom valuables. Ostensibly inalienable, these heirlooms can, in fact, be lost in the payment of debts when a house is pressed for a valuable and has no other resources to draw from. But to be completely devoid of valuables means a great loss of status and power. Just as when a house is stingy and does not give valuables to its *lolat*, so too when a house is empty of valuables, it is said that the "*lolat* will not be afraid [and] will not come [to them]" (*lolat wol rbobar, wol rmaa*). Any house that has pretensions to being big in the game of exchange, then, must negotiate this tension between giving and retaining, between the dispersal and concentration of valuables.

Yet the value of heirlooms is not in their retention or accumulation, as such. Heirlooms are, rather, a kind of concentration of value that is immobilized at the center of named houses, and the weight of such valuables anchors the house as an enduring source of life. At the same time, the permanence of such an anchorage makes possible the movement of other valuables that foster the extension of life outside and on the periphery (cf. Weiner 1985).

Just as a named house will strive to retain its heirloom valuables, so too a row will attempt to protect itself against the loss of the big named valuables that its member houses hold. Such valuables will often be targeted in bridewealth negotiations, especially if the woman's *dua* feel they can press their case. If one house along the row has a big named valuable, those lower down on the pathway will attempt to "stand and block it" (*rdir teri ia*) so it will not be diverted from their row. They will try to use smaller, less important valuables to fulfill the redemption request. Those who stand in a position to receive the bridewealth may, of course, refuse to accept a smaller valuable, in which case those along the row may be forced to pass on the redemption request until it reaches the house in question, although this by no means assures that the valuable will move. The problem, here, is that if a big piece is sidetracked off onto a small sisters and aunts pathway it may well be permanently lost to the row that holds it. The people who are concerned with such valuables are highly unlikely to let them disappear from their sight in this way.

Indeed people who handle big named valuables are greatly reluctant to let such pieces pass out of the rows and be used to redeem men of their bridewealth debts. For such a valuable falls in status and value if it is used to redeem men. When a big named valuable is kept moving along the rows as "fish and palmwine set traveling," it is weighty (*aleman*), its "name is big" (*naran dawan*), or it is "made big" (*fadawan ia*). But if it is sidetracked onto smaller pathways and used to redeem men of bridewealth debts, then "its body falls" (*tenan nleka*), "its name falls already one step" (*naran nlek rang isaa roak*), or "its name is already light" (*naran maraan roak*). Rather, for a big named valuable, "its nobility is to stay in its own place" (*ni mela na'a waan obi*), where it can be used "to give weight to the row" (*al rta'i lolat*).

Like heirlooms in a named house, the valuables that are retained within a row represent a concentration of value, the value of the specific set of relations between houses along that row. They demonstrate the nobility of the relations that continue to stand as an enduring source of life—which is evident not only in all that has issued forth from these relations but also in the sheer number, weight, and names of valuables that continue to move back through them, giving tangible proof of their fecundity.

The Marriage of Valuables

Rarely renewed through the marriages of persons, relations of alliance along the rows are renewed through the movement of valued objects. Yet when big named valuables move along the rows, the character of the exchange is paradoxical. For, on the one hand, the exchange is expressly objectified in terms of buying and selling (with implications for equivalency that undermines the hierarchical impetus of the relation). On the other hand, and despite the market metaphor, the valuables themselves become personified. Here, it is the valuables that court and marry each other.

A male valuable given from *lolat* to *dua* must eventually be passed on to the house master of the latter, who will in turn pass it on to his own house master. In this way it will proceed from wife-taking to wife-giving houses according to the manner in which they are linked to one another along the row. Similarly, a female valuable given from *dua* to *lolat* is destined to travel to the *lolat* of the latter, and on along the row from wife-giver to wife-taker.

As the valuables move in their opposite directions from house to house along the row, they do not move except in exchange for an opposite-gender piece of equivalent value. Let us take, for example, a named breast pendant (a male valuable) that has been given to one's house master as the great sail prestation for a *vat dua*. Eventually one's house master must pass the pendant on to his own house master as "fish and palmwine set traveling." Yet it will not travel on in haste. Such a valuable must "rest" (*nyari*) for some time in each house through which it is destined to pass. A valuable will rest in a house sometimes for many years. It waits, bides its time, and "searches for its spouse" (*ndava awan*).[8] Only when the house master of this house comes into possession of a female valuable that is considered its "match" or "equal" (*noka*) will an exchange be contemplated, and then only if some suitably weighty occasion presents itself — as I have said, the house-raising or death feast of a high-ranking person. During the exchange negotiations, the male and female valuable will be placed side by side in the same dish. If they are considered one another's match, they are said to "marry one another" (*rsifaa*). As a result, each valuable "stands up" (*ndiri*) and moves to the other house. If they are not one another's match, however, one will not stand, and the exchange will be blocked. One valuable should not move without its counterpart moving in the opposite direction: one should replace the other (*rsiwaul ira*), so as not to empty a house altogether of the valuables that give it weight.[9] Should one valuable be given without a counterpart being received, the former cannot yet be considered "dead" or the exchange completed (*nmata*) until the latter has been received. Each valuable will rest again for some time in its new home and will not travel on to the next house until it has found its match, upon which the two will marry and move on. In this way, famous named valuables move only exceedingly slowly up and down the rows they travel, resting for years or even decades in one house after another.

The impetus to objectify relations between named houses in terms of objects rather than persons, therefore, contains its own opposite: the personification of objects, which are seen to act with human sensibilities. Yet this personification is delimited and encompassed by the general characterization of such exchanges in terms of a market metaphor of buying and selling.

It has already been noted that *dua* say "we buy before we receive"

8. Cf. Malinowski 1961:356, for a similar metaphor concerning the marriage of valuables as they cycle through the kula ring.

9. One person told me, however, that big named valuables should not be immediately exchanged in this fashion. One should be given and the two valuables should "sleep together" (*rsilu'uk ira*) for a while before the other is given in exchange.

(*tfaha betii tala*), with the understanding that it is the *dua* who must make some additional effort in relation to their *lolat* — by giving women or valuables — in order to revitalize the relationship and renew the hierarchical superiority of the source of life over that which has issued forth from it. However, this hierarchical superiority is immediately challenged in the nature of the exchange, which is characterized as one wherein "we buy and sell with each other" (*tsifeddi sifaha ita*). The implication is that the exchange must be immediate, balanced, and strictly equivalent. The contrast, here, is with relations between *ura-ava* and *ura-memi*, for whom exchanges are motivated because "we have compassion and are embarrassed with each other" (*tsilobang sima'it ita*). The implication, in this case, is that bridewealth exchanges between such people are never immediately closed, balanced, or strictly equivalent.

Although valuables move slowly along the rows, there is an insistence upon immediate closure and a strict equivalence in the exchange. In a move not anticipated by Mauss, this effects a resolution of the tension between separation and encompassment inherent in the gift and its return. It thereby collapses the asymmetric relation between source and sprout into a symmetric relation between two sides that are simultaneously source and sprout to each other.

It is this symmetry of relation between two sources that gives shape to what we might otherwise call the relations of equality. Equality is the point where the asymmetry between source and sprout turns back upon itself and establishes a symmetry of relation in which the sprout becomes a source in its own right. And, it is the negotiation of this transformation of asymmetry into symmetry, and hierarchy into equality, that is part of what the buying and selling along the rows is all about.

In contrast to this buying and selling, the compassion and embarrassment characteristic of exchanges between *ura-ava* and *ura-memi* is expressive of the continued tension between separation and encompassment that is the mark of hierarchy and the requirement for the extension of life out from the source. This tension is temporarily resolved along the open rows in a move that negotiates and transforms relations of hierarchy into those of equality. This move is also simultaneously one that slows the flow of life, turns its outward trajectory back upon itself, and, in the process, begins to establish a permanent anchorage for that outward flow. If, along the open rows, this tension between separation and encompassment, hierarchy and equality, is only temporarily resolved and must continually be negotiated, then the permanent resolution of these tensions is, as we shall see, the unique achievement of the double cycle of the Great Row, which forms the final and fixed point of anchorage for the entire system.

The Tastiness of Exchange

I once asked Falaksoru Ditilebit why anyone bothered with the kinds of exchanges made along the rows. After all, it was not as if anyone could accumulate a lot of valuables or really profit from the exchanges. At best one valuable simply bumped out another, replacing it when it moved into the next house along the row. After some consideration, Falaksoru finally said that one bothered because it was "tasty" (*manminak*), or more properly, "aesthetically pleasing."[10] Obviously, he said, one did not exchange for profit; one did it to "look for relation" (*ndava hubungan*). One exchanged in order to make noise, to make one's name "travel" (*nbana*), to make people sit up and take note that something momentous is happening. If one did not negotiate exchanges, he insisted, one might as well just go sit in the gardens and plant yams all the time. This is, of course, precisely what distinguishes forest people from village people. Yet exchanges are only aesthetically pleasing, he suggested, if the people party to them know the system and understand how to play it and how to move big named valuables along the rows without losing them. But, I asked, was not part of the aesthetic appeal of exchange that it was not too easy, that there was always some resistance? Would it be aesthetically satisfying if Yelar Vuarlela, when pressed a bit, simply gave over Mas Kubang or Lebit Fenu just like that? Obviously not, he replied, there must be some play for it to become a game.

Indeed, people do not expect famous named valuables to move often or with anything but the most stately and dignified slowness. They would never be "thrown out" on the gamble that they would return in due time. Such a valuable remains traveling along its row, giving weight to the row at the same time that its own weight, nobility, and value are given by the limits of its trajectory. The weight of a particular row and the value of the relations that constitute it are therefore manifest in both the quality and quantity of the named valuables that travel along the row, just as the weight and status of each house is evidenced by the named valuables that have married and rested within it and by the heirloom valuables that have been immobilized at its center.

Yet just as the movement of valuables gives weight and permanence to both a row and its houses, so it could also be said that the weight and permanence of a row and its houses make the movement of women and valuables difficult and slow. In this way, certain famous named valuables

10. *Manminak* literally means "tasty" or "delicious" when applied to food, as it most commonly is. However, it is also used with reference, for instance, to the singing of songs, to indicate that it has been aesthetically pleasing. This usage of *manminak* is similar to that of the Indonesian word *sedap*.

belong exclusively to the Great Row—the most weighty and permanent row of all—and their movement is restricted to an exceedingly slow circuit through the eight houses of this cycle.

Once, when talking with Falaksoru and Ma'ileba Ditilebit about the slowness of the movement of these valuables, I was surprised to hear them state quite frankly, and with an evident sense of regret, that they did not expect to see a big named valuable move through their hands again during their lifetime. They had seen a number of big pieces move at their fathers' death feasts, but they did not expect other valuables of that caliber to move until after they themselves had died. Possibly their sons would see such valuables move again. When they were talking, their thoughts wandered back to Seran Kuwai. They remembered how he waited in vain for the Ditilebits to release Lim Ila'a and how he had finally died, his desire to hold Lim Ila'a unfulfilled. Perhaps (although they did not say so) it is not just that a house is dignified and made weighty by holding on to big named valuables during the lifetime of its occupants, but that in holding them they also ensure that the valuables will be used at their death feast to make their name travel throughout the land with the same dignity and weight as the valuable itself.

The Great Row Weighs Anchor

While the perpetuity of a row, and of the alliances between the houses that constitute it, is founded upon the continued movement of valuables along the row, it is precisely this movement of valuables that makes possible the renewal of an alliance through marriage. Because of the massive number of valuables—both named and unnamed—that are required for the exchanges that accompany a *vat dua* marriage, it is said that the "row [must have] content/flesh" (*lolat ihin*) before such a marriage can be negotiated. Since there are always new women along new pathways and old rows, valuables continue to overflow—feeding into a row and giving it content—and it is this continued fecundity of the row that makes it possible to give flesh to old alliances.

A *vat dua* marriage presupposes not only that one's house master continues to provide women, lifeblood, and female valuables to members of one's house but also that one's *lolat*, as wife-takers, continue to pass along the male valuables received for women, such that these valuables overflow. The mutual implication of the ascending order of wife-givers and the descending order of wife-takers makes possible the renewal of an alliance.

In this way, the renewal of an alliance does not merely signify the importance of the link between the two houses concerned. It recognizes the enduring significance of every preceding marriage as the source of its own possibility, and of every succeeding marriage as the fulfillment of its own potential. Unlike a marriage with an other woman — in which the value of the woman, and of the lifeblood that flows through women, must be paid for and eaten — in *vat dua* marriages the value of the woman and flow of lifeblood has already been established: it is evident in the fullness of the row that issues from the original woman. This fullness — the continued movement of valuables along the row — reaffirms with each exchange the relation between houses as a one of enduring alliance and also allows for the renewal of the alliance in the form of the marriage of a man with his *vat dua*.

There is not only a difference in the extent that certain types of marriage imply the hierarchical order of relations between houses, there is also a difference in the extent to which *vat dua* marriages themselves are able to implicate the system of exchange pathways. For while the renewal of an alliance between *dua* and *lolat* along a single row implicates each alliance along that particular row, it is only in the renewal of the alliances along the Great Row (Lolat Ila'a) — and especially those that link the islands of Sera and Fordata — that the entire system of exchange rows is potentially implicated.

It will be remembered that the Lolat Ila'a comprises a double cycle of alliance: a cycle of four houses on Sera and a cycle of four houses on Fordata. The two cycles are further linked by two alliances in which one house on each island stands as wife-giver to one house on the other island (see figure 6.7). When an intraisland Lolat Ila'a alliance is renewed, the exchanging parties include not only the representatives of the houses belonging to the relevant cycle but also, and perhaps more important, the representatives of the houses that belong to all the rows that feed into these four houses. Such an alliance renewal is supported, on the one hand, by the movement and countermovement of male and female valuables that belong to the cycle itself. On the other hand, each of the four houses will mobilize valuables necessary from the houses along the rows that stand subordinate to them. It will be the "fullness of the rows" (*lolat ihin*) that will make it possible to launch the ceremonial boat. I was told, furthermore, that the *lolat* and elder-younger brothers of the houses that stand as wife-taker would engage in a kind of competitive gift exchange with the *lolat* and elder-younger brothers of the houses that stand as wife-giver (*rsia'ut ira*: "they give each other gifts").[11] In this way, the entire hierarchy

11. Cf. Valeri (1980:186), who reports that the exchanges accompanying certain marriage alliances in Huaulu mobilize the entire society, which is divided "into two reciprocating sides — one connected with the male group (hahamana), the other with the female group (hahapina)."

of exchange pathways that culminates in the four-house cycle of the island is made evident in the course of a single event.

However, only when the alliances that link the two islands are renewed is the entire interisland system of exchange mobilized and made manifest. Such marriages happen only rarely: two and four generations ago the house Ditilebit on Fordata took a woman from Kuwai on Sera. In the present generation, the house Vavumasa on Sera has taken a woman from Melatunan on Fordata, but at the time of my stay, they had not yet launched the ceremonial boat.

In such an alliance renewal, the two cycles and two islands would stand opposed—together with their *lolat*—as wife-giver to wife-taker, male to female. It is significant that the strongest positions in the system are occupied by the two houses in the Lolat Ila'a—Ditilebit on Fordata and Vavumasa on Sera—that stand as wife-takers to a house on the other island. Both these houses have, as one of their own *lolat*, a house that is called the "anchor" (*a'ur*) of the Lolat Ila'a cycle of their own island. On the Fordata cycle, Ditilebit's *lolat*, Bungaa, is the anchor; on the Sera cycle, Vavumasa's *lolat*, Fabeat, is the anchor.[12] A greater proportion of the rows that feed into the Lolat Ila'a converge upon these two anchor houses—Bungaa and Fabeat (see figures 6.7 and 6.8). When Ditilebit (accompanied by the other members of the Lolat Ila'a Fordata) goes to Sera to take a wife from Kuwai, it is said that they cannot set sail unless they weigh their anchor, Bungaa, and take along all the *lolat* that are pulled in by Bungaa—that is, unless they carry with them the concentrated weight and value of all their rows. "If the anchor is not taken up, the ship can not sail" (*A'ur wol nrata, kabal wol naflaa nala*). Similarly, I was told that without its anchor, Ditilebit—and the Lolat Ila'a Fordata, as a whole—would be swept away to sea: without the means to fix their bearings, they would have no bearing at all.

It is significant that the *lolat* of the four houses of Fordata are principally (though not exclusively) from the villages in the northern and eastern half of the Tanimbar archipelago, whereas the *lolat* of the four houses of Sera are principally (though not exclusively) from the southern and western half of the archipelago. When an alliance between the two islands is renewed, it therefore implicates the system of exchange pathways throughout the entire archipelago.

Built upon the relative, but irreversible opposition between male and female, life-giver and life-taker, the rows here culminate in, and make pos-

---

12. The integral position of the anchor provides a fifth point for each of the four-house cycles. The four-five (and the eight-nine) combination is common throughout Indonesia as an image of wholeness (see, for example, Jansen 1977:103).

sible, a double cycle that ultimately recomposes all oppositions into an image of reversibility and unity. Relative to the Ditilebit–Kuwai alliance, Sera and the southwestern half of Tanimbar are male, and Fordata and the northeastern half of Tanimbar are female. Relative to the Vavumasa–Melatunan alliance, male becomes female and female male. Together, the double cycle of the Great Row is — like the stone boat and the ancestral altar — a figure of transcendent unity that was otherwise witnessed only in the time before Atuf speared the sun to pieces.

The Sense of the Cycle

Tanimbarese think of the Lolat Ila'a cycle as a unique and, in a certain sense, an unnatural form. They stress that there is only one row that cycles in this way. Only with reference to the Lolat Ila'a do they claim that each house is strictly the equal of the other, that no one is more than any other (*isaa wol nrahi isaa*). Moreover, unlike any other row, in the Lolat Ila'a people say that each house is simultaneously *dua* and *lolat* to *each other*.

The overwhelming sense one has of the Tanimbarese system of marriage is its pervasive asymmetry — the directionality and irreversibility of the flow of blood and women. This flow is seen as a process of growth originating from and grounded in a source and expanding ever outward in a multitude of sprouts that issue forth from women.[13] The continued encompassment of the sprouts by the source gives a hierarchical form to the asymmetric relations between houses linked along pathways of exchange.

Against this backdrop, the Lolat Ila'a cycle appears as a startling anomaly. Here the directionality and irreversibility of the flow of blood and women has been turned back upon itself: sprouts do not expand outward, but reverse the outward directionality of growth and, in an unnatural movement, return to the source. The identity of source and sprout creates the conditions for equality in a system that is otherwise pervasively hierarchical. It declares, moreover, that sustained equality is a singular form, as rare as it is profoundly paradoxical and difficult to establish.

The unnaturalness of the Lolat Ila'a is expressed in a story about its

---

13. Traube notes that "when Mambai represent the alliance system as a totality, they project blood imagery onto an imaginary space that is structured like a tree, oriented around a center source and forking outward along multiple paths. Neither at the level of ideals nor in their social practices do Mambai appear concerned with the eventual return of blood to its source. Rather, the indigenous model is of blood that 'flows continually outward until it reaches its final bit,' and no special value is placed on closing cycles of marital exchange" (1986:95).

origin. According to Sa'intii Kora of Sera, the Lolat Ila'a did not grow out of the movement of women and lifeblood at all, but was established through a kind of contract. He told me that it was So'u Melatunan — the same Rumya'an man who had dealings with the "Portugis" (see chapter 3) — who founded the Lolat Ila'a. According to Sa'intii, So'u called a meeting, to which he invited the heads of the four houses of Sera and the four houses of Fordata, along with all their big *lolat*. Together they created the double cycle of the Lolat Ila'a, agreed upon how it would run, and provided each cycle with an anchor that drew in a large number of rows to support the alliances that linked the two cycles. So'u then initiated the cycle by giving his sister Titi Ma'i in marriage to a man named Itran Duanyaru of the house Vavumasa in Sera.

Knowing the difficulties Tanimbarese have in agreeing to any organized activity, especially when it would so obviously benefit certain houses, it is hard to imagine such a meeting being called, let alone any such contract being agreed upon. Whether So'u in fact created the Lolat Ila'a in this way is immaterial. What is more interesting is that people could even conceive that it might have been formed in this way.

In a system where all form is seen as the result of a process of growth maintained by the successive extraction of women from a source that they might give issue, the idea of the creation of form through contract is surprising indeed. In such a history, the Lolat Ila'a is represented as an astonishing conflation of opposites and hierarchical order, which could only be created and sustained in this world by a process so totally other as to appear to contradict the most basic premises concerning the genesis of life and growth.[14]

In the context of an otherwise thoroughgoing asymmetry and directionality, the Lolat Ila'a cycle indeed looks as if it were the child of an unnatural act: a reversal in the direction of marriage or, to put it more succinctly, marriage with a sister. If to close a cycle before four generations is to marry a sister, then the Lolat Ila'a cycle manages to come as close to sister marriage — and therefore incest — as respectably possible without quite committing itself to such an act. It does so by closing each cycle with four instead of three houses.[15] Like the passage of four generations, the cycle of four houses in each half of the Lolat Ila'a represents the point at

14. There is another, complicated story concerning the origins of the Lolat Ila'a which features an original brother-sister pair. The sister is transformed into a dog and is then given in exchange to a man. It is the descendants of this man and his woman-dog (by day she is a dog, by night a beautiful woman) who eventually found the Lolat Ila'a cycles. This story also points to the unnatural origins of the Lolat Ila'a.

15. Cf. Boon (1977:119–44), who discusses the significance of incestuous brother-sister twin marriages in marking the apex of the hierarchical order in Bali.

which identity becomes differentiated and differentiation can be recomposed into unity.

Here all oppositions—brother and sister, male and female, *dua* and *lolat*, source and issue, superior and inferior—articulate a point where unity and differentiation cannot be distinguished, where the two simultaneously ground one another and the potential of the entire system. Thus the double four-house cycle of the Lolat Ila'a approximates as closely as possible the divine unity of the sun-moon deity, Ubila'a, without destroying the very conditions of life. At the same time, it maintains only as much differentiation as is necessary to realize the potential for life without dissolving the power of the ultimate and original unity into an irreversible opposition.

It becomes clear, then, that two processes are necessary to the generation of life: one that extends the flow of life out from the source in a process of differentiation and dispersal; the other that anchors the flow of life in a process of unification, concentration, and encompassment. Whereas the differentiation necessary for the flow of life takes the form of asymmetry and hierarchy, the unification necessary to create an anchorage takes the form of symmetry and equality. The symmetry and equality of the Great Row resolves the tension between separation and encompassment that is crucial to the flow of life and, in the process, it creates a stoppage or counter to that flow. It is this unique ability to immobilize the flow and fold it back into itself that anchors and makes possible the hierarchical and asymmetric unfolding of life out from its source.

The Great Row exists as the final, and necessary, level of the global hierarchy of exchange pathways. Although egalitarian in form, it is, in fact, a kind of doubled hierarchy[16]—that which makes hierarchy itself possible. Neither the hierarchical order nor the whole (which is the same thing) would be possible without the Great Row. For as the unity of all opposites, the Great Row forms the base for the differentiation of these opposites in the hierarchical order of the rows and pathways that issue forth from it.

In this way, the Great Row demonstrates the manner in which hierarchy and equality elicit one another—indeed, cannot exist without one another. In order to create a base and anchorage for the hierarchical order, the hierarchical implications of asymmetric marriage must be destroyed by the egalitarian cycle. But in so destroying them, the cycle creates the very possibility of hierarchy. For if hierarchy implies differentiation, then the apex of the system must represent the ultimate unification of all parts

---

16. I am grateful to Marilyn Strathern for stressing the hierarchical nature of this otherwise apparently egalitarian form.

and potentialities of the whole. In an asymmetric marriage system, which requires the irreversible directionality and differentiation of opposites, that image of unity can only be achieved in the cycle, which denies directionality and recomposes differentiation into an image of transcendent unity. It is not surprising, then, that the original unity of brother and sister (and indeed of all oppositions), which was rendered asunder through the agency of Atuf and the sacred spear, should be thought to have been recomposed through the agency of Atuf's latter-day trickster successor, So'u Melatunan, and his cross-dressing sister, Titi Ma'i.

11   The Mobility and Immobility of Rank

The prince is not permitted to be active and is not allowed to leave the precincts of his palace (*sonaf*); it is his duty to remain "inside." Here he "eats and drinks," in other words, here he offers sacrifices as the principal officiant in charge of the state ritual. (Schulte Nordholt 1971:200)

If there was not the distinction between persons and houses, then the tripartite hierarchy demarcated by the Great Row, the open rows, and the sisters and aunts pathways would simultaneously outline the system of ranking of those persons who occupy the named and unnamed houses at these three levels. While it is because of the distinction between persons and houses that the hierarchy between named houses (and their *lolat*) and unnamed houses (and their *ura-ava* pathways) becomes manifest, nevertheless this same distinction means that the ranking of persons does not necessarily correspond to that of houses.

Named and unnamed houses are not the same weight. Neither are nobles, commoners, and slaves. Ideally, the two scales of differences should be congruent: nobles should occupy named houses and commoners should occupy unnamed houses — and slaves should move around the margins. The correlation, however, like everything else, is not automatic.

The status of one's house and one's personal rank combine in a statement of relative worth (*fiawan*). On the one hand, if one occupies a named house, the problem is to maintain the high rank of one's descendants through appropriate marriages. For if one occupies a named house but is personally of less than noble rank, then the combination has "no worth" (*wol fiawan*), and one will soon be replaced by a high-ranking person. On the other hand, if one is a noble, the problem is to maintain one's occupancy of a named house through the redemption of one's bridewealth debts. For if one is of noble rank but does not occupy a named house, then again the combination has no worth.

The status of houses has a permanence and indisputability that the rank of the people who occupy them does not have: the former remains more or less constant over the generations; the latter is potentially fluid and fluctuating. Where the two are not in accord, the latter is eventually made to conform to the former. In the end, the two together define a system whose core is formed by the weight and permanence of named houses occupied by nobles, whose middle ground is formed by the mobility and impermanence of unnamed houses and the commoners who constitute them, and whose extreme periphery is delimited by the absolute lightness and mobility of slaves (and witches).

In other chapters I have explored the various representations of named and unnamed houses. Here I wish to examine the categories of rank; the permutations of rank through marriage; the differential representations of nobles, commoners, and slaves; and the manner in which these articulate with the differential representations of houses.

Categories and Confidences

Tanimbarese generally recognize three main categories of rank, which, on Fordata, are known as *mela, iria-iwarin,* and *iria.*[1] *Mela,* the highest or noble rank, also means the "right side" of anything. Occasionally, this category is divided further into three levels: "elder noble" (*mel ya'an*), "middle noble" (*mel ifruan*), and "younger noble" (*mel iwarin*). In general, however, the grounds upon which such subdivisions might be made are extremely vague and they are rarely distinguished. *Iria-iwarin,* the middle or commoner rank, is a compound of the words for "slave" (*iria*) and "younger same-sex sibling" (*warin*), and thus demarcates a class of subordinates: slaves and juniors. Slaves, the lowest rank, are sometimes referred to as "slaves [who] run about/make haste" (*iria farlaan*), or "slaves [who are] sold and distributed" (*iria fadfeddi tantangang*).[2] Some people claim that what distinguishes "straight slaves and juniors" (*iria-iwarin malolan*) from slaves is that the latter are also witches (*iwangi*). Although it will become evident that there is some logic to the association, there is by no means agreement on this point,[3] since others claim

---

1. See Pauwels 1990 for the ranking system found in the village of Hursu (Fursuy) on the island of Selaru.

2. It should be made quite clear that slavery, and indeed rank divisions in general, have been officially abolished by the Indonesian state. I continue to refer to these rank categories — including slavery — in the present tense, however, because they are still very much a lively concern and Tanimbarese continue to think about people in these terms.

3. Drabbe also noted this tendency to treat witches as a category of rank, or even to confuse the category with that of slaves. Using the Yamdena terms, he states: "When one hears the Tanimbarese speak, one notices that they very frequently confuse the words *keswange* [witch] and *kawar,* slave. Formerly slaves were probably often mistaken for *keswange,* so that one often uses the word *keswange* when one means slave. And when one asks if slaves were then *keswange* per se, one receives a negative answer" (1940:384).

that witches constitute a separate rank, the lowliest of all, and still others assert that witches do not constitute a rank at all.

No subject is more delicate than that of a person's rank. Nor is there one on which a person is likely to hear more varied statements and contradictory claims. Certain questions of rank are fairly well agreed upon: there is little divergence of opinion regarding those considered to be slaves (or witches), and one can fairly well determine those who are considered to be commoners. But there is a vast range of people who seem to hover between noble and commoner status, and their rank is as ambiguous as it is covertly disputed.

Rank is not discussed publicly, and a person's rank is never mentioned in his or her presence, except under conditions of extreme anger. One would never ask a person point blank what his or her (or anyone else's) rank is. In conversations about other matters, a person is more likely than not to slant the evidence toward his or her own claims to high rank. But others, in other conversations, are just as likely to slant the evidence in the opposite direction. Usually statements about one's own or another's rank come out in the heat of disputes—either in flashes of fire-spitting anger or in the hushed tones of prideful disdain that follow not long thereafter. Almost no one is unsullied by such incidents; everyone seems to have a skeleton of some kind in the closet. It is unlikely that he or she will tell you about it. But it is highly probable that, in time, somebody will.

The delicate nature of the subject, the secrecy and the hushed tones in which it is veiled, the potential for insult and even violence, all make rank a particularly difficult matter to investigate and understand. Yet with time, the hushed tones assume the proportions of a whispered chorus of furies commenting upon actions past and ongoing, and one soon begins to perceive the course of the drama.

Permutations of Rank

Although guarded when talking about the rank of specific persons, people do not hesitate to talk about the theory of rank. When directly asked what determines rank, they will say that one's rank follows from that of one's father and, for married women, from that of one's husband. Thus it is said that "a man's nobility settles upon a woman, but a woman's nobility does not settle upon a man" (*brana ni mela ntebar na'a vata, na'akmaa vata ni mela wol ntebar na'a brana*). The explicit theory is this: if a higher-ranking man marries a lower-ranking woman, his high rank will cover her low rank; that is, his rank will be extended to both his wife and their children. If a higher-ranking woman marries a lower-ranking man, however, her high rank cannot cover his low rank; both she and her children will assume the lower rank of her husband. The weight of the man's rank over the woman's in determining the rank of their children is expressed in the saying: "We take our father ['s rank] in order to speak" (*Tala yamadida al tangrihi*). This means that the position from which one speaks is that of the rank of one's father, not one's mother. In other words, people say, "one's father before [there is] worth" (*yaman betii fiawan*): it is by one's father's rank that one's own worth is assessed.

This general theory of rank accounts for virtually all the possible permutations except those involving the unions of slave women with higher-ranking men. It should be noted, however, that at least on Fordata people claimed that slaves were not allowed to marry at all and, except in two cases I heard of, this seems indeed to have been true. Nevertheless, this did not prevent slaves from having affairs. Elsewhere in Tanimbar, according to Drabbe, it seems to have been more common for slaves to marry. Yet it is impossible to determine, in these cases, whether slaves were allowed to marry into a rank higher than their own.

In order to understand the system of rank, it is best to review the full range of permutations to see how they are conceptualized (figure 11.1). To begin from the perspective of a woman, it is obvious that if a noble woman marries a noble man, both their own rank and that of their children will remain noble. If, however, a noble woman marries a commoner man, it is said that "the woman's nobility dissolves" (*vata ni mela namwear*), and both her own rank and that of their children will fall to the rank of her husband. If a noble woman should marry a slave, a chasm between herself

MAN	WOMAN	WOMEN & CHILDREN
mela	mela	mela
mela	iria-iwarin	mela (tilted)
mela	iria	iria-iwarin
iria-iwarin	mela	iria-iwarin
iria-iwarin	iria-iwarin	iria-iwarin
iria-iwarin	iria	iria-iwarin (tilted)
iria	mela	iria
iria	iria-iwarin	iria
iria	iria	iria

Figure 11.1   Permutations of rank through marriage

and her family is irrevocably opened.[4] They would disown her (*rafena ia*) and demand, in lieu of bridewealth, that her body be replaced, part by part (*rtuvu ia*): "for her head a large earthenware jar, for her breast an antique piece of breast gold, for her back an elephant tusk, for her ribs an old sword, for her hair, hands, and feet ordinary gold earrings, for her eyes an antique gold earring, etc., etc., altogether a colossal amount" (Drabbe 1940:197–98). From the point of view of the woman's family, this is a death payment. The only other time when people pay off someone's body part by part (*rtuvu ia*) is when that peson has been murdered.[5] Thus, if a noble woman marries a slave, her family considers her as good as murdered. The payment made is not so much bridewealth, as it is the price of her death.[6] Or, to put it another way, it is a bridewealth prestation that effects the woman's complete severance and absolute alienation from her natal house. Her family will no longer recognize her existence or the existence of the female line that issues from her. Obviously, since the woman is considered dead, her noble rank dissolves therewith, and her children can only assume the rank of their father, who is a slave. It is extremely unlikely that such a marriage would be made, for a slave would not be able to mobilize such a vast array of valuables (if he were, he would not have been made a slave), and no master would, by choice, throw away so many valuables on this kind of marriage.

The consequences of the marriages that a noble woman may contract are thus clearly spelled out: she and her children will always assume the rank of her husband. The consequences of the various possible marriages of a noble man, however, are slightly less clear. It is explicitly claimed that a man's nobility settles upon a woman. Yet at the same time, it is said that if a noble man marries a commoner woman, the rank of their children will "tilt" (*natli'ik*) or "fall a little" (*nleka kedan*) — although they will

4. In Makatian, I was told that formerly there were two villages, with a wall separating them. On one side lived the nobles and on the other side lived the slaves. Marriage between them was strictly prohibited.

5. Drabbe mentions one other instance in which people *rtuvu* something. He says that if an extremely large sea creature, such as a whale, was caught, then they *rtuvu ia*, by laying a pair of earrings or other valuables next to it and telling it to return to the sea. A rough image of the beast was then cut out of sago palm stems and thrown into the sea (1940:392).

6. In discussing the Ambonese system of classification as it relates to the human body, Jansen notes that at "a marriage the bride's parents also make a symbolic human sacrifice: a gong for the head, *arak* [a distilled liquor] for blood, a *piring* [plate] for a belly and so on" (1977:113). Here again, the connection between the form of the prestations and the woman's symbolic death is made evident. Leach (1965:148) reports a similar series of prestations used in the settlement of a chief's blood feud in highland Burma, and Battaglia (1983:291) discusses the construction of an effigy of a corpse in mortuary rituals on Sabarl Island.

still be considered noble. In commentaries upon such marriages, people always intimate that the rank of the children is, indeed, not quite the same as the father, on account of the lower rank of the mother. This is most likely the reason for the subdivisions in the rank of nobility mentioned above.

We have already seen that when a noble man intends to marry a commoner woman, it is possible to have her unofficially adopted into a named house—preferably one which is the house master of her fiancé's house. Upon her marriage, she will be weighted down with valuables, "in order to make her noble" (*ala rot mela ia*). Where a commoner woman is married out of a named house to a noble man, it is said that her children will retain the noble rank of their father. Nevertheless, a good deal of ambiguity surrounds the consideration of their rank, and this ambiguity hinges upon the difference between houses and blood. By adoption, her brothers are nobles who occupy a named house; by blood, her brothers are commoners who occupy an unnamed house. Because of the adoption, the blood brothers should no longer be recognized as the *dua* of her husband and children. But in fact, this is rarely the case: for the blood connection cannot be broken and, people say, "blood demands" (*lara ntuntut*) that one's *dua* along bloodlines be recognized.

In the end, the question always turns on rival interpretations, all of which are true according to their own light. The commoner can claim superiority by virtue of his stance as the *dua* of a noble man (because of the female bloodline that links them). However, the noble man born of a commoner woman can claim superiority based on his father's rank. Moreover his mother was transformed with valuables into a noble woman. It may be that, in comparison with his father, he has fallen somewhat in rank, but he is still noble. Despite ambiguities, the contradiction engendered by the marriage of a noble man to a commoner woman is resolvable. The procedure by which a commoner woman can be married out from a noble house and weighted down with valuables is meant to override the contradiction, even if it is only partly successful.

The contradiction seems to become insurmountable, however, should a noble man marry a slave. Unlike a commoner woman, a slave woman could not be taken into a noble house, should she have prospects for being married off to a noble man. This would indicate that if a noble man did indeed marry a slave woman, their children could not be considered noble in rank, but rather would assume the rank of a commoner. In fact, a man who made such a marriage would likely be disowned from the named house he occupied, and his children would, in the end, constitute an unnamed house. The commoner status of the children of such a union is confirmed by Drabbe's comment that a slave is distinguished from a commoner in the following sense: "by slave is denoted someone who actually lives in bondage, whereas a *famudi* [Yamdenan: 'younger same-sex sibling' or 'commoner'] is often no longer a slave . . . on account of his mother, who is married to a *mele* [Yamdenan: 'noble'] or to a *famudi*" (1940:179). Thus where a slave woman marries either a noble or commoner man, their children would assume the rank of a commoner. In the former case, the contradiction is too great, and the children fall a full rank to that of commoner; in the latter case they follow the rank of their father. I was told, however, that even here their rank would tilt lower than that of their father.

Although Drabbe's statement concerning Yamdena would indicate that marriages between noble or commoner men and slave women were possible, people in Fordata told me that they were not. In each instance, when asked what the consequences would be of a relation between male or female slaves and persons of the commoner or noble rank, people said that the latter would be disowned if they did not break it off. Their housemates and *dua* would "refuse [to recognize] them" (*rafena ira*) and, as a consequence, their children would fall in rank.

In sum, as long as unions involve nobles and commoners, the rank and weight of the husband will settle upon his wife and their children. But when unions involve nobles or commoners and slaves, the contradiction is too powerful, and the rank and weight of the husband is no longer effective to overcome the difference in rank of the wife or constitute the rank of their children. Unions with slaves are disallowed, and those who engage in them are disowned.

Yet in the dynamics of rank and sinking status—where the prize is to maintain both high personal rank and one's place in a named house—it is not only the rank and status of one's mother and father that is important. The other crucial variable, as will be seen, is the ability to be fully redeemed of one's bridewealth debts and thus to maintain a fixed place in a named house.

The Mobility and Lightness of Slaves

Slaves were people who stood unredeemed—utterly severed from their source of life—whose absolute mobility was their most evident defining feature. I was told that a person was made a slave on account of a situation in which a man took a woman as his "lover" or "provisional spouse" (*ni dodu*), and his *dua* were either unable or unwilling to pay the separation fine necessary to "throw the woman off." Unlike bridewealth payments—the fulfillment of which can be stretched out over the course of a lifetime—the four portions of the separation fine must be paid together, and usually within a few days after the illicit union of the man and woman has been discovered. If a man's *dua* were either unable or unwilling to redeem this debt, then the *dua* of the woman could seize him, or one of his brothers or sisters, and sell him or her off as a slave. Thus, it is said, "they sold the person in order to cover the man's provisional spouse" (*rfeddi tomata ala rtutup brana ni dodu*).

Drabbe notes that people could be captured and sold into slavery on account of any debt, not simply one incurred in connection with a provisional union (1940:179–80; cf. Forbes 1884:15, and Forbes 1885: 312–13). He also makes it clear that men who were captured as slaves in this way usually originated from villages other than that of their captor.

> The manner in which one may become a slave is through capture on account of debt, which did not happen easily in one's village, but did happen with respect to strangers. One captures someone from whom one has, in vain, been awaiting the payment of one or another debt, at a moment when he is not expecting it and when none of his family is in the vicinity, and one takes him to one's own village. One waits for a time to see if his family or *stam* members will come to buy him back. In the meanwhile, he is not yet a slave. But as soon as one becomes tired of waiting, and sells the prisoner, then he becomes a slave. One puts a rope around his neck, from which all can see that he has become a slave and is being offered for sale. Or one goes to sell him in other villages. In the sixteenth [*sic*: seventeenth] century such slaves were even bought by men of the [Dutch East India] Company from the Tanimbarese. (1940:179–80)

It should be mentioned that, although in some areas prisoners of war were made slaves, this was not general practice. Instead, they were usually killed "because otherwise one individual would have the benefit of the common spoils of war" (Drabbe 1940:180).

The main reasons why a man might have found himself in a situation in which neither his brothers nor his *dua* could, or would, come to his rescue are insulting behavior or words, especially if directed toward his *dua*, and an affair or marriage with a "true sister," a slave, or a witch. The last, in particular, is likely to result in being disowned by both the members of one's natal house as well as one's *dua*.[7] Having so incurred the wrath of his *dua*, the latter would refuse to redeem him—whether he was able or not—and would block the redemption request from being passed

---

7. Since sexual contact with a witch makes oneself a witch, an affair or marriage with a witch would, in this case, result in a person who was both a slave and a witch. Such a situation is perhaps the basis of some people's claim that slaves are also witches.

further along the exchange pathway. Having alienated both his brothers and his *dua*, the man would be left defenseless.

A slave was thus a man whose relations to both his house of origin and his *dua* had been severed. His connection to the ancestors of the house—through which he held rights over the estates and patrimony of the house—was broken: he had neither land nor trees; neither *lolat* nor sisters; neither house nor heirloom. Moreover, the female bloodline that connected him to his *dua* was cut: he was no longer able to trace the female bloodline that marked his "place" (*waan*) in the world. He was a man whose origin and source of life had been lost to him; a man who had, indeed, no place in the enduring order of the world.

That a slave could no longer place his origins can be seen from the provisions concerning bridewealth paid for or on behalf of slaves (if they were allowed to marry)—since ordinarily it is the passage of redemption requests and bridewealth valuables along exchange pathways that marks out a person's place of origin. With the bridewealth paid for a slave, however, valuables no longer passed along pathways that held the memory of the origin and source of life. A slave's life rested, instead, in the hands of his master alone, and it was there that bridewealth began and ended. The bridewealth debts of a male slave were redeemed by those who owned him. The bridewealth valuables paid for a female slave were received by her owners, who could use them as they pleased. "They carried the value of the woman [i.e., her bridewealth] on their neck" (*Rsaka vat velin na'a boturira*): that is, her bridewealth "died" or "stopped" (*nmata*) with them, and did not need to be passed on further. Ordinarily bridewealth is said to die at the limits of the recognized bloodline of a person, after which it continues to travel along the row to which it is connected. In the case of a slave, the limits of the recognized bloodline were reached immediately, since the bloodline, itself, had been broken.[8] There was no line of continuity, no pathway to mark the memory of one's place in the world or the source from which one's life had flowed.

Indeed, a slave in Tanimbar was a person who had no fixed place. He was a person who ran about at the order of others and was sold and distributed at the will of others. Slaves are considered "light" (*maraan*), in contrast to nobles, who are "heavy, weighty" (*aleman*) and who have a fixed place in a house. Whereas it might be said of a noble, that he "leans against the ancestor statue" (*nebang tavu*) and takes support from the status and presence of his ancestors, a slave is denoted by saying that

8. I was told that, in reality, no bloodline could be broken, but because a person had been sold he was "embarrassed" and "humiliated" (*nma'it*). Since he could therefore never again recognize his blood relations, his bloodline was as good as broken.

he "comes from the space beneath the house" (*ntali rahan ni lavavan*) —
that is, the space reserved for animals. Although, in fact, a slave lived in
the house, as Drabbe notes, he "is not a real house member, and has no
say over the property or in the perkaras [the suits of the house]. If the
family must fight in a matter concerning the family itself, the slave is the
first [to be] sent off. In this way, he is also used for all kinds of work and
all kinds of errands in other villages" (1940:180). Slaves not only fought
in the front line of battles for their masters, they also ran messages hither
and yon and did the greater proportion of the work necessary for the provision of food. It was they who did the gardening, fishing, and hunting
in the forests and reefs outside the village, while their masters remained
in the village talking *adat*.

Slaves, then, having their origins lost to them, having no fixed place
in the world, were the epitome of mobility: they could be sold and moved
about at the will of others; they were the runners, the workers of the
world outside — beneath the house, beyond the village, within the forests
and the reefs. Broken away from both their house and their bloodline,
they were set adrift without a line to connect them back to the source of
life. They were light.[9]

The Shifting Status of "Slaves and Juniors"

People conceive of the origin of "slaves and juniors" in two
ways. Some slaves and juniors, who constitute the younger brother, unnamed houses attached to elder brother, named houses, are thought to
have been in existence since time immemorial — that is, since the time of
the migrations before the founding of villages. Others, however, have attached themselves to named houses within recent memory: these are the
ones who have been displaced from their natal houses because, for one
reason or another, they have not been redeemed of their debts. Although
these are the ways in which people conceive of the generation of slaves
and juniors, the possibility that the process of segmentation is covertly
implied by the existence of this rank will also be explored.[10]

---

9. The affinity between slaves and witches derives, at least in part, from this lightness.
Witches are considered light in the extreme, since their souls fly about through the air and
possess now one person and then another. Moreover, whereas the mobility of slaves follows
the will of their master, the mobility of the soul of the witch follows neither the will of others
nor that of the witch, but only its own desire. It is said that a witch's "soul" (*ngraan*) departs
from his or her own body, "pursues" (*naflaa orang*) a victim, or "flies onto" (*noru na'a*) and
enters another's body, where he or she proceeds to eat (*na'an*) out the victim's insides.

10. Drabbe (1940:180) poses yet another possibility. He suggests that once a male slave
married and acquired a *dua*, his children would no longer be considered slaves, but rather

Certain named and unnamed houses are thought to have been associated with one another during the time of the migrations, to have come to the present location and settled upon the land together, and subsequently to have moved to the village together. They are thought to have always been associated in this way and feel certain that they will always be so associated. They are conceived as "elder-younger brothers [who] treat each other well" (*ya'an-iwarin simaklivur*). There is no assumption that they share an ancestor in common: they have simply always been men whose actions — treating each other well — establish their performative brotherhood. In terms of rank considerations, the younger brothers are slaves and juniors who occupy unnamed houses that "harbor" beneath the named houses of their noble elder brothers. One senses that slaves and juniors of recent origin eventually come to be seen in terms of this kind of traditional, long-term association that has endured since the beginning of time.

Yet there are slaves and juniors whose more recent origins are still well known, even if the matter is never talked about openly. Their fate has been fixed in one way or another by the fact that they have not been redeemed of their bridewealth debts and have consequently lost their place in the natal house of their father. There are two possibilities here. First, one's relation to one's house and *dua* can be severed because of some offense (usually a mismarriage). Second, because of a divorce or failure to complete bridewealth exchanges, one can end up affiliating matrilaterally. In the latter case, the effect upon one's rank is ambiguous.

The main way people see a person falling to the rank of a slave and junior follows from a situation similar to that in which a man finds himself threatened with the possibility of becoming a slave. This happens when neither a man's own brothers nor his *dua* are able or willing to redeem him of his debts — presumably for the same reasons (i.e., insulting behavior or union with a slave, true sister, or a witch). He may then flee from his house or his village and seek out a big man of an important named house who is capable of offering him protection. Unlike a slave who is captured and sold, the refugee "sells himself" to the big man and "dons [the role of] a younger brother" (*neluk warin*) toward his protector. The two men will thus become "attached elder-younger brothers" (*ya'an-iwarin fareling*), or "elder-younger brothers [who] treat each other well."

---

the "slaves and younger brothers" of their master's house. This may well have been the case on Yamdena, but, as mentioned earlier, on Fordata people stressed that slaves were not allowed to marry, and, when pressed to speculate, said that the children of male slaves would all remain slaves. Indeed, once when the children of former slaves came to Awear they were still talked about as if they were slaves.

The refugee will come entirely dispossessed of the estates of his house — be it a noble or a commoner house; he will possess neither land nor trees, neither *lolat* nor sisters. His only hope of establishing himself once again is through the protection of an elder brother who belongs to an important named house. Either the man's new elder brother or the *dua* of the latter will assume responsibility for the payment of his debts. Such a refugee will establish an unnamed, younger brother house attached to his protector's named house within a single house-complex (*rahan ralan*).

These younger brothers will never be able to establish rights over the estates of the named house to which they are attached. Yet they are not totally bereft of the possibility of establishing estates — in the sense of plantations of trees and *ura-ava* pathways. True, they begin lacking trees as well as sisters. But as the younger brothers of noble men — under whose protection they stand — they gain access to village land on which to plant trees; and the sisters of the elder brothers become like sisters to them. In time, moreover, they will have daughters, who will be sisters to their sons; and if these "multiply their sprouts a thousandfold," there will eventually be sisters and aunts pathways that issue from their house. Just as the acquisition of a new *dua* and an elder brother rescues a man from a position of defenselessness, in which he has no hope of redemption, so the establishment of sisters and aunts pathways gives a man some stature in the world. For a man's position is gauged, at least in part, by women given in marriage and valuables received as bridewealth.

The second way in which the lack of redemption can affect one's status, if not one's rank, follows in the wake of matrilateral affiliation. Because of a provisional affair, a divorce, or the refusal to complete the rope of the dead prestations upon the death of one or another spouse, the children of such a union will affiliate matrilaterally, their place in their father's house having never been established. The general feeling is that such children do not fall in rank: if they are born of noble fathers, then they are still noble. But the problem is that they have "no fathers" (*wol yamar*). The significance of this came out in the context of the following event.

> One day, when T returned from negotiating an exchange in
> Rumya'an, he was more than a little tipsy and he had a male earring
> hanging from his pocket as an ostentatious sign of the success of his
> negotiations. Arriving in Awear, he encountered a group of people
> who were in the midst of a feast. He confronted the assembled
> guests by saying: "You all are talking of what nobility?" In this way
> he challenged them, suggesting that none of them were nobles or
> had anything noble to talk about. One of the guests quickly retorted
> that if it had not been for his own father, T would not be sitting in

the named house he currently occupied. This is because T's parents had wanted a divorce, but the man's father forced T's mother to remain with her husband. For if the "woman descends and leaves the house, her children have no father" (*vata nsut ntalik rahan, yananra wol yamarira*). The man mocked T with a reminder of what the resulting problem would have been, when he queried: "Who takes their mother ['s rank] to talk?" (*Iki nala renan al nangrihi?*).

To the extent that rank derives from the father and matrilaterally affiliated children have no official father, they can only assume the rank of their mother. Moreover, publicly, their position in the world is determined by their subordinate place within the house of their mother, and it is from this much inferior position that they must speak.

Even when people insisted that, by blood if not by house, matrilaterally affiliated children of a noble father were still noble, they maintained that "they have no rights over a house" (*na'ak wol rir hak na'a rahan*). "It is true they are noble, but it has no worth" (*Mel vali, na'ak wol fiawan*). That is, if one has lost one's rights to speak on behalf of a named house, one may well be a noble, but one has no worth in the enduring world of named houses.

Ultimately, the rank of the descendants of such children will depend upon whether the house to which they were matrilaterally affiliated was a named or an unnamed house. The likelihood that their nobility will continue to be recognized is much greater if they have affiliated to a named house. The descendants of a matrilaterally affiliated man in an unnamed house are much more likely, over time, to be considered commoners rather than nobles. Even where people insist that matrilaterally affiliated children would continue to be nobles, following their father, it is evident that, by living in an unnamed house, their status is greatly diminished, and that eventually their noble lineage would fade and be forgotten. The problem of matrilateral affiliation thus suggests that once one has lost one's place in a named house and become a member of an unnamed house, one's descendants will eventually assume the corresponding status of commoners — of slaves and younger brothers.

Another way in which commoner lines may be generated is through the process of segmentation of senior and junior lines within a named house — although it must be stressed that people do not talk about rank in this way. Such segmentation would result from disputes that cause rifts in the relation between brothers but do not threaten their relation with their *dua*. These disputes might include conflicts between their respective wives, insults, contention over land or valuables, and dissension concerning duties toward their *dua*, *lolat*, or *ura-ava*. Tremendous efforts are made to prevent a dispute between agnatic brothers from assuming such proportions that a break becomes inevitable. Nevertheless, breaks presumably do occur over time, in which case it would be the elder brother (unless it is he who is at fault) and his descendants who would retain rights over the estates of the house. The members of the junior line would lose rights over the *lolat* of the house, but they would retain rights over their own sisters; they would no longer be considered the masters of the land that belongs to the house, but would continue to claim ownership over their own trees. They would no longer be the custodians of the heirloom valuables of the house, nor would they represent the house or negotiate matters on its own behalf. They could appeal to their own "masters of their body" (*tenan dua*), but they could no longer appeal to the "masters of the house" (*rahan dua*). Presumably, such a junior line would eventually come to be considered an unnamed commoner house within the house-complex, the core of which is formed by the named house of their noble elder brothers. With time, the members of the senior and junior lines would no longer recognize a common source of lifeblood, and they would be thought of simply as attached elder-younger brothers who have been traditionally associated with one another and who, traditionally, "treat each other well."

"Slaves and younger brothers" — as the term suggests — is thus a composite category comprising traditional younger brothers, refugee men, and younger brothers who have lost their position within a named house. Unlike slaves, who are the essence of mobility, "slaves and younger brothers" are at least attached to a fixed place in the world, even if they themselves do not constitute such a fixed point. Often severed from a *dua* who is theirs by origin, they have found one who will assume his place; severed from brothers who share estates and lifeblood in common, they have found brothers who treat each other well. Although they have no *lolat*, they have, at least, sisters. Where they have no land, they have trees. Although there is no fixed pathway that remembers the founding source of lifeblood, there is nevertheless a point from which new pathways may grow and multiply.

The relationship between such elder and younger brothers exists in, and only in, the performative sense that they treat each other well and are protective of one another's well-being. "True brothers" may or may not treat each other well: they will remain brothers nonetheless, because they share a common source of blood, and blood cannot be severed. By contrast, the mutual regard that attached brothers have for one another, and the guarded attentiveness they show in demonstrating their solidarity and loyalty, reflects the extreme tenuousness of the underlying reality. Attached brothers are brothers only for as long as they act with gestures as bold as the relationship itself is fragile. The delicacy of the relation rests in the fact — understood but never openly expressed — that if the younger brother was not attached to the elder, he would have been the slave of someone else. As it stands, he is the commoner client of a noble house. It is not, perhaps, a tremendous difference, yet it is all the difference in the world.

The Fixity and Weight of Nobles

A noble is one whose high personal rank has been maintained by his father's marriage, and whose place in a named house has been fully established through the completion of all exchanges connected with his father's and his own marriage. As already noted, two alternative fates threaten the security of the descendants of a noble person in a named house: through a mismarriage his children can fall in rank, and through a failure of exchange his children can lose their place in a named house. Thus if a noble man marries a woman of lower rank or status, this can cause a change in the rank of his children. If the woman married is of the slaves and juniors rank, and especially if she has been married out of a noble house and weighted down with valuables, then the rank of the children will only tilt a bit from the rank of their father. Yet if a man marries a slave or a witch, then the status of their children will fall precipitously. If they are not disowned and expelled from the house altogether, it will nevertheless eventually become imperative that someone else, of noble rank, be lifted in to speak for the house and assume rights over the estates of the house in place of the original occupants.

When the reason for the adrogation is the decline in rank of the original occupants, a high-ranking noble man should be lifted into the house so that the *lolat* of the house will once again respect their *dua*.[11] Such a high-ranking man is then called a "lifted noble" (*mel saksikan*), or a "lontar bow" (*vuhur kalkau*) — that is, the strongest of all types of bows used in warfare. It is said that he "goes and strengthens the house" (*ntii nfang-rebat rahan*), for once again the rank of the occupant will be appropriate to the status of the named house. His presence will command the respect of his *lolat*, and the alliance between *dua* and *lolat* will no longer be threatened by a break in the flow of valuables or by the impossibility of marriage.

11. There seems to be considerable allowance given in the interpretation of a person's rank when the debated range is between noble (*mela*) and commoner (*iria-iwarin*). A line is drawn, however, and a real problem arises when the occupant of a house has been born of a slave (*iria*) or witch (*iwangi*). Such a person can no longer be recognized as a legitimate representative of a named house.

It can also happen that a man or his children can be dispossessed of their place in a named house if they fail to be fully redeemed of their bridewealth debts. If it is the father's redemption that remains incomplete, the result will be the matrilateral affiliation of the children. If it is a man's own redemption that is obstructed, he will be required to sell himself to a new *dua*. In either case, the man will ultimately become a commoner younger brother in an unnamed house attached to a noble elder brother of a named house.

Nobles, then, are those who stay in place, who do not move. To say they stay in place is to say they retain their ritual relation to, and speak for, the founding ancestor of the house and its estates and patrimony. To stay in place is to retain their position relative to those coordinates in the world that mark permanence as the arbitrator of ultimate value: named houses, heirloom valuables, land, house masters, and rows.

It is not surprising, then, to find Drabbe reporting that the highest rank is determined by reference to those marriages that embody the mark of permanence. Thus Drabbe states (using Yamdenan terms):

> With the true nobility there are, however, also grades, and people speak of *mel'silai* or high nobility. This refers to those who can point to nothing other than high nobility in their genealogy. The head of a *stam* will arrange to obtain for his eldest son, the daughter, preferably the eldest, of another *stam* head. The highest nobility is attained, then, if the family guardian [i.e., house master] of a *stam* head is also a *stam* head, and if one has always — up to the present day — remained faithful to the tradition of taking a daughter of this family guardian for the eldest son. (1940:179)

Here, the highest rank possible is constituted by the marriage (repeated over the generations) of the eldest son in the senior line of a named house with the eldest daughter in the senior line of a named house — where the house of the woman is the house master of the man's house. This would fix the position of the senior line along a row of enduring alliances that reaches back to the original source of life — the Lolat Ila'a.

Yet this image of the highest rank is based on an ideal order founded in the past. Its perpetuation presupposes a totally consistent realization of an asymmetric system of alliance. The paradox is this: if the asymmetric system of alliance were consistently realized — i.e., if everyone married his matrilateral cross-cousin — there would be no hierarchy, no differentiation in rank. Hierarchy does exist, however, because two brothers may not marry two sisters and only one brother can possibly take a wife from the traditional house master. Moreover, the highest nobility has not been realized because marriages between members of allied houses have never been consistently repeated over the generations. Indeed, it is as if Tanimbarese had replaced the potential for achieving the highest nobility (through a strict application of a matrilateral rule for eldest sons) with the pleasure they derive from the negotiation of differences and the movement of valuables (through which they continue to revitalize old alliances).

What this image of the highest nobility represents is the value of an achieved permanence in an otherwise mobile world. The fixity of persons is achieved relative to the permanence of houses, their estates and patrimony, their ancestors and alliances. The double permanence of noble persons and their named houses is evident in the enduring qualities of the gold valuables that give weight to their houses, that travel and marry along their rows, and that mark the histories of their marriages. If no one can achieve the highest nobility, they can at least approximate a nobility that is as resplendent with gold as the heavens of Ubila'a.

Centers in a Sea of Mobility

Whereas slaves have been disinherited from both their personal estates as well as the estates of their houses, commoners have been disinherited from the estates of their houses, at the same time as they retain their own personal estates, or begin to establish new ones. Nobles, on the other hand, maintain possession over the full complement of estates: *lolat* in addition to *ura-ava*; land in addition to trees; heirloom in addition to named house. With slaves, their connection to their *dua* and their brothers has been severed completely. A commoner's relation to his *dua* and his brothers is but of recent origin. Nobles, however, have kept intact the lines that relate them to their *dua* and their brothers, and these lines make evident their fixed relation not only to the ancestors of the house, the source of its patrimony, but also to the Lolat Ila'a and the source of life represented by Ubila'a. Anchored in this way, nobles are considered to be heavy or weighty—they are, essentially, immovable.

It is through the permanence they achieve in their relation to Ubila'a and the ancestors, to their house, its heirlooms, and estates, that the nobles of named houses hierarchically encompass those who have become dispossessed—the commoners of unnamed houses and the "slaves who just run about." In this, they embody the totality of that which defines humanity. This position is achieved through a privileged relation to the sociological conditions for its realization. For it is only the nobles of named houses who command the full range of types of marriage and modes of exchange—with their attendant consequences for effecting the ideal forms of residence and affiliation. Where commoners may marry "other women" and, at best, their matrilateral cross-cousins, it is only nobles who may, in addition, marry a woman of their house master to renew a permanent alliance along the rows. Where commoners engage in the quick and fleeting exchange of light valuables that are dispersed along sisters and aunts pathways, nobles may also engage in the slow and ponderous exchange of weighty valuables that are concentrated along the rows. Where the affiliation and residence of commoners is variable, that of nobles is, almost by definition, patrilateral and patrilocal. Finally, as the ultimate expression of their encompassing position, it is only the nobles of named houses along the double cycle of the Lolat Ila'a who have the potential for realizing the forms of marriage and exchange through which the weight of the entire system may be mobilized.

Named houses are described as "ships" (*kabal*); their younger brother unnamed houses are said to "harbor beneath the ship" (*rlau na'a kabal vavan*). They are like small outriggers sheltered under the protective bulk of a great ship at anchor. Indeed, one can see nobles and named houses as a kind of fixed and weighted center point in a sea of increasing mobility and lightness that is composed of true younger brothers, attached younger brothers, commoners, and slaves. At the center, the village people sit, make offerings to Ubila'a and the ancestors, and negotiate exchanges. Through their offerings and their negotiations, they create and recreate the enduring shape of the world: the order of people and houses founded by the ancestors and fixed in time. Around them, the commoners — the forest people — and the slaves who just run about move in a world of impermanence, outside and on the periphery, where forms shift with the seasons and dissolve in the mists of time.

12 Conclusion

The legacy of the spear was the differentiation of the self-contained unity of the world, the radical dispersal of its component parts, and the subsequent recomposition of synthetic images of transcendent unity that would anchor the productive activities of humans in a new cultural order. These unities — points where differentiation was folded back into itself, where motion was stopped, and where value was concentrated and held in reserve — gave villages their center in the stone boat, gave houses their center in the *tavu* complex, and gave exchange pathways their center in the Great Row. The legacy of the spear was to set in motion this double movement of differentiation and recomposition through which all creative action in the world is realized.

In contemporary life, it is exchange — as the analogue of the spear — that differentiates prior unities, separates them into their component parts and, in the process, establishes the relation between a source and that which issues forth from it. A process of differentiation is necessary for life, growth, and productivity in general, since such unities are, in themselves, unproductive. Yet life, growth, and productivity are made possible not only by the processes of differentiation and separation that extend life out from the source, but also by the processes of recomposition and encompassment that ground the source of life.

Each process contains the other, and their mutual implication is what creates hierarchy. The generation of hierarchy cannot be understood apart from its processual logic. This logic involves not only the existence of a prior transcendent totality and its subsequent differentiation (Dumont 1970: 243), but also, and integrally, the necessity for the recomposition of new synthetic and transcendent unities. Such a processual logic allows for an understanding of the generation of hierarchical forms and does not confine itself to a static description of contexts, levels, and the mechanical reversals that link them (Barnes, de Coppet and Parkin 1985). At the same time, the idea of reversal is itself transformed. For where the transcendent unity contains both opposed parts, which one becomes the encompassing source depends upon which part is extracted, and it is the process of extraction that defines the hierarchical relation between source and issue. Reversal is, then, the differential extraction of one or the other part. The whole must be seen to contain both potentialities. Thus in Tanimbar, with reference to the stone boat, it is the male aspect of an androgynous whole that is extracted; with reference to the *tavu* complex (and, ultimately, the Great Row), it is the female aspect that is extracted. Together, the two contain the totality of social life.

While the generation of hierarchy requires the realization of the complementary processes of differentiation and recomposition, separation and encompassment, in order to be made visible in the world hierarchy also requires an analogous set of processes that we have encountered throughout the analysis of Tanimbarese social life. What is at work here is a contrastive logic that poses the dispersal of value to its concentration, the particularization of relation to its generalization and abstraction, and the personification of relation to its objectification. With regard to both houses and exchange pathways, it is the relative ability to gather together and concentrate value in forms that are more generalized, abstracted, and objectified (e.g., named valuables, ancestor statues, rows, and certain forms of marriage) that gives weight and permanence to a place and constitutes it as a point of anchorage where movement stops and the flow of life is rooted in a source. It is, by contrast, the relative ability to disperse and disseminate value in forms that are more particularized (e.g., persons, bodies, blood, and other forms of marriage) that gives lightness and fluidity to the flow of life out from a source. Both processes are necessary to the creation of life and hierarchy, but it is the achievement of the former that transforms the relative hierarchy of persons and affines into the fixed hierarchy that subordinates unnamed houses and *ura-ava* pathways to named houses and their *lolat*.

Understanding hierarchy in terms of these processes, it is then possible to return to the issues raised in the beginning of the book and reconsider how the nature and import of asymmetric cycles and pathways, houses, and the differential forms of marriage and affiliation are illuminated by such an understanding.

The analysis of the asymmetry of Tanimbarese marriage and alliance began with those forms of marriage that extended asymmetry out along new pathways. It gradually proceeded toward the point, at the top and center, where asymmetry was folded back into itself in the form of the double cycle of the Great Row. Having worked our way to the top, as it were, it is nevertheless imperative to realize that to view the system of marriage and exchange from one direction only — either from the top down or the bottom up — provides only a partial picture. The dynamics of the system can only be understood by perceiving the whole from both perspectives simultaneously.

From the point of view of the double cycle, the extended lines of alliance and exchange that radiate out (and down) from the Great Row appear as a movement of differentiation, separation, and dispersal. Here the Great Row, as a synthetic image of the unity of all opposites (including the near incestuous unity of brother and sister) is differentiated by way of the injunction that at least some brothers must marry other women and some sisters must marry other men. There results the open, irreversible lines that relate houses as brother and sister, male and female, and source and issue — as the movement of life and blood through women reaches ever outward in new tendrils of growth.

Conversely, from the point of view of these extended lines of exchange — the open rows and the *ura-ava* pathways — the double cycle at the top of the system appears as a recomposition of the original androgynous unity of the world (including the incestuous unity of brother and sister). Here, the Great Row — embodying that rare form of asymmetry, the cycle — appears as the closest approximation possible to that dream with which Lévi-Strauss ends the *Elementary Structures of Kinship*: "a world in which one might *keep to oneself*" (1969:497).

Indeed, contrary to Lévi-Strauss' contention that it is the prohibition of incest that makes possible society and the system of reciprocity that underlies sociality, it could be said that it is a recomposed image of androgynous and incestuous unity (or its closest approximation) that stands at the very center of society and is the condition for both hierarchy and exchange. That is, "keeping to oneself," relatively speaking — as manifest in the "unnatural" enclosed form of the cycle — is the ground against which "giving away" — as manifest in the open and extended "natural" growth of the rows and pathways of exchange — receives value (Boon 1977; Weiner 1985).

Yet keeping to oneself and giving away should not be seen in terms of the logic of accumulation and the maximization of advantage that Lévi-Strauss' terminology sometimes evokes. It should rather be seen as the concentration of value that gives fixity, weight, and permanence to a source and makes possible the dispersal of value that extends life in the light and supple motions of growth. This concentration and dispersal of value is evident in the differential movement of both valuables and women. With regard to valuables, one finds the contrast between the heirloom valuables that have been immobilized within named houses, the named valuables that are restricted to a nearly imperceptible movement along the circuit of the Great Row, other named valuables that move at a dignified pace along the open extended rows, and the unnamed valuables that move with comparative swiftness along the sisters and aunt pathways. At one end of the continuum, there is the weight, the concentration of value, and the stoppage of movement that creates the ancestral source as an enduring and stable anchorage. At the other end of the continuum, there is the lightness, the dispersal of value, and the fluidity of movement that is the form taken by the expansion of life. Just as the immobility of the stone boat contains within itself the mobility of the village as a sailing boat, so too does the stillness of valuables at the center of houses and the Great Row contain within itself, and make possible, the movement of valuables along the rows and pathways of exchange. Yet reciprocally, the stillness of valuables at such centers would not be possible without the movement of valuables around the periphery, since the former represent the concentrated, generalized value of the latter.

Similarly, with regard to types of marriages, one finds the contrast between the marriages that renew house alliances along the Great Row, those that renew alliances along the open extended rows, those that renew affinal relations traced through persons (matrilateral cross-cousin marriages), and those that initiate new affinal relations between unrelated persons. At one end of the continuum, there is the concentration and replication of marriages along a single, deeply furrowed pathway that reaches back to the ancestral past and the source of life. At the other end, there is the dispersal of marriages along a multitude of newly created pathways that extends out into the future and fulfills the potential of life in the proliferation of descendants. By reference to this double movement, the forms of marriage find their differential value, at the same time that they mutually imply one another. The continuity of the old, permanent alliances that connect back to the past and the source of life is dependent, in part, upon the movement of valuables engendered by the initiation of new affinal relations that issue forth from outmarried women. Conversely, these latter are supported by the exchange that operates along the pathways and rows that trace established alliances.

Seeing the relation between the closed cycle and the open asymmetric pathway in terms of recomposition and differentiation, anchorage and flow, source and issue, makes it possible to view the relation between equality and hierarchy in a different manner. Equality derives neither from the breakdown in hierarchy (as Lévi-Strauss would have it) nor from a revolt against hierarchy (as Leach would have it). Equality is achieved at the point where differentiation is recomposed into an image of a prior unity, where the tension between encompassment and separation is resolved, where asymmetry between source and issue is folded back into the symmetry of two sources. Hierarchy is established where a prior unity is differentiated, where the tension between encompassment and separation is fostered, and where the asymmetry between source and issue is extended ever outward. Equality, in an asymmetric system (as manifest in the Great Row), is both the prior unity from which differentiation and hierarchy emerge and the point where hierarchy turns back upon itself and encompasses itself from within. In the process, a superordinate level emerges that fixes hierarchy as an enduring social form. This is to say that as much as equality contains hierarchy, hierarchy cannot endure without being grounded and encompassed by equality.

If the double movement of differentiation and recomposition, dispersal and concentration, makes sense of the relation between asymmetric cycles and open asymmetric pathways, it also makes sense of houses and the relation between houses. To see houses as discrete, bounded descent groups would be to miss the dynamics involved in their creation. A house is better seen as a prior androgynous unity — exemplified in the *tavu* complex — from which a core of males is created through the extraction of their own female aspect (their sisters, sister's husbands, and sister's children) and the female aspect of other houses (their own brothers, brother's wives, and children). The fact that their own female aspect remains encompassed by their house and is integral to its self-definition, and that they remain encompassed as the female aspect of other houses, makes it particularly difficult to draw the boundaries of a house.

It is through exchange that the tension between encompassment and separation is negotiated and the lines that demarcate or dissolve houses begin to emerge. Exchange, if successful, counters the potential for absolute incorporation (slavery) with separation, at the same time that it counters the potential for absolute alienation (death) with renewed encompassment. The life and continuity of a male core at the center of a house depends, therefore, not only upon the extraction and separation of the female aspect of their own and other houses (thereby resisting and answering the challenge of absolute incorporation). It also depends upon the encompassment of the female aspect of their own and other houses (thereby answering and resisting the challenge of complete alienation). Paradoxically, the definition of houses simultaneously requires both separation and encompassment.

The forms of affiliation and residence are given value by reference to this double movement of separation (countering incorporation) and encompassment (countering alienation). For where exchange successfully negotiates the tension between the two, patrilateral affiliation and patrilocal residence are the result. By contrast, where exchange remains incomplete, matrilateral affiliation and uxorilocal residence (or incorporation) are the result. Where exchange fails altogether, the result once was slavery (complete incorporation) and, even now, requires selling oneself as a younger brother to another house (complete alienation). Viewed in another light, the male core of a house can be seen as a concentration or gathering in of males in face of the constant potential for their dispersal.

Indeed, it is this contrast between concentration and dispersal that distinguishes named houses and unnamed houses. For named houses are those which have been able to concentrate, generalize, and objectify value in the form of heirlooms, *tavu*, and the enduring estates of land and rows of houses. Given weight in this way, they stand as fixed points where motion is stopped, where the connection back to the past and the ancestral source of life is most immediate, and where, therefore, growth may be rooted. Unnamed houses, by contrast, are those in which value is dispersed, particularized, and personified in their impermanent estates of trees and *ura-ava* pathways. Without weight to center themselves, they must attach themselves to other centers, for which they constitute the mobile peripheries.

In light of this contrast, the relation between the kinds of marriages that are the province of the nobles of named houses (and elder brothers) and the commoners of unnamed houses (and younger brothers) also becomes clear. The alliances that form the prerogative of nobles, named houses, and elder brothers are concentrated along old pathways of alliance that connect back to the past and to ancestral sources of life. Yet these alliances would not be possible except for the fact that the marriages that remain the province of commoners, unnamed houses, and younger brothers are dispersed along new pathways that extend growth into the future and are productive of a wealth of valuables that gives flesh to the old pathways of alliance.

In order to understand the dynamics of Tanimbarese social life, it has been necessary to move away from a theoretical framework that conceptualizes social units in terms of a priori, essentialist, and exclusive criteria. Within such a framework, not only have societies been characterized by reference to external categories but these categories have also been seen as exclusive of one another. It has been necessary to substitute a more dynamic conception of social relations that reveals (rather than conceals) the contrastive logic of relatively valued social forms and the processes by which they are brought into being. This move has been possible because a consideration of indigenous ideology has compelled a reevaluation of the analytic categories in which we have been tangled for so long.

A house society, at least in Tanimbarese terms, is not simply a random "compounding of forces which, everywhere else, seem only destined to mutual exclusion because of their contradictory bends" (Lévi-Strauss 1982: 184). It is, rather, the explicit and differential articulation of mutually implicating, contrastive social forms and processes. Nor is a house society a kind of monstrous child, born of the world of kinship, transfigured by the world of the market, and governed by the forces of an evolutionary logic external to it. It is, rather, an integral form governed by processes that have their own internal logic.

Like Atuf's spear, exchange is the activating and mediating agency through which the processes of differentiation and recomposition (and their analogues) are realized. If I have emphasized the role of exchange, it is because Tanimbarese themselves place it at the center of their social lives. It is the force with which they animate and actively shape their world. Atuf stands at the center of Tanimbarese conceptions of the origin of their world because he was the first one to understand and wield this force in its original form. With the sacred spear, Atuf was able to differentiate the self-contained unity of the world, to separate its complementary parts and set them in motion. Having abandoned the sacred spear, however, he was himself immobilized and contained within the fixity of stone. It remained the task of humans to recompose new transcendent images of unity—the stone boat, the *tavu* complex, and the Great Row—that would anchor the forces of the cultural order which they created, and continue to create, for themselves.

Appendices
Glossary
References
Index

Appendix 1
Affiliation and Residence in Awear

Given the complexity of the rules of affiliation and residence, it is remarkable the extent to which patrilateral affiliation and patri-virilocal residence are indeed realized. In the tables that follow, I set forth certain statistical data concerning affiliation and residence which, however, are not differentiated by reference to the possible types of marriage. The tables summarize the findings of a census I took in 1979 in the village of Awear on the island of Fordata; they may be compared to the data garnered from the 1927 census of Awear taken by Drabbe (1940:155–77).[1] It should be said that although the total population of Awear in 1979 was 267 persons, the figures shown here total only 238, because I have excluded the families of the school teachers who were resident in the village.

Table A1.1 shows the figures that relate to affiliation. The terms used in table A1.1 should be explained. Patrilateral refers to affiliation to the house of the father. Step-patrilateral indicates the affiliation of children of a pervious husband to the house of their mother's succeeding husband. Matrilateral signifies affiliation to the house of the mother's father or mother's brother. Adrogational refers to affiliation that results from the lifting of an adult man from one house to another. In-married signifies the affiliation of a person to the house into which he or she has married.

The figures clearly show that affiliation is overwhelmingly patrilateral for all males (both before and after marriage) and for females before marriage. After marriage, women affiliate to the house of their husband, unless they are thereafter "thrown off."[2] Previous to their adrogation, three of the four men who were lifted

1. Statistical data concerning affiliation and residence in 1927 can be compiled from Drabbe's census only after a painstaking study of the genealogies I collected. Although I began to compile such statistics, the effort proved far too time-consuming for the present study.

2. Within the category of married women I have included those women who have engaged in one or more provisional unions and have been thrown off, but who have children from such unions. These women will usually have returned to the house of their father or brother, to whose house they will remain affiliated until they marry again.

Table A1.1. Affiliation to houses in Awear (1979)

Affiliation	Males			Females		(B/A)	(B/A)
	Married	Un-married	Total	Married Before/After	Un-married	Total	Total
Patrilateral	38	67	105	51/ 1	66	117/ 67	222/172
Step-patrilateral	2	0	2	1/ 0	0	1/ 0	3/ 2
Matrilateral	2	2	4	3/ 0	2	5/ 2	9/ 6
Adrogational	4	0	4	0/ 0	0	0/ 0	4/ 4
Inmarried	0	0	0	0/54	0	0/ 54	0/ 54
Total	46	69	115	55/55	68	123/123	238/238

into other houses had been patrilaterally affiliated, and the fourth had been affiliated matrilaterally. Even when taken together, step-patrilateral, matrilateral, and adrogational affiliation accounted for only 8.7 percent of the total male population. For the female population, the figures are 4.9 percent (counting together unmarried women and married women before their marriage) or 1.6 percent (counting together unmarried women and married women subsequent to their marriage). Patrilateral affiliation, on the other hand, accounted for 91.3 percent of the total male population and 95.1 percent of the female population, when their affiliation is reckoned before their marriage. Thus, although affiliation is not automatic, the constitution of a house according to patrilateral affiliation (for men and children) is largely realized.

That the residential unit formerly comprised a core of agnatic brothers living with their families in the house of their father can be seen from the data collected in Drabbe's 1927 census of Awear. This residential and spatial unity has now been obscured with the current prevalence of nuclear family households – although the residence of the senior member of the house continues to hold the place as the central focus of this unity. In 1979, one married son would commonly reside patrilocally, while other sons would maintain separate, neolocal residences. Hence, of the forty-six married men, the residence of eighteen was patrilocal,[3] that of twenty-six was neolocal, and that of two was uxorilocal. The residence of both unmarried males and females is predominantly patrilocal (89 percent). Married women reside in the houses of their husbands in 87 percent of the cases, often even after the death of their spouses, although widowed women may also take up residence in the house of one of their children or grandchildren (in either the male or female line). Table A1.2 shows the statistics from 1979 regarding the types of residence found in the village of Awear.

Certain terms used in table A1.2 need explanation. I have used virilocal to refer to the residence of a woman with her husband, where the latter is living patrilocally. By contrast, neo-virilocal signifies the residence of a woman with her hus-

3. I have included among those living patrilocally not only those who reside with a living father but also those who live in the structure, or on the site, traditionally associated with a particular house.

Table A1.2. Residence patterns in Awear (1979)

Residence	Married males	Unmarried males	Total males	Married females	Unmarried females	Total females	Total
Patrilocal	18	61	79	3	61	64	143
Matrilocal	—	4	4	—	2	2	6
Neolocal	26	—	26	—	—	—	26
Uxorilocal	2	—	2	—	—	—	2
Virilocal	—	—	—	22	—	22	22
Neo-virilocal	—	—	—	26	—	26	26
Sorilocal	—	1	1	—	2	2	3
Fratrilocal	—	1	1	—	—	—	1
Other	—	2	2	4	3	7	9
Total	46	69	115	55	68	123	238

Table A1.3. Household size in Awear (1927 and 1979)

Number of persons per household	1927		1979	
	Number of households	Total persons	Number of households	Total persons
1	2	2	—	—
2	—	—	1	2
3	5	15	3	9
4	4	16	5	20
5	6	30	8	40
6	5	30	6	36
7	8	54	3	21
8	5	40	9	72
9	7	63	2	18
10	6	60	2	20
11	4	44	—	—
12	1	12	—	—
13	—	—	—	—
14	—	—	—	—
15	2	30	—	—
16	1	16	—	—
17	1	17	—	—
Total	57	429	39	238

band, where he is living neolocally. Sorilocal and fratrilocal refer to the residence of unmarried children with their married sister or married brother, where these latter are living neo-virilocally or neolocally.

The breakdown of the residential core of agnatic brothers into separate neo-local units is also evident in the comparative data concerning the number of people per household, the number of agnatic brothers per household, and the number of households per house. Table A1.3 demonstrates that in 1927 the average number of persons per household was 7.5 (with nine households containing more than ten people); in 1979 the average number of persons per household was 6.1 (and no household contained more than ten persons). In 1927, twenty-nine of the fifty-seven households held two or more agnatic brothers; while in 1979, only one of thirty-nine households contained two married agnatic brothers, and the majority either were single family households or were comprised of one married son living in the house of his father (with or without unmarried siblings). In 1927, only three of the named and unnamed houses comprised more than one household, as compared with 1979, when ten of the twenty-five named and unnamed houses comprised more than one household.

Despite the current prevalence for neolocal residence, the dominant form of residence in 1927 was patrilocal, as it continues to be today for unmarried children. In fact, the opposition of patrilocal residence to neolocal residence is not particularly significant: the relevant opposition is rather that of patrilocal/neolocal versus matrilocal and uxorilocal residence, and, in this case, the predominance of the first is quite obvious.

Appendix 2
Adrogations in Awear

In order to gain some idea of the prevalence of the practice of adrogation, I have gathered information (from both my own and Drabbe's reports) on all the adrogations that have taken place over the last three or so generations in the village of Awear. During this time, there was a total of thirty-three adrogations. Concerning the relation — before the move — of a man to the house into which he was lifted, five were related as *dua*, four as *lolat*, three as sister's son, six as one or another type of elder-younger brother, three by various other connections, two had no previous relation, and in ten cases the relation was unknown.

It is evident that out of thirty-five named houses in Awear (counting the ones that have already died out), nineteen houses have had men lifted into or out of them. More precisely, twelve houses have had men lifted in only, two have had men lifted out only, and five have had men lifted both in and out. Of the twenty-nine unnamed houses in Awear, five have had men lifted out and only one has had a man lifted in. The overall percentage is even higher if one takes only those houses that were still present in Awear in 1979. Of the fourteen remaining named houses, eleven have had men lifted into or out of them (seven houses have had men lifted in only and four houses have had men lifted both in and out). There remain twelve unnamed houses and, of these, only three have had men lifted out; none have had men lifted in. It may be mentioned that since 1927, when Drabbe's census was taken, only four men have been lifted into other houses.

Glossary

Terms are from the Fordatan language except where noted. Those nouns that take a possessive suffix — which marks the person and number of the possessor — are given with the third person singular possessive suffix (-n) appended to the root form (e.g., *ava-n*).

a'ur: anchor; the immediate *lolat* of the house on each cycle of the Great Row that is the traditional wife-taker of a house on the other cycle

a'a-n: elder same-sex sibling. See also *ya'an-iwarin*

aa warat duan: liana masters, spirits of the forest

aa-wa'ar: magical substances (lit., "wood-leaf"). *aa-wa-ar ngnea*, hot magical substances

abat: a tract of land. *abat dua*, master of the land. *abat ahu*, the village estates of a house, including rows of houses and sisters and aunts pathways. *abat nangan*: the forest estates of a house, including land and plantations of long-lived trees

adat (Indonesian): custom, customary law

af malmolinra: genitals (lit., "taboo things")

ahu: village. *ahu dua*: master of the village

alamin: raised platforms inside a house, used for sitting or sleeping. *alamin tavu murin*, in traditional houses, the raised platform behind the *tavu*, where unmarried girls slept

aleman: heavy, weighty, important. *rfalemang ia*, they make her/him/it weighty (i.e., with valuables)

arin: large communal yam gardens

arun: ward of a village

ava-n: aunt, including father's sister and mother's brother's wife. *avan yanan*, father's sister's children, the descendants of father's sister. *norang avan*, she follows her aunt, said of a woman who marries her father's sister's son

awa-n: spouse

baiyau: the adornments of a woman, i.e., the valuables given from wife-giver to wife-taker upon a woman's marriage, in particular the valuables given from *dua* to *lolat* in a *vat dua* marriage

bakan: indigenous woven sarong of various kinds, including, in order of value, *bakan mnanat, bakan maran,* and *bakan inelak. bakan ko'u,* small sarong (valuables given from wife-giver to wife-taker). *eman-bakan,* loincloth-sarong (i.e., textiles in general)

bareat: see **baiyau**

bati-n (Yamdenan): heart, pit, kernel, seed, eye (of something)

bebu-n: placenta. *ta'a bebun,* coconut shell

brana: man; male

da'uk: brother-in-law (man speaking); sister-in-law (woman speaking)

da'ut: rain

daa: landside (if the speaker is there)

danton (Indonesian): village militia leader

das ni mbaretar (Yamdenan): the heirloom valuables of a house (lit., the "riggings of the house")

dawan: big, great; important; as a noun, it can be used to refer to adults, elders, and nobles

dedan ulu: the central platform on the seaside of a house

didalan: the ritual center of a village

dii: *ni dii,* his/her/its base, trunk, bottom

diti: a black ring of coconut shell or Venetian glass that is added as the top ring of the most valuable of shell armbands

doal: seaside (if the speaker is there)

dodu: *ni dodu,* his/her provisional spouse or lover

dolan: box used to hold heirloom valuables

dompet (Indonesian): wallet

dua-n: master, owner; wife-giver, life-giver. *dua dawan,* big/important master (i.e., the wife-giver of a house rather than a person)

Duadila'a: the Supreme Deity (lit., "our great master")

eman: loincloth. *eman-bakan,* loincloth-sarong (i.e., textiles in general)

era: sago palm

etan: daughter-in-law

faa: mango

falfolat: door

famudi (Yamdenan): younger same-sex sibling, commoner

fanera: offerings made to the ancestors and Ubila'a

farea: weariness; a residual portion of bridewealth

fatnima: father's sister's son (woman speaking); mother's brother's daughter (man speaking)

fau tnanan: plantation of trees

fenreu: ritual language term for a noble man
fiawan: price, exchange value, worth
fidu: gate, gateway of a village
fini (Yamdenan): seedling
fndirin (Yamdenan): a kind of tree called "coldmaker," used in gardening rituals
fngear ulu: the front loft on the seaside of the house
fnita: stairs, steps. *fnit matan dardirin*: the carved portal at the entrance to a traditional raised house
frua-n: middle
fuat: fishnet; pattern of dots in an ikat textile design

hati (Indonesian): liver, seat of the emotions

ian: fish. *ian e tuat fabana*, fish and palmwine set traveling, said of valuables traveling along the rows from *lolat* to *dua* as well as of valuables after they have died, or stopped, with the appropriate *dua* and continue to travel on to the next *dua*. *ian e tuat nvoat watan*, fish and palmwine simply overflow, said of valuables given from *ura-ava* or *lolat* to *dua*
ifa'at: four
ihi-n: contents, flesh, harvest
ila'a: great, supreme
imut: branch, *imut ila'a* and *imut ko'u*, the great shading branch and the small shading branch, are prestations given from *lolat* to *dua* in connection with a *vat dua* marriage
inawaan: the entrance to a house
inetal: that which cuts through or by-passes; the subordinate cycles attached to named houses belonging to the Great Row
inobal: long-distance trading voyage; the boat used for such a voyage. *inobal ralan*, the crew of the boat
iria: slave. *iria fadfeddi tantangang*, slaves [who are] sold and distributed. *iria farlaan*, slaves [who] run about, make haste
iria-iwarin: "slaves and younger brothers," commoners. *iria-iwarin malolan*, straight slaves and younger brothers (as opposed to those who are also witches)
isaa: one
isua: betel nut
itai: mother (used of animals)
iwangi: witch

juru bahasa (Indonesian): spokesperson
juru batu (Indonesian): anchor person
juru mudi (Indonesian): steersperson

kabal: ship
kabaya (Indonesian): blouse

kakeat rela: a tie for the neck, a single-strand bead necklace worn by both men and women

kalulun inawaan: the roof beam on the entrance side of a traditional raised house

kalulun tavu: the roof beam on the *tavu* side of a traditional raised house

kamoa: eruption; the appendages on the top, base, and sides of a male earring

karbaa: buffalo

keladi (Indonesian): taro

kembili (Indonesian): a kind of tuber

kfuan: hearth

kilun: spiral pattern characteristic of Tanimbarese carvings and textile designs. *kilun etal*, the single spiral. *kilun ila'a*, the S-shaped double spiral

kmena: female earrings. *kmena ngelya*, shield earring. *kmena ni lean*, the string of beads that connects the two members of a pair of female earrings. *kmena vatu*, stone/pebble earring

knaa ila'a: the large beads joining the double strands of a woman's bead necklace

kobi: palmwine cup. *nfeffar ni kobi*, he shatters his palmwine cup. *nfatnemung ni kobi*, he joins together his palmwine cup [and makes it whole again]

kora: the carved boards on the front and back of a boat; the horn-shaped decorations extending from the roof of a raised house. *kora muri*, stern board of a boat; the rear of the *tnabar ila'a* dance formation. *kora ulu*, prow board of a boat; the front of the *tnabar ila'a* dance formation

kual: lead singer in a dance

kubania: community, communal

kukuwe (Yamdenan): small, carved ancestor statues

la'it: punting pole

laar: sail. *laar ila'a* and *laar ko'u*, great sail and small sail, are prestations given from *lolat* to *dua* in connection with a *vat dua* marriage

lalean: true

lamngatabu (Yamdenan): the carved, human-shaped altar inside and opposite the entrance to traditional named houses, also known as the *tabu*

langit (Yamdenan): sky, heavens

lanuun: earth, land

lara-n: blood. *lara numak ira*, blood asphyxiates them (when valuables travel wrongly or when people marry wrongly)

larlera: the ceremony of blocking the woman's path when she moves to the house of her husband

latlata: foundation, that with which something is raised off the ground. *latlata ulu/muri*, front/back foundation, are small prestations subsidiary to the main body of a bridewealth prestation

laun: the triangular mass of small beads that hangs from the center and bottom of a woman's bead necklace

lela: elephant tusk, ivory. *lel daa narut ita*, a tusk measuring from the fingertips of one hand to the middle of the one's body. *lel naran did tanuvur*, a tusk measuring from the fingertips of one hand to the wrist of the other. *lel refa*, a tusk measuring the full arm span of a man. *lel ti'i nala,* a tusk measuring from the fingertips of one hand to the elbow of the other

lemditi: ritual language term for a noble woman

lera: sun

lihir: side. *lihir brana,* the side of the man [or father], said of persons along the ascending female bloodline of one's father. *lihir vata,* the side of the woman [or mother], said of persons along the ascending female bloodline of one's mother

lingat: drinking house used by men

Liri Uat: star cluster (the Belt of Orion)

lolat: row; row of corn; row of allied (named) houses; the traditional wife-taker of a named house. *lolat dawan,* big (or long) row. *Lolat Ila'a,* the Great Row. *lolat ko'u,* small (or short) row. *lolat sivelik,* a row that alternates, takes turns, or turns back on itself, said of the Great Row and the *inetal* cycles. *norang lolat,* she follows the row, said of a woman who marries a man from a traditional wife-taking house linked to her own along a row

loran: male earrings. *loran dida,* male earrings made in Tanimbar (lit., "our *loran*")

lunur: a skid used for launching or beaching a boat

luvu: betelnut basket or pouch

malolan: straight

mangatanuk (Yamdenan): speaker

mangun: stranger, said of a girl who is born into a house but is destined to move to another house when she marries

mani-n: wing, the side appendage on a male earring

manminak: tasty, aesthetically pleasing

Manut: star cluster (lit., "bird")

maraan: light, inconsequential

marinyo (Indonesian): government herald

marumat: woman's bead necklace

masa: gold, gold breast pendant. *mas kubania:* the valuables belonging to a village as a whole (lit., "community gold")

mata-n: origin, source; eye; sprout, offshoot

matmatan waan: death place, stopping place; the *dua* with whom a woman's bridewealth "dies" or "stops" and no longer needs to be passed on

mavu: foreign

mela: noble, noble person; right (side of anything). *mela fwaak,* herald. *mela ngrihi,* speaker. *mela raa,* the traditional ritual officials of a village (lit., "landside nobles"). *mela roal,* the village officials appointed by the Dutch East India Company, the Dutch colonial government, or the Indonesian government (lit., "seaside nobles"). *mela snoba,* sacrificer. *mel kubania,* the traditional ritual officials of a village (lit., "community nobles"). *mel saksikan:* a lifted noble, one who has been adrogated into a named house because its occupants have fallen in rank. *nvalat mel vain,* a ritual official who "answers the voice of the [community] nobles"

mele (Yamdenan): noble

memi-n: uncle, including mother's brother and father's sister's husband

muri: back, rear, stern

muti-salah (Indonesian): a form of sard, a variety of reddish-orange chalcedony

nait: wind. *nait nforuk*, the wind blows (or sings)

nangan: forest. *nangan dua*, master of the forest

nara-n: name

nara: star

natar (Yamdenan): the ritual center of a village. *natar sori*, a ritual center in the shape of a boat

ngan-an (Yamdenan): female genitals

ngnea: hot

ngraa-n: soul

ngrihi: suit, case, negotiated exchange. *rfallak ngrihi*, they negotiate an exchange (lit., "they talk a suit/case")

ngrova (from verb *nangrova*): anger, a preliminary marriage prestation

nitu: the dead; the spirit of the dead. *nit botun*, the atlas and axis bones of an ancestor. *nit matmatan*, spirits of the dead. *nit ratan*, spirits of the above, free spirits

noka: match, equal (said of people and valuables)

nuhu: island, land

nuur: coconut

ombak (Yamdenan): earth

orang kaya (Indonesian): village head

pemali (Indonesian): taboo

pemerintah negeri (Indonesian): village head

raa: landside (if the speaker is not there)

radridan: cool, cold

rahan: house (as both a physical structure and a social unit). *rahan dua*, the master of the house, including the head of the house, the males born into a house (who are intended to sit or stay in the house), the heirloom valuables of the house, and the traditional wife-givers of a named house. *rahan matan*: a named house (alone or in connection with its affiliated unnamed houses); source or origin house. *rahan matan ifa'at Sera-Fordata*, the four named houses of Sera and the four named houses of Fordata that together compose the Great Row. *rahan namudut*, the house dies out (because valuables have traveled wrongly). *rahan nfakinan*, the house kills off [its occupants], in cases of excessive or unjustified bloodshed. *rahan ralan*: house-complex (lit., the "inside of a house"); the central portion of a house. *rahan ulu*, the head [or main portion] of the house, a prestation made by a man's *dua* to the master carpenter who has supervised the building of the man's house

rala-n: inside; insides (of a person) including the seat of emotions

ramat: spear; a portion of bridewealth

ranetan: son-in-law. *nafranetan*, he makes himself a son-in-law (i.e., lives uxorilocally)

rela-n: neck. *sierak rela*, those who sever necks, headhunters

rena-n: mother, including mother's sister and father's brother's wife

roal: sea; seaside (if the speaker is not there)

rubu-n: sprout, shoot, new growth (of a plant). *rmela ruburira rivun*, they multiply their sprouts a thousandfold

sa'ir: flag. *sa'ir muri*, rear flag (a residual portion of bridewealth). *sa'ir ulu*, front flag (a residual portion of bridewealth)

saksikat dii: the lifting of the bottom, a prestation presented by a man to his *dua* requesting that they redeem him of a portion of his wife's bridewealth

sala: wrong, wrongly

sebraa: a male or female spirit of the forest that entices humans [of the opposite gender] into sexual or commensal relations, thereby causing their death

shal: small piece of indigenously woven cloth worn by women over the shoulder (from the Dutch *sjaal*)

sikar: swaddling clothes

simaklivur: [they] treat each other well, said of attached elder-younger same-sex siblings

sinuun: chestcloth

sislau: shell armbands worn by women. *sislau uvur*, shell armbands that fit on the lower forearm of a woman or on the upper arms of a young girl. *sislau vetit*, shell armbands that fit on the upper arms of a woman

situan: to meet each other, come together; a named house that has several rows branching off from it

snguran: shrimp; the clasps of the chain of a gold breastplate

snibi: cork; a prestation, accompanying a bottle of palmwine, consisting of a pair of male earrings or a small amount of money or both

sori luri (Yamdenan): the ritual official who is the "bow of the boat"

suruk: sword; a portion of bridewealth

tanlain: ritual song, sung during a bridewealth negotiation or any ritual event

tavu-n: beginning, starting point, base of something. *al ntavu*, to begin. *ntavun*, she/he begins to clear [a garden plot]

tavu: the carved, human-shaped altar inside and opposite the entrance to traditional named houses. *tav dakdokun*, the bench in front of the *tavu*, where the head of the house sat. *tav dardirin*, the upright "standing" portion of the altar.

temar: bamboo

tena-n: body. *tenan dua*, the master of his body (i.e., the mother's brother and the wife-giver of a particular person)

tiniman: kin, relatives

tnabar ila'a: ritual dance performed when renewing an intervillage brotherhood alliance

tomata: person. *ni tomata*, his people (said by a *dua* of his *lolat* and *ura-ava*).

tomat ahu, village people, used to refer to nobles. *tomat liak*, other people, i.e., those who are not kinsmen or relatives. *tomat nangan*, forest people, used to refer to commoners. *tomata ramuu*, people die (because valuables travel wrongly)

tuan vain: the voice of the official, the fine paid when a man repudiates a woman with whom he has been in a provisional relation

tuat: distilled palm wine. *tuat nvoat watan*, palmwine simply overflows, said of valuables given from sister's son to mother's brother. *tuat watan*, just palmwine, a prestation consisting of a bottle of palmwine and its "cork" (a pair of male earrings or a small amount of money or both)

tufat: packets of cooked rice

tutuk: ceremonial perahu. *rtolar tutuk*, they launch a ceremonial boat, said of a marriage with a woman of one's master along the rows

tutul: end, tip

tuur nitu: rope of the dead, a prestation made after the death of either spouse to secure the patrilateral affiliation of their children

ubi (Indonesian): yam

Ubila'a: the Supreme Deity (lit., "great ancestor/descendant")

ubu: the place for offerings to Ubila'a inside a house

ubu-n: males and females of the second ascending and the second descending generation; grandparent, grandchild. *ubun yanan*, grandparent's children, descendants of father's father's sister

ubu-nusi: ancestors, descendants (lit., all males and females of the third and fourth ascending and descending generations)

ulu: coconut frond torch

ulu: front, head, bow (of a boat). *ulu-n*, head. *ulur relar ratnemu*, their heads and necks they join together, is a preliminary marriage prestation

ulur: breadfruit. *ulur vrea*, seedless breadfruit. *ulur watan*, breadfruit with seeds

ungrela: the most valuable of women's bead necklaces, having an additional strand of beads (called its tail, *kikurn*) that hangs down the back of the woman

ura-n: cross-sex sibling. *uran yanan* sister's children, the descendants of sisters

ura-ava: "sisters and aunts," the descendants of outmarried women; wife-takers along specific female bloodlines

ura-memi: "brothers and uncles," wife-givers along specific female bloodlines

vaa-n: a share (of bridewealth, of ritual offices, of land). *vaan dawan*, the larger shares of the bridewealth (i.e., bow and water). *vaan ko'u*, the smaller shares of the bridewealth (i.e., spear and sword)

vaha-n: fluid, liquid

vahi: paddle

vai-n: voice. *vai lolin*, voice of accord, a preliminary marriage prestation. See also *tuan vain*

vakul (Yamdenan): betelnut pouch

varat: west, west winds; year

vata: woman; female. *vat dua*, woman of one's master (i.e., a woman from an established wife-giving house along a row). *vat liak*, other woman (i.e., a woman from an unallied house). *vat mnelat*, unmarried girl. *vat velin*, the value of the woman (i.e., bridewealth)

vatu: rock, stone; stone seat in a ritual center, ritual office. *vatu ntafal ia*, "stone clings to, envelops him/her/it." *nfulak ia na'a vatu*, "she/he/it is transformed or changed into stone."

vavu: pig. *vavu ni malmoli*, the pig's tabooed parts, consumed by men after a successful pig hunt

vovar tutul: the tip of the bamboo container [used to tap palmwine], an initial offering in bridewealth negotiations that is not expected to be accepted

vua-n: fruit

vuhur: bow (used in hunting); a portion of bridewealth. *vuhur kalkau*: lontar hunting bow, a noble who has been adrogated into a named house because its occupants have fallen in rank

vulan: moon

Vun Itai: star cluster (the face of Taurus)

Vun Yanat: the Pleiades

vunut: spear. *vunut malmoli*, sacred/taboo spear. *vunut sakti*, spear of otherworldly powers

vurat: rice cake used as ceremonial offering

waa-n: place; place of origin (along ascending female bloodline)

wadu: catch. *wadu-bebun*, fish and pork that sisters and aunts are obliged to give their brothers and uncles

waha-n: face

wahat: portion (of bridewealth, of a catch, of a ceremonial meal). *brana ni wahat*, the portion of the man (i.e., the father's *dua*). *vata ni wahat*, the portion of the woman (i.e., the mother's dua). *wahat dua*: master of the [ritual] divisions

walu-n: image, picture

walut: small, carved ancestor statues

wari-n: younger same-sex sibling. See also *ya'an-iwarin*

wawaul: return prestation

wear: water; a portion of bridewealth. *wear-sus vahan*, water and breast milk, are prestations made in order to effect the adrogation of an unrelated man

wika sitana: the large gold chains of a gold breastplate

wilin: the rudder of a boat; a position in the *tnabar ila'a* dance formation. *wilin mela* and *wilin balit*, right and left rudders, positions in the *tnabar ila'a* dance formation; prestations given from *lolat* to *dua* in connection with a *vat dua* marriage

ya'an-iwarin: "elder-younger same-sex siblings" (from the terms *a'an* and *warin*); also, father's sister's son (woman speaking), mother's brother's daughter (man speaking), and the spouses of one's elder-younger same-sex siblings. *ya'an-iwarin fareling*, attached elder-younger brothers. *ya'an-iwarin simaklivur*, elder-younger brothers [who] treat each other well

yafu: fire
yaha: dog
yama-n: father, including father's brother and mother's sister's husband
yana-n: child. *yanan brana*, male child. *yanan vata*, female child
yanat: young offspring (used of animals)

References

Adams, M. J.
1974   "Symbols of the Organized Community in East Sumba, Indone-
           sia." *Bijdragen tot de Taal-, Land- en Volkenkunde* 130:324–47.
1980   "Structural Aspects of East Sumbanese Art." In *The Flow of Life:
           Essays on Eastern Indonesia*, ed. J. J. Fox, pp. 208–20. Cambridge:
           Harvard University Press.

Art of the Archaic Indonesians
1982   Dallas: Dallas Museum of Fine Arts.

Barbier, J. P.
1984   *Indonesian Primitive Art*. Dallas: Dallas Museum of Art.

Barnes, R. H.
1973   "Two Terminologies of Symmetric Prescriptive Alliance from Pan-
           tar and Alor in Eastern Indonesia." *Sociologus* 23:71–89.
1974   *Kédang: A Study of the Collective Thought of an Eastern Indone-
           sian People*. Oxford: Clarendon Press.
1977a   "Alliance and Categories in Wailolong, East Flores." *Sociologus*
           27:133–57.
1977b   "*Mata* in Austronesia." *Oceania* 47, no. 4:300–319.
1978   "Injunction and Illusion: Segmentation and Choice in Prescriptive
           Systems." *Anthropology* 2, no. 1:19–30.
1979   "Lord, Ancestor and Affine: An Austronesian Relationship Name."
           Nusa 7:19–34.
1980a   "Concordance, Structure, and Variation: Considerations of Alli-
           ance in Kédang." In *The Flow of Life: Essays on Eastern Indonesia*,
           ed. J. J. Fox, pp. 68–97. Cambridge: Harvard University Press.
1980b   "Marriage, Exchange and the Meaning of Corporations in Eastern
           Indonesia." In *The Meaning of Marriage Payments*, ed. J. L. Com-
           aroff, pp. 93–124. New York: Academic Press.

Barnes, R. H., D. de Coppet, and R. J. Parkin, eds.
1985   *Contexts and Levels: Anthropological Essays on Hierarchy.* Oxford: JASO.

Barraud, C.
1979   *Tanebar-Evav: Une société de maisons tournée vers le large.* Cambridge: Cambridge University Press.
1985   "The Sailing-Boat: Circulation and Values in the Kei Islands, Indonesia." In *Contexts and Levels: Anthropological Essays on Hierarchy,* ed. R. H. Barnes, D. de Coppet, and R. J. Parkin, pp. 117–30. Oxford: JASO.

Battaglia, D.
1983   "Projecting Personhood in Melanesia: The Dialectics of Artefact Symbolism on Sabarl Island." *Man,* n.s., 18:289–304.

Berger, J.
1979   *Pig Earth.* New York: Pantheon Books.

Bezemer, T. J., ed.
1921   *Beknopte encyclopaedie van Nederlandsch-Indië.* The Hague: Martinus Nijhoff.

Bickmore, A. S.
1869   *Travels in the East Indian Archipelago.* New York: Appleton and Co.

Bleeker, P.
1856   *Reis door de Minahassa en den Molukschen Archipel.* Batavia: Lange.

Blust, R.
1980a   "Early Austronesian Social Organization: The Evidence of Language." *Current Anthropology* 21:205–26.
1980b   "Notes on Proto-Malayo-Polynesian Phratry Dualism." *Bijdragen tot de Taal-, Land- en Volkenkunde* 136:215–47.

Boon, J. A.
1977   *The Anthropological Romance of Bali, 1597–1972: Dynamic Perspectives in Marriage and Caste, Politics and Religion.* Cambridge: Cambridge University Press.
1982   *Other Tribes, Other Scribes: Symbolic Anthropology in the Comparative Study of Cultures, Histories, Religions, and Texts.* Cambridge: Cambridge University Press.

Budaya-Indonesia
1987   *Budaya-Indonesia: Kunst en cultuur in Indonesië.* Amsterdam: Tropenmuseum.

Cappers, E.
1935   "25 Jaar Tanimbar-missie." *Annalen van Onze Lieve Vrouw van het Heilig Hart* 53:197–201.

Chijs, J. A. van der, ed.
1885–97   *Nederlandsch-Indisch plakaatboek, 1602–1811.* 16 vols. The Hague: Martinus Nijhoff.

Clamagirand, B.
1975   "La maison Ema." *Asie du Sud-Est et Monde Insulindien* 2:35–60.
1980   "The Social Organization of the Ema of Timor." In *The Flow of Life: Essays on Eastern Indonesia*, ed. J.J. Fox, pp. 134–51. Cambridge: Harvard University Press.

Colenbrander, H. T., and W. Ph. Coolhaas, eds.
1919–53   *Jan Pieterz. Coen, bescheiden omtrent zijn bedrijf in Indië.* 7 vols. The Hague: Martinus Nijhoff.

Collier, J. F., and S. J. Yanagisako, eds.
1987   *Gender and Kinship: Essays Toward a Unified Analysis.* Stanford: Stanford University Press.

Cooley, F. L.
1962   "Ambonese Kin Groups." *Ethnology* 1:102–12.

Coolhaas, W. Ph., ed.
1960–79   *Generale missiven van Gourverneurs-Generaal en Raden aan Heren XVII der Verenigde Oostindische Compagnie.* 7 vols. The Hague: Martinus Nijhoff.

Crab, P. van der
1862   *De Moluksche eilanden.* Batavia: Lange.

Crook, J.
1967   *Law and Life of Rome.* Ithaca: Cornell University Press.

Cunningham, C. E.
1967a   "Atoni Kin Categories and Conventional Behavior." *Bijdragen tot de Taal-, Land- en Volkenkunde* 123:53–70.
1967b   "Recruitment to Atoni Descent Groups." *Anthropological Quarterly* 40, no. 1:1–12.
1973   "Order in the Atoni House." In *Right and Left: Essays on Dual Symbolic Classification*, ed. R. Needham, pp. 204–38. Chicago: University of Chicago Press.

Daghregister gehouden in 't Casteel Batavia, anno 1624–1682
1896–1913   31 vols. The Hague: Martinus Nijhoff.

Dijk, T. van, and N. de Jonge
1987   "The House on the Hill: Moieties and Double Descent in Babar." *Bijdragen tot de Taal-, Land- en Volkenkunde* 143, no. 1:54–104.

Doren, J. B. J. van
1863   "De Tenimber-eilanden ten zuid-westen van de Keij-eilanden." *Bijdragen tot de Taal-, Land- en Volkenkunde* 11:67–101.

Drabbe, P.

1917   "De vrede van Larat." *Annalen van Onze Lieve Vrouw van het Heilig Hart* 35:113–14.

1923   "Het heidensch huwelijk op Tanimbar." *Bijdragen tot de Taal-, Land- en Volkenkunde* 79:546–68.

1925   "Dood en begrafenis en spiritisme op Tanimbar." *Tijdschrift van het Koninklijk Nederlandsch Aardrijkskundig Genootschap* 42:31–63.

1926a   "Spraakkunst der Fordataasche taal." *Verhandelingen van het Koninklijk Bataviaasch Genootschap van Kunsten en Wetenschappen* 67, no. 1:1–75.

1926b   "Spraakkunst der Jamdeensche taal." *Verhandelingen van het Koninklijk Bataviaasch Genootschap van Kunsten en Wetenschappen* 67, no. 2:1–93.

1927   "Waardigheden of ambten in de Tanimbareesche maatschappij." *Bijdragen tot de Taal-, Land- en Volkenkunde* 83:181–91.

1928   "Het Tanimbareesche Huis. Rahan Tnebar." *Volkenkundige Opstellen* 2:145–61.

1932a   "Woordenboek der Fordaatsche taal." *Verhandelingen van het Koninklijk Bataviaasch Genootschap van Kunsten en Wetenschappen* 71, no. 2:1–118.

1932b   "Woordenboek der Jamdeensche taal." *Verhandelingen van het Koninklijk Bataviaasch Genootschap van Kunsten en Wetenschappen* 71, no. 3:1–122.

1932c   "Beknopte spraakkunst en korte woordenlijst der Slaroeesche taal." *Verhandelingen van het Koninklijk Bataviaasch Genootschap van Kunsten en Wetenschappen* 71, no. 4:1–32.

1935   "Aanvulling van de spraakkunst der Jamdeensche taal." *Tijdschrift voor Indische Taal-, Land- en Volkenkunde* 75:625–33.

1940   *Het Leven van den Tanémbarees: Ethnografische studie over het Tanémbareesche volk.* Supplement to vol. 38 of *Internationales Archiv für Ethnographie.* Leiden: E. J. Brill.

Dumont, L.

1979   "The Anthropological Community and Ideology." *Social Science Information* 18, no. 6: 785–817.

1980   *Homo Hierarchicus: The Caste System and Its Implications.* Rev. English ed. Chicago: University of Chicago Press.

1982   "On Value" (Radcliffe-Brown Lecture 1980). *Proceedings of the British Academy* 66:207–41.

Ellen, R. F.

1986   "Conundrums about Panjandrums: On the Use of Titles in the Relations of Political Subordination in the Moluccas and along the Papuan Coast." *Indonesia* 41:47–62.

Errington, S.
1979   "The Cosmic House of the Buginese." *Asia* 1, no. 5:8–14.
1983   "The Place of Regalia in Luwu." In *Centers, Symbols, and Hierarchies: Essays on the Classical States of Southeast Asia*, ed. L. Gesick, pp. 194–241. New Haven: Yale University Southeast Asia Monographs no. 26.
1987   "Incestuous Twins and the House Societies of Insular Southeast Asia." *Cultural Anthropology* 2, no. 4:403–44.
1989   *Meaning and Power in a Southeast Asian Realm.* Princeton: Princeton University Press.

Evans-Pritchard, E. E.
1940   *The Nuer: A Description of the Modes of Livelihood and Political Institutions of a Nilotic People.* Oxford: Oxford University Press.
1951   *Kinship and Marriage among the Nuer.* Oxford: Oxford University Press.

Evens, T. M. S.
1989   "An Illusory Illusion: Nuer Agnation and First Principles." *Comparative Social Research* 11:301–18.

Feldman, J. A.
1979   "The House as World in Bawömatalua, South Nias." In *Art, Ritual and Society in Indonesia*, ed. E. M. Bruner and J. O. Becker, pp. 127–89. Papers in International Studies, Southeast Asia Series no. 53. Athens: Ohio University, Center for International Studies.

Firth, R.
1963a   *We, The Tikopia: A Sociological Study of Kinship in Primitive Polynesia.* 1936. Reprint. Boston: Beacon Press.
1963b   "Bilateral Descent Groups: An Operational Viewpoint." In *Studies in Kinship and Marriage*, ed. I. Shapera, pp. 22–37. Royal Anthropological Institute Occasional Paper no. 16.

Fischer, H. Th.
1935   "De aanverwantschap bij enige volken van de Nederlands-Indische archipel." *Mensch en maatschappij* 11:285–97, 365–78.
1936   "Het asymmetrisch cross-cousin huwelijk in Nederlandsch Indië." *Tijdschrift voor Indische Taal-, Land- en Volkenkunde* 76:359–72.
1938   "'Masculine' and 'Feminine' Presents." *Man* 38: 158–59.
1957   "Some Notes on Kinship Systems and Relationship Terms of Sumba, Manggarai and South Timor." *Internationales Archiv für Ethnographie* 48:1–31.

Forbes, A.
1888   "Reizen in den Indischen archipel." *Tijdschrift voor Nederlandsch Indië*, 4th ser., 17, no. 1:365–88; 17, no. 2:38–57.

Forbes, H. O.
1884   "On the Ethnology of Timor-Laut." *Journal of the Royal Anthro-*
              pological Institute 13:8–29.
1885   *A Naturalist's Wanderings in the Eastern Archipelago.* London:
              Sampson Low, Marston, Searle and Rivington.

Forde, C. D.
1963   "On Some Further Unconsidered Aspects of Descent." *Man* 63:12–13.

Fortes, M.
1969   *The Web of Kinship among the Tallensi: The Second Part of an*
              Analysis of the Social Structure of a Trans-Volta Tribe. Oxford:
              Oxford University Press.

Forth, G. L.
1981   *Rindi: An Ethnographic Study of a Traditional Domain in Eastern*
              Sumba. Verhandelingen van het Koninklijk Instituut voor Taal-,
              Land- en Volkenkunde, no. 93. The Hague: Martinus Nijhoff.

Fox, J. J.
1971   "Sister's Child as Plant: Metaphors in an Idiom of Consanguinity."
              In *Rethinking Kinship and Marriage,* ed. R. Needham, pp. 219–52.
              Association of Social Anthropologists Monograph no. 11. London:
              Tavistock.
1980a   "Introduction." In *The Flow of Life: Essays on Eastern Indonesia,*
              ed. J. J. Fox, pp. 1–18. Cambridge: Harvard University Press.
1980b   "Obligation and Alliance: State Structure and Moiety Organiza-
              tion in Thie, Roti." In *The Flow of Life: Essays on Eastern Indone-*
              sia, ed. J. J. Fox, pp. 98–133. Cambridge: Harvard University Press.
1987   "The House as a Type of Social Organization on the Island of
              Roti." In *De la hutte au palais: Sociétiés "à Maison" en Asie du*
              Sud-Est insulaire, ed. C. Macdonald, pp. 171–78. Paris: Éditions
              du Centre National de la Recherche Scientifique.

Fox, J. J., ed.
1980c   *The Flow of Life: Essays on Eastern Indonesia.* Cambridge: Har-
              vard University Press.

Friedberg, C.
1980   "Boiled Woman and Broiled Man: Myths and Agricultural Rituals
              of the Bunaq of Central Timor." *The Flow of Life: Essays on Eastern*
              Indonesia, ed. J. J. Fox, pp. 266–89. Cambridge: Harvard Univer-
              sity Press.

Friedman, J.
1975   "Tribes, States, and Transformations." In *Marxist Analysis in So-*
              cial Anthropology, ed. M. Bloch, pp. 161–202. New York: John
              Wiley and Sons.

Geertz, H., and C. Geertz
1975   *Kinship in Bali.* Chicago: University of Chicago Press.

Geurtjens, H.
1910   "Le cérémonial des voyages aux îles Kei." *Anthropos* 5:334–58.
1917   "Reisindrukken van de Tenimber-eilanden, III." *Annalen van Onze Lieve Vrouw van het Heilig Hart* 35:66–69.
1921a   "Tanimbareesche feestviering." *Almanak van Onze Lieve Vrouw van het Heilig Hart* 31:70–76.
1921b   *Uit een vreemde wereld, of het leven en streven der inlanders op de Kei-eilanden.* 's-Hertogenbosch: Teulings' Uitgevers-Maatschappij.
[1941]   *Zijn Plaats onder de Zon.* Roemond: J. J. Romen.

Glickman, M.
1971   "Kinship and Credit among the Nuer." *Africa* 41, no. 4:306–19.

Goody, E. N.
1971   "Forms of Pro-Parenthood: The Sharing and Substitution of Parental Roles." In *Kinship,* ed. J. Goody, pp. 331–45. Harmondsworth, Middlesex: Penguin Books.

Goody, J.
1969   "Adoption in Cross-Cultural Perspective." *Comparative Studies in Society and History* 11, no. 1:55–78.

Gordon, J. L.
1980   "The Marriage Nexus among the Manggarai of West Flores." In *The Flow of Life: Essays on Eastern Indonesia,* ed. J. J. Fox, pp. 48–67. Cambridge: Harvard University Press.

Gregory, C. A.
1982   *Gifts and Commodities.* London: Academic Press.

Heine-Geldern, R.
1966   "Some Tribal Art Styles of Southeast Asia: An Experiment in Art History." In *The Many Faces of Primitive Art,* ed. D. Fraser, pp. 165–221. Englewood Cliffs, N.J.: Prentice-Hall.

Hocart, A. M.
1952   *The Life-Giving Myth and Other Essays.* London: Methuen.

Hoëvell, G. W. W. C. van
1890   "Tanimbar en Timorlaoet eilanden." *Tijdschrift voor Indische Taal-, Land- en Volkenkunde* 33:150–86.

Hoog, J. de
1959   "Nieuwe methoden en inzichten ter bestudering van de funktionele betekenis der beelden in het Indonesisch-Melanesisch kultuurgebied." *Kultuurpatronen: Bulletin van het Delfts Etnografisch Museum* 1:1–98.

Izikowitz, K. G. and P. Sørensen, eds.
1982   *The House in East and Southeast Asia: Anthropological and Architectural Aspects.* Scandinavian Institute of Asian Studies, monograph no. 30. London: Curzon Press.

Jacobsen, J. A.
1896   *Reise in de Inselwelt des Banda-Meeres.* Berlin: Mitscher und Röstell.

Jansen, H. J.
1977   "Indigenous Classification Systems in the Ambonese Moluccas."
            1933. Reprint in *Structural Anthropology in the Netherlands*, ed.
            P. E. de Josselin de Jong, pp. 101–15. The Hague: Martinus Nijhoff.

Josselin de Jong, P. E. de
1952   *Minangkabau and Negri Sembilan.* The Hague: Martinus Nijhoff.
1975   "The Dynastic Myth of Negri Sembilan (Malaya)." *Bijdragen tot
            de Taal-, Land- en Volkenkunde* 131:277–308.
1981   "Ruler and Realm: Political Myths in Western Indonesia." *Mededel-
            ingen der Koninklijke Nederlandse Akademie van Wetenschap-
            pen, Afd. Letterkunde*, n.s., 43, no. 1:3–19.

Kan, C. M. and P. J. Veth
1878   "Voyages of the Steamer 'Egeron' in the Indian Archipelago, Includ-
            ing the Discovery of Strait Egeron, in the Tenimbar, or Timor Laut
            Islands." *Journal of the Royal Geographical Society* 48:294–301.

Kana, N. L.
1980   "The Order and Significance of the Savunese House." In *The Flow
            of Life: Essays on Eastern Indonesia*, ed. J. J. Fox, pp. 221–30. Cam-
            bridge: Harvard University Press.

Kantor Sensus dan Statistik Propinsi Maluku
1980   *Pemetaan Desa Sensus Penduduk Propinsi Maluku.* Ambon: Kan-
            tor Sensus dan Statistik Propinsi Maluku.

Karp, I., and K. Maynard
1983   "Reading the Nuer." *Current Anthropology* 24, no. 4:481–503.

Kipp, R. S.
1983   "A Political System of Highland Sumatra, or Rethinking Edmund
            Leach." In *Beyond Samosir: Recent Studies of the Batak Peoples
            of Sumatra*, ed. R. S. Kipp and R. D. Kipp, pp. 125–38. Athens:
            Ohio University, Center for International Studies.

Klerks, J.
1912   "De expeditie op de Tanimbar-eilanden." *Annalen van Onze Lieve
            Vrouw van het Heilig Hart* 30:276–78.

Kolff, D. H.
1840   *Voyages of the Dutch Brig of War Dourga.* London: James Madden
            and Co.

Kroef, J. M. van der
1952   "Some Head-hunting Traditions of Southern New Guinea." *Ameri-
            can Anthropologist* 54:221–35.
1954   "Dualism and Symbolic Antithesis in Indonesian Society." *American
            Anthropologist* 56:847–62.

Kuper, A.
1982a   "Lineage Theory: A Critical Retrospect." *Annual Review of Anthropology* 11:71–95.
1982b   *Wives for Cattle: Bridewealth and Marriage in Southern Africa.* London: Routledge & Kegan Paul.

Labby, D.
1976   *The Demystification of Yap: Dialectics of Culture on a Micronesian Island.* Chicago: University of Chicago Press.

Lando, R. P.
1983   "Hierarchy and Alliance in Two Sumatran Societies: Toba Batak and Minangkabau." In *Beyond Samosir: Recent Studies of the Batak Peoples of Sumatra,* ed. R. S. Kipp and R. D. Kipp, pp. 53–81. Athens: Ohio University, Center for International Studies.

Leach, E. R.
1963   "Alliance and Descent among the Lakher: A Reconsideration." *Ethnos* 2, no. 4:237–49.
1965   *Political Systems of Highland Burma.* 1954. Reprint. Boston: Beacon Press.
1969   "Kachin and Haka Chin: A Rejoinder to Lévi-Strauss." *Man* 4:277–85.
1971   *Rethinking Anthropology.* 1961. Reprint. London School of Economics Monographs on Social Anthropology no. 22. University of London: Athlone Press.

Lehman, F. K.
1970   "On Chin and Kachin Marriage Regulations." *Man* 5, no. 1:118–25.

Lévi-Strauss, C.
1969   *The Elementary Structures of Kinship.* 1949. Translation. Boston: Beacon Press.
1982   *The Way of the Masks.* Seattle: University of Washington Press.
1987   *Anthropology and Myth: Lectures, 1951–1982.* Oxford: Basil Blackwell.

Lewcock, R., and G. Brans
1975   "The Boat as an Architectural Symbol." In *Shelter, Sign, and Symbol,* ed. P. Oliver, pp. 107–16. London: Barrie and Jenkins.

Lienhardt, G.
1961   *Divinity and Experience: The Religion of the Dinka.* Oxford: Clarendon Press.

MacCormack, C.P., and M. Strathern, eds.
1980   *Nature, Culture, and Gender.* Cambridge: Cambridge University Press.

Macdonald, C., ed.
1987   *De la hutte au palais: Sociétés "à maison" en Asie du Sud-Est insulaire.* Paris: Éditions du Centre National de la Recherche Scientifique.

Malinowski, B.
1961   *Argonauts of the Western Pacific.* 1922. Reprint. New York: Dutton.

Mauss, M.
1967   *The Gift: Forms and Functions of Exchange in Archaic Societies.*
                1925. Translation. New York: W. W. Norton.

Maxwell, R.
1981   "Textiles and Tusks: Some Observations on the Social Dimensions
                of Weaving in East Flores." In *Five Essays on the Indonesian Arts,*
                ed. M. J. Kartomi, pp. 43–62. Special issue of the AIA-CSEAS
                Winter Lecture Series. Melbourne: Monash University, Geography
                Department.

McKinnon, S.
1987   "The House Altars of Tanimbar: Abstraction and Ancestral Pres-
                ence." *Tribal Art* (Bulletin of the Barbier-Mueller Museum, Geneva)
                1:3–16.
1988   "Tanimbar Boats." In *Islands and Ancestors: Indigenous Styles of
                Southeast Asia,* ed. D. Newton and J. P. Barbier, pp. 152–69. New
                York: Metropolitan Museum of Art.
1989   "Flags and Half-Moons: Tanimbarese Textiles in an 'Engendered'
                System of Valuables." In *To Speak with Cloth: Studies in Indone-
                sian Textiles,* ed. M. Gittinger, pp. 27–42. University of California,
                Los Angeles: Cultural History Museum.

Metcalf, P.
1982   *A Borneo Journey into Death: Berawan Eschatology from Its Rit-
                uals.* Philadelphia: University of Pennsylvania Press.

Moyer, D. S.
1983   "Cultural Constraints on Marriage: Anti-Exchange Behaviour in
                Nineteenth Century South Sumatra." *Bijdragen tot de Taal-, Land-
                en Volkenkunde* 139:247–58.

Needham, R.
1956   "A Note on Kinship and Marriage on Pantara." *Bijdragen tot de
                Taal-, Land- en Volkenkunde* 112:285–90.
1957   "Circulating Connubium in Eastern Sumba: A Literary Analysis."
                Bijdragen tot del Taal-, Land- en Volkenkunde 113:168–78.
1966   "Terminology and Alliance, I: Garo, Manggarai." *Sociologus* 16:
                141–57.
1967   "Terminology and Alliance, II: Mapuche, Conclusions." *Sociolo-
                gus* 17:39–53.
1968   "Endeh: Terminology, Alliance, and Analysis." *Bijdragen tot de
                Taal-, Land- en Volkenkunde* 124:305–35.
1970   "Endeh, II: Test and Confirmation." *Bijdragen tot de Taal-, Land-
                en Volkenkunde* 126:246–58.

1980   "Principles and Variations in the Structure of Sumbanese Society."
                In *The Flow of Life: Essays on Eastern Indonesia*, ed. J. J. Fox,
                pp. 21–47. Cambridge: Harvard University Press.

Nieuwenhuis, L.
1912   "Brief van den Weleerw. Pater L. Nieuwenhuis, uit Amsterdam."
                Annalen van Onze Lieve Vrouw van het Heilig Hart 30:279–83.

van Nouhuys
1924   "Verslag betreffende het Museum voor Land- en Volkenkunde en
                het Maritiem Museum 'Prins Hendrik' over het jaar 1923." In *Ver-
                slag omtrent den Toestand van het Museum voor Land- en Volken-
                kunde en Maritiem Museum 'Prins Hendrik', te Rotterdam over het
                Jaar 1923*. Rotterdam.

Nugent, D.
1982   "Closed Systems and Contradiction: The Kachin In and Out of
                History." *Man* 17, no. 3:508–27.

Oliver, P., ed.
1975   *Shelter, Sign, and Symbol*. London: Barrie and Jenkins.

Ossenbruggen, F. D. E. van
1930   "Verwantschaps- en huwelijksvormen in den Indischen archipel."
                Tijdschrift van het Aardrijkskundig Genootschap 47:212–29.
1935   "Het oeconomisch-magisch element in Tobasche verwantschaps-
                verhoudingen." *Mededeelingen der Koninklijke Akademie van Wet-
                enschappen*, Afd. Lett. ser. B, 80:63–125.

Parmentier, R. J.
1984   "House Affiliation Systems in Belau." *American Ethnologist* 11:
                656–76.

Parry, J. P.
1979   *Caste and Kinship in Kangra*. London: Routledge and Kegan Paul.

Pauwels, S.
1990   "From Hursu Ribun's 'Three Hearth Stones' to Metanleru's 'Sailing
                Boat'; A Ritual after the Harvest." *Bijdragen tot de Taal-, Land-
                en Volkenkunde* 146, no. 1:21–34.

Renes, P. B.
1977   "Circular Connubium in the Leti Archipelago." In *Structural Anthro-
                pology in the Netherlands*, ed. P. E. de Josselin de Jong, pp. 225–30.
                The Hague: Martinus Nijhoff.

Riedel. J. G. F.
1883   "De Tenimber- en Timorlaut-eilanden." *Tijdschrift voor Neder-
                landsch Indië*, 4th ser., 12, no. 2:463–68.
1885   "Eenige opmerkingen over de recente ethnologische, linguistische,
                geographische en ornithologische mededeelingen omtrent de
                Tanembar- en Timorlao-eilanden. *Tijdschrift Nederlands Aard-
                rijkskundig Genootschap*, 2d ser., 1:721–25.

1886   *De sluik- en kroesharige rassen tusschen Selebes en Papua.* The Hague: Martinus Nijhoff.

Robert, W. C.
1973   *The Dutch Explorations, 1605–1756, of the North and Northwest Coast of Australia.* Amsterdam: Philo Press.

Rosaldo, M. Z.
1980   *Knowledge and Passion: Ilongot Notions of Self and Social Life.* Cambridge: Cambridge University Press.

Rosaldo, M. Z., and L. Lamphere, eds.
1974   *Women, Culture, and Society.* Stanford: Stanford University Press.

Rubin, G.
1975   "The Traffic in Women: Notes on the 'Political Economy' of Sex." In *Toward an Anthropology of Women*, ed. R. R. Reiter, pp. 157–210. New York: Monthly Review Press.

Sahlins, M. D.
1965   "On the Ideology and Composition of Descent Groups." *Man* 65:104–7.
1972   *Stone-Age Economics.* Chicago: Aldine Press.
1981   "The Stranger-King." *Journal of Pacific History* 16, no. 3:107–32.

Schneider, D. M.
1984   *A Critique of the Study of Kinship.* Ann Arbor: University of Michigan Press.

Schulte Nordholt, H. G.
1971   *The Political System of the Atoni of Timor.* Verhandelingen van het Koninklijk Instituut voor Taal-, Land- en Volkenkunde, no. 60. The Hague: Martinus Nijhoff.
1980   "The Symbolic Classification of the Atoni of Timor." In *The Flow of Life: Essays on Eastern Indonesia*, ed. J. J. Fox, pp. 231–47. Cambridge: Harvard University Press.

Sherman, D. G.
1987   "Men Who Are Called 'Women' in Toba-Batak: Marriage, Fundamental Sex-Role Differences, and the Suitability of the Gloss 'Wife-Receiver.'" *American Anthropologist* 89:867–78.

Singarimbun, M.
1975   *Kinship, Descent and Alliance among the Karo Batak.* Berkeley: University of California Press.

Southall, A.
1986   "The Illusion of Nath Agnation." *Ethnology* 25, no. 1:1–20.

Stanley, O.
1842   "Notes of a Cruise in the Eastern Archipelago in 1841." *Journal of the Royal Geographical Society* 12:262–65.

Steinman, A.
1946   "The Ship in Textile Art." *Ciba Review* 52:1870–96.

Stokes, J. L.
1969   *Discoveries in Australia*. 1846. Reprint. Australia Facsimile Edi-
            tions no. 33. Adelaide: Libraries Board of South Australia.

Strathern, M.
1988   *The Gender of the Gift: Problems with Women and Problems with
            Society in Melanesia*. Berkeley: University of California Press.

Tambiah, S. J.
1985   *Culture, Thought, and Social Action: An Anthropological Per-
            spective*. Cambridge: Harvard University Press.

Taylor, L. R.
1968   *Party Politics in the Age of Caesar*. Berkeley: University of Califor-
            nia Press.

Thomas, N.
1985   "Forms of Personification and Prestations." *Mankind* 15, no. 3:
            223–30.

Tiele, P. A., and J. E. Heeres, eds.
1886–95   *Bouwstoffen voor de geschiedenis der Nederlanders in den Male-
            ischen Archipel*. 3 vols. The Hague: Martinus Nijhoff.

Traube, E. G.
1980a   "Affines and the Dead: Mambai Rituals of Alliance." *Bijdragen tot
            de Taal-, Land- en Volkenkunde* 136:90–115.
1980b   "Mambai Rituals of Black and White." In *The Flow of Life: Essays
            on Eastern Indonesia*, ed. J. J. Fox, pp. 290–314. Cambridge: Har-
            vard University Press.
1986   *Cosmology and Social Life: Ritual Exchange among the Mambai
            of East Timor*. Chicago: University of Chicago Press.
1989   "Obligations to the Source: Complementarity and Hierarchy in
            an Eastern Indonesian Society." In *The Attraction of Opposites:
            Thought and Society in the Dualistic Mode*, ed. D. Maybury-
            Lewis and U. Almagor, pp. 321–44. Ann Arbor: University of
            Michigan Press.

Valeri, V.
1975–76   "Alliances et échanges matrimoniaux à Seram Central (Moluques)."
            L'Homme 15, nos. 3–4:83–107; 16, no. 1:125–49.
1980   "Notes on the Meaning of Marriage Prestations among the Huaulu
            of Seram." In *The Flow of Life: Essays on Eastern Indonesia*, ed.
            J. J. Fox, pp. 178–92. Cambridge: Harvard University Press.
1982   "The Transformation of a Transformation: A Structural Essay on
            an Aspect of Hawaiian History (1809–1819)." *Social Analysis* 10:
            3–41.

1985   "The Conqueror Becomes King: A Political Analysis of the Hawaiian
               Legend of Umi'." In *Transformations of Polynesian Culture*, ed.
               A. Hooper and J. Huntsman, pp. 79–103. Memoir no. 45. Auck-
               land: Polynesian Society.

Vries, J. H. de
1900   "Reis door eenige eilanden-groepen der Residentie Amboina." *Tijd-
               schrift van het Nederlandsch Aardrijkskundig Genootschap* 2d ser.,
               17:467–502, 593–620.

Vroklage, B. A. G.
1936   "Das Schiff in den Megalithkulturen Südostasiens und der Süd-
               see." *Anthropos* 31:712–57.
1940   "De prauw in culturen van Flores." *Cultureel Indie* 2:193–204.

Wagner, R.
1967   *The Curse of Souw: Principles of Daribi Clan Definition and Al-
               liance.* Chicago: University of Chicago Press.
1975   *The Invention of Culture.* Englewood Cliffs, N.J.: Prentice-Hall.
1977   "Analogic Kinship: A Daribi Example." *American Ethnologist* 4:
               623–42.
n.d.   "The Fractal Person." Paper presented at the Symposium on Great
               Man and Big Man Societies. Paris, 1988.

Waterson, H. R.
1986   "The Ideology and Terminology of Kinship among the Sa'dan To-
               raja." *Bijdragen tot de Taal-, Land- en Volkenkunde* 142, no. 1:
               87–112.
1990   *The Living House: An Anthropology of Architecture in South-
               East Asia.* Singapore: Oxford University Press.

Weiner, A. B.
1985   "Inalienable Wealth." *American Ethnologist* 12, no. 2:210–17.

Wouden, F. A. E. van
1968   *Types of Social Structure in Eastern Indonesia.* 1935. Translation.
               Koninklijk Instituut voor Taal-, Land- en Volkenkunde, Transla-
               tion series, no. 11. The Hague: Martinus Nijhoff.
1977   "Local Groups and Double Descent in Kodi, West Sumba." 1956.
               Translation in *Structural Anthropology in the Netherlands*, ed. P. E.
               de Josselin de Jong, pp. 184–222. The Hague: Martinus Nijhoff.

Wurm, S. A., and S. Hattori, eds.
1981–83   *Language Atlas of the Pacific Area.* Canberra: Australian Acad-
               emy of the Humanities in collaboration with the Japan Academy.

Index

Adoption, 134, 240n6

Adrogation, 99–100, 100n18, 107, 134, 220, 228, 239–43, 240n6, 242n7, 273, 287, 288, 291. *See also* Awear; Gender; Rank

Affiliation: contrastive forms, 18, 26, 28–32, 33, 98, 134–35, 156, 228, 278, 281, 287–88; and exchange, 28, 99, 156, 195; patrilateral, 28–29, 98, 156–57, 157–58, 161, 162, 195, 209, 237, 239, 276, 281, 287–88; matrilateral, 28–29, 98, 156–57, 158–59, 162, 178, 237, 238, 269–71, 274, 281, 287–88; in marriage with an other woman, 156–61; in-married, 157; step-patrilateral, 159–60; in matrilateral cross-cousin marriages, 208–9; in *vat dua* marriages, 236–39; and rank, 269–71, 274, 275–76; in Awear, 287–89

Affinal relations: continuity of, 112, 114, 117, 119–20, 199–203, 208; form of reciprocity between, 187–89; dissolution of, 203, 209; reversal of asymmetry in, 203, 211–16, 219–20, 222

Africa, 28, 29n6

Agricultural rituals: and village identity, 71, 71n12; for planting, 185; at harvest, 186–87

Alliance: Leach and Lévi-Strauss on, 18–22; and closed cycles, 12, 16, 17, 19–25, 33, 124–27, 125n14, 223, 224, 255–58, 279; and hierarchy and equality, 17, 19–23, 24, 124–27; and open pathways, 19–25, 33, 279; reciprocity

along pathways of, 200–1; renewal of, 217, 252; vs. marriage, 222; permanence of, 229; reversal of, 255–58. *See also* Great Row; Exchange; Houses; Marriage; Rows

Ancestors: bones of, 94n11, 96; as unity of opposites, 109; definition of, 109; as source of life and death, 109–10; offerings to, 179, 181–82, 184–85; power of, 190.

Androgyny: and unity, 35; in Ubila'a, 42–44, 45, 45n8, 108; of Atuf and Inkelu, 47, 48–50

Atuf: differentiation of world, 45–46, 50, 51–53, 54, 62, 139, 154–55, 255, 258, 283; origins of, 47; and Inkelu, 47–49, 54, 54n16, 58; acquisition of spear, 50–51, 56; turns to stone, 52–54, 61. *See also* Bridewealth; Spear

Autochthones: from Olsuin, 39–42, 50–51, 56; dispersal of, 54–56, 62; names of settlements, 55; deception of, 58; history regarding, 67n6

Awear: population of, 12; on Selaru, 56; spatial organization of, 66; adrogation in, 100, 287, 288, 291; residence and affiliation in, 287–89

Balau, 29n6

Bali: and *dadia*, 29n6; marriage types in, 134, 227, 256

Barnes, R. H., 26, 30

Birth, 108–9

Blood: and movement of women, 96; flow

317